JAMES BEARD... COOKERY

"The most authoritative... —*House Beautiful*

MORE CULINARY COUPS IN THE JAMES BEARD
TRADITION OF COOKING EXCELLENCE

- **More than 500 recipes for 85 different kinds of shellfish, saltwater, and freshwater fish.**
- **How to create a taste-tempting variety of fish stews and chowders.**
- **How to whip up 48 flavor-enhancing sauces and savory stuffings.**
- **How to prepare some lesser-known, highly flavored varieties of fish.**
- **How to find the best fresh or frozen fish on the market.**

Books by James Beard

Hors d'Oeuvres and Canapés
Cook It Outdoors
Fowl and Game Cookery
The Fireside Cookbook
Paris Cuisine (with Alexander Watt)
Jim Beard's New Barbecue Cookbook
The Complete Book of Outdoor Cookery
(with Helen Evans Brown)
How to Eat Better for Less Money
(with Sam Aaron)
The James Beard Cookbook
James Beard's Treasury of Outdoor Cooking
Delights and Prejudices
Menus for Entertaining
How to Eat (and Drink) Your Way Through a French
(or Italian) Menu
James Beard's American Cookery
Beard on Bread
Beard on Food
James Beard's New Fish Cookery

JAMES BEARD'S NEW
FISH COOKERY

JAMES BEARD'S NEW FISH COOKERY

A Revised and
Updated Edition
of James Beard's
Fish Cookery

WARNER BOOKS

A Warner Communications Company

Warner Books Edition
Copyright © 1954, 1976 by James A. Beard
All rights reserved

This Warner Books edition is published by arrangement with
Little, Brown and Co. Inc., 34 Beacon Street, Boston, Massachusetts 02106.

The author is grateful to E. P. Dutton & Co., Inc., for permission to quote the
recipe for roasting a pike from *The Compleat Angler* by Izaak Walton, Everyman's
Library Edition; and to Charles Scribner's Sons for permission to reprint "Minorca
Gopher Stew" from *Cross Creek Cookery* by Marjorie Kinnan Rawlings. Copyright
1942 by Marjorie Kinnan Rawlings.

Illustrations by Earl Thollander

Warner Books, Inc., 666 Fifth Avenue, New York, NY 10103

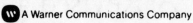 A Warner Communications Company

Printed in the United States of America
First Warner Books Printing: March 1987
10 9 8 7 6 5 4 3

Library of Congress Cataloging-in-Publication Data

Beard, James, 1903-
    James Beard's new fish cookery.

    Reprint. Originally published: Boston : Little,
Brown, c1976.
    Includes Index.
    1. Cookery (Fish)   I. Title.
TX747.B35   1987   641.6'92   86-26646
ISBN 0-446-38152-7 (U.S.A.) (pbk.)
        0-446-38153-5 (Canada) (pbk.)

Foreword

This rich land of ours is richer still because of the living things that swim or crawl in its waters. In the seas and gulfs along our shores, in our innumerable lakes and ponds, and in our rivers and lesser streams are hundreds of different sorts of edible fish and shellfish. Yet I suppose that of this great variety the average American has cooked no more than three or four kinds. Few people have tasted all the species that are sold in our markets. Many Americans eat fish regularly without really knowing what fish they are eating.

For centuries the French, Italians, Russians, and Chinese have been great fish cooks. It is regrettable that skill in cookery is not an inherited trait among human beings, and that the art of preparing fish could not have been transmitted effortlessly from Old World generations to those of the New. But then, of course, there would have been no need for this book, the purposes of which are to encourage Americans to eat more fish and to help them enjoy it more through the expedient of cooking it well.

All my life I have been fond of fish, and I have been fortunate in having lived where fish were plentiful. I was brought up in the Pacific Northwest, a region that is remarkable in its range of both salt- and freshwater fish. Later, in California, New York, and Europe, I managed to eat every form of seafood I could catch or buy.

Nearly all the recipes I offer were tested at one time or another in my own kitchen. Through the years I have had much expected pleasure and many exciting surprises in cooking varieties of fish that were new to me, in trying new recipes, and in refining traditional ones. I urge you to be adventurous, as I have tried to be, in your approach to fish cookery. And I suggest only one general rule: Don't overcook fish.

— JAMES A. BEARD

Introduction

Since I first wrote this fish book, there have been great ecological changes, and there have been great shortages of some of our favorite fish. There will continue to be, I am afraid, until many of the problems that have to do with raising, caring for, and harvesting fish are settled. Some of our shellfish are almost extinct. Some of our favorite fish are in short supply. On the other hand, there are fish being used and publicized which we never dreamed of using before that have rather distinct and varied flavors that we have not experienced. It is wise to acquaint yourself with those fish in your markets that are permanently in short supply nowadays and those that are in fairly plentiful supply, because one can then judge what will be your mainstays in fish for the future.

In New England there is still haddock, cod, scrod, lemon sole, and small sole. Around New York, we have the same fish, plus a great plenitude of striped bass, and we also get red snapper, pompano, trout, salmon, and halibut. Along the Atlantic Coast, you will find very much the same things. There are shortages of crab and of lobster, but so far no shortages of shrimp and scallops, especially bay scallops, which seem more or less at a premium.

On the West Coast, I think you will still find the dabs, the rex sole, and the petrale sole; in the Northwest, the ling cod, true cod, sablefish, to some extent the sturgeon and the sea trout, and what is known on the West Coast as red snapper, which differs from that on the East Coast. In the rivers and lakes there are no tremendous shortages, though I don't think fish are quite as plentiful as they once were. Yet the variety seems to continue in its satisfying way. We are using many fish now that were not in common usage before, such as squid and octopus, and various other smaller fish. As the science of aquaculture develops, we can look forward to increased varieties and to new flavors from the sea that are totally alien to us now.

It is with a certain sense of excitement, and a certain sense of loss, that I look to the future in fish cookery. I hope the revisions in this book will assist you in adapting to the new tastes we will all have in the coming years.

We wish to thank the Canadian Fisheries Council for their revolutionary discovery in fish cookery. And thanks to Carl Jerome for retesting a major portion of the recipes. Also, I will grant kudos to Emily Gilder and Marilyn Mangas for their assistance with the manuscript of this book. Our thanks to Marc Parson for his suggestion that inspired the addition of a section to the book.

Contents

Foreword vii

Introduction ix

General Information about Fish

Buying and Preparing Fish 3

Cleaning and Dressing Fish 5

Cooking Methods 6

Serving Wine with Fish 13

Court Bouillons and Essences of Fish 17

Sauces for Fish 21

Stuffings and Fish Forcemeat 39

Fish Stews, Chowders, and Soups 42

Suggestions for Using Leftover Fish 62

Saltwater Fish

Barracuda 69

Black Drum 72

Blowfish (Sea Squab) 73

Bluefish 74

Butterfish 77

California Black Sea Bass 80

California Kingfish 82

California Pompano 83

California Whitefish 84

Cod 85

Croaker 102

Cusk	103
Eels	103
Fluke	110
Groupers	111
Grunion	112
Haddock	113
Hake	122
Halibut	123
Herring	132
Kingfish	141
Ling Cod or Long Cod	144
Mackerel	146
Mullet	152
Ocean Perch	154
Ocean Sunfish	159
Pollock	160
Pompano	161
Porgy, or Scup	163
Redfish	164
Red Snapper	167
River Herring	171
Sablefish	172
Salmon	176
Sand Dabs	206
Sardines	208
Sculpin	213
Sea Bass	214
Sea Trout	217
Shad	219
Sheepshead	225
Skate	226
Smelt	228

Sole and the Flounder Family   233
Spanish Mackerel   261
Spot   264
Squid   265
Striped Bass   266
Sturgeon   272
Surf Perch and Sea Perch   279
Swordfish   280
Tautog   285
Tuna and Related Fish   286
Whitebait   294
Whiting   296
Yellowtail   300

Freshwater Fish

Bass   305
Bluegill Sunfish   306
Bowfin   307
Buffalo Fish   307
Burbot   308
Carp   308
Catfish   318
Chub   321
Crappies   321
Lake Herring   322
Pike and Pickerel   323
Pike Perch   331
Sheepshead   333
Suckers   333
Trout   335
Whitefish   344
Yellow Perch   350

Shellfish

Abalone   353
Clams   355
Conch   368
Crab   369
Crawfish or Crayfish   386
Lobster   388
Mussels   413
Oysters   419
Scallops   437
Shrimp   444

Terrestrial Animals Prepared like Fish

Frogs' Legs   469
Snails   473
Turtle, Tortoise and Terrapin   476

Index   481

General Information
About Fish

Buying and Preparing Fish

FRESH FISH

Like other kinds of food, most varieties of fish have their seasons — the particular times when they are in most abundant supply, at their best, and cheapest. These seasons vary greatly from coast to coast and from fish to fish. Everything considered, the best authority on when to buy fresh fish is your own fish dealer. In a number of respects, however, you must supplement his advice with your own judgment.

When you buy whole fish, make sure you are getting the freshest by checking these points:

1. The eyes must be bright, clear, and bulging.
2. The gills should be reddish or pink, clean, and fresh-smelling.
3. The scales should be bright, shiny, and tight to the skin.
4. The flesh should be firm and should spring back when pressed.
5. There should be no strong or unpleasant odor.

Fish spoils easily. As soon as it comes from the market, wrap it in moistureproof paper or place it in a covered dish and store it in the refrigerator.

FROZEN FISH

The frozen-food companies now produce a wide variety of frozen fish, and their selections are excellent buys. If you live far from the fresh supply, or if you have your heart set on a fish that is not at the height of its season, the frozen product can solve your problem with little or no sacrifice in flavor or texture. The amount per person is the same as for fresh fish: ⅓ to ½ pound of edible fish per person. Keep frozen fish, packaged in its original container, in the freezing unit or the frozen-food compartment of your refrigerator until you intend to use it. Thawed fish must be used at once.

To thaw: Fillets, steaks and dressed fish may be cooked without thawing, but you must allow additional time in the cooking process (see page 8). If you wish to bread or stuff the fish, take it out of the package and place it in the refrigerator (not the freezing compartment), allowing it to thaw slowly at 37° to 40°. Thaw it just enough to make it easy to handle. Thawing is always necessary for whole fish in order to clean it. Whole fish may be thawed more quickly by placing it under cold running water. Thawing at room temperature is unwise, as the fish is apt to become shapeless and soggy.

HOW MUCH TO BUY

You will need about ⅓ to ½ pound of fish for each person, but this means edible fish. Do not count the bones, head, tail, and so on. As a general rule, figure on buying about 1 pound of whole fish per person.

Cleaning and Dressing Fish

Much of the fish sold today in the markets is already cleaned and dressed, filleted, or steaked. If you are a fisherman and catch your own, or if you are fortunate enough to have sportsmen friends who give you some of their catches, then you need to know just how to clean and prepare fish for cooking. Here is the process (for further directions for blowfish, see pages 73–74).

1. *Scaling:* Place the fish on a table, holding it firmly by the head with one hand. In the other hand hold a sharp knife, and starting at the tail, scrape toward the head, taking off the scales. Be sure to remove all scales around the fins and the base of the head. Wet fish can be scaled more easily than dry, so you can simplify this job by soaking the fish in cold water for a few minutes before you begin work.

2. *Cleaning:* With a sharp knife slit the belly of the fish the full length from the vent (anal opening) to the head. Remove the intestines. Next, cut around the pelvic fins (those on the underside toward the head) and pull them off, being careful not to tear the fish.

Take off the head by cutting above the collarbone; also remove the pectoral fins (on either side just back of the gills). If the backbone is large, just cut through to it on each side of the fish; then place the fish on the edge of the table so the head hangs over and snap the backbone by bending the head down. Then cut any remaining flesh that holds the head to the body.

Cut off the tail. Next remove the dorsal fin (the large one on the back of the fish). Cut along each side of it and give a quick pull forward toward the head to remove the fin and its root bones. Take out the ventral fins (at the back on the underside) in the same way. Do not take fins off with shears, for simply trimming them will not remove the little bones at the base.

Now wash the fish in cold running water, being sure it is free of any membranes, blood, and viscera. It is now dressed and ready for cooking. Large fish may, of course, be cut crosswise into steaks.

3. *Filleting:* With a sharp, supple knife cut along the back of the fish from the tail to the head. Next, cut down to the backbone just back of the head on one side of the fish. Then, laying the knife flat, cut the flesh down one whole side, slicing it away from the ribs and backbone. Lift the whole side off in one piece. Turn the fish over and repeat on the other side.

4. *Skinning:* Many people like their fillets skinned. Place the fillets skin side down on the table. Hold the tail tightly and with the knife cut down through the flesh to the skin about ½ inch from your fingers. Flatten the knife against the skin and cut the flesh away by sliding it forward while you hold the tail end of the skin firmly.

Cooking Methods

THE CANADIAN COOKING THEORY

The consumption of fish has grown a great deal since I first wrote this book and our knowledge of fish is far greater. There has been a great deal of experimenting on fish, most importantly on cooking time. The Department of Fisheries of Canada went through a long period of testing and made what is probably the most important announcement in fish cookery of the last century, certainly since Mary Evelene Spencer* of the University

* See page 309.

of Washington gave her ideas. The basic principle of the Canadian rules for cooking is that fish is measured at its thickest point — its depth, not across the fish — and that it be cooked, no matter how, at exactly 10 minutes per inch. We have a little diagram for this so you will get the feeling for it more clearly.

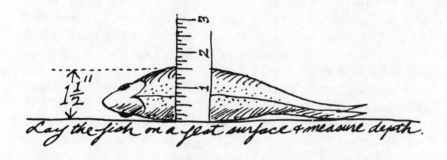

Lay the fish on a flat surface & measure depth.

This applies to fillets, whole fish, and steaks, and it applies to baking, broiling, braising, sautéing, frying, poaching, steaming — every sort of preparation of fish. When cooking rolled fillets, measure the diameter of the fillet after you have rolled it. When poaching fish, wait until it reaches the simmering point after you put it into the boiling water, then count your 10 minutes per inch. In sautéing or frying, measure a fillet or a fish, and give it 10 minutes per inch or any fraction thereof. In baking, bake it at 10 minutes per inch in a 450° oven. In braising, do the same thing. And in pan frying or broiling, follow the same rule. The Canadian cooking theory does not apply when cooking shellfish or crustaceans. Elsewhere, it works like a charm and is completely foolproof. Remember, measure the fish at its thickest point, when it's on its side, not erect, and then give it 10 minutes per inch, no matter how you cook it. I have used this method for over seven years, both in classes round the United States and Europe and in demonstrations. I assure you that with it you get better fish without all of that testing and flaking, which often causes mutilation and overcooking.

The Canadian theory works equally well with fresh fish and frozen fish. If you are cooking frozen fish, do not thaw it, but cook the fish frozen. Instead of counting 10 minutes per inch, simply count 20 minutes. Thus a fish measuring 2½ inches would take 50 minutes. (If the fish were fresh and measured 2½ inches, it would cook for 25 minutes.)

Any fish may be cooked by any of the methods given in this section. Sometimes you may hear people say that such and such a fish is "too fat" to broil or that another fish is "too dry" to eat with mayonnaise. These are silly notions. Don't believe them.

Fish is most responsive to flavoring during the actual cooking process. Some varieties of fish require special flavors to complement natural flavors that are somewhat neutral. Others need only salt and pepper to make them outstanding. And don't forget that good butter, olive oil, sweet cream, sour cream, and wine enhance fish and give it added goodness.

BAKING

Measure the fish at its largest point. Allow 10 minutes cooking time per inch of thickness. If fish is frozen, double the cooking time. Bake in a very hot oven (425°–450°). When baking stuffed fish, stuff the fish as usual and measure the stuffed fish at its thickest part. Bake it as already explained, allowing 10 minutes per inch for fresh fish, 20 minutes per inch for frozen fish.

Cooking fish in foil or paper. When cooking fish in either foil or paper, measure the thickness of the fish as already explained and bake in a hot oven (450°), allowing 10 minutes cooking time per inch thickness for fresh fish and 20 minutes cooking time per inch thickness for frozen fish, *plus* additional time for the heat to penetrate the paper or foil. Count on 5 extra minutes for fresh fish and 10 extra minutes for frozen fish.

BROILING – CHARCOAL GRILLING

There is no doubt about it – fish grilled over charcoal has an entirely "different" flavor. Use a hinged grill so the fish will stay in place, and be sure the grill is hot and well oiled when you put the fish into it – it should be hot enough to mark the fish.

Whether whole, half fillets, or steaks, the fish should be well floured and oiled before grilling and should be brushed well with oil several times during the cooking process. Steaks or fillets without skin will need more lubrication than whole fish. Allow 10 minutes cooking time per inch thickness for fresh fish, and 20 minutes cooking time per inch thickness for frozen fish.

OVEN BROILING

Measure the thickness of the fish or pieces of fish and place them on the oiled rack of a broiling pan. Baste with melted fat or basting sauce. Place the broiling pan in a preheated oven, so that the fish is approximately 2 to 4 inches from the heating unit. If fish is frozen, it will have to be placed lower in the oven to prevent overcooking the surface before the interior is cooked. Leave the door ajar if using an electric oven, unless the manufacturer's directions state otherwise. When fish has browned on one side, turn. Brush with melted fat again. The total cooking time should be 10 minutes per inch thickness for fresh fish, and 20 minutes cooking time per inch thickness for frozen fish. Cuts of fish ¾ to 1 inch have less tendency to dry out during broiling than thinner cuts. Thin cuts of fish may be broiled *without* turning.

Fillets: Flour the fillets and rub them well with butter, oil, or other fat. Place them about 2 inches from the heat and baste them once or twice during the cooking process. Do not turn them. Allow 10 minutes cooking time per inch of thickness.

Steaks: Dust the steaks with flour and dot them well with butter or brush them with oil. Place them on the oiled rack or flat pan about 2 inches from the heat. Steaks should be turned once during the broiling, and it is wise to allow more of the cooking time after the turning than before; then the serving side will have a nice brown color. Baste once or twice, and be sure to give the steaks an extra basting after you turn them to help them brown well. Season steaks after removing from the broiler. Allow 10 minutes cooking time per inch of thickness or fraction thereof.

Split fish: You may split fish at home or have the fish dealer do it for you. I like a fish broiled with its backbone intact — it seems to make a difference in the juiciness and the flavor. Place the fish skin side down on the oiled broiling rack or in a separate pan. Dust it with flour and dot it heavily with butter or brush it with oil. Broil it 2 to 3 inches from the heat. Very delicately meated fish, such as carp, pike, and whitefish, should be placed a bit farther away. Baste it several times during the cooking and be sure you do not turn it. Allow 10 minutes cooking time per inch of thickness. Season the split fish after cooking.

Whole fish: A whole fish with the head on will be much juicier than one without the head. Dust the fish with flour, and butter or oil it well on one side. (Oil the second side after turning.) Place smaller fish about 3 inches from the heat, larger ones about 6 inches away. Allow 10 minutes cooking time per inch of thickness, turning once. Fluke, flounder, and sole are usually not turned. Baste often and season after cooking.

PAN FRYING OR SAUTÉING (SAUTÉ MEUNIÈRE)

If necessary, cut fish into serving-sized pieces. Prepare as directed by your recipe. Heat 1/4 inch of melted butter or oil or a combination of butter and oil in a frying pan. Have it very hot, but not smoking. Fry the fish until golden brown on one side; turn and brown on the other side. The complete cooking time will be approximately 10 minutes per inch in thickness. For sauté meunière, proceed as above, remove fish to a hot platter, and add to it the butter from the pan along with a goodly sprinkling of lemon juice and chopped parsley.

DEEP FRYING

Heat the fat in your deep fryer to 375°. Dip the fish in beaten egg and roll in flour, corn meal, or bread crumbs. Place in the frying basket and lower into the fat. Cooking time will be approximately 10 minutes per inch of thickness. Drain on absorbent paper and season to taste.

Be sure the temperature of the fat goes back to 375° before frying other pieces of fish. Be careful not to overcook. Fish done this way can be deliciously juicy and tender or it can resemble sawdust. Deep frying is perhaps the riskiest way to cook fish.

BRAISING

This method is little known in this country but very popular in France. If you've never tried it, I urge you to make the experiment. The results are excellent.

Cut 3 carrots, 2 stalks of celery, 3 onions, and a clove of garlic into thin strips. Sauté them in 3 tablespoons of butter for 5 minutes. Arrange them on the bottom of a baking dish, fish boiler, or saucepan. Place your fish on the bed of vegetables, salt and pepper it, and place a few strips of bacon or salt pork across the top. Add enough liquid — red or white wine or a mixture of wine and fish bouillon — to half cover the fish. Let it come to a boil; either cook it very slowly on top of the stove or put it in a 350° oven. In either case baste carefully during the cooking process. The total cooking time will be about 10 minutes per inch of thickness from the time the liquid reaches a boil.

Fish cooked in this manner is usually served with a sauce made of the cooking liquid, put through a sieve and mixed with other ingredients. Sometimes part of the skin is removed after cooking and the fish is decorated with garnishes — mushrooms, truffles, pickles, lemon slices, anchovy fillets.

POACHING

Whether you are going to poach your fish in water or milk, or in any of the court bouillons in this book, the timing is exactly the same. Bring the water or milk to the boiling point; place the fish in it. When it returns to the boiling point, begin timing the fish. Allow 10 minutes cooking time per inch thickness for fresh fish, about 20 minutes cooking time per inch thickness for frozen fish.

Most whole fish are prepared with the head and tail on the fish, but scaled and with the fins run. For ease in handling, wrap the fish in cheesecloth. Leave long ends on the cloth to serve as tabs at each end of the fish and grasp these when you lift it.

Neither fish nor shellfish should not be left in bouillon after they are cooked. They will be overdone and tough.

When you cook fish in court bouillon, the critically important point to remember is that the liquid should never boil or bubble after the fish goes in. Do not discard the broth. It may be used for sauces, aspics, and in any way you use fish stock. If fish is left to cool in the bouillon, the cooking time should be reduced so as not to overcook.

SOUPS AND CHOWDERS

For these methods of cooking, see the section on fish stews, chowders, and soups (pages 42–62).

Serving Wine with Fish

Most fish dishes are enhanced by well-chilled dry white wine. This is neither rule nor ritual but simply a time-tested expression of popular taste and preference. Fish generally has a delicate texture, and its flavor is often elusive. Dry white wines, lacking the roundness and robust taste of the reds, improve the flavor of the fish but do not overwhelm it.

Not everyone agrees. If you are among those people who genuinely like red Burgundy with broiled halibut or sauternes with bouillabaisse, then these preferences are your own special pleasures. No one can say for certain that you are "incorrect." If, however, you are serving fish to guests whose tastes are unfamiliar to you, probably the wise procedure would be to accompany the dish with the traditional dry white wine.

What if the fish has been cooked in red wine or the sauce contains red wine? Should the cook set aside a jug of red "cooking wine," distinct and separate from the wine that is to be served with the fish?

The existence of "cooking wine" is a culinary myth. Wine is used in cooking as a flavoring agent; the better the wine, the better the flavor. And so some authorities say that it makes good sense to serve the same wine that was used in cooking the fish. I think it might be more accurate to say that the predominating flavors of a dish, and the intensities of these flavors, should determine what sort of wine is served. If the sauce for a fish is pungently accented with herbs, spices, and garlic, then red wine or rosé may be preferable to white. For example, the famous California dish cioppino is customarily served with red or rosé wine. A number of highly seasoned baked fish dishes — red snapper, redfish, sea trout — are sometimes served with a light red.

There are also some other exceptions to the traditional affinity between fish and dry white wine. Some salmon dishes, for example, are perfect with rosé and also go well with a light red wine. The same is true of some of the heavier fish stews. Many people enjoy rosé or light red wine with swordfish, since its texture is heavier than that of most fish and its flavor rather "meaty."

Champagne is happily married to all fish dishes — hors d'oeuvre, stews, entrées. Besides champagne, pleasant accompaniments for hors d'oeuvre based on fish and shellfish are dry sherry, rosé, and dry white wine. All should be chilled.

FRENCH WINES

There are no greater wines than the great French wines, and there is no greater complement to a fine fish dish than one of the superb white wines of the Côte de Beaune. The great French wines are readily available in good wine shops in New York, Boston, San Francisco, and other large American cities, but they are often hard to find in smaller cities.

Where French wines are available, fish lovers have this advantage: Generally speaking, the finest of France's dry white wines and rosés are less costly than the very great reds. Superb white wines, the greatest in the world, may be had for less than $15–$18, and many excellent white wines of less distinction may be obtained for around $4–$6.

Champagne. Complementary to all fish, but never cheap. Among the famous names are Pommery and Greno, Dom Perignon, Louis Roederer, Bollinger, Veuve Clicquot, Pol Roger, Taittinger. The dryest champagne is labeled *brut* and *English Market*. Despite the implication, *extra dry* is not the dryest.

White Bordeaux. The white wines of Graves, once popular in England and the United States, are no longer so eagerly sought by wine lovers. A notable exception, almost a curiosity, is the very dry Château Haut-Brion Blanc, regrettably scarce and expensive. A good dryish Graves is Château Olivier. In general, sauternes and Barsac are too sweet for fish dishes.

White Burgundy. Perfect with fish. The communes that are world-famous for dry whites include Vougeot, Aloxe-Corton,

Meursault, Chassagne-Montrachet, Puligay-Montrachet. In a special class of its own is Chablis, greenish golden and dry as flint. It is superb with oysters. Not sufficiently appreciated by Americans is Pouilly-Fuissé, excellent with all fish and quite reasonable.

Rhone. The Hermitage white wines are excellent with fish. One of the most charming white wines in the world is Clos de Chante-Alouette. Try it with a delicate sole dish.

Loire. For a pleasant experience with fish, try Pouilly-Fumé, which is fresh and fruity, with a taste of the soil. Also pleasant, and very reasonable, is Muscadet.

Alsace. For wonderful summer drinking, especially with cold fish try Gewurztraminer, Traminer, Riesling.

Rosé wines. The Travel rosé wines are delicious when chilled. To a somewhat lesser extent than champagne, they are congenial with nearly all fish dishes.

GERMAN WINES

The Rhine and Moselle districts of Germany produce some of the world's most famous white wines. Rhine wines tend to be full-bodied and long-lived, while the Moselles are lighter and often delightfully fragrant and delicate. Personally, I have never considered German wines to be the equal of the fine French white wines, yet I must acknowledge that they are highly prized and that the renowned bottlings, such as Schloss Johannisberg and Bernkasteler Doktor, command exceptional prices. Many of the dry German wines are excellent with fish, and the Moselles, especially, are delicious with cold fish dishes served on warm summer days.

Some of the most expensive Rhine wines are exceedingly rich and sweet, and these, of course, are not congenial with fish. German wines labeled *Auslese* (selected picking of the grapes) and *Spätlese* (late picked) tend to be dryish.

AMERICAN WINES

The white wines produced in the United States must be judged and enjoyed in proper perspective. In the last ten years they have increased in stature and in quality and are now equal to fine white wines in any country of the world. American wine is interesting, varied, and delicious and goes especially well with fish dishes. Their prices do not differ much from those of imported wines, but in many communities one finds inexpensive and good American wines that are perfectly reasonable table wines.

There are some interesting wines in New York State and there are great developments in Oregon and Washington and in many other states, but we find the greatest number of available wines from California. The best ones are named for their variety, such as Johannisburg Riesling, Riesling, Pinot Blanc, Pinot Chardonnay, Sauvignon Blanc, Sylvaner, Traminer, and Gewurztraminer. Most of these come from the counties around San Francisco Bay and the Livermore, Napa, Sonoma, and Santa Clara valleys. These geographic names are also generally clues to quality.

The native wines of New York are distinctly different from those of California. There has been a great deal of work done with hybrid grapes to banish the rather foxy, or grapy, flavor that was distinctive to the wines of New York State and one finds some excellent white wines coming along.

The same varietals that are used in California are used to great advantage in Oregon and Washington. If you find them, give them a sampling.

With American wines, it's true that the label describes what you're buying. Varietal wines are tops, although there are some bulk bottled wines called Chablis or Rhine wines that are not too bad and should be tasted. They can be considered as everyday table wines, to be enjoyed without spending a great deal of money. If in doubt, consult your wine merchant or the many books that have recently been published on American wines.

ITALIAN WINES

Italian wines have become more and more popular in this country within the last ten to twelve years. We have some deliciously simple, rather romantic wines such as Verdicchio. Also good are the white Chiantis, red and white Corvo, and red and white Orvieto. Italian wines are generally not as distinguished as French ones, nor are they always as good as fine American wines, but they're gay, enjoyable wines to drink, especially in the summer and they lend themselves to fish beautifully. If you eat cold fish or take fish on a picnic, remember good Italian wines.

OTHER WINES

There are some very interesting wines from Hungary and Yugoslavia that use the same varietals as the Rieslings and Pinot Chardonnays of California, France, and Italy. Some of them are excellent buys and offer great drinking pleasure. Don't be afraid to experiment.

Court Bouillons and Essences of Fish

Fish differs greatly in flavor, texture, gelatinous content, and delicacy of meat. Some fish and shellfish need strong bouillon to bring out and complement their flavors. Others have such distinctive flavors in themselves that they need practically nothing to enhance them.

SIMPLE COURT BOUILLON I

Sea bass, striped bass, red snapper, and other similar fish should be poached in a simple salt and water bouillon. They have distinction and flavor in themselves and should not be assaulted with artificial seasonings. Other flavors and seasonings will come directly from the sauces served with these fish.

SIMPLE COURT BOUILLON II

This bouillon can be used for whiting, halibut, cod, and many of the small white fish. Combine equal quantities of milk and water with just a little salt. Bring to a boil before adding the fish. Reduce the bouillon over a fairly brisk flame after the fish is cooked and you can use it for sauces.

COURT BOUILLON FOR COLD FISH DISHES

If you are doing a large piece of salmon, or a whole one, or a large piece of any fish to be served cold, you then want a bouillon that has a pleasant blending of flavors and is well punctuated with herbs and seasonings. Such a court bouillon may be used as the basis for a remarkably good aspic. Reduce the court bouillon after removing the fish. Clarify by adding white of egg and eggshell to the broth.*

For a large fish:

3 quarts water	3 onions
1 quart white wine	9 cloves
1 cup wine vinegar	4 carrots, finely cut

* Note: Add the eggshells and egg whites, and over high heat beat constantly with a wire whisk until the aspic reaches a boil. Then turn off the heat and let the aspic settle for approximately 10 minutes. Strain, very carefully, through a sieve lined with a linen towel, being sure not to disturb the liquid as it drips through the towel (this can cause the aspic to cloud).

<table>
<tr><td>2 stalks celery</td><td>4 to 5 sprigs parsley</td></tr>
<tr><td>1 bay leaf</td><td>1 tablespoon salt</td></tr>
<tr><td>1 teaspoon thyme</td><td></td></tr>
</table>

Put 3 cloves in each onion. Combine all ingredients and bring to a boil. Simmer for an hour before adding the fish.

RED WINE COURT BOUILLON

This is really an essence of fish, for it uses the bones and heads to make a richer bouillon. It is an excellent base for aspics or sauces, or it may be cooked down to about a third of its volume and used as a flavoring agent or glaze for fish dishes.

2 pounds fish bones and heads	2 stalks celery
3 quarts water	1 onion stuck with cloves
1 quart red wine	3 carrots cut in quarters
Bouquet garni (thyme, parsley, leck)	1 tablespoon salt

Cook the bones and heads of fish in 2 quarts of water for 30 minutes. Add the remaining water and all the other ingredients and continue cooking for 20 minutes. Add the fish and cook according to the recipe.

RICH WHITE WINE COURT BOUILLON
FOR ASPICS

1 pound fish bones and heads	2 carrots, diced
1 quart water	2 cloves garlic
1 quart dry white wine	1 bay leaf
1 teaspoon dried thyme	Salt
2 onions stuck with cloves	Freshly ground black pepper

Cook the fish bones and heads in the water for 30 minutes. Strain through fine cloth. You should have about a quart of bouillon. Add all the other ingredients, bring to a boil, and simmer for 20 minutes before adding the fish. For aspic, reduce the bouillon over high heat after the fish is removed. Clarify it with egg white and shells (page 18).

COURT BOUILLON FOR SHELLFISH

Use either the red or the white wine court bouillon for any of the shellfish. If, however, the shrimp, lobster, langouste, or crayfish are to be served with a highly flavored sauce, it is often more desirable to poach the fish in a plain salt and water bouillon — or in seawater, if available.

FISH ESSENCE

This can be used for flavorings, aspics, soups, and — if reduced to a heavy jelly — glazes.

2 cups mirepoix (carrots, onions, celery)
3 tablespoons butter
Salt
Freshly ground black pepper

2 quarts white wine
2 pounds fish bones and heads
4 sprigs parsley
1 teaspoon thyme

Make the mirepoix by cutting the vegetables in very fine julienne and cooking them in the butter until they just begin to color. Salt and pepper to taste. Add the wine and the fish bones and heads. Bring to a boil, remove any surface scum, and add the parsley and thyme. Simmer for 2 hours.

Clarify and strain through a very fine sieve or linen napkin (page 18).

Sauces for Fish

SAUCE VELOUTÉ

2 tablespoons flour
2 tablespoons butter
1 cup fish stock

Salt
Freshly ground black pepper

Combine the flour and butter and cook together until they are slightly browned or yellowish in color. Gradually stir in the fish stock; continue stirring until it thickens. Simmer 10 minutes and season to taste. This makes 1 cup of velouté.

It is customary when you serve a plain velouté to add cream and egg yolks to the sauce. To 1 cup of velouté add 1 cup of cream and 3 egg yolks. Beat the cream and egg yolks together well and gradually stir into the basic sauce; continue stirring until the sauce is properly thickened and heated through. Be careful not to let the mixture boil after the egg yolks have been added. This will make 2 cups of sauce velouté.

VARIATIONS

Shrimp Sauce. To 1 cup sauce velouté add ½ cup finely chopped cooked shrimp.

Lobster Sauce. To 1 cup sauce velouté add ½ cup finely chopped cooked lobster meat.

Oyster Sauce. Use ¼ to ½ cup oyster liquor in making the basic sauce velouté and add ½ cup chopped oysters.

Clam Sauce. Use ½ cup clam liquor in making the basic sauce velouté and add ½ cup minced clams.

Crabmeat Sauce. To 1 cup sauce velouté add ½ cup flaked, cooked crabmeat.

SAUCE AURORE

1 cup sauce velouté   ½ cup cream
½ cup tomato paste   2 egg yolks

Combine the sauce velouté with the tomato paste. Gradually add the cream and egg yolks, which have been well mixed. Stir until thickened and smooth, but take care the mixture does not boil. Taste for seasoning.

SAUCE MORNAY

1½ cups sauce velouté   ½ cup (more or less) cream
½ cup grated Parmesan cheese   Few grains cayenne pepper

When the sauce velouté has thickened, stir in the grated cheese and continue stirring lightly until the cheese is melted. Dilute with cream, if needed. Season with cayenne and taste for salt.

FRENCH CURRY SAUCE

This is a good choice if you like a mild flavor of curry. It is also easier to make than the regular curry sauce.

2 cups sauce velouté   Curry to taste
½ cup cream

Combine the sauce velouté with the cream and as much curry as you like; heat well. Use on any type of fish.

SAUCE SOUBISE

1 large onion, finely chopped   1 cup sauce velouté
Butter

Steam onion in butter until soft and transparent. Add to sauce.

BASIC SAUCE BÉCHAMEL

4 tablespoons butter   Salt
3 tablespoons flour   Freshly ground black pepper
½ cup fish broth   Nutmeg
1 cup milk

Melt the butter, add the flour, and cook until slightly colored. Add the fish broth and stir until smooth. Gradually add milk and continue stirring until nicely thickened. Cook 5 minutes and season to taste with salt, pepper, and nutmeg.

VARIATIONS

Tomato Sauce. Add 3 tablespoons tomato paste.

Tomato-Curry Sauce. To the tomato sauce add 1 to 1½ tablespoons curry powder.

Anchovy Sauce. Add 2 or more tablespoons anchovy paste, 1 tablespoon butter, and the juice of half a lemon.

Cheese Sauce. Add 1 cup grated Cheddar or Gruyère cheese, a few grains cayenne, and ½ teaspoon dry mustard.

Egg Sauce. Add 3 hard-cooked eggs, thinly sliced.

Parsley Sauce. Add ⅓ cup finely chopped parsley. Flavor, if you wish, with 1 tablespoon onion juice.

Piquant Sauce. Add 1 tablespoon finely chopped onion, 1 finely chopped hard-cooked egg, 1 finely chopped dill pickle, and 1 tablespoon finely chopped parsley.

Mustard Sauce. Add 1 tablespoon Dijon mustard and 1 teaspoon or more dry mustard.

White Wine Sauce. Stir in ½ cup white wine and 2 egg yolks. Heat through, stirring constantly, but do not let the sauce boil.

Dill Sauce. Add 1 teaspoon chopped fresh dill.

Cream Sauce. Follow the basic sauce béchamel recipe, but substitute cream, or half cream and half milk, for the fish broth and milk.

SAUCE CARDINAL

1 cup fish stock
1 truffle (optional)
½ cup heavy cream

1½ cups sauce béchamel
4 tablespoons lobster butter
(page 32)

Using a high heat reduce the fish stock to ½ cup. While it is reducing, you may add a truffle to the stock, if you wish. Combine the stock with the cream and the béchamel. When it is smooth and thickened, remove it from the fire and stir in the lobster butter.

HORSERADISH SAUCE

½ cup grated fresh horseradish
1 cup sauce béchamel

Juice of ½ lemon

Add the horseradish to the sauce, blend well, and add the lemon juice. If you use bottled horseradish, be sure you drain it well before you mix it with the sauce, and omit the lemon juice.

SAUCE POULETTE

1 cup white sauce
2 egg yolks

Juice of ½ lemon
Chopped parsley

Make a basic white sauce, add the egg yolks, and blend well with a wooden spoon or whisk. Season with lemon juice and parsley. Be careful not to let the sauce boil after the egg yolks are added.

SAUCE BOURGUIGNONNE

1 small onion	Salt
6 mushrooms	Freshly ground black pepper
4 tablespoons butter	Beurre manié (page 475)
2 cups fish stock	Chopped parsley
1 cup red wine	

Chop the onion very fine and slice the mushrooms very thin. Sauté them in butter until they are cooked through. Add the fish stock and the wine and let it simmer until reduced by half. Correct the seasoning and thicken with beurre manié (balls of butter and flour kneaded together). Add chopped parsley just before serving. Serve with poached fish such as salmon, salmon trout, or sturgeon.

VARIATION

Add anchovy paste to taste along with a dash of lemon juice.

SAUCE HOLLANDAISE

This is sometimes called sauce Isigny. The secret of a good Hollandaise is to use the finest of sweet butter, to be sure the pan in which you make it does not touch the water below, and to be sure that the water never boils. Use either a wooden spoon or a wire whisk (I think the latter is better).

3 egg yolks	Few grains cayenne pepper
1 or 2 teaspoons water	Few grains salt
¼ pound (½ cup) butter, cut into small pieces	Lemon juice *or* tarragon vinegar

Combine the egg yolks and water in the upper part of a double boiler and whisk over hot water until the eggs are well mixed and slightly thickened. Gradually add the butter. Whisk all the time, and be certain that the water below does not boil. If your sauce becomes too thick, dilute it with a little water. If it curdles, you can bring it back with a little boiling water. When it is properly emulsified, add the cayenne and a few grains of salt and the lemon juice (or vinegar) to taste.

SAUCE MOUSSELINE

This is a combination of equal parts of Hollandaise and whipped cream. It is one of the most delicate sauces in cookery.

SAUCE BÉARNAISE

This is prepared exactly like a Hollandaise except that it has some added flavorings. Take 2 teaspoons of chopped fresh tarragon or 1 teaspoon of dried, 2 teaspoons of finely chopped shallots or green onions, a small pinch of salt and a pinch of black pepper. Add these to 3 tablespoons of wine vinegar and cook it down until it is practically a glaze. Add this glaze to the egg yolks and then proceed as for Hollandaise. Flavor with finely chopped tarragon, parsley, and chervil, and a speck of cayenne. Add more lemon juice or tarragon vinegar, if you like.

BÉARNAISE TOMATE

This is a blend of Béarnaise and tomato paste, flavored with a little salt and pepper and a bit of tarragon.

DUXELLES

1 medium onion	1 teaspoon chopped parsley
½ pound mushrooms	Salt
6 tablespoons butter	Freshly ground black pepper

Chop the onion very fine. Chop the mushrooms — caps and stems — very fine and press them in a cloth or sieve to release any natural moisture.

Melt the butter in a skillet. Add the onion and let it become just transparent. Add the mushrooms and let them cook down to almost a paste. Add the parsley, salt, and pepper to taste, and cook until there is practically no moisture left. This may be stored in the refrigerator and used for various sauces or stuffings.

SAUCE DUXELLES

This is a very practical sauce as it can be served with a great number of fish dishes.

¾ cup white wine	3 tablespoons flour
¾ cup fish stock *or* bouillon	½ cup strong stock (fish or
2 tablespoons chopped shallots	meat)
or onions	½ cup tomato paste
3 tablespoons butter	3 tablespoons duxelles

Combine the wine, the fish stock, and the chopped shallots or onion. Bring to a boil and let it reduce by half. Melt the butter in a large saucepan or skillet, combine with the flour, and let it cook until lightly colored. Gradually stir in the additional stock, the tomato paste, and the reduced wine and broth mixture. Stir until thickened and well blended. Add the duxelles and blend again. Taste for seasoning.

SAUCE À L'AMÉRICAINE

3 tablespoons butter
1 small chopped onion
6 chopped shallots *or* green
    onions
5 ripe tomatoes, peeled, seeded,
    and chopped
1 clove garlic, chopped
3 tablespoons chopped parsley

1 tablespoon chopped fresh
    tarragon *or* 1 teaspoon dried
    tarragon
1½ teaspoons thyme
Salt
Freshly ground black pepper
3 tablespoons tomato paste

Melt the butter and sauté the onion for a few minutes. Add the shallots, tomatoes, garlic and herbs and simmer for 1 hour. Season to taste and let cook down and blend thoroughly. Add the tomato paste at the last.

NOTE: Actually, sauce à l'Américaine is usually added to fish (generally shellfish) as it cooks in white wine. During the cooking process the sauce and the wine blend. The fish is then dished out on a platter and the liquid poured over and around it. The amount of sauce given above will blend with 1½ cups of wine or fish stock.

SAUCE ITALIENNE

Brown roux
12 mushrooms
3 tablespoons butter
1 cup tomato paste *or* 1 can
    condensed tomato soup

¾ cup fish stock
2 tablespoons chopped herbs
    (parsley, tarragon, chervil or
    dill)

Make a brown roux by browning 4 tablespoons of flour and combining with an equal amount of butter.

Chop the mushrooms very fine and cook them down in the butter until they are a paste.

Heat the tomato paste and the fish stock, which should be reduced a bit; when this has almost reached the boiling point, stir in the mushrooms and the roux and continue stirring until properly thickened. Add the chopped herbs and taste for seasoning.

CURRY SAUCE

⅔ cup grated coconut *or*
    ground almonds
1 cup milk
2 onions
1 apple, cored but unpeeled
2 tomatoes, peeled and seeded

4 tablespoons butter
2 tablespoons curry powder
Salt
1 cup white wine
Cream, if needed

Put the coconut or almonds to soak in the milk.

Chop the onions, apple, and tomatoes. Melt the butter in a skillet and cook the onion until just soft. Add the apple, tomatoes, curry powder, and salt to taste. Cook slowly until the vegetables are tender. Add the wine and simmer for 15 minutes; then add the coconut or almond milk and simmer for 15 minutes more. Force the sauce through a fine sieve, return it to the stove, and let it cook down for a few minutes until well blended and thickened. Add a little cream if necessary. Taste for seasoning.

SAUCE DIABLE

6 shallots *or* 1 small onion with
    1 clove garlic finely chopped
3 tablespoons butter
2 tablespoons Dijon mustard
½ cup consommé *or* fish broth
½ cup white wine
2 tablespoons tomato paste

1 teaspoon salt
Cayenne pepper
Juice of ½ lemon
½ teaspoon Tabasco
1 teaspoon freshly ground black
    pepper

Sauté the shallots or onion and garlic in butter. Add mustard. Gradually add the consommé and wine, blending well. Add remaining seasonings and taste.

BARBECUE SAUCE

2 medium-sized onions, finely
  chopped
¼ cup olive oil
1 cup tomato sauce
1 teaspoon salt
1 teaspoon basil

½ cup steak sauce
¼ cup Worcestershire sauce
1 teaspoon dry mustard
½ cup strained honey
½ cup red wine

Sauté the onions in olive oil until lightly browned. Add the tomato paste, salt, basil, steak sauce, Worcestershire sauce, mustard, and honey. Allow to simmer 5 minutes, stirring constantly. Add the wine and allow the sauce to come just to the boiling point. Taste for seasoning. Strain through a fine sieve.

ANCHOVY ONION SAUCE

2 large or 4 medium-sized
  Spanish onions
4 tablespoons olive oil
10 anchovy fillets
¼ cup chopped parsley

Thyme
Fresh or dried basil
1 cup Italian tomato paste
¼ cup white wine

Peel the onions and chop them fine. Sauté them until delicately golden, but not brown, in olive oil. Add the anchovy fillets, each cut into 2 pieces. Mix very carefully with the onions and add the chopped parsley and a few leaves of thyme and basil. Stir in the tomato paste mixed with the wine and let the entire sauce cook down very slightly. Taste for seasoning. Whether you need additional salt depends on the saltiness of the anchovies.

SAUCE PROVENÇALE

¾ cup finely chopped onion
6 cloves garlic, very finely
  chopped

½ cup olive oil
1 32-oz. can Italian plum
  tomatoes

1½ teaspoons salt
3 tablespoons chopped fresh
   basil *or* 1½ teaspoons dried
   basil

1 teaspoon freshly ground black
   pepper
3 heaping tablespoons tomato
   paste
¼ cup chopped fresh parsley

Sauté the onions and garlic in the oil over medium-high heat. Add the tomatoes and seasonings, bring to the boil, reduce heat, and cook slowly for 15 minutes, stirring occasionally. Correct seasonings. Add the tomato paste and simmer for 15 minutes, stirring occasionally. Finally, add the parsley and stir together.

BROWNED BUTTER (BEURRE NOISETTE)

This is really browned butter. Heat the butter in a small skillet or pipkin, turning the pan from side to side, until it is a delicate brown but not burned.

BEURRE MAITRE D'HOTEL

Beurre noisette (browned butter) with lemon juice to taste.

BLACK BUTTER (BEURRE NOIR)

Heat 6 tablespoons of butter until well browned. Add lemon juice or wine vinegar to taste and blend well.

LEMON BUTTER

Heat the amount of butter needed and add lemon juice to taste.

Lime Butter. Substitute lime juice for lemon juice.

LOBSTER BUTTER

Grind or pound cooked lobster shells until very fine. Combine with the quantity of butter needed for the recipe and force through a fine strainer. To each ¼ pound of butter add the shells from a 1-pound lobster.

ANCHOVY BUTTER

Cream ½ cup butter until it is light. Fold in 6 anchovy fillets, finely chopped, or use anchovy paste to taste. Add a few drops of lemon juice and 1 teaspoon chopped parsley.

VARIATION

You may melt the butter and stir in the anchovy paste. Season with a few drops of lemon juice.

CAVIAR BUTTER

Cream 6 tablespoons of butter until light and add 1 tablespoon of caviar (more or less, according to your taste). Season with a few drops of lemon juice.

HERB BUTTER

Cream ¼ pound of butter and blend in 1 tablespoon each of finely chopped parsley, chives, chervil and tarragon. If you use the dried tarragon and chervil, use 1 teaspoon each.

VARIATIONS

Tarragon-Chive Butter. Cream butter and add chopped chives and tarragon to taste.
Parsley Butter. Cream butter and add chopped parsley to taste.

SAUCE AÏOLI

This sauce is a regular Friday dish for many people living in the South of France. It was formerly made by pounding the garlic in a mortar, but you can make it much more easily with a blender or food processor.

12 cloves garlic
3 cups olive oil, plus 3 tablespoons

4 egg yolks
Salt
Lemon juice

To prepare in a blender, blend the garlic in the container with 1 egg yolk and 3 tablespoons olive oil. Combine this paste with a very heavy mayonnaise, made with 3 egg yolks and 3 cups olive oil, depending on the size of the eggs. Season with the salt and lemon juice to taste.

To prepare in a food processor, combine 6 to 8 cloves garlic, 1 whole egg, 2 tablespoons lemon juice, salt, and freshly ground black pepper in the beaker. With the metal chopping blade in place, process, gradually adding 1½ cups olive oil.

To prepare in a mortar, pound the garlic in the mortar; gradually add the egg yolks and finally pound in the olive oil, a tablespoon at a time (approximately 3½ cups), until the consistency of a thick mayonnaise is reached. Season with salt and lemon juice to taste.

SAUCE MAYONNAISE

2 egg yolks
1 teaspoon salt
½ teaspoon dry mustard

1 pint peanut *or* olive oil
Lemon juice *or* vinegar

Beat the egg yolks, salt, and mustard together and gradually add the oil, beating constantly until well thickened and stiff. Thin with lemon juice or vinegar to taste.

If your mayonnaise starts to curdle, begin over with another egg yolk and a little oil, and gradually add the curdled mixture. I find that it is important to have your eggs and oil at the same temperature.

You may make mayonnaise with a fork, a rotary beater, a whisk, or an electric blender or mixer, or a food processor.

VARIATIONS

Sauce Andalouse. To 1 cup mayonnaise add ½ cup tomato paste and 2 pimientos, finely chopped. Season with ½ teaspoon paprika.

Mayonnaise with Jelly. Combine equal quantities of mayonnaise and aspic — either lemon or fish, when the jelly is very thick before it has actually jelled. Beat it well with a wire whisk and chill. Use it for masking fish, or as decoration piped through a pastry tube.

Green Mayonnaise (Sauce Verte). To 2 cups mayonnaise add 1 cup mixed herbs (spinach, watercress, parsley, chives, tarragon) that have been chopped very fine, almost to a powder. Blend well.

SAUCE RÉMOULADE

2 cups mayonnaise
2 cloves garlic, finely chopped
1 tablespoon finely chopped
   tarragon
1 teaspoon dry mustard
1 tablespoon capers

2 hard-cooked eggs, finely
   chopped
1 tablespoon finely chopped
   parsley
1 teaspoon anchovy paste

Mix all the ingredients thoroughly and let stand for 2 hours before serving.

RUSSIAN DRESSING

2 cups mayonnaise
2 tablespoons finely chopped
   onion

1 tablespoon Dijon mustard
2 ounces caviar

Blend well and let stand for 2 hours before serving.

THOUSAND ISLAND DRESSING

2 cups mayonnaise
2 tablespoons finely chopped
   onion
1 finely chopped hard-cooked
   egg

1 teaspoon dry mustard
⅓ cup chili sauce
1 tablespoon capers
2 tablespoons finely chopped
   parsley

Blend well and let stand for 2 hours before serving.

TARTAR SAUCE

3 tablespoons finely chopped
   onion

2 cups mayonnaise
2 teaspoons lemon juice

| 2 tablespoons finely chopped dill *or* 3 tablespoons finely chopped dill pickle | 2 tablespoons finely chopped parsley |

Blend well and let stand for 2 hours before serving.

LOUIS DRESSING

1 cup mayonnaise	2 tablespoons chopped parsley
2 tablespoons grated onion	Few grains cayenne pepper
¼ cup chili sauce	⅓ cup heavy cream, whipped

Mix the mayonnaise, onion, chili sauce, parsley, and cayenne thoroughly. Let them blend while whipping the cream. Fold in the cream until it is well mixed with the mayonnaise mixture. This is excellent on cold shellfish.

VINAIGRETTE

Vinaigrette is nothing more than oil, vinegar, salt, and pepper, the oil and vinegar being apportioned according to your taste. I prefer 3 to 4 parts of oil to 1 of vinegar.

It is often erroneously called "French dressing" in this country.

SAUCE GRIBICHE

This sauce is often mistakenly called "vinaigrette."

3 yolks of hard-cooked eggs	1 tablespoon wine vinegar
1 teaspoon dry mustard	3 egg whites, hard-cooked and finely chopped
1 teaspoon salt	
½ teaspoon freshly ground black pepper	1 tablespoon finely chopped pickle
1 cup olive oil	1 teaspoon finely chopped capers

2 tablespoons finely chopped   tarragon, chervil)
  mixed herbs (chives, parsley,

Crush the egg yolks with a fork and blend well with the mustard, salt, and pepper. Gradually stir in the oil. When it is all absorbed, add the vinegar, egg whites, and the other seasonings. Let the sauce stand for at least an hour to bring out the flavors.

BOILED SALAD DRESSING

2 tablespoons sifted flour
3 tablespoons sugar
1 teaspoon dry mustard
1 cup white wine
1/4 cup lemon juice or vinegar

2 eggs, separated
1/2 cup olive oil
Salt
Freshly ground black pepper
1/2 cup sour cream

Combine the flour, sugar, mustard, white wine, and vinegar or lemon juice together in the top of a double boiler. Add the egg yolks, oil, and salt and pepper to taste. Heat over hot water until the mixture thickens. Beat the egg whites until stiff. Add the sour cream and the stiffly beaten egg whites to the mixture and beat with a whisk or wooden spoon until the dressing is thoroughly blended. This can be used hot or cold.

CUCUMBER SAUCE

1 cup sour cream
1/2 cup seeded, grated cucumber
1/2 teaspoon salt
1 tablespoon finely chopped

fresh dill
2 tablespoons chopped chives
1/2 teaspoon freshly ground
  black pepper

Blend all the ingredients well. Allow the sauce to stand for 1 or 2 hours in the refrigerator before serving.

SOUR CREAM SAUCE

Season 1 cup of sour cream to taste with salt and freshly ground black pepper. Add grated onion or chopped chives if you wish.

COCKTAIL SAUCE I

½ cup chili sauce
1 tablespoon Worcestershire
  sauce
½ cup tomato catsup
½ teaspoon dry mustard

½ teaspoon salt
1 tablespoon horseradish
1 teaspoon freshly ground
  black pepper

Blend all ingredients well.

COCKTAIL SAUCE II

6 tomatoes, peeled, seeded, and
  chopped
1 green pepper, seeded, and
  chopped
1 medium onion *or* 4 shallots,
  peeled and chopped
1 teaspoon dry mustard

1 tablespoon horseradish
1 teaspoon freshly ground
  black pepper
2 teaspoons lemon juice
Salt to taste
½ cup olive oil

Chop the vegetables very fine, add the seasonings and olive oil, and mix thoroughly. Chill before using.

Stuffings and Fish Forcemeat

Stuffings for baked fish vary from the simple to the elaborate — from a bit of chopped onion and parsley to the complicated fish forcemeat. There are plain bread stuffings, vegetable stuffings, and stuffings that include meats or other fish or shellfish.

The recipes listed here are a few general favorites, the ingredients of which may be varied to suit your own taste. You may also select any of a number of stuffings given in various recipes throughout the book. In making your selection, keep in mind the other foods you plan to serve at the meal and the sauce, if any, that you will serve with the baked fish.

SIMPLE BREAD STUFFING

2 large onions, sliced
4 tablespoons butter
1 cup bread crumbs
¼ cup finely chopped parsley
½ teaspoon thyme

2 tablespoons chopped celery leaves
1 teaspoon salt
1 egg, well beaten

Sauté the onions in the butter until soft. Add all the other ingredients and mix thoroughly.

VARIATIONS

1. Add sautéed chopped mushrooms.
2. Omit the thyme and celery and add chopped toasted almonds.

VEGETABLE STUFFING

2 onions
1 clove garlic
Butter
1 green pepper, seeded and
  chopped

4 ripe tomatoes, peeled, seeded,
  and chopped
Chopped parsley
Salt
Freshly ground black pepper

Sauté the onions and garlic in butter just until soft. Add the green pepper, tomato, parsley, and salt and pepper to taste.

Fish baked with this stuffing is especially good served with a tomato sauce made with red wine.

PUNGENT STUFFING

½ cup finely chopped onion
4 tablespoons butter
2 tablespoons olive oil
2 cups dry bread crumbs *or*
  zwieback crumbs
1 cup ground cooked ham

¼ cup chopped parsley
1 teaspoon dried *or* 1 tablespoon fresh tarragon
Salt
Freshly ground black pepper

Sauté the onion in butter and oil until soft; add the other ingredients and blend thoroughly. If the stuffing is too dry, add a little dry vermouth or sherry.

OYSTER STUFFING

6 green onions, chopped
¼ cup celery, minced
¼ cup green pepper, minced
5 tablespoons butter
1½ cups bread crumbs

½ pint oysters and liquor
½ cup chopped parsley
Salt
Freshly ground black pepper
Thyme

Sauté the onions, celery, and green pepper in butter until just soft. Add the crumbs and oysters with their liquor and cook for 3 or 4 minutes. Add the parsley and season to taste with salt, pepper, and thyme.

CRABMEAT STUFFING

2 cups cracker crumbs
½ cup chopped celery
½ cup chopped onion
¼ cup chopped green pepper
½ cup crabmeat

3 eggs
1 teaspoon salt
Dash of cayenne pepper
1 teaspoon dry mustard
½ cup melted butter

Mix all the ingredients together.

VARIATION

You may substitute chopped shrimp for the crabmeat.

SCANDINAVIAN STUFFING

Stuff the fish with anchovy fillets and pieces of uncooked bacon.
This is especially good if you baste the fish with white wine
during the cooking.

FISH FORCEMEAT

This is one of the most complicated stuffings. It is very flavorful
and is used in several ways: as a stuffing for baked fish, as a
spread on rolled fillets, or as small fish balls poached in court
bouillon.

1 cup soft bread crumbs
Milk, about ½ cup
1 pound pike *or* other white
  fish
1 egg
4 egg yolks

Salt
Freshly ground black pepper
Thyme
Tarragon
Heavy cream

Soak the bread crumbs in milk until all the milk is thoroughly
absorbed. Grind the fish several times or pound it in a mortar.
It must be exceedingly pasty. Add the bread crumbs to the fish;

add the egg, egg yolks, seasonings, and enough cream to smooth the mixture. Work it in a mortar or with a heavy wooden spoon over ice until smooth and thoroughly blended.

Fish Stews, Chowders, and Soups

It seems to be human nature to like stews, chowders, and heavy soups made of many ingredients. Almost every country has produced its specialty, and perhaps the most famous of all is the bouillabaisse. This splendid concoction is usually associated with the port of Marseilles, but it has been known for centuries, in one form or another, to the residents of the whole of Southern France.

BOUILLABAISSE

Certain Mediterranean fish, not available in this country, are traditional in the bouillabaisse, but excellent substitutes can be found. A good selection for an American bouillabaisse is haddock or bass for the hearty fish, then lemon sole, whiting, red snapper, flounder — practically any other fish you want. And always eel. For shellfish, use lobster, mussels, sea urchins. For a large bouillabaisse:

3 pounds fish:
  1 pound eel
  1 pound haddock *or* sea bass
  1 pound red snapper
  Or you may use a large variety
  of fish — ½ pound each of 6
  different kinds
3 pounds lobster
3 dozen mussels
3 leeks
2 large onions, chopped
3 cloves garlic

3 tomatoes
⅓ cup olive oil
Bouquet garni (thyme, bay leaf,
  parsley, celery, rosemary)
Pinch of saffron
Water *or* fish broth
Salt
Freshly ground black pepper
Cayenne pepper
Croutons fried in garlic-flavored
  olive oil

Cut the fish into small serving-sized pieces. Keep the richer, heavier fish — eel, haddock, cod, bass — separate from the more delicate types. Cut the live lobsters into pieces (page 390). Wash and clean the mussels.

Cut the white part of the leeks into small pieces. Chop the onion and the garlic. Peel and seed the tomatoes.

Heat the olive oil in a large kettle. Add the vegetables and let them cook well together. Add the bouquet garni and the heavier fish. Let this cook about 7 or 8 minutes. Add the lighter fish, the lobster, and a good pinch of saffron. Cover with the water or fish broth, season to taste with salt, pepper, and cayenne, and bring to a boil. Cook 8 to 10 minutes. Add the mussels and cook until they open. Place the fish in a deep serving dish and pour the hot liquid over it. Serve the croutons separately.

VARIATIONS

1. Boil the heads and bones of the fish with water and white wine — 3 quarts of liquid to 3 pounds of heads and bones — for ½ hour. Then simmer until the liquid is reduced to 1½ quarts. Strain, clarify, and use as a liquid for the bouillabaisse.

2. Substitute ½ cup of butter for the olive oil. The result is a more delicate dish.

AIGO-SAU

This is similar to bouillabaisse and is also native to the South of France. It is simple to prepare and has interesting variations.

1½ pounds fresh fish	Freshly ground black pepper
5 or 6 potatoes, peeled and sliced	Seasonings (bay leaf, fennel, parsley, celery, grated orange rind)
2 tomatoes	⅓ cup olive oil
1 onion	Boiling water
2 cloves garlic	Dry bread
Salt	

Arrange the fish, cut into serving-sized pieces, in a large saucepan and cover with the potatoes. Add the tomatoes, onion, and garlic — all peeled and finely chopped. Add the seasonings — salt, pepper, and herbs. Pour the olive oil on this and add enough boiling water to cover. Boil quickly for 20 minutes or until the potatoes are tender. Pour the broth into dishes over slices of dry bread — toasted or not, as you wish — that have been well rubbed with garlic. Serve the fish and the potatoes on a separate plate. This recipe serves 4 to 6 people.

This dish is sometimes served with what is called "rouille," which is not a sauce, but more of a condiment.

Rouille

In a mortar, pound 4 cloves garlic, 2 small red peppers, 2 tablespoons bread crumbs, and a little bouillon; stir in 2 tablespoons olive oil. For color, one may add a little tomato paste and paprika. If too thick, add a little more bouillon. The rouille should be served in a sauceboat and may be eaten with any of the bouillabaisse recipes or soupe de poisson Marseillaise. If using a food processor, combine all the ingredients in the beaker and process to a smooth paste. If too thick, add a little more bouillon.

VARIATION

You may prepare aigo-sau with only one fish or with as many as you please. It is also made without fish, with eggs poached in the broth just before serving. In this case it is sometimes called bouillabaisse borgne.

COTRIADE — A BRETON BOUILLABAISSE

4 large potatoes, peeled and
    quartered
4 large onions, peeled and
    quartered
Fish heads
Bouquet garni (thyme, bay leaf,

rosemary, parsley)
Salt
Water, about 1 pint per person
3 pounds fish (mackerel, eel,
    fresh sardines, mullet, cod)

Put the potatoes, onions, fish heads, bouquet garni, and salt in a pot and cover with water — a pint per person. Bring to a boil and simmer for 20 minutes. Remove the fish heads. Add the fish, which has been cut into serving-sized pieces. Cook until the potatoes are tender and the fish cooked through, about 15 minutes.

Serve in two bowls, one for the broth and the other for the fish and vegetables.

BOURRIDE

There are about as many types of bourride as there are of bouillabaisse. It is difficult to offer one recipe that is representative, so I suggest two that are very different.

BOURRIDE I (CHIBERTA)

2 onions
2 cloves garlic
2 tomatoes
Bouquet garni (thyme, bay leaf, fennel, parsley)
2 quarts water
Salt
2 tablespoons olive oil

1½ pounds small fish (sole, smelt, sea bass)
Pinch of saffron
6 fillets sole *or* flounder
6 large slices day-old bread, fried in garlic-flavored olive oil
2 egg yolks
Sauce aïoli (pages 33–34)

Peel and chop the onions and garlic. Peel, seed, and chop the tomatoes. Add these with the bouquet garni to the water. Add salt to taste and the olive oil. Bring to a boil and add all the fish except the fillets. Simmer for 15 minutes and add a pinch of saffron.

Remove the fish to a hot dish and allow the bouillon to cook down for a few minutes. Strain it and rub the vegetables and seasonings through a fine sieve. Reheat the bouillon and poach the fillets until they are just cooked through. Remove them to a hot plate and keep the bouillon hot.

Fry the bread in garlic-flavored olive oil until nicely browned.

Beat the egg yolks well and stir them into the bouillon. Do not let it boil. Place each piece of fried toast in a soup plate, top each one with a fillet and cover with sauce aïoli. Surround with the rest of the fish and the broth.

BOURRIDE II

2 pounds fish (bass, haddock, flounder)
1 medium onion, finely chopped
Bouquet garni (thyme, bay leaf, fennel, peel of half an orange)
Salt
Freshly ground black pepper
Boiling water
12 slices bread
Garlic
2 cups sauce aïoli (pages 33–34)

Prepare the fish — fillets will do. Cut them into small serving-sized pieces. Place them in the bottom of a saucepan and cover with the onion, bouquet garni, and salt and pepper to taste. Add boiling water to cover and a little above and let it boil for 10 minutes.

While the fish is cooking, toast the bread and rub well with garlic. Place it in a large tureen or deep platter. Then prepare enough sauce aïoli to use 1 cup in the sauce and have enough left (at least another cupful) to serve separately. You may estimate 1 egg and ¼ cup of oil per person.

When the fish is cooked, remove it and keep it warm. Strain the bouillon and combine it, little by little, with 1½ to 2 cups of the aïoli. Mix well without letting it curdle. When it is all mixed, put it in a saucepan over very low heat or over hot water and stir with a wooden spoon until the sauce just coats the spoon. *It must not boil.* Pour this sauce over the pieces of toast and serve the fish separately with additional aïoli.

BOUILLINADE DES PECHEURS

This is a fisherman's dish that is a combination of French and Spanish cuisine, and while it shows some relationship to the Provençal dishes, it has a personality quite its own. It is properly made in an earthenware pot, but since few people have much success in top-of-the-stove cookery in earthenware, I think it is better to use copper, stainless steel, or aluminum.

⅓ cup olive oil
⅓ cup butter
1 onion, finely minced
3 cloves garlic, finely minced
2 large minced sweet red peppers *or* pimientos, cut in fine julienne
1 pound potatoes, peeled and sliced or quartered

2 pounds fish (haddock, sea perch, sea bass, red snapper)
6 to 8 soft-shelled crabs *or* 2 hard-shelled crabs broken into pieces
2 to 3 dozen mussels
⅓ cup flour
Sauce aïoli (pages 33–34)

Place the olive oil and butter in the bottom of the pan (the Rousillon natives like rancid lard, but the flavor is not pleasant to our palates); add to this the onion and garlic, the peppers or pimientos, potatoes, and fish cut into small serving-sized pieces, Top this with the crabs and mussels and sprinkle with flour. Cover the fish completely with water. Bring it to a boil and boil for about 15 minutes or until the potatoes are soft.

Thicken the sauce with aïoli as in the preceding recipe. (The traditional way to make the sauce and thickening for this dish is to pound the liver of the fish with garlic, oil and egg yolks; however, we seldom get fish livers in this country and the method I give you is far simpler.)

This recipe will serve 6 to 8 people.

ZUPPA DI PESCE

This is an Italian version of the dishes above.

½ cup olive oil
1 large onion, finely chopped
Herbs (bay leaf, fennel, parsley)
½ cup white wine
1 teaspoon salt
Freshly ground black pepper
2 pounds fish (eel, sea bass,
  skate, red snapper, or cod,

with lobster, clams, or mussels)
2 quarts boiling water
6 to 12 slices of stale bread
  fried in olive oil
Chopped parsley
Garlic, finely minced

Heat the olive oil in a deep kettle; add the onion and herbs and let them cook for a few minutes. Add the wine, salt, and pepper and let it all blend thoroughly.

Cut all the fish into pieces for serving and cut the live lobster into sections. Wash the clams and wash and clean the mussels. Add the heavier fish to the hot olive oil mixture and cook for just a minute. Add boiling water and cook for 4 minutes. Add the lighter fish and the shellfish and cook for 5 to 6 minutes more. Taste for seasoning.

Meanwhile, brown 6 to 12 pieces of stale bread in olive oil until crisp. Remove the cooked fish to a tureen. Let the broth cook down for a few minutes and pour it over the fish. Sprinkle with chopped parsley, a little garlic, and a dusting of black pepper. Serve on top of the fried bread in soup bowls.

CIOPPINO

This is a California dish with a noble history that is now tarnished by commercialism. It was originally made by the Portuguese fishermen along the coastal counties of California; much care went into its preparation. In recent years, a bastardized version has become standard fare in many seafood restaurants — one of those "specialties of the house" resting for hours on a steam table.

1 sea bass *or* striped bass
1 pound shrimp
1 quart clams *or* mussels

¼ pound dried mushrooms
  (Italian variety)
1 West Coast crab *or* lobster

3 or 4 tomatoes	3 tablespoons chopped parsley
1 green pepper	1/3 cup tomato paste
1/2 cup olive oil	1 pint red wine
1 large onion, chopped	Salt
2 cloves garlic, chopped	Freshly ground black pepper

Cut the raw fish into serving-sized pieces. Shell the shrimp, leaving the tails intact. Clean and steam the mussels or clams and save the liquid. Soak the mushrooms in cold water. Break the crab apart, or if you use lobster, cut it in pieces. Peel and chop the tomatoes and chop the green pepper.

Place the olive oil in a deep pot; when it is hot add the onion, garlic, parsley, mushrooms, and green pepper and cook for 3 minutes. Next add the tomatoes and the paste, the wine, and the liquid from the mussels or clams. Salt and pepper to taste, cover, and let it simmer for 30 minutes. Add the cut-up fish, the shrimp and the crab or lobster, and cook until done. Serve with plenty of red wine and garlic bread.

VARIATION

Helen Evans Brown of the *West Coast Cook Book* adds oregano and basil to her recipe, which give it an Italian touch. She also says that there are recipes calling for white wine, sherry, and other wines.

It is my opinion that cioppino is a result of the various Mediterranean cuisines that met on the shores of California.

SOLIANKA

This rather interesting stew is found often in the Northwest where it was introduced by the White Russians, who arrived via China after the Russian Revolution. It is particularly suited to this part of the country, where salmon abound.

2 pounds fish bones and heads, or 2 pounds bony fish, with head	1 1/2 quarts water
	Salt
	Freshly ground black pepper

3 large, ripe tomatoes, peeled,
  seeded, and chopped
3 tablespoons butter
1½ pounds salmon, cut in strips
1 tablespoon each of chopped
  black olives and chopped
  green olives
4 dill pickles, finely chopped

2 teaspoons capers
2 onions, finely chopped
1 bay leaf
4 tablespoons additional butter
Chopped parsley, additional
  chopped olives, and lemon
  slices, for garnish

Cook the fish bones and heads in the water, seasoned with salt and pepper, for 1½ hours. Drain off the broth and reserve. Simmer the tomatoes in butter for 15 minutes. Season to taste. Arrange the salmon strips in a deep pot with the onions, pickles, tomatoes, capers, and chopped olives. Cover with the fish broth, add the bay leaf, and simmer 12 to 15 minutes. Add 4 tablespoons of butter. Serve in bowls, garnished with chopped olives, chopped parsley, and lemon slices.

NOTE: A tablespoon or more of chopped fresh dill or two teaspoons dill weed make this a most appetizing soup with another accent.

RUSSIAN FISH STEW

1 pound flounder *or* sole
1 pound pike
½ lemon
6 potatoes cut in ½-inch slices
3 large onions, sliced
2 carrots cut in fine julienne

2 quarts water
1 bay leaf
1 teaspoon salt
Freshly ground black pepper
Paprika

Slice the fish in serving-sized pieces. Cover them with lemon juice and place in the refrigerator for several hours.

Prepare a bouillon with the vegetables, water, and seasonings. Cook for nearly an hour. Add the fish and simmer for about 15 minutes. Serve very hot.

UKHA

2 quarts water	2 pounds carp
Bouquet garni (leek, celery,	1 pound pike
carrot, onions, bay leaf,	1 pound eel
thyme)	Lemon juice
Salt	Croutons
Freshly ground black pepper	Garlic-flavored oil or butter
1 pint white wine	

Combine the water, bouquet garni, and seasonings and simmer
for 30 minutes. Add the wine and the carp and simmer until the
fish begins to fall apart — about 35 to 40 minutes. Strain and force
the fish and the seasonings through a fine sieve. Return the
broth to the pan and bring it to a boil. Add the pike and eel
cut into small serving-sized pieces. Simmer for 15 minutes. Taste
for seasoning and add lemon juice (about 4 tablespoons) just
before serving. Serve with croutons fried in garlic-flavored oil
or butter.

MATELOTE OF EELS NORMANDIE

Mirepoix (see page 20)	2 egg yolks
2 pounds eel	½ cup cream
1½ cups cider	Fresh sorrel (if available) *or*
Parsley	lemon juice
Tarragon	12 small onions
1 teaspoon salt	Butter
3 tablespoons butter	Fried croutons
3 tablespoons flour	

Prepare a mirepoix and put it at the bottom of a large saucepan. Cut the eel into serving-sized pieces and place it on top.
Add the cider, parsley, tarragon, and salt. Bring to a boil and
simmer for about 20 minutes. Remove the eel to a hot platter
and keep hot.

    Reduce the bouillon to 1 cup. Strain. Melt the butter in a
saucepan or double boiler and blend in the flour. Add the bouillon gradually, stirring constantly, until the sauce is thick and

smooth. Remove from the heat and add the egg yolks and cream; stir until well blended and taste for seasoning. If available, add a few leaves of chopped sorrel — or a good squeeze of lemon juice. Pour the sauce over the eels and surround with small white onions that have been browned in butter and steamed until tender. Serve fried croutons, or slices of bread fried in butter and flavored, if you wish, with garlic.

CRAB GUMBO

There seems to be great differences of opinion about this famous dish and I cannot tell who is right. So I give a New Orleans version and a Western version and will let you fight it out on your own stove.

CRAB GUMBO, NEW ORLEANS VERSION

12 crabs (either hard- or soft-shelled)
3 tablespoons butter
1 large onion, chopped
1 pound okra
6 ripe tomatoes, peeled and chopped
Seasonings (thyme, bay leaf, parsley, salt, cayenne pepper)
Water
Boiled rice

Clean the crabs. If you use the hard-shelled variety, break off the claws and cut the body in quarters. If you use soft-shelled, leave them whole.

Melt the butter in a large pot and cook the onion until lightly browned. Add the okra and tomatoes, cover and cook for 15 minutes. Uncover and add the seasonings, the crabs, and enough water to cover and a little over. Simmer for 40 minutes.

Serve very hot in bowls with boiled rice.

CRAB GUMBO, WESTERN VERSION

2 Dungeness crabs
4 tablespoons butter
2 large onions, coarsely chopped
5 large tomatoes, peeled and
  chopped
1 green pepper cut in julienne
¼ pound smoked ham, diced

Salt
Freshly ground black pepper
3 quarts boiling water
1 pound okra cut into 1-inch
  lengths
Boiled rice

Clean the crabs and remove all the meat from the shells. Melt the butter in a large kettle and sauté the onions until they are golden; add the tomatoes, green pepper, ham, salt, pepper, and the boiling water. Cover and simmer for 20 minutes. Uncover and add the okra. Cook for 10 minutes. Add the crabmeat and cook until gelatinous. If you like it thicker, add a little beurre manié.

Serve with boiled rice and a good white wine, well-chilled.

NOTE: It is my opinion that these dishes, authentic as they are, overcook the crab. I believe that you will enjoy the dish more if you do not add the crab until about 5 minutes before serving. Or add only part of it to flavor the gumbo and the rest just at the last. The fish will then retain the texture and flavor of crabmeat and will not end up merely as part of a mush.

NEW ORLEANS COURT BOUILLON

This is not to be confused with the court bouillons that are used generally in cooking fish and shellfish. This is a particularly interesting development in regional cookery. It is definitely related to the court bouillon of French cookery and more distantly to the bouillabaisse; it has also the heaviness of Indian and Negro adaptations of foreign dishes that have sprung up in the South.

1 cup flour
½ cup olive oil
¼ pound butter

2 pounds onions
4 stalks celery
3 cloves garlic

2 sweet peppers
12 ounces tomato paste
1½ quarts boiling water
1 pint red wine
1 tablespoon Worcestershire
  sauce
1 lemon, sliced

1 bunch parsley
2 bay leaves
Salt
Freshly ground black pepper
3 pounds filleted red snapper
Fried croutons

Prepare a roux with the flour and oil. When it is well thickened, add the butter, and the onions, celery, garlic, and peppers, all of which have been chopped very fine. Stir constantly so as not to scorch the roux; add the tomato paste and gradually add the boiling water. Add the wine and other seasonings. Simmer gently for 30 minutes. Add the fillets of snapper, and cook just until they flake easily with a fork. Correct the seasoning and serve with fried croutons and a chilled white wine.

SOUPE DE POISSON MARSEILLAISE

2 medium onions
2 leeks
4 tablespoons olive oil
2 tomatoes, finely chopped
2 cloves garlic
Bouquet garni (fennel, bay leaf,
  oregano, parsley)
3 quarts water
Fish bones and heads

2 pounds fish
½ pound orzo *or* acini di pepe
Salt
Freshly ground black pepper
A large pinch of saffron
Croutons rubbed in garlic
Grated Parmesan cheese
Rouille (page 44)

Pare the onions and leeks and mince very fine. Cook in olive oil 4 to 5 minutes. Add the tomatoes, garlic, and the bouquet garni. Add the water, fish bones and heads, and fish and simmer 15 to 20 minutes. Remove fish. Discard the bones and heads and put fish through a food mill. Return to the pot and bring to a boil. Add orzo and season to taste. Add saffron. Boil until the pasta is very soft. Serve with garlic croutons, grated Parmesan cheese, and rouille.

SOUPE DE POISSON À LA MARSEILLAISE

4 quarts of rockfish (sea bass, blackfish, etc.)
1 cup olive oil
Salt
Freshly ground black pepper
4 large onions, grated or finely chopped

20 tomatoes, peeled and chopped
½ pound vermicelli
1 pinch saffron
½ pound grated Swiss cheese

Clean and wash the fish (no scaling is necessary) and cook it in ¾ cup of the olive oil, stirring often to prevent burning and to flake the fish. When the fish is reduced to pieces, fill the pot with water, add salt and pepper to taste, and cook as long as you deem it necessary in order to extract all the flavor.

In another pot, put the remaining ¼ cup of olive oil and cook the onions until they are soft (not brown). Add the tomatoes and cook for 15 minutes.

Strain the fish through a fine mesh strainer or squeeze it through a piece of cloth. Add the resulting broth to the vegetables and bring to a boil. Add ½ pound of medium-sized vermicelli, cut small, and when almost cooked, add a pinch of saffron. Let it simmer for a few minutes. This should give 8 quarts of soup. When serving, sprinkle each bowl with grated Swiss cheese.

Toasted fried bread and rouille (page 44) are good accompaniments.

CLAM CHOWDER

This, among fish soups, is my oldest love. It was the first fish soup I ever had and it has remained my favorite through the years. It can be made with either the minced razor clams of the Pacific Coast or the littlenecks of the East Coast.

With the littlenecks: Place 1 quart of clams in a saucepan with a little white wine or water. Cover and steam until they open. Pour off the liquid and strain it. Remove the clams from their shells and set aside. If you use the minced razor clams (fresh or canned), you will need about 1½ cups of clams, drained. Save the broth, of course.

3 or 4 slices salt pork *or* bacon, cut in fine pieces	2 cups light cream
1 medium onion, finely chopped	Clams (about 1½ cups, drained) and clam liquor
2 medium potatoes	Thyme
Salt	Paprika
Freshly ground black pepper	Chopped parsley

Try out the salt pork or bacon. Remove it when it is crisp, and lightly brown the onion.

Peel and dice the potatoes and cook them in boiling water until just tender. Take them out and let the water cook down a bit. Combine the bacon, onion, potato, and potato water in a saucepan, and add the clam juice. Bring this to a boil and let it simmer for 5 minutes. Season to taste. Add, gradually, the cream, and when it has just come to the boiling point, add the clams. Just let them heat through. Sprinkle with the merest pinch of finely rubbed thyme.

Serve in heated cups with a dash of paprika and a little chopped parsley.

VARIATION

You may add more clam broth and use milk instead of cream. The result is a lighter, less hearty soup.

MANHATTAN CLAM CHOWDER

3 dozen medium cherrystone clams, shucked (with 2 to 3 cups reserved liquor)	1 can (16 ounces) stewed tomatoes
½ cup onions, chopped	½ cup cooked rice
½ cup green pepper, chopped	½ teaspoon thyme
2 cloves garlic, minced	¼ teaspoon oregano
4 thick slices bacon, crisp-fried and coarsely crumbled (bacon drippings reserved)	Salt
	Freshly ground black pepper
	Parsley

Strain clams, reserving liquid, and chop finely. Sauté onion, green pepper, and garlic in 3 tablespoons of the reserved bacon fat until tender but not browned. Add reserved clam liquid, tomatoes, rice, thyme, and oregano. Season to taste. Simmer 5 minutes. Just before serving, add the chopped clams and bring to a boil. Garnish with crumbled bacon and parsley.

WIN'S CLAM CHOWDER

This rich and unusual version of New England clam chowder is the recipe of Irwin Chase, an excellent Yankee cook.

¼ pound salt pork
2 medium onions, finely
  chopped
1 green pepper, finely chopped
6 medium potatoes
1 pint quahogs *or* other clams,
  chopped, with liquid

2 tablespoons salt
¼ teaspoon white pepper
¼ teaspoon garlic powder
¼ teaspoon celery salt
1 pint water
Sour cream

Dice the salt pork and fry it until brown. Add the onions and green peppers to the salt pork and drippings. Let them sauté to a light brown. Dice 3 of the potatoes. Add the quahogs with their liquid and the diced potatoes to the salt pork, onion, and pepper. Add the seasonings and let it all simmer until the potatoes are done.

Cut the remaining 3 potatoes into small pieces, put them in a blender with the water, and blend until creamy. Add this to the clam mixture and simmer for 5 more minutes. Serve with a dab of sour cream.

FISH CHOWDER

This is a hearty dish for a number of people. It can be cut in half, if you wish, but I like it best for a big party.

10 pounds fish, plus heads and
bones
½ pound salt pork
½ cup butter
1 cup chopped onion
2 to 3 pounds potatoes, sliced

about ⅜ inch thick
2 to 3 quarts milk
Salt
Freshly ground black pepper
Thyme

Use several kinds of fish and order the heads and bones as
well; cover these with water and simmer them for 1 hour. Strain
the broth.

Cut the salt pork into small dice and try it out until crisp in 2
tablespoons of butter. Add the onion and brown lightly. Boil
potatoes in salted water till just tender.

Cut the fish into small fingers and simmer these in the fish
broth for about 15 to 20 minutes. Add the potatoes, onions, and
salt pork and let it come to the boiling point. Add the milk and
season to taste. Let the mixture come just to the boil and simmer
for 5 minutes. Add the butter and a sprinkling of thyme.

Fish chowder is usually served with pilot crackers, but I prefer fried bread with mine.

CARIBBEAN CHOWDER

¼ pound salt pork *or* bacon
Butter
2 cloves garlic, chopped
1 large onion, chopped
1½ pounds fish (grouper, snapper)
3 large potatoes

Milk *or* light cream
Salt
Freshly ground black pepper
Oregano
Thyme
1½ pounds lobster
½ pound shrimp

Cut the salt pork into small dice and try it out in a little butter. Add the garlic and onion and brown lightly.

Chop the fish or put it through a fine grinder. Cook the potatoes in boiling salted water until just tender. Put the potatoes
and the chopped fish through a puree machine or force them
through a fine sieve. Add them to the salt pork and onion mixture, and add enough milk or light cream to make a soup. Season to taste with salt, pepper, oregano, and thyme.

Cook the lobster and shrimp in boiling salted water for 5 minutes. Shell the shrimp and cut them into small pieces. Remove the lobster meat from its shell. Add the lobster and chopped shrimp to the soup and heat it to the boiling point. Correct the seasoning.

VARIATIONS

1. Add ½ cup of sherry or Madeira to the soup before serving.
2. Blaze the lobster and shrimp meat with brandy before adding it to the soup.

MARGARET JENNINGS'S CRAB SOUP

This is one of those soups that, seasoned by mistake, became a notable gastronomic discovery.

1 pound crabmeat
½ cup milk
2 tablespoons butter

2 cups sauce béchamel (pages 23–24)
1 cup cream, or more
⅓ cup Scotch whisky

Heat the crabmeat in the milk and butter. Prepare a light béchamel and add the cream to it after it has come to the boiling point. Add the crabmeat and heat again until it reaches the boiling point. Season to taste, and add more cream if it needs thinning. Just before serving, stir in the Scotch. Serve in heated cups with a sprinkling of finely chopped parsley.

CREAM OF SEAFOOD SOUP

12 shrimp
4 cups court bouillon (page 20)
12 crayfish *or* 1 small lobster
¼ pound butter
12 mussels

½ cup white wine
Bouquet garni (onion, parsley, thyme)
12 oysters
3 tablespoons flour

Salt	2 cups cream
Freshly ground black pepper	3 egg yolks
Cayenne pepper	Croutons

Shell the shrimp; poach just the shells in court bouillon for 3 minutes. Leave the shells in the broth. Poach the lobster or crayfish for 8 minutes. If you are using lobster, remove the meat from the shell and cut it into small pieces. (With crayfish, remove the meat from the tails.)

Grind the lobster (or crayfish) shells or pound them in a mortar and mix with 4 tablespoons of butter. Force this through a fine strainer.

Put the mussels in a large pan with the wine and the bouquet garni. Cover and steam until they open. Remove the meat from the shells and strain the broth.

Remove the oysters from the shells.

Reduce the court bouillon and add the broth from the mussels and any oyster liquor there may be. Strain the bouillon — you should have about 4 cups.

Prepare a velouté with the flour and 4 tablespoons of butter, gradually stirring in 2 cups of the bouillon until the sauce is thickened. Add the remaining bouillon, bit by bit, and taste for seasoning. Mix the cream and egg yolks and stir into the soup. Add the various seafoods. Heat until the oysters are heated through, but do not let it boil. Finally, stir in the lobster butter. Serve with croutons.

VARIATIONS

1. Add a healthy slug of either sherry or Madeira just before serving.

2. Make substitutions or additions to the list of seafood: clams, scallops, crabmeat, or others.

3. Make the soup with only one fish, if you prefer. Be sure, however, that you adjust the amounts of the other ingredients.

BISQUE

No matter what your seafood happens to be, the procedure for making bisques is the same. The recipe I suggest here is based on lobster.

Mirepoix (onion, carrot, celery, leek)
3 tablespoons olive oil
1 lobster, 1½ to 2 pounds
1 cup white wine
¼ cup cognac
½ cup rice

1 quart stock *or* fish bouillon
Salt
Freshly ground black pepper
1 cup heavy cream
3 or 4 tablespoons butter
Cayenne pepper

Prepare a mirepoix by cutting the vegetables into very fine julienne and sautéing them for 2 or 3 minutes in 3 tablespoons of olive oil. Add the live lobster which has been cut in half. Toss it around with wooden spoons until its shell turns red. Add the wine and cognac and simmer for about 6 minutes. Remove the meat from the lobster shell and keep it warm. Pound the shells in a mortar, or break them up and put them through the grinder. Return them to the pot.

Meanwhile, cook the rice gently in broth or stock for about 45 minutes. Combine the cooked rice, the mirepoix, and the ground lobster shells and put all through a puree machine or fine sieve. Dilute the mixture with stock or bouillon until it is the consistency of a very thick soup. Season to taste. Reheat, adding the cream and 3 or 4 tablespoons butter. Add a few grains of cayenne and serve with the finely cut pieces of lobster meat and a little chopped parsley. This will serve 6 people.

Tiny quenelles (pages 325–327) are sometimes used for garnish with various bisques. This is a lot of work, but may be worth while for an extra special occasion.

VARIATIONS

Crayfish, Shrimp, or Clam Bisque. This same procedure may be followed for crayfish (use about 18), for shrimp (use about 15 to 18), and for clams (use about 24). In using clams, save the juice for the broth. Do not try to crush the shells. Instead, combine them whole with the rice, and then strain it. Add the clam broth to the stock in which the rice is cooked.

Oyster Bisque. Heat 1 pint of oysters with the mirepoix and when they are plumped, chop them very fine. Add the rice, which has been cooked in stock with the oyster liquor added. Force all through the puree machine or sieve and proceed as above. Serve several oysters in each dish as a garnish. (As with clams, do not try to crush the oyster shells.)

Suggestions for Using Leftover Fish

Aside from serving cold fish with mayonnaise or vinaigrette or making a fish loaf, there are many savory and attractive ways to use small quantities of fish for a second meal. These are some of my favorites.

QUICHE

Any of the quiche recipes in this book can be adapted to use with leftovers by substituting 1½ cups flaked cooked fish — any variety, with skin and bones removed — for the fish called for in the recipe.

MARC PARSON'S FISH HASH

½ cup chopped onions
½ cup finely chopped potatoes
¼ cup butter

1 cup cold, cooked fish, flaked and diced
Salt
Freshly ground black pepper

Cook the onions and potatoes in the butter until the mixture is soft. Add the fish and cook over high heat until the hash begins to brown, stirring to spread the crispy portion. Season with salt and pepper to taste.

FISH PIE

Fish pie can be made by adding a little cream to the fish hash mixture and baking it in a crust.

STEAMED FISH (HALIBUT) PUDDING OR TIMBALE

Irma Rombauer was surely beloved by thousands — or probably millions — of young Americans, and her cookbook, *Joy of Cooking,* is now edited by her daughter.

This fish pudding was one of Irma Rombauer's favorites as a child, and she has graciously passed it on to me for this book. It it a perfect way of using up leftover fish. This recipe is for 6 people. If you wish to serve 3, cut the ingredients in half and steam the pudding in a 1-pound coffee tin or a small mold.

2 cups flaked or ground halibut *or* other fish	2 teaspoons lemon juice *or* 1 teaspoon Worcestershire sauce
¾ cup bread crumbs	Salt
¼ cup melted butter	Paprika
3 eggs, separated	

Combine the fish, crumbs, butter, egg yolks, and seasonings. Beat the egg whites stiff and fold them into the mixture. Pour into a well-buttered timbale mold or pudding tin and steam for 1 hour. Unmold onto a hot platter and serve with cream sauce flavored with Worcestershire, or a mustard or tomato sauce (page 24).

PICKLED FISH

Cold halibut, cod, tuna, striped bass, and swordfish may be pickled by covering them with a mild wine vinegar. Add 1 large thinly sliced onion, 12 to 14 peppercorns, and 1 tablespoon chopped fresh dill or 1 teaspoon dill weed. Cover and let stand in the refrigerator for 24 to 36 hours before serving. It may be served as is or combined with a green salad, a rice salad, or mayonnaise.

FISH AND COLESLAW SALAD

Shred a 2-pound cabbage. Mix with 1 cup mayonnaise, 1 tablespoon mustard, and ⅔ cup sour cream (if you want a sweet-sour sauce, add 1 tablespoon sugar). Let stand 30 minutes. Fold in 1 to 2 cups cooked, flaked cold fish, any variety or combination. Garnish with watercress or chopped parsley.

FISH CAKES

1½ cups cooked, cold flaked fish, skin and bones removed	1 tablespoon grated onion
	Salt
2 cups well-seasoned mashed potatoes	Freshly ground black pepper
	Ground ginger

Mix together the fish, potatoes, and onion and add seasonings to taste. Form into fish cakes about 3 inches in diameter and 1½ inches thick. Sauté in butter or bacon fat until golden brown.

Garnish with bacon slices or tomato sauce, if desired.

FLORENTINE BEAN SALAD

3 20-ounce cans cannelini beans,
  drained and washed
2½ cups mixed, cooked fish *or*
  2 7-ounce cans white meat
  tuna fish
3 garlic cloves, finely chopped
¼ cup finely chopped parsley

1 tablespoon finely chopped
  fresh basil, or 1 teaspoon
  dried basil
Olive oil
Vinegar
Salt
Freshly ground black pepper

Mix the beans and fish with the garlic, parsley, and basil. Add the olive oil, vinegar, salt, and pepper to taste. Mix well and chill several hours. Sprinkle with chopped parsley.

ESCABECHE

This isn't really a dish you can make with leftovers but, if you have some extra fresh or frozen fish fillets, salt them lightly on both sides and marinate in lemon and lime juice, barely to cover, for about an hour. Pour off the marinade and reserve. Dry the fish well, and dust very, very lightly with flour, a little more salt, and some pepper. Melt 3 tablespoons butter and 2 tablespoons oil in a skillet. Sauté the fish very quickly on both sides, until heated through and delicately brown. Remove to a serving dish. Sprinkle with 2 to 3 finely chopped garlic cloves, 1 tablespoon paprika, 1 teaspoon dried cumin seed, 1 teaspoon oregano, 3 or 4 canned green chiles cut into strips, 1 large red Italian onion sliced paper-thin, and about 2 tablespoons chopped parsley. Add about ½ cup olive oil and 1 to 2 tablespoons of the reserved juice. Taste and refrigerate, covered, for 24 hours, until the fish is imbued with the various flavors.

Remove the fish and garnish with shredded lettuce, stuffed olives, and perhaps some little green onions, cut in long shreds.

Saltwater Fish

Barracuda

Sometimes called a sea pike or *brochet de mer,* which it resembles, barracuda is eaten principally on the Pacific Coast and is seldom marketed elsewhere. Anglers respect it as a game fish. It has treacherous teeth, and there are occasional reports of its striking at bathers close to shore.

Those who have eaten barracuda — their number is not impressively large — regard it as a good dish. It is a fat fish and I think it is exceptionally fine when smoked. The food barracuda averages 12 to 15 pounds, but some of the species may weigh as much as 100 to 150 pounds.

In some parts of the country barracuda is considered poisonous. This is an old wives' tale.

BROILED BARRACUDA

Use either steaks or fillets. Follow the directions for broiling (pages 9–10). Serve with mustard sauce (page 23), black butter (page 31), or parsley butter (page 33).

CHARCOAL-BROILED BARRACUDA

Barracuda is really best baked, for my taste, but I do think it is wonderful broiled over charcoal. In that case, follow this California method.

Use a small whole fish, clean it, and place it in an oiled hinged grill. Broil according to the Canadian cooking theory (page 10). Baste it with soy, sesame, or peanut oil and whiskey (bourbon is best) or sherry — using equal parts of the oil and liquor. Add any seasonings you wish to the basting sauce. Sometimes you may like a few slivers of ginger or perhaps you would enjoy crushed garlic. Serve the sauce separately.

SAUTÉED BARRACUDA

Follow the basic rules for sautéing on page 10. Serve with sour cream sauce (page 38), mustard sauce with tarragon added (page 23), or a tomato-curry sauce (page 23).

BAKED BARRACUDA

The directions for baking salmon (page 179) or halibut (page 125) apply equally well to barracuda.

BAKED BARRACUDA CALIFORNIA

Select a small whole barracuda and clean it. Make a basting sauce as for charcoal-broiled barracuda (see recipe above). Place the fish in an oiled baking dish, pour the sauce over it, and bake at 425°–450° according to the Canadian cooking theory (page 8). Baste frequently with the sauce during the cooking process. When the fish is about half done, sprinkle it liberally with sesame seeds. If you have a baking thermometer, cook the fish to 140° internal temperature. You will find it deliciously juicy.

BAKED BARRACUDA NIÇOISE

Olive oil
2 cloves garlic
1 medium onion
4 barracuda steaks
Flour
Salt
Freshly ground black pepper

Anchovy fillets
Tomatoes, pealed and sliced
Black olives
1 cup red wine
Chopped parsley
Fresh tarragon

Oil a baking dish well. Chop the garlic and onion and sprinkle on the bottom of the dish. Dip the steaks in flour and place them on top of the garlic and onion. Season with salt and pepper. Arrange anchovy fillets and sliced tomatoes over the top and sprinkle with black olives. Add red wine and bake at 425°–450° according to the Canadian cooking theory (page 8), basting about three times during the process.

Sprinkle wtih chopped parsley and a little fresh tarragon, if available. Serve with a mound of buttered rice.

BRAISED BARRACUDA SANTA BARBARA

6 tablespoons butter
4 barracuda steaks
Flour
Salt
Freshly ground black pepper
1 bay leaf

3 cloves
2 slices onion
Milk
Gruyère cheese, grated
Paprika

Melt the butter in a baking dish or casserole. Dust the steaks with flour and brown them in the butter. Salt and pepper them to taste, add the bay leaf, cloves, onion slices, and enough milk to cover three-quarters of the thickness of the fish. Sprinkle with grated cheese and paprika. Bake at 425°–450° according to the Canadian cooking theory (page 8).

BARRACUDA ROE

1½ pounds barracuda roe
Court bouillon (page 18)
¼ cup butter
1 clove garlic
4 tablespoons flour
½ cup white wine

1 cup cream
Salt
Freshly ground black pepper
Rosemary
Buttered crumbs

Poach the roe for 10 minutes in court bouillon. Melt the butter, add the garlic, and cook it for 2 minutes. Remove the garlic and add the flour to the butter, blending well. Cook for 3 minutes. Gradually stir in the white wine, ½ cup of the court bouillon, and the cream. Season to taste with salt, pepper, and a trace of rosemary.

Cut the poached roe into fairly small pieces. Arrange them in baking shells and cover with the sauce. Top with buttered crumbs and bake at 425°–450° for 10 minutes.

VARIATION

Poach the roe as above and serve in a Newburg sauce (pages 396–397) made with 1 cup heavy cream, ¼ cup sherry, 3 egg yolks for thickening, salt, and cayenne pepper.

Black Drum

These are probably the most musical of all fish. They are loud and harmonious, and on a quiet evening a school of them can put on an impressive symphonic program.

Black drums are also gluttons. They often stand on their heads, sometimes with their tails showing above the water, while they suck up great quantities of clams, the shells of which they crush as they gorge.

Drums grow to a large size, but those marketed average only

8 to 20 inches long. They are more popular in the South, especially in Texas and Louisiana, than in other parts of the country.

BROILED DRUM

The drum is a rather dry fish, so oil it well before broiling and baste it frequently with oil or butter. Follow directions for broiling, pages 9–10. Serve with tartar sauce (pages 35–36), lemon butter (page 31), parsley butter (page 33), or browned butter (page 31).

BAKED DRUM

Follow any of the recipes for baked redfish.

Blowfish (Sea Squab)

Also called the puffer or globefish, this creature can suck in water and air and enlarge itself until it is nearly round. Only the meat around the spine is eaten. In Eastern markets you will see the prepared fish looking something like large chicken drumsticks from which the skin has been pulled. In this form it is known commercially as sea squab. It's good eating but expensive.

If you catch your own blowfish, there is a special procedure for extracting the edible portion. Hold the tail of the fish in your left hand, and with a sharp knife cut right through about 1 inch back of the eyes, removing the head. Then peel the skin back, stripping it off the fish. Cut away the entrails. This will leave you one solid round piece of meat with the spine bone running through it—a sea squab.

SAUTÉED SEA SQUAB

Follow directions for sauté meunière, page 10.

BROILED SEA SQUAB

Follow directions for broiling, pages 9–10.

FRIED SEA SQUAB

Follow directions for deep frying, page 11.

Bluefish

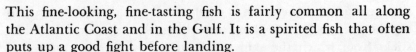

This fine-looking, fine-tasting fish is fairly common all along the Atlantic Coast and in the Gulf. It is a spirited fish that often puts up a good fight before landing.

Bluefish may run up to 10 pounds, but about 3 to 6 pounds is its usual weight. It is nicely meated and may be prepared a number of ways, although I think it is best broiled or baked. Bluefish is so delicate in flavor that it does not need heavy seasonings to enhance it. Simple herbs, white wine, salt, and freshly ground pepper are the only additions necessary.

BROILED BLUEFISH

You may either split the fish or broil it whole, whichever you prefer. Follow the Canadian cooking theory for broiling (pages 9–10).

(pages 9–10)

VARIATIONS

1. Serve the broiled fish on a bed of dried herbs: thyme, fennel, bay leaf, parsley. Pour ¼ cup cognac or rum over the fish and herbs and ignite it. Let it burn, smoking the herb flavors into the fish. Serve with lemon butter and plain boiled potatoes.

2. Split the fish, dot it with butter, and add bacon strips. Broil it about 4 inches from the flame until the bacon is crisp and the fish cooked through.

SAUTÉED BLUEFISH

Small whole bluefish or pieces of bluefish may be sautéed à la meunière (page 10) or à l'Anglaise (page 142).

Avoid the highly spiced sauces for this delicate fish. Serve with something simple, such as lemon butter (page 31), parsley butter (page 33), or anchovy butter (page 32).

BAKED BLUEFISH

Clean and split a bluefish and place it on an oiled baking dish or pan. Dot it heavily with butter, sprinkle with salt and pepper, and bake at 425° according to the Canadian cooking theory (page 8). Serve with lemon or parsley butter.

VARIATIONS

1. Stuff the bluefish with crabmeat; sprinkle the stuffing with salt, pepper, and butter. Tie the fish up, place it on an oiled baking dish, dot with butter, and season with salt and freshly

ground black pepper. Bake at 425° according to the Canadian cooking theory (page 8). Serve with lemon butter (page 31).

2. Arrange a split bluefish on an oiled baking dish. Lay strips of bacon or salt pork across the top of the fish. Bake at 425° as above. Serve with lemon wedges, boiled potatoes, and a cucumber salad made with a sour cream and dill dressing.

3. Stuff a bluefish with a few sprigs of parsley, fresh dill, and 2 or 3 lemon slices. Dot the interior with butter and sprinkle with salt and freshly ground black pepper.

Oil a baking dish and cover the bottom with 3 shallots and 4 green onions, finely chopped. Lay the stuffed fish on top, dot with butter, and sprinkle with salt and pepper. Add 1 cup white wine. Bake at 425° as above, basting often. Remove the fish to a hot platter.

Take out the herbs and add them to the pan juices. Put the juices through a sieve or a food mill. Return to the stove and add ½ cup heavy cream and 2 egg yolks. Stir until thickened, but do not let it boil. Taste for seasoning and pour the sauce over the fish. Sprinkle with chopped parsley and dill.

BABY BLUES

The small bluefish, called "baby blues," which are caught late in the summer, are bluefish that have not yet grown to full size. They should be cleaned and cooked whole. Follow the recipes for broiled or sautéed bluefish.

Butterfish

These small silvery fish are among the most delicately meated and thoroughly pleasing fish in the sea. They are caught in great quantities and are available in Eastern markets throughout most of the year.

BROILED BUTTERFISH

Since butterfish are very small — some weighing as little as ¼ pound — they should be broiled very quickly. My preference, as usual, is to sauté them. However, if you do broil them, use plenty of butter and oil and place them near the flame. Serve with a sauce Béarnaise (page 26).

SAUTÉED BUTTERFISH

Follow the directions for sauté meunière (page 10). Serve with lemon wedges or lemon butter. A strong sauce is not good with this delicate fish.

VARIATION
Add buttered toasted almonds to the pan at the last minute.

BUTTERFISH NIÇOISE

Sauté butterfish as for sauté meunière, but substitute olive oil for the butter. Grill or sauté tomatoes in olive oil and season them with a little tarragon and garlic. Arrange the fish on a bed of the tomatoes, top them with strips of anchovies, and garnish with ripe olives. Serve this with sautéed potatoes and a bountiful salad and you will have a satisfying meal.

BUTTERFISH WITH CURRY AND TOMATOES

Sauté 1 medium onion, finely chopped, in butter. Dip 4 small butterfish in flour that has been heavily seasoned with curry powder and salted to taste. Sauté the fish in the pan with the onion. Remove the fish to a hot platter and rinse the pan with a little white wine. Serve with rice and a tomato sauce laced with more curry (page 23).

BUTTERFISH IN CASES

This is definitely a party dish.

To prepare a breadcase, remove the crusts from an unsliced loaf. Cut bread into a rectangle large enough to hold an entire fish comfortably with a 1-inch margin on all sides. Scoop out some of the crumbs, butter the case well, and dry it out in a 300° oven until it is a delicate brown.

Make a sauce duxelles (page 27). For each fish, sauté 3 large mushroom caps in butter.

Flour the fish and sauté them according to the directions for sauté meunière (page 10). Spread a little sauce duxelles in each bread case, place a fish in each case, add more sauce, top with the mushroom caps, and garnish with chopped parsley. Serve with additional sauce.

PAN-FRIED BUTTERFISH

Dip in seasoned flour, then in beaten egg, and roll in any of the following: buttered crumbs, cracker crumbs, corn meal, chopped nuts mixed with crumbs, or sesame seeds. Sauté quickly in butter or olive oil and serve with lemon wedges.

VARIATIONS

1. Sauté whole slices of orange, peel and all, with the fish and serve as a garnish.

2. Add 1 teaspoon of tarragon to the pan and rinse it with ¼ cup of white wine. Pour over the fish.

BUTTERFISH EN PAPILLOTE

Butterfish (1 per serving)	Butter
Cooking parchment	Salt
Ham slices (1 per serving)	Freshly ground black pepper
Anchovy butter	Thick tomato paste
Grated onion	Chopped parsley

Cut heart-shaped pieces of cooking parchment big enough to accommodate the fish. On each piece of parchment, place a slice of ham near one edge. Spread it with anchovy butter and a little grated onion. Top with a butterfish, dot with butter, season with salt and pepper, add a teaspoon of tomato paste, and sprinkle with chopped parsley. Fold the other side of the parchment over this and crimp the edges together so that they are tightly sealed. Bake at 425° according to the Canadian cooking theory (page 8).

SMOKED BUTTERFISH

Smoked butterfish is found in many delicatessens and fish shops. It is delicate and very pleasant. Try it as a first course for dinner or as a light luncheon dish. Serve it with lemon, a sprinkling of capers if you like, or chopped onion.

California Black Sea Bass

This Pacific Coast fish is sometimes called the jewfish, but it is not the same as the Florida jewfish or giant sea bass. It is a good game fish and is sold to a certain extent for food. The flesh is flaky, white, and well flavored. The fish is large, weighing as much as 700 to 800 pounds, and is usually sold as steaks or fillets.

Two smaller fish, the cabrilla and the grouper, are sold in fillets in California markets as "golden bass." The rock bass, averaging about 18 inches in length, is popular in the West both as a game and a commercial fish.

BROILED CALIFORNIA SEA BASS

Follow directions for broiling, pages 9–10.

SEA BASS FILLETS PACIFIC

See recipe on page 215.

BAKED CALIFORNIA SEA BASS

Follow directions for baking on page 8.

BARBECUED SEA BASS STEAKS CALIFORNIA

¼ cup melted butter	1 clove garlic, crushed
2 tablespoons soy sauce	2 pounds sea bass steak
Juice of 1 lemon	½ cup sesame seeds
2 ounces whiskey or brandy	Lemon or lime wedges

Prepare a basting sauce with the butter, soy sauce, lemon juice, liquor, and garlic. Brush the steaks with this, place them in an oiled hinged grill, and cook over a charcoal fire according to the Canadian cooking theory (page 9), basting often and turning. When nearly done, sprinkle heavily with sesame seeds and continue cooking until the seeds are toasted. Serve with lemon or lime wedges.

JEWFISH STEAKS TROPICAL

3 cups toasted crumbs	4 tablespoons heavy cream
2 tablespoons chili powder	6 to 8 rashers bacon
2 teaspoons paprika	1 clove garlic
1 teaspoon salt	3 pounds jewfish steaks
1 teaspoon oregano	Flour
3 eggs	

Roll the crumbs fine and combine with the chili powder, paprika, salt, and oregano. Beat the eggs lightly and add the cream. Try out the bacon and add the garlic to the bacon fat. When the bacon is crisp, remove it to absorbent paper. Brush the fish steaks with flour, dip them in the eggs and cream, and then cover them thoroughly with the crumb mixture. Sauté them gently in the bacon fat according to the Canadian cooking theory (page 10). Serve with tomato sauce (page 23) and a bacon garnish.

California Kingfish

In order to avoid confusion, I must resort here to Latin: the California kingfish is a *Genyonemus lineatus,* which means that it is a different fish from the East Coast fish, which is a *Scomberomorus Cavalla* and closely resembles the Spanish mackerel (page 261). The West Coast fish is sometimes mistaken for tomcod, a similar fish.

California kingfish range from about 3/4 to 1 1/4 pounds and are usually eaten whole. The meat is excellent.

BROILED CALIFORNIA KINGFISH

Broil the fish whole or split, according to the directions on pages 9–10.

FRENCH-FRIED CALIFORNIA KINGFISH

Clean, wash, and dry the fish. Dip it in flour, then in milk, and roll it in corn meal. Heat fat in a deep-fat fryer to 375°. Fry the fish according to the Canadian cooking theory (page 11). Drain on absorbent paper, season with salt and paprika, and serve with tartar sauce (pages 35–36) or mustard sauce (page 23).

BAKED CALIFORNIA KINGFISH WITH ANCHOVIES

Split 2 kingfish and stuff them with anchovy fillets, sliced onions, and chopped parsley. Fold them over, place on an oiled baking dish, dot with butter, and sprinkle with freshly ground black pepper. Bake at 425° according to the Canadian cooking theory (page 8). Serve with lemon quarters.

BAKED CALIFORNIA KINGFISH ITALIAN

Split the fish and stuff them with finely chopped onion, parsley, and thyme. Place them on a well-oiled baking dish and brush with olive oil. Add ½ cup of white wine and bake at 425° according to the Canadian cooking theory (page 8), basting once or twice during the cooking. Season with salt and freshly ground black pepper and serve with tomato sauce (page 23) or lemon quarters.

California Pompano

This fish is not the true Florida pompano, but is a relative of the butterfish. It is found only on the California coast. It is always served whole and is a delicious and delicate morsel.

Prepare it according to the recipes for Florida pompano, pages 161–162.

California Whitefish

This is an entirely different fish from the freshwater whitefish of the Great Lakes. It is a good game fish and is sought by anglers as well as commercial fishermen. Fairly large, it comes to the market whole, filleted, and in steaks.

BROILED CALIFORNIA WHITEFISH

Broil steaks or fillets according to the directions on pages 9–10. Serve with butter flavored with tarragon or sauce Béarnaise (page 26).

BAKED CALIFORNIA WHITEFISH AU GRATIN

3 pounds whitefish fillets
Court bouillon (page 18)
2 cups sauce béchamel (page 23)
Tarragon

¼ cup chopped parsley
Swiss or Cheddar
   cheese, grated

Cut the fillets into strips 1 inch wide. Poach them in court bouillon for 3 minutes, then remove them to an oval baking dish or casserole. Using the fish broth and some cream, make 2 cups sauce béchamel. Season it with tarragon and parsley and pour over the fish. Sprinkle with grated cheese and bake at 450° for 7 minutes. Serve with buttered noodles and chopped spinach seasoned with a little garlic.

POACHED WHITEFISH HOLLANDAISE

Poach 3 pounds of whitefish fillets or steaks in salted water for 5 or 6 minutes, or until the fish flakes easily. Serve with Hollandaise sauce (pages 25–26), boiled parsley potatoes, and green beans.

VARIATION

You may substitute shrimp (page 21), lobster (page 21), or poulette sauce (page 24) for the Hollandaise.

Cod

One of the most important food fishes in the world, cod comes mainly from the banks of Newfoundland, from New England waters, and from the coast of Norway. Close cousins of the Atlantic cod are caught in North Pacific waters and other relatives are taken in the colder regions of the southern hemisphere.

An average cod weighs about 10 pounds, but specimens weighing 50 pounds and more are sometimes caught. It is an active hunter with an excellent appetite, preying relentlessly on shellfish and on practically any fish that live on the bottom or close to it. Sharks and dogfish are among the few species that can cope successfully with a husky cod.

The annual haul of cod is over a billion pounds, and it is sold as flakes, shredded, pickled, green, or smoked, in salted slabs, whole, in steaks, and in frozen and fresh fillets. Cod is also the source of cod-liver oil, a fact of slight gastronomic interest.

I am so fond of salt cod that I sometimes forget that fresh cod can be prepared in many interesting ways, and that the so-called "scrod," which is a young cod weighing 1½ to 2½ pounds, is fine eating.*

* Young haddock, pollock, and other similar fish are also often called scrod.

If you live near the source of supply, you can buy the whole fish, steaks, or center cuts. Most unsalted cod, however, comes to market as fresh or frozen fillets, and these can be prepared in any of the ways given for ocean perch or haddock (see pages 154–159 and 113–120). Here are other recipes for fresh cod:

BROILED CODFISH

Broil either steaks or fillets according to the directions on pages 9–10.

BROCHETTES OF COD ITALIAN

Cut 2 to 3 pounds of cod into small cubes about 1½ to 2 inches square. Alternate them on skewers with mushroom caps. Sprinkle them with salt and freshly ground black pepper, dip in flour, brush with butter or egg yolks, and roll in crumbs. Then sauté them quickly in oil or butter according to the Canadian cooking theory (page 10) or until they are nicely browned on all sides. Serve with a rich tomato sauce (page 23) and risotto.

SAUTÉED COD

Either steaks or fillets may be used. Follow the directions on page 10. Serve with your favorite sauce.

COD SAUTÉ, INDIAN STYLE

1 large onion, chopped	6 to 8 tomatoes, peeled, seeded,
⅓ cup olive oil	and chopped
1 clove garlic	Salt

Freshly ground black pepper
Sweet basil
1 large eggplant, peeled
and diced
1½ cups rice, cooked

2 pounds cod fillets
Flour
Curry powder
Butter *or* oil
Tomato sauce *or* parsley butter

Heat the olive oil and sauté the onion. Add the garlic and tomatoes. Season to taste with salt, pepper, and basil. Cook for 10 minutes and add the eggplant. Cover and cook for 20 minutes, or until the eggplant is tender and the tomatoes cooked down.

Cut the cod fillets into strips 2 inches wide and roll them in flour and curry powder. Sauté them quickly in butter or oil according to the Canadian cooking theory (page 10).

Make a ring of the rice on a large platter, heap the fish in the center, and make a border of the tomatoes and eggplant. Serve with a tomato sauce (page 23) flavored with more curry powder, or parsley butter (page 33) with curry added.

CODFISH STEAKS IN WINE

4 cod steaks, 1 inch thick
Salt
Freshly ground black pepper
1½ cups white wine

6 tablespoons butter
Chopped parsley
Lemon slices

Arrange the steaks in a baking dish, season to taste, and cover with white wine. Let them soak in the refrigerator for several hours.

When ready to cook, dot the steaks heavily with butter and bake at 425° according to the Canadian cooking theory (page 8). Baste often during the cooking process. Sprinkle with chopped parsley and garnish with lemon slices. Serve with small artichoke hearts and fresh peas.

BAKED COD

Cod may be baked in any of the ways given for striped bass or halibut (see pages 269 and 125).

BAKED STUFFED COD

1 whole cod (2 to 4 pounds)	½ pint oysters and liquor
Lemon	½ cup chopped parsley
6 green onions, chopped	¼ teaspoon freshly ground
¼ cup minced celery	black pepper
¼ cup minced green pepper	1 teaspoon salt
5 tablespoons butter	½ teaspoon thyme
1½ cups bread crumbs	Butter or bacon fat

Clean and split the fish. Rub the interior with lemon.

Sauté the onions, celery, and green pepper in butter until just tender. Add the crumbs, the oysters and their liquor, and cook for 3 or 4 minutes. Add the parsley and season to taste with salt, pepper, and thyme. Stuff the fish with this mixture, secure it with toothpicks and string, and place it in an oiled baking dish. Season with salt and pepper, dot with butter or bacon fat, and bake at 425° according to the Canadian cooking theory (page 8).

Serve with lemon butter (page 31) or with sauce béchamel (page 23) to which you have added onion and parsley.

NEW ENGLAND TURKEY

This is one of the truly authentic American dishes.

Clean and split a whole cod and stuff it with your favorite bread stuffing. Sew it up or secure it with toothpicks and string. Arrange it in an oiled baking dish in an S-shaped design. Cover with strips of salt pork from head to tail and bake at 425° according to the Canadian cooking theory (page 8). Baste with the pan juices during the cooking.

Remove to a hot platter, garnish with plain boiled potatoes and green peas, and serve with an egg or parsley sauce (both page 24).

COD IN THE FASHION OF THE BAKER

For this recipe you may use either a medium-sized whole fish or a large center cut of cod.

Steam 12 to 18 small potatoes in butter until almost tender. Brown 12 small white onions in butter, cook until nearly done. Clean the fish, arrange it in a greased baking pan, and sprinkle it with salt, freshly ground black pepper, thyme, and powdered bay leaf. Surround it with the potatoes and onions and pour over it the melted butter in which the vegetables were cooked. Bake at 425° according to the Canadian cooking theory (page 8), basting every 5 minutes with the pan juices. Garnish with chopped parsley and lemon slices.

BAKED COD WITH CREAM

Use either a whole fish or a large center cut.

Clean the fish, place it on an oiled baking pan, and dot heavily with butter. Add 1 cup of fish broth or chicken broth. Season to taste and bake at 425° according to the Canadian cooking theory (page 8). Baste often with the pan juices. Arrange the fish on a hot platter and surround it with a ring of sautéed potatoes.

Thicken the pan juices with beurre manié (page 475) and add ½ cup of heavy cream. Pour the sauce over the fish.

POACHED COD

In Norway poached cod is usually cooked in salt water and served with an egg sauce and boiled potatoes, and always with red wine.

You may poach a whole fish, a center cut, steaks, or fillets. Wrap the fish in cheesecloth and poach in boiling salted water or in a court bouillon (page 18) according to the Canadian cooking theory (page 12). Serve with lemon butter (page 31), Hollandaise sauce (pages 25–26), or an egg sauce made by adding chopped hard-cooked egg and a bit of sherry to sauce béchamel (page 23).

CODFISH CUSTARD

1½ teaspoons cornstarch	Salt
1½ cups milk	Freshly ground black pepper
2 eggs, well beaten	1½ pounds cod, poached and
¼ cup melted butter	flaked

Dissolve the cornstarch in the milk, add the eggs, butter, seasonings to taste, and the fish. Pour into a buttered casserole and bake at 350° for about 40 minutes, or until the custard is not quite set in the middle. This is a Rhode Island dish and is often served with their native johnnycake.

COD LOAF

2 cups cooked, flaked cod	Salt
¼ cup each chopped onion, celery, green pepper	Freshly ground black pepper
½ cup chopped walnuts	1 teaspoon tarragon
¼ cup chopped parsley	2 eggs, separated
1 cup sifted toasted crumbs	½ cup milk
	½ cup melted butter

Combine the fish, vegetables, nuts, parsley, crumbs, salt, pepper, and tarragon. Beat the egg yolks and add them to the mixture with the milk and melted butter. Fold in the stiffly beaten egg whites and pour into a buttered mold or pan. Set in a pan of hot water and bake at 375° for about 40 minutes, or until set. Unmold on a hot plate and serve with egg sauce (page 24) or Hollandaise sauce (pages 25–26).

COD FLORENTINE

Poach 1 fillet of cod for each serving in boiling salted water. Arrange the poached fillets on a bed of chopped cooked spinach lightly flavored with nutmeg. Top with sauce Mornay (page 22), sprinkle with grated Parmesan cheese, and run under the broiler for a few minutes to brown.

COLD POACHED COD

Cold poached cod is delicious if it is firm and not overcooked. Serve it with mayonnaise, sauce gribiche (pages 36–37), sauce rémoulade (page 35), tartar sauce (pages 35–36), or Russian dressing (page 35).

If you wish to serve the fish in aspic, follow the directions on pages 18–20.

Salt Cod

My favorite codfish dishes are based on the salt cod. In preparing salt cod, it is always necessary, of course, to remove the salt. There are two ways to do this. You may soak the fish for several hours; or you may cover it with cold water, bring the water to a boil very slowly, and then rinse the fish in cold water. Here are recipes that demonstrate the versatility of the salt cod.

POACHED CODFISH WITH VARIOUS SAUCES

Soak 1 pound of salt codfish in cold water for 4 hours. Rinse the fish thoroughly. Place it in a skillet or shallow saucepan and cover it with cold water. Bring slowly to a boil and let it boil feebly for about 15 minutes. Remove the fish to a hot platter and surround with plain boiled potatoes sprinkled with parsley. Serve with:

1. Melted butter
2. Parsley sauce (page 23)
3. Hollandaise sauce (pages 25–26)
4. Egg sauce (page 23)

CODFISH BÉCHAMEL

1 pound salt codfish
2 cups sauce béchamel (page 23)

Chopped parsley
Toast fried in olive oil

Soak the codfish in cold water for 4 hours. Remove, rinse, place in cold water, and bring to a boil very slowly. Taste for tenderness; the fish may have to simmer for a few minutes. Remove the fish from the water and cut into small pieces or flake with a fork. Combine with sauce béchamel and serve hot over fried toast. Sprinkle with parsley. Plain boiled potatoes are a natural accompaniment.

VARIATIONS

1. Prepare the codfish béchamel as above and pour into a flat baking dish or gratin dish. Sprinkle with buttered crumbs and grated Gruyère cheese and place under the broiler for a few minutes.

2. Sauté 1 medium onion in 4 tablespoons butter; when it is

just light-colored, add 1 tablespoon curry powder and ½ teaspoon black pepper. Combine with the cooked codfish and season to taste — possibly you may want additional curry. Serve with rice. French-fried onion rings, very crisp, are good with this.

3. Combine 1 cup of grated Cheddar or Gruyère or Swiss cheese with sauce béchamel and mix well with the codfish. Pour into a flat baking dish or gratin dish and sprinkle with grated Parmesan cheese. Run under the broiler for a few minutes. Serve accompanied by plain boiled potatoes with butter and parsley.

4. Sauté ½ pound sliced mushrooms, 2 tablespoons finely chopped onion, and 4 tablespoons chopped parsley and combine with the fish. Mix with the sauce béchamel and serve in patty shells or in a large vol-au-vent. (This is an overgrown patty shell. You may order one from a good French baker if you wish to serve something spectacular.)

5. Sauté ½ cup blanched shredded almonds in 4 tablespoons butter until crisp and brown. Combine with the fish and sauce béchamel. Serve with large baked potatoes topped with paprika.

6. Add 4 sliced hard-cooked eggs and ¼ cup finely chopped parsley to the sauce béchamel after combining with the fish. Add to this 1 tablespoon paprika and blend well. Serve with buttered noodles.

ARMENIAN CODFISH

1 pound salt codfish	Freshly ground black pepper
8 tomatoes, peeled and	Vinegar
finely chopped	6 green peppers cut in julienne
6 tablespoons oil	5 tablespoons butter
Salt	4 tablespoons oil

Put the fish to soak in cold water for 4 hours. Combine the tomatoes with the oil and let them cook down to a paste. Add salt and pepper to taste and a touch of vinegar to cut the oil. Sauté the peppers in butter until tender.

When the fish has soaked, rinse it and put it in a skillet with cold water and bring to a boil. Drain off the water, add 4 table-spoons of oil, and sauté the fish according to the Canadian cooking theory (page 10). Serve on the tomato paste topped with the sautéed peppers. Pass rice and additional tomato sauce, if you wish.

CODFISH, SPANISH STYLE

1 pound salt codfish	6 to 8 tomatoes,
2 medium onions, chopped	peeled and chopped
2 cloves garlic, chopped	Beurre manié (page 475)
2 green peppers	Pimientos, chopped
cut in julienne	Parsley, chopped
½ cup olive oil	Toast points, fried in olive oil

Soak the codfish in cold water, rinse, and poach according to the Canadian cooking theory (page 12). Brown the onions, garlic, and pepper in the olive oil. When tender, add the tomatoes and a little of the fish broth. Thicken with beurre manié. Let it cook down for ½ to 1 hour, add the pieces of codfish and the pimientos, and heat again. Serve in a flat dish topped with chopped parsley and garnished with fried toast points.

CODFISH SOUFFLÉ

1½ cups flaked salt codfish	Freshly ground black pepper
4 tablespoons butter	4 egg yolks, beaten
4 tablespoons flour	6 egg whites
1 cup milk	Sauce béchamel (page 23)
Nutmeg	or Hollandaise (pages 25–26)

Soak the codfish in cold water, rinse, and poach according to the Canadian cooking theory (page 12). Flake into shreds.

Combine the butter and flour in a saucepan; when they are well blended, gradually add the milk, stirring until it is thickened. Season with a little nutmeg and black pepper. Add the egg yolks, blend well, and add the codfish. Beat the egg whites until stiff and fold into the mixture. Pour into a buttered soufflé dish and bake at 375° for 35 to 45 minutes or until puffy and brown. Serve with a béchamel or Hollandaise sauce — and forget you ever ate a fish cake.

FRIED CODFISH STRIPS

1 pound filleted salt codfish	Fat for frying
Flour	Tartar sauce (pages 35–36)
Freshly ground black pepper	

Soak the codfish in cold water for several hours. Rinse and cut in diagonal strips about 1 to 1½ inches wide. Roll in flour, sprinkle with pepper, and fry in deep fat at 375°. Drain on absorbent paper and serve hot with tartar sauce.

CODFISH LYONNAISE

Naturally the combination of onion and codfish is elegant. So it is not surprising that there should be a Lyonnaise version, for the traditional dishes of that city use onions a great deal.

1 pound salt codfish	Butter *or* oil
6 medium potatoes, sliced	Chopped parsley
2 medium onions, sliced	

Soak the codfish in cold water for several hours. Sauté the potatoes and onions as you would for Lyonnaise potatoes. Flake the codfish and brown it nicely in butter or oil; combine with the potato-onion mixture and let it cook down for a few minutes. Sprinkle generously with chopped parsley. This is a wonderful Sunday breakfast dish.

CODFISH CARCASSONNE

1½ pounds salt codfish
1½ pounds small new potatoes
Butter *or* fat
2 cloves garlic, finely chopped

3 to 4 tablespoons flour
Freshly ground black pepper
Chopped parsley

Soak the codfish for several hours and poach for about 15 minutes. Cut into small pieces.

Scrape or peel the potatoes and brown them in butter or fat until they are just golden. Add the garlic and sprinkle with the flour. Season with the pepper and a bit of parsley. Add broth from the fish and water mixed in equal parts — enough to cover the potatoes. Let them simmer until tender. About 4 or 5 minutes before you remove them from the heat, add the codfish and let it all blend well together.

CODFISH MARSEILLAISE

Here is another tasty way of combining salt cod and potatoes:

1½ pounds salt codfish
Flour
½ cup olive oil
1 large onion, chopped
1 clove garlic, chopped
5 large or 6 medium tomatoes,
    peeled, seeded, and chopped

Freshly ground black pepper
Sage
Thyme
Salt
6 potatoes cut in quarters
White wine
Chopped parsley

Soak the codfish. When it is freshened, cut it into even-sized squares. Roll these in flour and sauté them in hot oil until nicely browned. Remove them from the pan and in the same oil sauté the onion and garlic until they are light-colored and soft. Add the tomatoes, black pepper, a pinch of sage, a bit of thyme, and let this simmer about 15 minutes. Season to taste with salt.

Oil a casserole, put the quartered potatoes in the bottom, pour the sauce over them, and add just enough white wine and water mixed to cover. Add the pieces of cod, cover the casserole, and bake at 350° for 30 minutes, or until the potatoes are tender. Remove the cover and sprinkle with chopped parsley.

CODFISH PORTUGAISE

2 pounds dried salt codfish,
  soaked 12 hours, or overnight,
  in cold water
6 to 8 potatoes

cream
⅓ cup olive oil
3 cloves garlic, minced
½ cup buttered crumbs

Drain the codfish and pull apart into small pieces. Put in a small saucepan, cover with cold water, and bring to a boil. Simmer for 5 minutes, or until flaky and tender. Drain well and cool. When cool enough to handle, shred or chop very fine and pound in a mortar.

Meanwhile, steam the potatoes and mash, adding a very little cream. Beat in the codfish, oil, and garlic to make a light fluffy mixture. Taste for seasoning. (Codfish is salty, so you might not need any more salt.)

Turn into a well-buttered baking dish or casserole and sprinkle with crumbs. Bake in a 350° oven until very hot, about 35 minutes.

CODFISH SALAD

3 tablespoons cold poached salt
  codfish, broken into large flakes
2 cups sliced, boiled potatoes
  (preferably waxy, new potatoes)
1 cup finely chopped or thinly
  sliced onions
¼ cup chopped parsley

Dressing
½ cup olive oil
3 tablespoons vinegar
½ teaspoon freshly ground black
  pepper
1 clove garlic, crushed
½ teaspoon dry mustard

This salad undoubtedly came from the Portuguese on Cape Cod or Nantucket.

Combine the fish, potatoes, onions, and parsley in a salad

bowl. Blend the dressing thoroughly. Pour over the salad and let it mellow an hour or so before serving.

CODFISH CROQUETTES

1 cup salt codfish, soaked, poached, and flaked
¾ cup sliced mushrooms, sautéed
1 teaspoon freshly ground black pepper
1 tablespoon chopped parsley

Dash of nutmeg
1¼ cups heavy white sauce
Sifted bread *or* cracker crumbs
1 egg, beaten
Oil or fat for frying

Mix the codfish, mushrooms, and seasonings and combine with the heavy white sauce. Let it cool thoroughly and form into balls, cylinders, or pyramids. Let these chill for an hour or so. Heat the fat in your fryer to 375°. Dip the croquettes into crumbs, then into beaten egg, and finally cover thoroughly with crumbs again. Fry 3 or 4 minutes or until nicely browned. Drain on absorbent paper.

VARIATIONS

1. Add another cup of codfish and omit the mushrooms.
2. Use sautéed onions in place of the mushrooms. The onions should be finely chopped and sautéed until just soft. Use ½ cup of onions to 1¼ cups of codfish flakes.

CODFISH CAKES I

There are as many recipes for this delicacy as there are counties in all the New England states. One of the newest has come to me from Charles Triggs, who is an authority on fish and a man who knows codfish. His recipe is:

1 pound salt codfish
7 or 8 medium-sized potatoes

1 egg
Fat for frying

Cut the codfish across the grain into about ½-inch pieces. Pick the pieces apart, place in a skillet, cover with hot water, stir, and drain. Repeat two or three times, then cover with cold water and let it come to a boil. Change the water, let it come to a boil again, and simmer for a few minutes.

Boil and mash the potatoes. Drain the codfish and mix with the mashed potatoes, using a wire masher. When thoroughly mixed, add the egg and beat with a fork. Take a tablespoon of the mixture at a time and drop into deep fat, or into a frying pan with a fair amount of fat. Drain on absorbent paper.

NOTE: This recipe can be changed according to taste — some may prefer a larger percentage of codfish, some less.

CODFISH CAKES II

This is a recipe from Martinique that is served in a pleasant restaurant in Paris specializing in food from the Antilles.

2½ cups flour	Beer, enough to make a batter
1 teaspoon baking powder	(about 1 cup)
1 clove garlic, finely chopped	½ pound codfish, soaked,
4 shallots, finely chopped	poached, and shredded
2 tablespoons chopped parsley	Fat for deep frying
Freshly ground black pepper	

Sift the flour and baking powder together. Add the garlic, shallots, parsley, and a good grind of black pepper. Stir in enough beer to make a batter and add the shredded codfish.

Heat the fat in your fryer to 375°. Drop the batter by spoonfuls into the hot fat and fry until nicely browned. Drain on absorbent paper.

CODFISH CAKES III

The mixture of equal quantities of mashed potatoes and cooked shredded codfish is the traditional codfish cake. Some like less potato, and others like more. Vary it to suit yourself.

1 cup shredded cooked codfish	Freshly ground black pepper
1 cup mashed potatoes	Butter *or* hot fat
1 or 2 eggs	Flour *or* crumbs (if desired)

Mix the codfish, potatoes, eggs, and pepper and form into cakes. Sauté in plenty of butter or bacon fat, or roll in flour or crumbs and fry in deep hot fat.

VARIATIONS

1. A teaspoon of ground ginger or a little finely chopped green ginger does wonderful things for codfish balls. This is a recipe that my mother's old chef used, and the codfish balls he made were always in demand. He added plenty of butter to the mashed potatoes and then sautéed the codfish balls, spiked with ginger, in additional butter. They were crisp and rich with the mixed flavors of butter, ginger, and salt cod.

2. Southerners are apt to add finely chopped green onion to the traditional codfish cake mixture, which gives it a different flavor. Sometimes a bit of finely chopped green pepper is also added.

3. For cocktails, make the cakes very small, roll them in flour and crumbs, and deep fry them for about 3 minutes at 390°. A demitasse spoon is perfect for dropping this size ball into the basket for frying.

BRANDADE DE MORUE

1 pound salt codfish	½ teaspoon freshly ground
⅔ cup olive oil	black pepper
⅓ cup heavy cream	Toast triangles fried in olive oil
2 cloves garlic	

Soak the codfish for several hours. Wash it and bring it to a boil in cold water. Reduce the heat and simmer for about 10 minutes. Drain the fish and shred it very fine, removing any bits of bone.

Heat the olive oil and the cream separately. Crush the garlic — in a mortar if you have one — and add the fish; if you don't have a mortar, put both garlic and fish through the food grinder twice, using the fine blade. The fish must be very fine, so if two grindings do not seem enough, work it with a heavy wooden spoon in a bowl. This brandade can be prepared quickly and easily in a food processor. When the mixture is practically a paste, put it in a heavy saucepan over very low heat and stir well with a fork. Now add the olive oil and the cream alternately and work them both in well. Continue until all the oil and cream are absorbed and the mixture has the consistency of mashed potatoes. Season with the pepper, heap it up in the center of a serving dish, and surround it with fried toast triangles.

VARIATION

Beat mashed potatoes into the mixture. This gives a completely different texture to the dish and a more delicate flavor. It is called Benedictine, and the true eggs Benedictine are served on a bed of this. Eggs Benedict is another dish entirely.

Croaker

This fish gets its name from the air bladder it uses to give off tuneful sounds. There are a number of varieties on both coasts, and in some localities they are marketed. The croaker is a good game fish.

BROILED CROAKER

Broil whole croakers according to the Canadian cooking theory (pages 9–10). Serve with any of the fish butters — anchovy, lemon, or parsley (pages 31–33).

CROAKERS SAUTÉ MEUNIÈRE

To my taste, this method of preparation is usually preferable to pan frying. Dust the fish with flour and sauté lightly in plenty of butter. Season to taste and serve the fish with chopped parsley, lemon, and more butter.

PAN-FRIED CROAKERS

Roll the fish in seasoned crumbs or corn meal and sauté in butter or oil. Serve with a sauce rémoulade (page 35) or tartar sauce (pages 35–36).

Cusk

Even more streamlined than the hake, this fish is distinguished by a long black fin extending from just behind the head to the tail. It is found in northern waters and is nearly always caught on line. It puts up a good fight when hooked.

You will not often see the whole fish in the markets, but quite a bit of it is sold as fillets that are labeled something else besides cusk. It has good flavor and texture and ought to be more popular in its own right.

Cusk may be prepared in any of the ways you prepare haddock or fresh cod.

Eels

Eels are erroneously called freshwater fish by most French authorities. They are both freshwater and marine. All the European and American eels are born in the same place, a deep spot in the ocean south of Bermuda. From there they migrate to localities previously frequented by their parents — European eels go to Europe, and American eels to America. They ascend the freshwater streams, stay for a while, and then return to the spawning grounds in the Atlantic.

Eels are a traditional dish during the Italian celebration of Christmas Eve, and they are in greatest demand at the holiday season. Smoked eels are available all year and fresh eels can now be bought the year round in markets that maintain tanks in which to keep them.

PAN-FRIED EELS

First, the eels must be skinned. The traditional method is to nail the head of the eel to a wall and then skin it with one full sweep of the hand. You may also cut the eel skin around the head, and peel it back very slowly. You may need the aid of pliers to get it started. Once the eels are skinned, remove the intestines, wash the fish, and cut them into 3-inch pieces. Dip these in flour and sauté them in butter or oil until delicately browned. Season to taste and serve plain or with tartar sauce (pages 35–36).

EELS SAUTÉ PROVENÇALE

2 large eels or several small ones	Salt
	Freshly ground black pepper
Flour	3 cloves garlic, chopped
6 tablespoons olive oil	¼ cup chopped parsley

Skin and clean the eels, cut in 3-inch pieces, and dredge with flour. Heat the olive oil in a skillet and sauté the pieces of eel quickly according to the Canadian cooking theory (page 10). When they are done, season to taste and add the garlic and parsley. Toss them about in the pan for a minute or two. Serve the eel with the garlic and parsley poured over the top.

EELS NAPOLITANA

2 or 3 large eels	1 teaspoon salt
2 cups browned crumbs	1 teaspoon cinnamon

1½ teaspoons sugar
Flour
Beaten egg

Butter
Lemon wedges

Skin and wash the eels and cut into pieces. Mix the crumbs, salt, cinnamon, and sugar. Dip the eels in flour, then the beaten egg, and finally in the crumb mixture. Sauté quickly in butter according to the Canadian cooking theory (page 10). Serve with lemon wedges.

NOTE: The traditional way of preparing this dish is to tie the eel on a spit and roast it in front of the fire, basting it with its own juices. However, this is a little involved for most people.

EELS COMMACHIO

The Italians, like many Europeans, are very fond of eels. In fact, true international gourmets find it difficult to understand why Americans neglect this delicious fish. Here is a famous Italian recipe that does justice to it.

6 eels
½ cup olive oil
1 large onion, sliced fine
Salt

Freshly ground black pepper
1 teaspoon sage
1 cup tomato paste
1 cup white wine

Skin and clean the eels and cut them in 3-inch lengths. Heat the olive oil in a skillet. Add the onion, sage, and the pieces of eel. Sauté according to the Canadian cooking theory (page 10) until nicely browned. Season to taste; add the tomato paste and white wine. Cover and simmer until the eel is tender. Serve with rice baked in broth.

MATELOTE OF EELS NORMANDIE

See pages 51–52.

MATELOTE PROVENÇALE

This is prepared in the same way as the preceding recipe, except that white wine and water (half and half) are used in place of cider and 3 cloves of garlic are added. Sautéed mushroom caps are used as garnish along with the onions and croutons.

OLD-FASHIONED NEW ENGLAND EEL STIFLE

6 eels	Freshly ground black pepper
6 fairly large potatoes, peeled and sliced	Flour
	Salt pork
4 large onions, peeled and sliced	Butter

Skin and clean the eels and cut them into 4-inch lengths. In a buttered baking dish or casserole, place a layer of the potatoes, a layer of the onions, and a layer of eels. Sprinkle each layer lightly with pepper and flour. Cover the top with small bits of salt pork, dot with butter, and add almost enough water to cover. Cover and bake at 375° until tender, approximately 45 to 50 minutes, or cook slowly on top of the stove until done.

EELS BORDELAISE

This dish is usually made with the lampreys caught near Bordeaux. It is a specialty of the house in one of the famous restaurants in Saint Émilion, where some of the finest wines of that district are used to prepare the food, and, of course, are drunk with it. Strangely enough, Saint Émilion is famous for another gastronomic delight — macaroons.

3 pounds eels	Pinch thyme
Carrot, thinly sliced	1 leaf and stalk of celery
Onion, thinly sliced	Several sprigs parsley
1 clove garlic	1 bay leaf

1 teaspoon salt
1 teaspoon freshly ground black
  pepper
Red wine to cover

6 to 8 pieces of the white of leek
⅓ cup diced raw ham
3 tablespoons butter
4 tablespoons flour

Skin and clean the eels and cut them in 4-inch pieces. Line a skillet or saucepan with sliced carrot and onion. Put the pieces of eel on top. Add garlic, thyme, celery, parsley, bay leaf, salt, pepper, and red wine to cover. Cover the skillet, bring it to a boil, and simmer for 10 minutes.

Meanwhile, brown the pieces of leek in butter. Add the ham and the cooked eel. Make a roux of the butter and flour and add it to the broth in which the eel was cooked. Simmer for 20 minutes. Force this sauce through a sieve onto the eel, leeks, and ham. Simmer this all together for 15 or 20 minutes, stirring occasionally. Taste for seasoning.

Arrange the fish and leeks on a serving dish. Thicken the sauce with beurre manié (page 475) if necessary, and pour it over the eel.

BAKED EELS, NEW ENGLAND FASHION

Skin and clean 6 eels but do not split them. Cut them in lengths of 3 to 4 inches. Remove the intestines with a fine-pointed knife, or a fork or skewer. Arrange the pieces on an oiled baking pan, season, and top with slices of onion and salt pork. Bake at 450° according to the Canadian cooking theory (page 8).

POACHED EELS

Skin and clean eels and cut them into 3-inch lengths. Poach them in a court bouillon (page 18). They should be tender in about 8 or 9 minutes. Remove them to a hot dish, reduce the broth, and use it to prepare a sauce velouté (page 21). Pour this over the eels and garnish with chopped parsley.

1. Prepare a curry sauce (page 29). Pour the sauce over the poached eels and serve with rice and chutney.

2. Poach the eels. Prepare the sauce velouté and lace it heavily with paprika. Serve with buttered noodles.

3. Poach the eels in white wine. Sauté 24 mushroom caps in butter. Brown ½ cup of artichoke hearts in butter. Arrange these in a baking dish or casserole with the eels. Add 3 pimientos cut in fine strips. Prepare a white wine sauce with the broth (page 24), season it with paprika, and pour it over the eels and vegetables. Heat in a 350° oven for 12 minutes.

4. Cut the eels into lengths of 5 or 6 inches and poach in a court bouillon for about 6 minutes. Let them cool in the broth. When cool enough to handle, wipe them well, dip in flour, then in beaten egg yolk, and roll in crumbs. Grill or broil until nicely browned. Served with tartar sauce (pages 35–36).

MARINATED EELS

Red wine	Pinch thyme
Garlic	1 leek
1 carrot	Salt
1 onion stuck with cloves	Freshly ground black pepper
1 stalk celery	3 eels
3 or 4 sprigs parsley	

Prepare a marinade of all the ingredients except the eels. Skin, clean, and cut the eels in pieces. Soak them in the marinade. Poach them in the marinade for 15 or 20 minutes. When tender, remove them to a hot dish. Reduce the broth and put it through a fine sieve or food mill. Reheat and pour over the pieces of eel.

COLD EEL (EELS IN JELLY)

6 large eels
White wine court bouillon
    (pages 18–19)
3 cloves garlic
Olive oil

Chopped parsley
1 envelope gelatin (if desired)
Sauce rémoulade (page 35) *or*
    sauce gribiche (pages 36–37)

Skin and clean the eels, and cut them in 3-inch pieces. Prepare the court bouillon. Poach the eels until tender, remove them, and arrange in a mold.

Chop the garlic and sauté in olive oil until brown. Add to the mold. Sprinkle chopped parsley over the pieces of eel.

Reduce the bouillon and strain. It should make a good jelly without the addition of gelatin. However, if you will feel safer, use 1 envelope dissolved in ¼ cup of water. Stir it into 2 cups of the hot broth. Chill slightly and pour over the pieces of eel. Stand in the refrigerator until firm. Unmold on a platter with your favorite garnishes and serve with sauce rémoulade or sauce gribiche.

FLEMISH GREEN EELS

This is certainly one of the finest of cold dishes. I like it as an hors d'oeuvre or as a full course for a summer buffet.

3 pounds eels
6 tablespoons butter
¼ pound chopped sorrel *or*
    spinach
½ cup chopped parsley
¼ cup chervil
1 tablespoon fresh *or* 1 tea-
    spoon dried tarragon
Savory

Rosemary
Sage
Thyme
Salt
Freshly ground black pepper
White wine
4 egg yolks, slightly beaten
1½ tablespoons of lemon juice

Skin and clean the eels, and cut them into 3-inch pieces. Brown them in the butter; when they are just colored add the herbs. Mix the herbs well with the pieces of eel, add salt and pepper to taste, and cover with white wine. Cover the pan and poach just until the eel is tender. Remove the fish to a large earthenware or glass dish.

Stir the egg yolks into the broth, and continue stirring and cooking until lightly thickened. Be careful not to let the sauce boil. Taste for seasoning, add lemon juice, and pour over the eel. Chill and serve cold.

SMOKED EEL

Smoked eel is excellent as a cocktail snack, as a first course, or as part of a smoked fish platter at a buffet or supper party. You may buy it by the pound.

It is not necessary to skin it and cut it up for serving, but it does make a nicer appearance that way. Its oily flesh takes well to a sprinkling of freshly ground black pepper and a little squeeze of lemon juice.

CANNED EEL

There are several different varieties of canned eel in jelly, and they are all good for cold snacks and summer luncheons. Serve on a bed of greens with a garnish of thinly sliced onions. Use a sauce rémoulade (page 35) or green mayonnaise (page 34).

Fluke

This is a fish that has become popular with summer fish enthusiasts along the lower Northeastern Coast. It is also known as the summer flounder and is in fact a member of the flounder family. It has much more spirit, however, than its close relatives, and this accounts for its appeal as a game fish.

In some local areas in southern New England, especially on the island of Nantucket, fluke is called plaice, although it bears no relationship to the European fish of that name. It is found in the markets only during the summer months, when it comes close to shore to feed.

Because of its somewhat poor taste and texture, it is not held in esteem by fish enthusiasts.

Although fluke can grow to 25 pounds, the average size caught is 1 to 5 pounds. It is a delicious food fish with white meat of an unusually delicate texture. Prepare it in any of the ways suggested for sole or flounder (pages 234–261).

Groupers

The many varieties of groupers are all members of that large family of fish known as sea bass, which is so common all through the Atlantic coastal area, and in fact, common all over the world. The red grouper is probably the best known, and it is important commercially from Virginia on south. The Nassau grouper is found around Florida, while the yellowfish and black grouper and the gag are mainly Gulf fish.

An interesting characteristic of the grouper family is the ability of its members to conceal themselves by taking on the color of their surroundings. In coral or seaweed they camouflage themselves with stripes. When they rise to the surface of the sea, they turn pale, almost colorless, blending with the water. Apparently this ability is something they can flash on and off at will, for they can turn on their colored bands when they see a fish of a different species approaching.

Another interesting fact about groupers is that they seem to be very friendly. One scientist who made underwater investigations some years ago found that red groupers he had been feeding would let him handle them and would even poke around in his pockets in search of tidbits.

Groupers can weigh as much as 40 pounds, but the market fish generally weigh from 5 to 15 pounds. They are sold whole, in steaks or fillets.

Groupers can be cooked in any of the ways suggested for sea bass or red snapper (pages 214–216, 167–171).

Grunion

These amusing fish are *gathered* on shore instead of being hooked or netted in the sea. During their spawning season, grunions come up on the beach and dig holes in the wet sand, where they deposit their eggs. Their floundering antics have always reminded me of a disorderly, unrehearsed ballet.

The grunion "run" can be forecast from year to year, and the seasonal sport of gathering them has many followers on the West Coast. I have never encountered grunions on the Atlantic seaboard. The fish is small, delicate, and flavorful, and somewhat resembles the smelt.

BROILED GRUNIONS

Clean the fish, dip them in flour, dot well with butter, and broil under a hot flame according to the Canadian cooking theory (page 10). Brush with oil or butter during the cooking process. Season to taste and serve with a tartar sauce (pages 35–36).

FRIED GRUNIONS

Here are grunions at their best.

Heat the fat in your French fryer to 375°. Clean the fish, dip them in flour, then in beaten egg, and roll them in corn meal. Fry according to the Canadian cooking theory (page 11) until brown and crisp. Drain on absorbent paper and season to taste with salt and freshly ground black pepper.

Serve with lemon butter or parsley butter and lemon quarters.

Haddock

The haddock and the cod are close relatives, but you can easily tell them apart once you have seen them side by side in the market. The haddock is usually smaller, the average market fish weighing about 2½ to 3 pounds; its mouth is smaller than that of the cod; and it has a black, rather than a whitish, lateral line.

A great deal of haddock is sold in fillets, either fresh or frozen, and like ocean perch and cod, it is shipped frozen all over the country. Americans now consume over one hundred million pounds of haddock a year.

Finnan haddie — or smoked haddock — is an extremely popular dish of Scottish origin. Years ago it was known as Findon haddock, after the Scottish fishing port of Findon.

Fresh Haddock

BROILED HADDOCK

See directions for broiling fish, pages 9–10.

SAUTÉED HADDOCK

See directions for sauté meunière, page 10. For fillets, see recipes for ocean perch, pages 154–159.

FRIED HADDOCK

See directions for frying fish and fillets, page 11.

HADDOCK TURBANS WITH LEMON SAUCE

6 haddock fillets	Court bouillon
½ pound shrimp	Sauce velouté (page 21)
Fresh dill	1 tablespoon lemon juice
Parsley	

Place one or two shelled, uncooked shrimp on each fillet and a little fresh dill and parsley. Roll the fillets and secure with toothpicks. Poach them in court bouillon according to the Canadian cooking theory (page 12). Remove to a hot serving dish. Reduce the stock, prepare the sauce velouté, and add the lemon juice at the last minute. Pour the sauce over the fillets.

HADDOCK FILLETS VÉRONIQUE

6 haddock fillets	Sauce velouté (page 21)
Court bouillon (page 18)	½ cup white seedless grapes
White wine	Half-whipped cream

Poach the fillets in court bouillon and white wine according to the Canadian cooking theory (page 12). Arrange them in a shallow baking dish. Make a sauce velouté with the bouillon and some heavy cream and add the grapes. Pour this over the fillets.

Dribble a little half-whipped cream on top, and run under the broiler for a minute or two to give it a glaze.

FILLETS OF HADDOCK IN CREAM SAUCE

Sauce béchamel (page 23)
2 tablespoons sherry *or* Madeira
Fresh fennel *or* fennel seeds

6 haddock fillets
Chopped parsley

Prepare the béchamel and flavor it with sherry or Madeira and the fennel or fennel seeds. Place the fillets in a flat baking dish and pour the sauce over them. Bake at 425°–450° according to the Canadian cooking theory (page 8). Remove and sprinkle liberally with chopped parsley. Serve with crisp fried potatoes and a cucumber salad.

BAKED HADDOCK FILLETS IN WHITE WINE AND TARRAGON

6 haddock fillets
Fresh *or* dried tarragon
Salt
Freshly ground black pepper

1½ cups white wine
Butter
½ cup heavy cream
3 egg yolks

Arrange the fillets in a shallow baking dish and sprinkle liberally with tarragon. Salt and pepper to taste. Add the wine and dot with butter. Bake at 425°–450° according to the Canadian cooking theory (page 8). Remove fish to a hot platter. Reduce the wine to ¾ cup and combine with the cream mixed with the egg yolks. Stir until the sauce is thickened, but do not let it boil. Season to taste, pour over the fillets, and sprinkle with additional tarragon.

STUFFED FILLETS IN WHITE WINE

Fish forcemeat (page 41)   1 cup white wine
6 haddock fillets   Butter
Chopped shallots *or* green onions   18 cooked, shelled shrimp

Prepare a fish forcemeat or your favorite stuffing for fish. Spread this on the fillets and fold them over. Arrange the stuffed fillets on a bed of chopped shallots or green onions in a baking dish and add the wine. Dot with butter and bake at 450° according to the Canadian cooking theory (page 8). Baste often with the pan juices. Remove the fish to a hot platter, and prepare a wine sauce with the pan juices. Pour this over the fillets and garnish with the shrimp.

HADDOCK FILLETS IN PAPER CASES

½ pound mushrooms   Dash of lemon juice for each
5 tablespoons butter   fillet
Salt   Finely chopped green onion
Freshly ground black pepper   Butter
6 haddock fillets   Mustard sauce (page 24)

Chop the mushrooms and sauté slowly in 5 tablespoons of butter until they are black and rich. Salt and pepper to taste. Spread each fillet with this mixture, add a dash of lemon juice and a little chopped onion and fold over.

Cut large heart-shaped pieces of cooking parchment or foil, and place one fillet on each piece, putting it toward the edge so that you can fold a layer of paper over the top. Dot the fillets with butter, spread with a little mustard sauce, and fold the paper over the top. Crimp the edges so that you have a tightly closed bag. Arrange on a baking sheet and bake at 450° according to the Canadian cooking theory (page 8).

BAKED STUFFED HADDOCK

Clean a 3-pound haddock and split it for stuffing. Leave the head and tail on the fish.

Prepare the following clam stuffing:

½ cup chopped onion	¼ cup finely chopped parsley
¼ cup butter	Salt
2 cups buttered crumbs	Freshly ground black pepper
1 can (7 ounces) minced clams with liquid	Nutmeg
	2 eggs, well beaten

Sauté the onion in butter and mix with all the other ingredients. Stuff the fish with this, sew up the sides, and put strips of bacon or salt pork on top. Place on an oiled baking dish and bake at 425° according to the Canadian cooking theory (page 8). Serve with a tartar sauce (pages 35–36) or with lemon butter (page 31).

HADDOCK PROVENÇALE

1 good-sized haddock	Freshly ground black pepper
1 large onion cut in paper-thin slices	½ cup olive oil
	Fennel seeds
12 to 16 anchovy fillets	Sliced tomatoes
2 cloves garlic, finely chopped	3 tablespoons tomato paste
18 to 20 ripe olives	1½ cups red wine
1 green pepper, finely shredded	Chopped parsley
Salt	Chopped tarragon

Clean and split the haddock. Mix together the onion, anchovies, garlic, olives, and green pepper. Salt and pepper to taste.

Pour over this the olive oil and a sprinkling of fennel seeds. Stuff the fish with the mixture, sew it up, and place it in a well-oiled pan or baking dish. Top with sliced tomatoes and pour over it the tomato paste and red wine mixed together. Bake at 450° according to the Canadian cooking theory (page 8), basting the fish often with the tomato-wine mixture. Just before serving, sprinkle well with the chopped parsley and tarragon, mixed.

STUFFED WHOLE HADDOCK

1 haddock
1 cup fine bread crumbs
¼ cup chopped parsley
¼ cup finely chopped green
    onions *or* chives
1 teaspoon salt, or more

½ cup melted butter
1 teaspoon fennel *or*
    tarragon
2 eggs
White wine court bouillon
    (pages 19–20)

Choose a 3-pound haddock, or larger. Have your fish dealer make a gash in the fish and remove all the meat and bones, leaving the skin intact and the head and tail on. Grind the meat well and combine it with all the other ingredients except the court bouillon.

Blend well, stuff the fish skin with this mixture, and sew it up after pressing it into shape.

Poach in the court bouillon according to the Canadian cooking theory (page 12). Remove the fish to a hot platter and serve with a white wine sauce (page 23) prepared with the court bouillon after reducing it.

BOILED HADDOCK, NEW ENGLAND STYLE

Split a 3-to-4-pound haddock, clean it, and rub the inside well with salt. Let it stand for 3 hours. Rinse it and wrap it in cheese-cloth, leaving long ends of the cloth for handles. Simmer in boiling salted water according to the Canadian cooking theory (page 12). Remove it to a hot platter, garnish with crisp bits of salt pork, and surround with boiled potatoes and boiled buttered beets. Serve with parsley sauce or egg sauce (page 23).

HADDOCK CUSTARD

5 eggs, well beaten
2 cups light cream
2 teaspoons finely grated onion
2 tablespoons finely chopped
  parsley

Salt
Freshly ground black pepper
Nutmeg
2 cups flaked, cooked haddock

Beat the eggs thoroughly, add the cream, beat another minute, and then add all the seasonings. Arrange the flaked fish in a well-buttered baking dish and pour the custard over it. Bake at 350° for about 40 minutes or until it is just set in the middle. Serve with crisp fried potatoes and a distinctive relish.

VARIATIONS

1. Line a deep pie tin with pastry and pour the mixture into this. Bake at 400° for 10 minutes. Then reduce to 350° for 25 minutes or until the custard is just set. Serve with a shrimp sauce (page 21).

2. Line a 12-inch pie tin with pastry. Arrange the flaked fish, chopped parsley and onion, and bits of crisp bacon in the bottom. Add a good sprinkling of grated Swiss or Parmesan cheese or a mixture of the two. Pour the custard over this and bake at 375° for 35 minutes or until the custard is just set.

HADDOCK LOAF

2 cups flaked cooked haddock
1 cup fine bread crumbs
¼ cup finely chopped green
  onions *or* scallions
1 cup chopped toasted almonds
  (canned)

¼ cup finely chopped parsley
Salt
Freshly ground black pepper
3 egg yolks, well beaten
3 egg whites, beaten stiff

Combine all the ingredients except the eggs. Then blend in the egg yolks, and finally fold in the egg whites. Turn into a well-buttered mold and bake at 375° for 35 to 40 minutes or until set. Serve from the mold, or unmold on a hot platter and serve with a shrimp or oyster sauce (page 21).

COLD HADDOCK

Follow the recipe for cold ocean perch, pages 158–159.

Finnan Haddie

Finnan haddie — or smoked haddock — comes in fillets and whole fish, and there is great argument over the merits of each type. Sometimes I think that the whole fish has a better flavor and other times I think that the fillets I happen to be eating are as good as anything could possibly be.

BROILED FINNAN HADDIE

Arrange fillets or a whole fish on a broiling rack over a little hot water. Dot the fish with butter and broil according to the Canadian cooking theory (pages 9–10).

FINNAN HADDIE BROILED IN MILK

Place a whole fish or fillet in a broiling pan and dot with butter. Pour warm milk over the fish to cover the bottom of the pan. Broil according to the Canadian cooking theory (pages 9–10). Baste it often with the milk. Serve with boiled potato.

POACHED FINNAN HADDIE

Poach the finnan haddie in milk, or in half milk and half water, or in a mild court bouillon (page 18). Serve with parsley butter (page 33).

VARIATIONS

1. Poach the finnan haddie, flake it, and combine with ¼ cup butter in a saucepan. Add 1 cup heavy cream, 4 sliced hard-cooked eggs, and flavor with cayenne pepper, nutmeg, and freshly ground black pepper. Blend thoroughly.

2. Combine flaked, poached finnan haddie with sauce béchamel (page 23), sprinkle with buttered crumbs, and run under the broiler for a few minutes.

3. Combine flaked, poached finnan haddie with sauce Mornay (page 22), sprinkle with grated Swiss cheese, and brown under the broiler.

4. Combine 2 cups flaked, poached finnan haddie with 1½ cups sauce béchamel, ¼ cup chopped pimiento, ½ cup chopped olives, 3 sliced hard-cooked eggs, and 2 teaspoons onion juice. Arrange in a baking dish, sprinkle with grated cheese, and brown under the broiler for a few minutes.

FINNAN HADDIE SOUFFLÉ

1½ cups flaked, poached finnan haddie
¾ cup heavy sauce béchamel (page 23)
4 egg yolks
Salt
Freshly ground black pepper
Nutmeg
6 egg whites
Butter

Combine the finnan haddie with the sauce béchamel. Beat in the egg yolks. Season to taste with salt and pepper and add a few grains of nutmeg. Beat the egg whites until stiff and fold them into the mixture. Pour into a buttered soufflé dish and bake at 375° for 35 to 40 minutes or until well puffed and brown. Serve with a sauce Mornay (page 22) or a sauce béchamel.

FINNAN HADDIE CAKES

1½ cups flaked, cooked finnan
  haddie
1½ cups seasoned mashed
  potatoes

½ teaspoon ginger
1 egg, well beaten

Combine the finnan haddie with the mashed potatoes — potatoes which have been mashed with plenty of butter and well seasoned with salt and freshly ground black pepper. Add the ginger and egg. Form into small flat cakes and sauté in butter until nicely browned on both sides. Serve with crisp bacon.

FINNAN HADDIE VINAIGRETTE

2 to 3 cups cold poached finnan
  haddie
1 cup cold sliced potatoes
1 cup cold sliced onions
1 cup cold sliced cucumbers

Garlic-flavored vinaigrette
Black olives
Hard-cooked eggs
Parsley
Dill

Combine the finnan haddie with the potatoes, onions, and cucumbers. Toss with the vinaigrette and garnish with the olives and hard-cooked eggs. You may sprinkle this with parsley and dill, if you wish.

Hake

A tremendous amount of hake is marketed all over the country, but I suspect that the number of people who actually recognize the fish when they see it on the stands is amazingly small. Filleted and salted, it is sold, along with haddock, cod, and other white fish, as "deep sea fillets."

The whole fish is readily identified. It is long and streamlined, with large eyes and only two dorsal fins, the second being very long. It is also equipped with a feeler.

The flesh of the hake is delicate, soft, and white. Prepare it in any of the ways you would cod or haddock.

COLD HAKE

To me, a cold hake is one of the most delicate and delightful dishes.

Poach the fish in a court bouillon (page 18) and serve it, chilled, with your favorite sauce. My choice with hake is mayonnaise, but many people may prefer something more highly seasoned.

SALT HAKE

A great deal of the salted codfish sold throughout the world is actually salted hake. Salt hake can be prepared in the same manner as salt cod (pages 91–101).

Halibut

The halibut is popular, but not nearly so popular as it ought to be. It resembles the famed turbot of Europe,* and many of the fine turbot recipes may be used in its preparation.

The Latin name for halibut is most appropriate — *Hippo-*

---

* Some people claim there is no turbot in American waters, but it is sometimes caught off the coast of Oregon.

glossus hippoglossus. An ordinary halibut may weigh 50 to 100 pounds. Some weigh as much as 600 pounds. Small members of the species, known as chicken halibut, are caught occasionally on the West Coast and still less frequently on the East Coast.

Halibut is usually bought in steaks, sometimes in fillets. For an unusual occasion, such as a very large gathering, you might buy a whole fish. Halibut cheeks are available from time to time on the West Coast, where they are cooked in the same way as salmon cheeks.

BROILED HALIBUT

A steak about 1½ to 2 inches thick seems to me to be the ideal piece for broiling. Follow the Canadian cooking theory for broiling fish steaks (page 9), brushing well with butter and lemon juice several times during the cooking process. Sprinkle with salt and paprika before serving.

Serve with maître d'hôtel butter (page 31), lemon butter (page 31), Hollandaise sauce (pages 25–26) or parsley butter (page 33).

HALIBUT SAUTÉ

Select a halibut steak about 1 to 1½ inches thick. Dip it in flour and sauté it gently in butter or oil according to the Canadian cooking theory (page 10), turning once during the process. Salt and pepper well and serve with lemon butter or parsley butter (pages 31, 33).

VARIATIONS

1. Dip the halibut steak into flour mixed with 1 teaspoon salt, 1 tablespoon paprika, and 1 teaspoon freshly ground black pepper. Sauté as above, sprinkling with additional paprika if needed. Remove to a hot platter. Add 1 cup sour cream to the

pan and blend well. Heat through but do not let it boil. Pour the sauce over the fish and serve with steamed rice.

2. Dip the halibut steak in lemon or lime juice, then in flour, again in lemon or lime juice, and then in fine bread crumbs. Or dip in beaten egg and crumbs. Sauté very quickly in butter or, preferably, olive oil according to the Canadian cooking theory (page 10). Salt and pepper to taste and remove to a hot platter. Serve with plenty of chopped parsley, boiled potatoes, and peas.

3. Follow the preceding recipe. When you have removed the fish to a hot platter, add to the pan ¼ cup Worcestershire sauce, ¼ cup white wine or sherry, 1 tablespoon prepared mustard, and 1 teaspoon dry mustard. Blend well with the pan juices. Pour the sauce over the fish.

4. Sauté the halibut steak in butter according to the Canadian cooking theory (page 10); add 1 teaspoon dried tarragon or 1 tablespoon fresh tarragon, salt, and freshly ground black pepper. When the fish is cooked and nicely browned, remove it to a hot platter and add ½ cup white wine to the pan. Let it cook down very quickly and pour over the fish.

BAKED HALIBUT

You may bake either a large piece of the fish or steaks, depending on the number you are feeding. Bake according to the Canadian cooking theory (page 8).

BAKED STUFFED HALIBUT STEAKS

Choose 2 good-sized halibut steaks, about 4 pounds each or more. Prepare the following stuffing:

¼ cup finely chopped onion
4 tablespoons butter

½ cup sliced mushrooms
½ cup dry bread crumbs

¼ cup finely chopped parsley
½ teaspoon freshly ground black
  pepper

1 teaspoon salt
¼ teaspoon thyme
Heavy cream

Sauté the onion in the butter. Add the mushrooms, bread crumbs, parsley, pepper, salt, and thyme. Mix thoroughly and moisten with a little heavy cream.

Oil a baking dish and put one of the fish steaks on the bottom. Spread it with the stuffing and top with the second steak. Secure the two steaks together with toothpicks or tie lightly with string. Brush with butter or oil and sprinkle with salt and pepper. Bake at 425° according to the Canadian cooking theory (page 8). Baste often during the process. Serve with a sour cream cucumber sauce (page 37) or with parsley sauce (page 23).

Tiny buttered new potatoes and green peas bonne femme are excellent with this.

VARIATIONS

1. Begin the preparation of a stuffing with 6 rashers of bacon cut in bits and tried out until crisp; remove to absorbent paper. Add 1 large onion, finely chopped, to the fat and sauté gently until soft. Add ½ cup bread crumbs, 1 7-ounce can minced clams with the liquor, 1 teaspoon salt, 1 teaspoon coarsely ground black pepper, and ½ teaspoon thyme or more. Mix well, adding a few more bread crumbs if the stuffing seems too soft. Finally, add the crisp bacon pieces. Spread this on one steak, cover with the other, and place in a baking dish or pan. Top with strips of bacon and bake at 425° according to the Canadian cooking theory (page 8). Serve with parsley butter (page 33).

2. Stuff the fish with your favorite stuffing and place in an oiled baking dish or pan. Cover with sour cream and bake as above. Sprinkle well with paprika and chopped parsley just before serving.

3. Stuff the fish with your favorite stuffing, place in an oiled baking dish and brush with butter. Add ½ cup white wine to the pan and bake as above. Baste with additional butter and white wine. Remove the fish to a hot platter, add balls of beurre manié (page 475) to the liquid in the pan, and stir until thick-

ened. Add ½ cup of heavy cream and heat thoroughly. Serve with the fish.

4. Prepare a stuffing with 1 small onion, finely chopped and sautéed in butter with ½ green pepper, finely chopped. Add ¾ cup bread crumbs, 1 teaspoon salt, 1 teaspoon freshly ground pepper, and 1 cup chopped oysters. Blend well, stuff the steaks, and place them in a well-oiled baking dish. Brush with butter and bake as above, basting every 10 minutes. Serve with a sauce béchamel (page 23) prepared with some of the oyster liquor. At the last moment add ½ pint of oysters to the sauce and taste for seasoning. The oysters should be small, or else they should be cut in several pieces.

5. Place a halibut steak on an oiled baking dish. Top with a layer of paper-thin onion slices, a layer of peeled tomatoes sliced very thin, a layer of thinly sliced green pepper, a layer of chopped parsley, and another layer of sliced onions. Dot each layer with a little butter and sprinkle lightly with salt. Top the whole with the second steak and brush well with butter or oil. Add 1 cup of red wine to the pan and bake as above. Remove the halibut to a hot platter. Add an additional ⅔ cup of wine to the pan juices and bring it to a boil. Add to this ¼ cup each of finely chopped parsley and green onion or scallion. Season to taste and, if you wish, thicken the sauce with small balls of beurre manié.

6. Stuff the halibut with a layer of thick tomato paste, a layer of finely chopped garlic, a layer of anchovy fillets, a layer of ripe olives, a layer of pimientos, and another layer of the tomato puree. Add some fennel or basil, salt, and freshly ground pepper. Place in an oiled baking dish and add 1 cup of tomato paste mixed with 1 cup of red wine. Bake as above. Serve with the juices in the pan and sprinkle lavishly with chopped parsley and sliced black olives.

7. Chop very fine ½ cup fresh dill sprigs, 1 cup parsley sprigs, and 6 to 8 green onions or scallions. Blend with ¼ cup butter and spread on a halibut steak. Season to taste and top with another steak. Brush with butter and bake as above. Serve with

boiled potatoes and a tartar sauce (pages 35–36) heavily flavored with dill.

FRIED HALIBUT

Buy halibut steaks cut about ¾ inch thick. Cut them into fingers about the same width, roll them in flour, dip in beaten egg and crumbs, and deep fry according to the directions on page 11. Serve with a rémoulade sauce (page 35).

POACHED HALIBUT

Halibut is firmly meated but has a certain delicacy that lends itself well to poaching. Have a piece about 1½ to 2 inches thick cut for you, and poach it in a well-seasoned court bouillon (page 18). See note on poaching on page 12. Serve it in any of the following ways:

VARIATIONS

1. Serve with Hollandaise sauce (pages 25–26). Pass boiled potatoes with parsley.

2. Serve with aïoli (pages 33–34). Serve with parsley potatoes, string beans, and tomatoes Provençale.

3. Prepare a sauce velouté (page 21) with the court bouillon and a little cream added. Spike it with lemon or lime juice.

4. Add ½ pound shelled shrimp to the court bouillon for the last five minutes of cooking. Remove the shrimp and halibut. Reduce the bouillon and make a sauce béchamel (page 23). Add the shrimp to the sauce and season it well with chopped fresh dill and freshly ground black pepper.

5. Prepare a sauce béchamel, using oyster liquor and some of the court bouillon. Add ½ pint or more of small or chopped oysters to the sauce and let them just heat through.

6. Poach the halibut in salted water instead of the bouillon.

Prepare a sauce béchamel using clam juice, and add 1 7-ounce can of minced clams and some chopped parsley to the sauce.

7. Poach the halibut in salted water. Prepare a curry sauce (page 29) and serve with a ring of saffron rice; garnish with chutney, bits of crisp bacon, and chopped hard-cooked eggs.

8. Poach the halibut in salted water. Serve with a highly seasoned tomato sauce, baked rice, and a cucumber salad.

HALIBUT MOUSSE

1 pound halibut	Nutmeg
3 eggs whites	Cayenne pepper (if desired)
1 cup heavy cream	Finely chopped fresh dill (if
Salt	desired)
Freshly ground black pepper	

Chop the halibut or put it through a fine grinder. The preferred method is to grind it and then pound it in a mortar or work it with a heavy wooden spoon. Place the bowl with the fish over cracked ice and gradually beat in the egg whites, using a whisk or wooden spoon to smooth the fish and make it absorb all the liquid. Then gradually stir in the cream, making sure every bit of it is absorbed as you work it in. Add salt, pepper, and a little nutmeg — you may add cayenne or finely chopped fresh dill if you wish. Let it stand over the ice for an hour.

Butter a fish mold and stir the mixture thoroughly before pouring it into the mold. Cover it with waxed paper or buttered brown paper and place it in a pan with about 1 inch of hot water. Bake at 350° for 25 minutes or until the mousse is firm.

Serve with a sauce mousseline (page 26), a sauce béchamel with shrimp or lobster added (page 23), or with a cucumber sour cream sauce (page 37). Tiny new potatoes and sliced cucumber salad are good accompaniments.

HALIBUT AU GRATIN

Poach a 3-to-4-pound halibut steak. Prepare a sauce Mornay (page 22). Place the fish in a flat baking dish and cover it with the sauce. Sprinkle with buttered crumbs and finely grated Swiss or Cheddar cheese and run under the broiler for a minute to brown.

HALIBUT SOUFFLÉ

Prepare as you would salmon soufflé (page 192). Serve with a Hollandaise, shrimp, or oyster sauce (pages 25–26, 24).

HALIBUT WITH LOBSTER

1 large lobster (2 to 2½ pounds)	Heavy cream
	Salt
Court bouillon	Freshly ground black pepper
2 halibut steaks (4 pounds)	Chopped parsley
2 tablespoons flour	Artichoke hearts filled with peas
2 tablespoons butter	Potato balls browned in butter

Poach the lobster in court bouillon (page 18). When it is cool, remove the meat from the shell, setting aside the tomalley and coral, if any. Return the shells to the bouillon. Cut the lobster meat into pieces and keep it warm.

Poach the halibut steaks in the bouillon according to the Canadian cooking theory (page 12). Remove them to a hot platter. Strain the court bouillon and reduce it to 1 cup. Prepare a sauce velouté (page 21) using the bouillon, flour, butter, heavy cream, and seasonings; add the lobster tomalley and the coral. Arrange the lobster meat on one of the steaks, top with the other, and sprinkle with chopped parsley. Garnish the platter with artichoke hearts filled with tiny green peas and small potato balls browned in butter. Serve the sauce separately.

COLD HALIBUT

Court bouillon (page 18)
Large piece of halibut or 2
  halibut steaks
1 egg white
2 envelopes gelatin
2 cups well-seasoned mayonnaise

Sliced cucumbers, hard-
  cooked eggs, or other garnish
Vegetable salad (mixed vegetables, finely cut, small
  whole tomatoes and green
  peppers)

Prepare a rich court bouillon with fish bones and heads. Poach a large piece of halibut or 2 halibut steaks. For cold dishes, some people prefer one or two large pieces without bones. Others like the appearance of one large piece cut right through the center of the fish with the bone left in.

When the fish is done, remove it to a plate to cool. Reduce the bouillon to 4 cups for a large piece of fish. When the liquid is reduced, strain, and clarify it with the white of an egg (see page 18). Strain it again, this time through a linen napkin. Return it to the stove, bring it to a boil and add the gelatin which has been softened in ½ cup of cold water. Stir well and cool.

Skin the fish and arrange it on a serving dish. When the gelatin mixture is almost set, combine 1 cup of it with the mayonnaise and mask the fish with it. Decorate the top with slices of cucumber, ripe olives, hard-cooked eggs, tarragon leaves, or anything you like.

Prepare a mixed vegetable salad. Mix it with some of the jellied mayonnaise. Hollow out a few small tomatoes and small green peppers and fill them with the vegetable salad. Surround the fish with these. When the first coating of jelly is almost firm on the fish, add a coating of the plain jelly. Brush the tops of the stuffed tomatoes and peppers with jelly and chill thoroughly. When ready to serve, chop the remaining jelly and sourround the fish with it. Serve with a mayonnaise sauce (page 34).

VARIATIONS

1. Poach halibut in a simple court bouillon (page 18) or in plain salted water. Serve cold with mayonnaise and a potato and cucumber salad.

2. Poach the halibut and serve with a sauce rémoulade (page 35), cole slaw, and sliced tomatoes.

3. Poach the halibut and serve with parsley, hard-cooked eggs, and a mayonnaise heavily spiked with dill.

4. Serve the poached halibut with a Russian dressing, a tossed green salad, sliced cucumbers, and hard-cooked eggs.

Herring

Herring is one of the most plentiful catches in the Atlantic. There is no great demand for it fresh, but it is enormously popular in other forms — smoked, pickled, salted, kippered. Every year millions of herring find themselves in cans labeled "sardines." The young fresh herrings, however, are considered a great delicacy in the spring, so much so that on almost every street corner in Holland herrings are held by the tail and devoured to the finger by adults and children alike.

For centuries herring have been a mainstay of commercial fishermen, and for many more centuries they have been the prey of practically every voracious fish in the sea. So great is the general chase for herring that the supply fluctuates sharply, and no one can accurately predict the catch.

Fresh herring weighing over a pound are seldom found in the markets. In fact, they are usually much smaller. They can be cooked whole or cut into fillets. Plan one or two fish per serving, depending on the size of the fish.

Fresh Herring

GRILLED HERRING

Split the fish and remove the backbone. Brush well with butter or oil, sprinkle with salt and freshly ground black pepper and a dash of paprika. Grill according to directions on page 9.

VARIATIONS
1. The whole fish may be grilled without splitting. Be sure to turn it once during the cooking process.
2. Baste with butter, and sprinkle dried fennel or thyme on top a few minutes before the fish is done.

HERRING SAUTÉ MEUNIÈRE

Clean and trim the fish. Roll in flour and follow the directions for sauté meunière on page 10.

HERRING, ENGLISH FASHION

Split and remove the bones from 8 small herring. Dip them in milk, then in finely rolled crumbs, and sauté quickly in 6 table-spoons of butter. Turn once. Salt and pepper to taste and sprinkle with lemon juice. Serve with tartar sauce (pages 35–36).

VARIATIONS
1. Dip the herring in milk and then in corn meal seasoned with salt, curry powder, and a little chopped garlic. Sauté as above and serve with mayonnaise blended with chutney.

2. Add finely chopped tomato to the pan while you are sauté-ing the fish. Or add ½ cup tomato paste to the pan after the fish are removed. Heat the paste, add 4 tablespoons sherry or red wine, let it cook up, and pour over the fish. Sprinkle with chopped parsley.

FRIED HERRING

Clean the fish and fillet them. Dip them into beaten egg and then into crumbs, and deep fry according to directions on page 11.

BAKED HERRING BOULANGÈRE

Oil

4 large herring

Butter

4 large or 6 medium potatoes

2 large onions

Salt

Freshly ground black pepper

Pinch of dried thyme

Oil a flat oval baking dish. Clean the fish and arrange them in the dish. Dot them with butter, covered with a layer of thinly sliced potatoes and then a layer of thinly sliced onions. Dot with butter again, season with salt, pepper, and a little dried thyme. Bake at 350° until the potatoes are cooked through. Baste from time to time with the pan juices.

VARIATION

Omit the potatoes and cover the herring with 3 large onions, thinly sliced and steamed in butter for 15 minutes. Dot with but-ter and season with salt and pepper. Bake at 450° according to the Canadian cooking theory (page 8), basting often. A few minutes before the fish is done, sprinkle the top with grated Gruyère or Swiss cheese. Serve with plain boiled potatoes.

SMOTHERED HERRING

6 shallots *or* green onions
4 tablespoons butter *or* oil
8 split, boned herring *or*
    fillets
Butter

Salt
Freshly ground black pepper
White wine
Beurre manié (page 475) (if
    desired)

Chop the shallots very fine and sauté them in the butter or oil for 5 minutes. Place the herring, or herring fillets, on top of this. Dot them with butter and season with salt and pepper. Cover them with white wine. Bring to a boil over medium heat; reduce the heat and simmer according to the Canadian cooking theory (page 12).

Remove the fish to a hot platter. Reduce the liquid by half and pour over the fish. If you wish a thicker sauce, add beurre manié to the pan juices and stir over low heat until smooth and well blended.

BAKED SPICED HERRING

Butter
3 carrots, chopped
3 onions, chopped
1 clove garlic, chopped
4 sprigs of parsley, chopped
Salt
Freshly ground black pepper
White wine
1 bay leaf

Sprig of thyme
6 peppercorns
Pinch of allspice
2 cloves
12 small herring
Rings of sliced onion
Thin slices of carrot
¼ cup wine vinegar

Butter a large baking dish or casserole and cover the bottom with the chopped carrots, onions, garlic, and parsley. Salt and pepper to taste, add white wine to cover; add the bay leaf, thyme, peppercorns, allspice, and cloves. Bring to a boil and simmer for 20 minutes, or until the vegetables are tender.

Clean the fish and place them on top of the vegetables. Cover with onion rings and carrot slices; add the wine vinegar and more wine — enough to cover. Bake at 425° according to the Canadian cooking theory (page 8). Let the fish cool in the liquid, and serve them chilled as a main course for lunch or as a first course for dinner.

VARIATIONS

1. Add ½ cup of olive oil and ½ cup of tomato sauce to the mixture.

2. Add 2 tablespoons of curry powder, ½ cup of tomato sauce, and 4 pimientos cut in strips.

COLD HERRING HORS D'OEUVRE

4 large tomatoes, peeled, seeded, and chopped
3 medium onions, chopped
2 cloves garlic, chopped
6 tablespoons olive oil
4 or 5 pimientos cut in julienne

1 teaspoon fresh basil
1 teaspoon salt
1 teaspoon freshly ground black pepper
¼ cup tomato paste
8 small herring

Sauté the tomatoes, onion, and garlic in the olive oil until soft. Add the pimientos, basil, salt, pepper, and tomato paste. Oil a baking dish, arrange the herring in it, top with the sauce, and cover tightly. Bake at 425° according to the Canadian cooking theory (page 8). Let the fish cool in the sauce.

Serve cold on greens with lemon slices, capers, and chopped parsley.

HERRING ROE

Herring roe, like the roe of salmon, shad, and whitefish, is excellent when poached or sautéed. See shad roe, pages 222–224.

Herring in Brine

If your family likes cured fish, you will find herring in brine one of the most versatile foods you can buy. The 9-to-10-pound kegs of the Holland or German variety are excellent. But before using this fish, you must freshen it in cold water for 24 hours. Change the water several times. After the fish has soaked, cut off the head, split the fish in half, bone it, and, if you wish, skin it.

ROLLMOPS

To make 12 rollmops:

6 herring in brine	2 bay leaves
12 sweet *or* 3 dill pickles	1 clove garlic
4 medium onions	1 teaspoon thyme
1 cup vinegar	3 or 4 allspice
1 cup water	3 or 4 cloves
2 tablespoons brown sugar	8 peppercorns

Prepare the herring as above, but do not skin them. Rinse them well; on each half herring place 1 sweet pickle or ¼ dill pickle. Roll up and fasten with a toothpick. Arrange the rollmops in a large bowl or crock that has a cover. Top with a layer of thinly sliced onions.

Combine the vinegar, water, sugar, bay leaves, garlic, thyme, and spices. Bring to the boiling point. Pour this hot pickle over the rollmops and cover them. Chill in the refrigerator for 48 hours. Serve as a luncheon dish or as hors d'oeuvre.

MARINATED HERRING

6 herring in brine
Sliced onions
Diced raw apple
Bay leaves

Dry mustard
Freshly ground black pepper
White wine
Sour cream

Soak and prepare the herring as above. Arrange a layer of the herring halves in the bottom of a glass or earthenware dish. Add a layer of sliced onions, ½ apple diced, a bay leaf, a sprinkling of mustard and pepper, and 3 tablespoons of white wine. Arrange another layer of the fish and repeat. When all the ingredients are used, cover the whole with heavy sour cream.

Cover the dish and chill for 24 hours. Serve as an appetizer or as a main course at luncheon with rye bread and beer.

VARIATION

Chop the herring into small dice and place in a large jar with 2 chopped onions and 1 chopped apple. Add 2 bay leaves, crushed, 3 tablespoons of vinegar, and ½ cup of dill and parsley mixed. Top with sour cream, cover, and chill for 24 to 36 hours. Serve as hors d'oeuvre.

PICKLED HERRING

6 herring in brine
Onion slices
Bay leaves
Cayenne pepper
Sliced lemon

1 cup wine vinegar
½ cup white wine
2 tablespoons prepared mustard
1 teaspoon sugar

Prepare the herring as above. Place a layer of the fish in a large dish, add a layer of onion, a bay leaf, a dash of cayenne, and a layer of lemon slices. Repeat.

Mix the vinegar, wine, mustard, and sugar and bring to a boil. Pour this over the fish. When cool, cover and chill for several days.

VARIATIONS

1. Omit the vinegar and sugar and double the white wine.
2. Arrange the herring in the dish with onion rings. Blend ⅔ cup of Dijon mustard with ½ cup olive oil. Season with a dash of cayenne pepper and 2 tablespoons chopped fresh dill. Add ½ cup white wine. Pour this sauce over the fish, cover, and chill for 2 days.

HERRING SALAD

There are many versions of this dish, all good and all excellent changes from the usual supper or buffet dish.

3 herring in brine	½ cup olive oil
4 potatoes, cooked and diced	¼ cup wine vinegar
5 beets, cooked and diced	1 tablespoon sugar
2 tart apples, sliced	Coarsely ground black pepper,
1 onion, diced	to taste
1 or 2 dill pickles, diced	Hard-cooked eggs
1½ cups cooked veal, diced	

Wash, soak, and prepare the herring as above. Remove both the bones and the skin. Cut the flesh into small dice and combine with all the other ingredients. Mix well; chill thoroughly.

Serve on a bed of greens and garnish with hard-cooked eggs.

Smoked Herring

Smoked herring come in fillets. They are rather heavily smoked and should be trimmed and soaked in water, water and milk, or white wine for several hours. The length of time you soak them will depend on how much smoky taste you like. I recommend soaking the fillets in a mixture of half water and half milk.

HERRING IN OIL

This is the customary way to serve smoked herring. After they
have soaked for 2 hours or more, remove them from the liquid
and dry them. Arrange a layer of the fillets in a dish, top with a
layer of sliced onions and then sliced carrots. If you wish to be
elaborate, scallop the edges of the carrot slices. Add several bay
leaves. Repeat these layers. Cover the fish and vegetables with
olive oil and chill for 48 hours.

Serve the fillets on lettuce with lemon quarters. Have some
good German or French potato salad — made by pouring oil and
vinegar over the hot sliced potatoes.

HERRING SALAD, RUSSIAN STYLE

Make a potato salad: Mix sliced cooked potatoes with finely cut
onion and parsley and dress with oil and vinegar. Arrange this
on a large platter. Top with a layer of sliced tart apple dressed
with oil and vinegar. Arrange the herring fillets on top in a lat-
tice design. Surround with quartered hard-cooked eggs, quartered
tomatoes, and sliced cucumbers marinated in a sweet-sour dressing. Serve with sauce vinaigrette (page 36) heavily laced with
grated horseradish.

KIPPERED HERRING AND BLOATERS

Both kippers and bloaters are herring. The bloaters are simply
older and fatter. I think that the kippers available in the fish
markets are far superior to the canned variety.

Both kippers and bloaters are best if heated through. They
may be placed in a baking dish, skin side up, dotted with butter,
and warmed in the oven. Or you may dot them with butter and
heat under the broiler flame. Be careful not to overcook them or
they will be decidedly dry and uninteresting.

Serve them with scrambled eggs and crisp toast and you have

a very good breakfast. Personally I prefer tea, rather than the usual coffee, with this breakfast menu.

Kingfish

This giant, which may weigh as much as 75 pounds, is a relative of the Spanish mackerel. It preys upon lesser fishes off Florida and in the Gulf. It is strong, fast, and gamy, with sharp teeth that can easily ruin fishing gear. Sometimes it is seen leaping as high as ten feet out of the water. (See also California kingfish.)

Gastronomically, the kingfish has a distinguished flavor. It is sold from November to March, whole, filleted, or in steaks.

BROILED KINGFISH STEAKS

Select good-sized steaks and brush them well with olive oil. Broil according to directions on pages 9–10.

VARIATIONS

1. Broil thick steaks, basting them with oil. Add salt and freshly ground black pepper to taste. When they are done, arrange them on a bed of dried thyme, rosemary, and fennel and top with parsley. Pour ⅓ cup of rum over the fish and ignite. Let it blaze until the herbs have burned down and flavored the fish steaks.

2. Broil thick steaks. Season with salt and freshly ground black pepper, sprinkle well with paprika, and dot with buttered crumbs. Serve with a sauce diable (page 29).

SAUTÉED KINGFISH

Use either steaks or fillets, dip them in flour and proceed as for sauté meunière (page 10).

SAUTÉED KINGFISH À L'ANGLAISE

Dip steaks into flour, beaten egg, and crumbs, and sauté in butter or bacon fat according to the Canadian cooking theory (page 10). Salt and pepper to taste and serve with a tartar sauce (pages 35–36) or a sauce rémoulade (page 35).

BAKED KINGFISH STEAKS AU GRATIN

Choose 1 steak per person. Dip in flour and arrange in an oiled baking dish. Dot with butter and sprinkle with salt and freshly ground black pepper. Bake at 425° according to the Canadian cooking theory (page 8). When they are cooked through, cover with a sauce velouté (page 21) and sprinkle with buttered crumbs and grated Parmesan cheese. Brown under the broiler for 3 or 4 minutes.

VARIATIONS

1. Proceed as above, but add 1 cup of seedless grapes to the sauce velouté before pouring it over the fish. Omit the cheese.

2. Arrange the steaks in the oiled dish. Top with paper-thin slices of onion and a slice of tomato. Salt and pepper and dot with butter. Bake at 425° according to the Canadian cooking theory (page 8), basting often. Serve with a tomato sauce (page 23).

BAKED WHOLE KINGFISH

If you find a smaller-sized fish, one that you can cook whole, stuff it with your favorite stuffing and bake in an oiled baking pan with red wine. Bake at 425° according to the Canadian cooking theory (page 8). Baste frequently with the red wine and serve with a tomato sauce (page 23).

KINGFISH STEW

4 leeks, well cleaned	Several sprigs of parsley
2 carrots	1½ pints fish stock
3 stalks celery	6 slices kingfish, 1 inch
4 tomatoes, peeled and seeded	thick
2 medium onions	Butter
1 green pepper	½ pound shelled shrimp
6 tablespoons olive oil	1 pint oysters
2 cloves garlic	Salt
1 bay leaf	Freshly ground black pepper
Sprig of thyme	

Cut the vegetables in julienne strips. Sauté them in the olive oil. Add the garlic, bay leaf, thyme, parsley, and the fish stock made from the heads and tails of fish.

Brown the kingfish slices lightly in butter and add them to the stock and vegetables. Simmer for 10 minutes. Add the shrimp and oysters and cook for 3 minutes longer. Season to taste.

Pour into a large tureen or bowl, garnish with lemon slices, and serve with garlic bread.

COLD KINGFISH

Poach a whole kingfish (or a large piece of kingfish) in a court bouillon (page 18). When it has cooled, remove the skin and serve with mayonnaise and cucumbers, or with a sauce rémoulade (page 35).

Ling Cod or Long Cod

Despite the name, this Pacific Coast fish is not a member of the cod family, nor does it resemble the cod. It is a greenish fish with brown spots, and its flesh has a greenish cast.

Ling cod averages about 12 pounds. It is sold whole and in steaks and fillets. The fresh fish sells well in West Coast markets; the smoked ling cod is popular, too.

BROILED LING COD

Use steaks or fillets and follow directions for broiling, pages 9–10. Serve with lemon butter (page 31), parsley butter (page 33), Hollandaise sauce (pages 25–26), or sauce Béarnaise (page 27).

BAKED LING COD FINES HERBES

Split and bone a small ling cod. Place it in a well-oiled baking dish, flesh side up, and sprinkle with chopped chives, tarragon, and parsley. Season with salt and pepper, dot with butter, and bake at 425° according to the Canadian cooking theory (page 8).

BAKED DEVILED LING COD

Split and bone a small ling cod. Place it in a well-oiled baking dish, flesh side up. Season with salt and freshly ground black pepper, cover with crisp crumbs, and dot with butter. Bake at 425° according to the Canadian cooking theory (page 8), adding melted butter to the crumbs during cooking, if necessary. At the last minute, run it under the broiler flame to brown. Serve with sauce diable (page 30).

BAKED LING COD MORNAY

Split and bone a small ling cod. Place in a well-oiled baking dish, dot with butter, and add ½ cup of white wine. Bake at 425° according to the Canadian cooking theory (page 8). Baste with the wine in the pan during the cooking process. When it is done, cover the fish with sauce Mornay (page 22) and sprinkle with grated Gruyère cheese. Run under the broiler flame to melt the cheese and brown the top.

POACHED LING COD

Follow the recipes for poached striped bass (page 270).

LING COD TIMBALES

1 pound cooked ling cod	Salt
3 egg yolks	Freshly ground black pepper
3 egg whites	White wine *or* sherry
¼ cup heavy cream	

Flake the fish and pound it in a mortar, or mash it well. Blend in the egg yolks. Beat the egg whites until just light and gradually work them in with a wooden spoon. (It is better to do this over a bowl of ice.) Add the heavy cream and work it in thoroughly. Season to taste with salt and pepper and add a dash of sherry or white wine.

Pour the mixture into a buttered mold and place it on a rack in a pan of hot water. Bake at 300° until the fish is firm, but be careful not to let the water boil. Keep the top from browning by placing several thicknesses of cooking parchment over the mold. Unmold and serve with shrimp or oyster sauce (page 21).

Mackerel

Every spring the first mackerel boats are eagerly awaited by those who fancy this regal, well-flavored fish. The first taste of it is every bit as good as that of the year's first shad and salmon.

Not so many years ago, salt mackerel was a standard dish for Sunday breakfast, along with boiled potatoes and fresh hot biscuits. Nowadays, since the fresh fish is available the year round thanks to freezing, the salt variety has become rare.

Mackerel comes in sizes up to about 16 inches long. You may buy the whole fish, cuts, fillets, and frozen fillets.

BROILED MACKEREL

Split the fish and broil according to the directions on pages 9–10.

FRIED MACKEREL

See fried fish, pages 10–11.

MACKEREL FILLETS SAUTÉ MEUNIÈRE

See directions for sauté meunière, page 10.

POACHED MACKEREL I

Mackerel may be poached whole in court bouillon (page 18), or you may poach it as slices or fillets.

Poach 6 mackerel fillets in court bouillon according to the Canadian cooking theory (page 12). Remove to a hot dish and surround with thin slices of fried eggplant covered with a tomato sauce. Reduce the bouillon and add it to a sauce Mornay (page 22) well seasoned with cayenne pepper and dry mustard. Pour the sauce over the fillets and sprinkle with grated Gruyère or Swiss cheese. Brown the whole platter under the broiler for a few minutes.

VARIATION

Add 2 tablespoons of curry powder to the sauce Mornay.

POACHED MACKEREL II

Poach 6 mackerel fillets in court bouillon (page 18) and remove to a flameproof serving dish. Reduce the bouillon by half and use it to prepare a rich velouté (page 21). Season the sauce heavily with paprika. Cover the fillets with mushrooms sautéed in butter and seasoned with paprika. Add the sauce, sprinkle with more paprika, and run under the broiler flame to glaze.

Add 1 cup of sour cream to the sauce at the last moment. Pour over the mackerel and glaze under the broiler flame. Serve with fried toast and a cucumber salad.

MACKEREL ITALIAN

6 mackerel fillets	¼ pound sliced mushrooms
Flour	6 or 8 chopped shallots *or* green
Beaten egg	onions
Crumbs	Tomato sauce
Olive oil	Parmesan cheese

Dip the fillets in flour, then in beaten egg, and roll in crumbs. Sauté them in hot olive oil according to the Canadian cooking theory (page 10). Arrange in a flat baking dish. Add to the pan the mushrooms and shallots or green onions. Sauté them lightly and arrange on top of the fish fillets. Cover the fish and vegetables with a rich tomato sauce (page 23).

Sprinkle with crumbs and Parmesan cheese and brown under the broiler for a few minutes. Spaghetti with oil and garlic is excellent with this dish.

SAUTÉED MACKEREL FLORENTINE

2 pounds spinach *or*	Pinch of nutmeg
2 packages frozen spinach	6 mackerel fillets
4 tablespoons butter	Beaten egg
Grated onion	Crumbs
1 teaspoon salt	Butter for sautéing
Juice of 1 lemon	French-fried onions

Wash the spinach and cook, or prepare the frozen spinach. Drain, squeeze, chop, and mix with the butter, onion, salt, lemon juice, and nutmeg. Oil a baking dish and arrange the spinach in a layer on the bottom.

Dip the fillets in beaten egg and then in fine crumbs. Sauté lightly in butter according to the Canadian cooking theory (page 10), or until browned. Place the cooked fillets on the bed of spinach and top with a layer of crisp French-fried onions. Serve with a tartar sauce (pages 35–36) and plain boiled potatoes dusted with chopped parsley.

VARIATIONS

1. Mix 3 cups of rich mashed potatoes with 2 egg yolks. Arrange in mounds, or pipe through the large rosette end of a pastry tube onto the bottom of a greased baking dish. Brush with butter and brown under the broiler flame. Place the sautéed fillets on top of this potato bed, sprinkle with chopped parsley, and dress with lemon butter. Serve with a mustard sauce (page 23).

2. Serve the fillets on a bed of sautéed onions. Top with grated Swiss and Parmesan cheese mixed. Run under the broiler to glaze. Surround with broiled tomatoes and garnish with anchovy fillets and black olives.

ESCABECHE OF MACKEREL, HELEN EVANS BROWN

This is an excellent hors d'oeuvre or summer supper dish.

6 mackerel fillets
Lemon *or* lime juice
Flour
6 tablespoons butter
2 cloves garlic, crushed
⅓ clup olive oil

3 tablespoons lemon *or* lime juice
⅓ cup orange juice
¼ cup green onions *or* scallions, chopped
Dash of Tabasco sauce
Salt

Dip the mackerel in lemon or lime juice, then in flour, and sauté in butter according to the Canadian cooking theory (page 10) until golden. Arrange the cooked fillets in a flat serving dish.

Prepare a sauce with the garlic, olive oil, lemon or lime juice, orange juice, green onions or scallions, and a dash of Tabasco sauce. Season to taste with salt. Pour over the fish and chill for 24 hours. Serve garnished with quartered limes or lemons and ripe olives.

VARIATIONS

1. Sauté the fillets in ⅓ cup olive oil. Remove to a serving dish. Add to the oil in the pan 5 cloves crushed garlic, 1 finely chopped onion, and one shaved carrot. Cook until they are just colored. Add ¼ cup vinegar, ¼ cup water, ¼ cup white wine, 1 teaspoon salt, 2 tablespoons finely chopped green pepper, a sprig of thyme, and ¼ cup chopped parsley. Simmer for 10 minutes. Pour over the fish and chill for 24 hours.

NOTE: This recipe may be used for almost any filleted fish.

2. You may add any of the following seasonings to the sauces in either of the two preceding recipes: ground coriander; finely chopped Chinese parsley, or fresh coriander, or cilantro; toasted coriander seeds.

BAKED MACKEREL

Clean a mackerel weighing 2 to 4 pounds. Oil a large oval baking dish or pan and place the fish on it. Dot with butter, sprinkle with salt and freshly ground pepper, and bake 425° according to the Canadian cooking theory (page 8). Baste often. Serve with Hollandaise sauce (pages 25–26) or a tomato sauce (page 23).

BAKED STUFFED MACKEREL I

Stuff the cleaned fish with thinly sliced onions, tomatoes, green peppers, and parsley. Sprinkle with salt and freshly ground black pepper and dot with butter. Sew the fish or tie it securely with string. Cook as above.

BAKED STUFFED MACKEREL II

1 whole mackerel	2 tomatoes, seeded and
2 medium onions, finely	chopped
chopped	3 eggs
8 mushrooms, finely chopped	Salt
1 clove garlic, chopped	Freshly ground black pepper
Butter	

Sauté the onions, mushrooms, and garlic in butter. Mix with the tomatoes and lightly beaten eggs. Salt and pepper to taste. Stuff the mackerel with this mixture, sew it up or tie securely. Bake as above and serve with a mustard (page 24) or a tomato sauce (page 23).

BAKED STUFFED MACKEREL WITH WHITE WINE

1 whole mackerel	White wine
Stuffing for fish	4 tablespoons butter
Thinly sliced onions	4 tablespoons flour
Salt	Cayenne pepper
Freshly ground black pepper	½ cup heavy cream

Clean and stuff the fish with your favorite stuffing. Arrange a bed of thinly sliced onions in the bottom of an oiled baking dish. Season and cover with white wine. Place the fish on top and bake as above. When the fish is cooked, remove it to a hot platter. Put the onion and wine mixture through a fine sieve. Melt the butter in a saucepan, blend in the flour, and gradually add the strained pan juices. Stir until smooth and thickened. Taste for seasoning, add a little cayenne and the cream. Blend thoroughly. Pour over the fish.

MACKEREL, CHINESE STYLE

1 2-pound mackerel	1 clove garlic, chopped
4 stalks celery, chopped	¼ cup bland oil
4 green onions, finely sliced	2 tablespoons soy sauce

Clean the mackerel and make diagonal slits on each side, slashing it to the bone. Mix the celery, onions, and garlic with the oil (preferably sesame or peanut oil) and soy sauce. Arrange this mixture on the bottom of a flat pan and place the fish on top. Cover, place in a bain marie, and steam gently for a half hour, or until the meat separates easily from the bone. Serve with rice and something crisp — bean sprouts with almonds, perhaps, or asparagus cooked in the Chinese manner.

NOTE: The Chinese steam such dishes on the platter, plate, or bowl in which it is to be served.

Mullet

The mullet, of which there are about a hundred varieties, has appealed to the tastes of the most diverse civilizations. The Egyptians cultivated it in the deltas of the Nile. The Romans were fond of it and planted it successfully in freshwater ponds and lakes. It was also a favorite of the Polynesians and of the early settlers of Hawaii, where it was similarly cultivated. Today the mullet is the principal food fish of the South.

The striped, or jumping, mullet is the species that is so plentiful in the coastal waters of the Carolinas and Florida. A beautiful silvery acrobat, it is so active that fishermen locate schools of the fish at night by listening for splashing sounds.

Mullet is marketed chiefly in the South, but occasionally you find it elsewhere. It is usually sold whole, and averages 2 to 3 pounds in weight.

BROILED MULLET

The small whole fish are the best for broiling. Follow directions on pages 9–10. Serve with lemon wedges, lemon butter (page 31), or parsley butter (page 33).

SAUTÉED MULLET

Either the small whole fish or the fillets may be sautéed. Follow directions for sauté meunière, page 10.

BAKED MULLET À L'ANGLAISE

Allow 1 small fish per serving or 1 medium fish for two. Clean the fish, dip in milk, and roll in crumbs. Place on an oiled baking dish, season with salt and freshly ground pepper, and dot with butter. Bake at 450° according to the Canadian cooking theory (page 8).

Serve with maître d'hôtel butter (page 31), lemon butter (page 31), or tartar sauce (pages 35–36).

BAKED SPLIT MULLET

1 whole mullet, 4 to 5 pounds	Salt
1 cup lightly sautéed onion	Freshly ground black pepper
rings	Butter
½ cup chopped parsley	Finely chopped parsley
Thyme	

Clean and split the mullet. Place it on an oiled baking pan and top it with the onion rings. Sprinkle with the chopped parsley, a little thyme, salt, and pepper. Dot with butter and bake at 425° according to the Canadian cooking theory (page 8).

Serve with the pan juices and a little additional butter kneaded with finely chopped parsley.

NOTE: Recipes for striped bass (pages 266–272) may be used in preparing mullet.

Ocean Perch

The term "ocean perch" appearing on frozen fillets is the official trade name for rosefish, redfish, red perch, and sea perch. The fillets are apt to be any of these. Together, these fish account for a large proportion of the fish eaten in this country. The flesh is firm and rather coarse and the flavor is delicate. Ocean perch is ideal for those who do not like a strong fish flavor but who enjoy the texture of fish. Since it is so bland, it adapts well to all sorts of cookery and sauces and different combinations of foods.

The fillets run about 6 to a pound and are practically boneless. They will thaw overnight in the refrigerator or in 3 or 4 hours if left out. They may be cooked frozen if you allow additional cooking time.

Some ocean perch fillets will have the skin on. Refer to page 6 if you wish to remove the skin before cooking.

BROILED OCEAN PERCH FILLETS

Butter the fillets well and follow directions for broiling fish on pages 9–10. Serve wtih lemon wedges, lemon butter (page 31), parsley butter (page 33), or Hollandaise sauce (pages 25–26).

OCEAN PERCH SAUTÉ MEUNIÈRE

Flour the fillets and follow the directions for sauté meunière on page 10. Serve with chopped parsley and lemon wedges.

OCEAN PERCH AMANDINE

8 to 12 ocean perch fillets
Lemon juice
Flour
6 tablespoons butter *or* oil

⅔ cup slivered blanched
   almonds
Salt
Freshly ground black pepper
Chopped parsley

Thaw the fillets. Dip them in lemon juice and then in flour. Sauté in butter or oil according to the Canadian cooking theory (page 10). Remove to a hot platter. Add the slivered blanched almonds to the pan and let them brown very quickly. Salt and pepper to taste; add a dash of lemon juice and the chopped parsley. Pour this over the fillets.

FRIED OCEAN PERCH FILLETS

Follow the directions for deep frying fish on page 11. Serve with a very highly seasoned tartar sauce (pages 35–36).

VARIATION

Marinate the fillets in lemon juice for 2 hours before frying them.

BAKED PERCH ESPAGNOLE

1 large or 2 medium onions,
   chopped
5 tablespoons butter *or* oil

1 clove garlic, chopped
½ cup chopped celery
¼ cup chopped green pepper

1½ cups tomato paste
2 cloves
1 bay leaf
2 carrots, grated
½ cup white wine

Salt
Freshly ground black pepper
12 ocean perch fillets
Grated Parmesan cheese

Sauté the onions in the butter or oil. Add the garlic, celery, and green pepper and cook until tender. Add the tomato puree, cloves, bay leaf, carrots, wine, and salt and pepper to taste. Simmer for ¾ hour.

Oil a large baking dish and arrange the fillets on the bottom. Season with salt and pepper, top with the sauce, and bake at 425° according to the Canadian cooking theory (page 8). Sprinkle with grated cheese and serve with noodles or rice.

OCEAN PERCH FILLETS POLONAISE

Crumbs
Flour
Salt
Freshly ground black pepper
8 ocean perch fillets

3 medium onions, sliced
Fresh dill *or* dill pickles
Sour cream
Chopped parsley

Line a well-oiled loaf pan with crumbs. Dredge the fillets in flour and season them with salt and pepper. Place a fillet or two in the bottom of the pan, top with onion slices, then chopped fresh dill (or thinly sliced dill pickle), and cover with sour cream. Repeat these layers until all the fillets are used. Mask the top thoroughly with sour cream and bake at 375° for 25 to 30 minutes, or until the cream is a golden color. Unmold the loaf and sprinkle with chopped parsley and fresh dill, if available.

Serve with boiled potatoes topped with parsley, and cole slaw.

DEVILED FILLETS

½ cup Worcestershire sauce	1 teaspoon freshly ground black
Juice of 3 lemons	pepper
¼ cup beefsteak sauce	12 ocean perch fillets
½ cup chili sauce	Salt
¼ teaspoon cayenne pepper	Buttered crumbs
1 teaspoon dry mustard	Butter

Mix the Worcestershire sauce, lemon juice, beefsteak sauce, chili sauce, cayenne, mustard, and pepper and spread this mixture on the fillets. Let them stand for ½ hour.

Oil a baking dish and place the fillets in it. Bake at 425° according to the Canadian cooking theory (page 8). A few minutes before the fish is done, season to taste with salt. Remove the pan from the oven, sprinkle with buttered crumbs, dot with butter, and run under the broiler to brown.

Serve with a sauce diable (page 29) or mustard sauce (page 23).

FILLETS MORNAY

Poach 12 fillets in a court bouillon (page 18) according to the Canadian cooking theory (page 12). Remove them to a hot platter and reduce the bouillon. Prepare a sauce Mornay (page 22), using some of the bouillon. Arrange the fillets in a baking dish and cover with the sauce. Sprinkle the top with grated cheese (Gruyère, Cheddar, or Swiss) and run the dish under the broiler to melt the cheese and brown the top.

CURRIED OCEAN PERCH FILLETS

12 ocean perch fillets	5 tablespoons butter
Court bouillon (page 18)	1½ tablespoons curry powder
½ cup chopped onion	½ cup white wine
½ cup chopped apple	Beurre manié (page 475)
½ cup chopped green pepper	

Poach the fillets in court bouillon as above. Remove them to a hot platter and reduce the bouillon to 1½ cups.

Sauté the onion, apple, and green pepper in butter until tender. Add the curry powder and white wine and simmer for 10 minutes. Add the reduced bouillon and cook 5 more minutes. If you wish a thicker sauce, add beurre manié, and stir until smooth and well blended. Pour the sauce over the fillets.

Serve with rice, chutney, and chopped toasted almonds.

STUFFED FILLETS FOYOT

8 to 10 ocean perch fillets	Freshly ground black pepper
1 tablespoon chopped onion	Court bouillon (page 18)
½ cup chopped mushrooms	3 tablespoons butter
4 tablespoons butter *or* oil	3 tablespoons flour
1 tablespoon chopped parsley	½ cup cream
1 cup crabmeat	1 egg yolk
Salt	Lemon juice

Thaw the fillets. Sauté the chopped onion and mushrooms in butter or oil until tender. Add the chopped parsley, crabmeat, and salt and pepper to taste. Blend well. Spread this mixture on the fillets, roll them, and fasten with toothpicks.

Poach the fillets in court bouillon as above. Remove them to a hot platter and reduce the bouillon to 1½ cups. Add the butter and flour blended together to the bouillon; stir until thickened and smooth. Gradually stir in the cream mixed with the egg yolk. Heat thoroughly but do not let boil. Taste for seasoning and add lemon juice. Pour over the fillets.

Serve with tiny boiled new potatoes and sautéed mushroom caps.

COLD OCEAN PERCH FILLETS

This is an excellent dish for a buffet supper. You can make it as simple or as decorative as you wish.

12 ocean perch fillets
Court bouillon (page 18)
Egg white and shell
1 envelope gelatin

¼ cup cold water
Garnish of tarragon leaves,
  olives, hard-cooked egg

Poach the fillets in court bouillon according to the Canadian cooking theory (page 12). Remove to a platter and let them cool. Reduce the bouillon to 2 cups, clarify with egg white and shell (page 18), and strain.

Dissolve the gelatin in the water and add to the boiling court bouillon. Cool, and when it is almost set, cover the bottom of a large platter or serving dish with part of the jelly. Arrange the fillets on top. Decorate them with tarragon leaves, olives, and hard-cooked egg cut into designs. You may make these as elaborate as you wish. (For suggestions on decorating cold fish, see page 131.) Brush the top of the decorated fillets gently with some of the jelly and set aside to chill thoroughly.

Serve with garnishes of salade Russe (page 372), stuffed eggs and olives, and sauce rémoulade (page 35).

Ocean Sunfish

This is a peculiar round, flat fish that appears to be mostly head and very little tail. It tends to grow quite large, about 8 to 10 feet across the flat side, and has a habit of lying almost motionless near the surface of the water. This trick has earned it the popular name of "floater."

Ocean sunfish are found in warm and temperate waters, but they seem to be considered food fish only in California, where commercial fishermen occasionally bring them in. Their average size is 20 to 24 inches across, and two will serve four to six people. But the skin and the flesh are tough and leathery, and special preparation is required.

OCEAN SUNFISH ITALIAN

Sunfish	Freshly ground black pepper
Olive oil	Lemon juice
2 cloves garlic, crushed	White wine
Salt	1 cup tomato sauce

First, split the fish in two very carefully and cut the flesh away from the skin. Put the flesh into a kettle with a little boiling water and simmer slowly for an hour to release the fat and the excess gelatinous material. Heat olive oil in a large skillet; add the garlic and the pieces of sunfish meat. Salt and pepper to taste, sprinkle with lemon juice, pour on a little white wine, and simmer slowly for a few minutes. Add the tomato sauce cooking until the fish is tender, about another 5 minutes.

Pollock

A relative of the haddock and the cod, pollock is one of the great sources of fillets for frozen fish sales. It is a well-flavored white fish of good texture that holds up well under freezing. You will find it marketed throughout the country as "ocean-fresh fillets," "deep-sea fillets," and with other similar labels. In New England it was once called "Boston bluefish," but somehow the name failed to stick.

You may prepare pollock in any of the ways given for haddock or cod.

Pompano

Many people — I am not among them — think that pompano is the finest fish caught in American waters.

Most of the catch obtained off Florida and in the Gulf is consumed locally. Some is shipped north and sold to luxury restaurants. It is not a cheap fish. Pompano is thin, with a deeply forked tail and a beautiful silvery skin.

BROILED POMPANO

You may broil either a whole pompano or fillets. The fish should be well oiled or buttered, and the broiling rack should be piping hot and oiled before the fish is placed on it. Broil the fish about 3 inches from the flame or charcoal. Season to taste after cooking. For detailed procedures see pages 9–10.

Serve with lemon wedges, lemon butter (page 31), anchovy butter (page 32), or parsley butter (page 33).

POMPANO SAUTÉ MEUNIÈRE

Roll the fish in flour and follow the directions for sauté meunière, page 10.

BAKED POMPANO

Clean the fish, place it on an oiled baking dish or pan and dot heavily with butter, season with salt and freshly ground pepper, and add a few slices of lemon. Bake at 425° according to the Canadian cooking theory (page 8).

Serve with lemon butter (page 31), anchovy butter (page 32), or Hollandaise sauce (pages 25–26). My favorite is a good Béarnaise (page 26), with a side dish of very crisp julienne potatoes and grilled tomato.

POMPANO EN PAPILLOTE

This is one of the most elegant ways of preparing pompano. You may use either the whole fish or fillets. For each serving you will need 1 fillet or small whole fish, a heart-shaped piece of cooking parchment that is big enough to wrap the fish in, 2 tablespoons of sauce duxelles, and 3 mushroom caps.

Mushroom caps	Salt
Butter	Freshly ground black pepper
Fillets or small whole fish	Sauce duxelles (page 27)
Cooking parchment	Chopped parsley

Sauté the mushrooms lightly in butter. Butter the fish well. Place the fish on the parchment, toward one edge. Season to taste, top with the sauce duxelles and the mushroom caps, dot with butter, and sprinkle with chopped parsley. Fold the parchment over the top of the filling and crimp the edges together securely. Bake in a 425° oven according to the Canadian cooking theory (page 8), adding 5 minutes for the paper. Serve with shoestring potatoes and lemon wedges.

VARIATION

Place a thin slice of broiled ham on the parchment and top with the fish. Dot with butter, add 2 or 3 shrimp, a little chopped parsley, and, if available, a bit of chopped truffle. Proceed as above.

Porgy or Scup

This fish is found in nearly all Atlantic Coast waters and sometimes in the Gulf. There are a number of different varieties of the fish, all very popular as game fish. It has great commercial value, but is more readily obtainable in coastal markets than inland because it is so seldom filleted. It usually weighs from ¾ to 2 pounds.

SAUTÉED PORGY

Follow the directions for sauté meunière on page 10.

PAN-FRIED PORGY

Roll the fish in seasoned flour, crumbs, or corn meal and fry in butter or oil. Serve with tartar sauce (pages 35–36).

Redfish

The redfish or red drum is a valuable commercial fish used extensively in Southern cookery. On the West Coast it is known as spot bass. In both the West and South it is regarded as a fairly good game fish.

Something of a gourmet in its own right, the redfish likes shrimp and crab, occasionally varying its diet with mullet and minnows. Redfish comes whole, in steaks, and in fillets. The fish vary in size from about 2 to 25 pounds.

BROILED REDFISH

You may broil steaks, fillets, or whole fish according to the directions on pages 9–10. Serve with lemon (page 31) or parsley butter (page 33) or with a sauce Italienne (page 29), diable (page 29), or Provençale (pages 30–31).

PAN-FRIED REDFISH

Use steaks or fillets for pan frying. Dust the fish with flour, dip in beaten egg, and roll in crumbs or corn meal. Sauté in butter or oil according to the Canadian cooking theory (page 10). Salt and pepper to taste, and serve with lemon wedges, lemon butter (page 31), or tartar sauce (pages 35–36). I like plain boiled potatoes with plenty of butter and cole slaw with this particular dish.

BAKED REDFISH CREOLE

4 slices bacon	2 cloves
3 tablespoons butter	½ teaspoon thyme
2 large onions, chopped	Salt
1 clove garlic, chopped	Freshly ground black pepper
3 cups cooked *or* canned	1 4- or 5-pound redfish
tomatoes	Sliced hard-cooked eggs
1 bay leaf	Olives

Try out the bacon until crisp. Drain on absorbent paper and set aside. Add the butter to the bacon fat. Sauté the onions and garlic in the butter and bacon fat until tender. Rub the to-matoes through a sieve or put them through a food mill and add them to the onions and garlic. Add the bay leaf, cloves, thyme, and salt and pepper to taste. Simmer this for 30 minutes.

Clean the fish, but leave the head and tail intact. Salt and pepper the interior of the fish and place it in an oiled baking pan. Pour the sauce over the fish and bake in a 425° oven ac-cording to the Canadian cooking theory (page 8). Baste often during the cooking.

Remove the fish to a hot platter and garnish it with the bacon slices, sliced eggs, and black olives. Pour the sauce around it. If the sauce seems too thick, dilute it with a little red wine.

With this serve saffron rice, garlic bread, and a salad of mixed greens dressed with garlic and oil. Amazingly enough, a rosé wine seems to be an excellent accompaniment.

CREOLE COURT BOUILLON

Follow the recipe for New Orleans court bouillon (pages 53–54), substituting redfish for red snapper.

POACHED REDFISH

You may poach either a whole redfish, a large piece, or fillets. Cook in a court bouillon (page 18), and serve with any of the sauces used for similar fish: Hollandaise (pages 25–26), Béarnaise (page 26), Mornay (page 22), or oyster, shrimp, or lobster sauce (page 21).

COLD REDFISH

Serve poached redfish cold with sauce rémoulade (page 35), sauce gribiche (pages 36–37), mayonnaise (page 34), or vinaigrette sauce (page 36).

COLD REDFISH BAYOU

1 3-pound piece of redfish	¼ cup chopped celery
1 sliced onion	1 teaspoon dry mustard
Salt	1 tablespoon lemon juice
Freshly ground black pepper	1 envelope gelatin
¼ cup chopped green onion	¼ cup cold water
¼ cup chopped green pepper	

Poach the redfish in boiling water with the sliced onion and salt and pepper, according to the Canadian cooking theory (page 12). Remove it from the broth, and when it is cool enough to handle, skin it and take out the bones. Add these to the broth, and let it cook down one third.

Break the fish into small pieces and mix with the green onion, green pepper, and celery. Moisten the mustard with the lemon juice, and blend it into the fish and vegetable mixture. Soak the gelatin in the cold water and stir it into 2 cups of the boiling fish broth. Mix the fish into the broth and gelatin, pour it all into a mold or loaf pan, and chill thoroughly.

When ready to serve, slice the fish loaf and arrange the slices

on a bed of green. Serve with a sauce rémoulade (page 35) or
with vinaigrette sauce (page 36).

Red Snapper

This delicate Gulf fish should not be confused with the more
oily and less meaty West Coast snapper, a fish that abounds on
the West Coast, especially around Astoria, Oregon. The red
snapper is a magnificent fish, 2 or 3 feet long and weighing up to
30 pounds. To see one resting on the ice in a market showcase
is most attractive, and its fine flavor is just as appealing to the
appetite.

Red snappers weighing around 5 pounds are often sold whole.
The larger ones are cut into steaks and fillets. The meat is excellent prepared in almost any manner.

Other species of snapper, smaller and less colorful, are caught
in the Gulf region, but are usually marketed locally. These include the yellowtail of Key West, the gray snapper, the mutton-
fish, and the schoolmaster. All are fine eating.

In general, snapper may be prepared according to any of the
recipes suggested for sea bass (pages 214–216).

BROILED RED SNAPPER

Follow directions for broiling, pages 9–10.

SAUTÉED RED SNAPPER
Follow directions for sautéing, page 10.

VARIATIONS
1. Just before removing the fish from the pan, add chopped
garlic and parsley in equal proportions.

2. When the fish is almost cooked, add to the pan 1 teaspoon fresh or dried tarragon and ½ cup white wine. Swirl this around for a few seconds and pour it over the fish. Parsley is a pleasant addition.

FILLET OF RED SNAPPER AMANDINE

4 fillets of red snapper	Butter
Flour	½ cup blanched almonds
Salt	¼ cup melted butter
Freshly ground black pepper	1 tablespoon lemon juice

Dip the fillets in flour, season with salt and pepper, and sauté in butter according to the Canadian cooking theory (page 10). Meanwhile, chop the almonds and brown them in melted butter. Remove the fillets to a hot platter and add the almonds to the pan in which the fish was cooked. Add the lemon juice, heat the mixture through, and pour over the fillets.

VARIATION

Add ¼ cup dry white wine to the pan juices along with the almonds and the lemon juice. Quickly bring to a bubbling boil and pour over the fillets.

RED SNAPPER STUFFED WITH SEAFOOD

1 4-pound red snapper	1 cup chopped raw shrimp
Salt	1 cup chopped green onions
Freshly ground black pepper	1 cup chopped raw oysters
Butter	½ cup chopped celery
Flour	Bacon
1 cup dry bread crumbs	

Wash and clean the fish for stuffing. Season the inside with salt and pepper, rub it with butter, and sprinkle with flour. Mix the bread crumbs, shrimp, onions, oysters, celery, and season to taste. Add a lump of butter to the mixture and stuff the fish lightly. Sew it up and arrange it on well-greased baking pan.

Sprinkle the fish with salt and pepper. Score the skin in two or three places and strip with bacon. Place the fish in a 425° oven and bake according to the Canadian cooking theory (page 8). Baste often during the cooking.

BAKED STUFFED RED SNAPPER

1 4-pound red snapper	4 cups dry bread crumbs
Salt	1 cup minced cucumber
Freshly ground black pepper	½ cup chopped toasted almonds
Butter	1 teaspoon thyme
1 large onion, chopped	White wine *or* sherry
1 clove garlic, minced	

Prepare the fish for baking. Rub the inside with salt, pepper, and butter. Sauté the onion and garlic in butter until they are soft, then add them to the bread crumbs, cucumber, and almonds. Season all with salt, pepper, and thyme, and moisten, if you wish, with white wine or sherry. Stuff the fish lightly and sew it up.

Place the fish on a well-greased baking pan, season it with salt and pepper, and add a little white wine or sherry to the pan. Bake the fish in a 425° oven according to the Canadian cooking theory (page 8). Baste occasionally with the pan juices, adding more wine and butter if necessary.

BAKED SNAPPER FLORIDA

This fine dish calls for a red snapper weighing 5 to 7 pounds. I first tasted it in the South, and the experience was memorable.

1 medium onion, finely chopped	2 cloves garlic, minced
1 large green pepper, finely chopped	Bacon fat

2 cups dry bread crumbs

Fresh dill or dill seeds

3 eggs, beaten

Bacon strips (optional)

1½ cups red wine

3 tablespoons flour

½ cup tomato paste

Salt

Freshly ground black pepper

Chopped parsley

First clean and split the fish, leaving the head intact. To prepare the stuffing, sauté the onion, pepper, and garlic in the bacon fat. Add the bread crumbs, a touch of fresh dill or a few dill seeds, the eggs, and another tablespoon of bacon fat. Stuff the fish with this mixture and sew or secure it with toothpicks.

Arrange it in an oiled baking pan and brush it with bacon fat or strip it with bacon. Add 1 cup of the red wine to the pan and bake at 425° according to the Canadian cooking theory (page 8). Remove the fish to a hot platter while you prepare the sauce.

Blend the flour with the pan drippings; add the tomato paste and the remaining ½ cup of red wine. Stir constantly until the mixture is smooth and thick. Season the sauce with salt, pepper, and parsley, and serve with the fish.

This delicious dish should be accompanied by plain boiled potatoes and a chilled rosé wine.

POACHED RED SNAPPER

For one of the most elegant fish dishes in the country, poach a good-sized red snapper according to the directions for poaching fish (page 12). Use a mild court bouillon (page 18), and serve with a sauce mousseline (page 26) or sauce Béarnaise (page 26).

Cold poached red snapper, jellied or plain, is very delicate. Serve with a good olive oil mayonnaise or rémoulade (pages 34, 35). For a spectacular summer dish, serve a cold poached red snapper on a platter with cold lobster, the whole garnished with cold jumbo shrimp and greens. Sauce verte (page 34) is the ideal accompaniment.

QUENELLES MADE WITH RED SNAPPER

The finest quenelles are made with a combination of red snapper, sea bass, and pickerel. The snapper gives them a body and flavor approximating the qualities of the famous French quenelles.

½ pound filleted red snapper
¼ pound sea bass
¼ pound pickerel *or* pike
2 pounds beef kidney fat
1½ quarts very heavy, rich
  cream

6 egg yolks
Salt
Freshly ground black pepper
Nutmeg
8 egg whites

Pound the fish in a mortar or grind it several times until it is pureed. Also grind or pound beef kidney fat until it is creamy. Combine the kidney fat and the fish, then work in 1 quart of the cream to which you have added the egg yolks. Season to taste with salt, pepper, and a little nutmeg. Blend with the stiffly beaten egg whites, and then force the mixture through a fine sieve. Put the mixture in a bowl, set the bowl in ice, and work it with a wooden spoon, gradually adding 1 pint of extra-heavy cream. The mixture must be quite stiff so that you can then mold it into egg-shaped pieces.

Poach the quenelles in boiling salted water for a few minutes and let them dry on a paper towel. They may be dropped into sauce at once, or they may be kept in the refrigerator and re-heated in sauce later.

Quenelles may be served in a white wine sauce (page 23).

River Herring

There are two species of river herring along our Atlantic Coast, the alewife, or branch herring, found chiefly in the North, and the blueback, whose range extends south to Florida. Like the salmon, river herring come into freshwater streams to spawn. They are small and bony, weighing on the average about ½ pound. They are seldom sold fresh, but support a large industry engaged in preserving them in salt, curing them in vinegar, smoking and canning them.

The river herring may be prepared in any of the ways given for sea herring, pages 133–136, or for sardines, pages 209–210.

Sablefish

Sometimes miscalled Alaska black cod, sablefish is an extraordinarily good Pacific Coast fish that has been greatly neglected. It has a peculiar gelatinous fat — I find it delicate and very tasty.

Especially when it is kippered or smoked, the sablefish has few rivals. The smoked meat can be eaten raw or may be cooked in various fashions.

The fish is sold whole, in steaks and fillets, and in cured forms.

BROILED SABLEFISH

You may broil the whole fish, steaks, or fillets. Brush the fish well with oil and follow the directions for broiling on pages 9–10. Serve with lemon butter (page 31), white wine sauce (page 23), or mustard sauce (page 23).

DEVILED SABLEFISH

Broil sablefish steaks until not quite done. Press crisp buttered crumbs on top and finish cooking, browning the crumbs well. Serve with sauce diable (page 29).

SAUTÉED SABLEFISH

Use steaks or fillets. Flour the fish well and sauté according to the directions on page 10. Serve with lemon butter (page 31) or lemon quarters.

SABLEFISH À L'ANGLAISE

Dip sablefish steaks or fillets into flour, then into beaten egg, and roll in crumbs. Sauté in butter according to the Canadian cooking theory (page 10). Serve with sauce soubise (page 22) or a tomato sauce with curry added (page 23).

BAKED SABLEFISH

Bake the whole fish, a section of the fish, or steaks. Place the fish on an oiled baking dish, dot with butter, and season with salt and pepper. Bake at 450° according to the Canadian cooking theory (page 8).

KIPPERED SABLEFISH

You may eat the kippered fish plain or use it in any of the recipes given for finnan haddie (pages 120–122).

BAKED SABLEFISH CREOLE

When I was a child we often had this fish with an imitation Creole sauce.

2-to-3-pound piece of sablefish
Salt
Freshly ground black pepper
⅔ cup red wine
2 medium onions, chopped

1 or 2 cloves garlic, chopped
6 tablespoons butter
6 to 8 tomatoes, peeled, seeded, and chopped
Chopped parsley

Place the fish in an oiled baking dish, season, and add the wine. Bake at 425° according to the Canadian cooking theory (page 8), basting with the wine frequently.

Sauté the onions and garlic in butter until they are just soft. Add the tomatoes and simmer until the mixture is thoroughly soft and well blended. Season to taste and serve poured around the fish. Top with chopped parsley.

POACHED SABLEFISH

Poach the fish in boiling salted water or in a highly seasoned court bouillon (page 18). Serve with Hollandaise sauce (pages 25–26), sauce Mornay (page 22), white wine sauce (page 23), shrimp sauce (page 21), or oyster sauce (page 21).

CURRIED SABLEFISH

Poach sablefish and arrange it on a bed of rice. Serve with curry sauce prepared from the bouillon (page 18). Pass chutney and crisp French-fried onions.

SMOKED SABLEFISH

Serve the smoked fish as you would smoked salmon (pages 203–205).

BROILED SMOKED SABLEFISH

Brush with oil and broil as you would fresh sablefish. Serve with lemon quarters.

SMOKED SABLEFISH IN CREAM

Smoked sablefish
1¾ cups thick cream
3 egg yolks

Dash of lemon juice
Freshly ground black pepper
Chopped parsley

Remove the skin and arrange the fish in a gratin dish or oval baking dish. Put the fish in a 250° oven to heat while you are making a heavy cream sauce.

Pour 1½ cups of the thick cream in a pan and let it come just to a boil. Remove it from the stove and gradually stir in 3 egg yolks beaten with the remaining ¼ cup heavy cream. Place it over low heat and stir until thickened, but do not let it boil. Add a dash of lemon juice.

Pour this sauce over the fish, sprinkle with pepper and chopped parsley, and run under the broiler to glaze.

VARIATION

Sprinkle with grated Swiss cheese before running under the broiler.

Salmon

~~~~~~~~~~~~~~~~~~~~~~~~~~~~

Salmon has an international reputation, richly deserved, as gourmet food. Like beef, it is also popular among people of plain taste, and it is eaten even by some members of that minority of Americans who dislike fish in general. Both fresh and quick-frozen salmon are readily obtainable. Smoked, kippered, salted, canned, and potted salmon may be purchased nearly everywhere.

The bulk of the salmon eaten in this country now comes from the Columbia River, Puget Sound, and Alaska. There was once a time when salmon was also plentiful along the eastern seaboard, but our forefathers fished the rivers so ruthlessly that the eastern catch has become commercially insignificant. Nearly all eastern salmon offered in the markets comes from Canada's Atlantic seaboard. In New York especially, smoked Nova Scotia salmon is sold as an expensive delicacy.

The decline of salmon fishing in the East has at least set an example for the West Coast. Eager to prevent its own extinction, the Far West salmon industry has cooperated with the government in efforts to perpetuate the great "runs" of salmon that appear each year in western rivers. The migrations are not as large as they once were, but they are still awe-inspiring spectacles.

The salmon of the North Pacific is basically a saltwater fish. It spends most of its life span in the open sea, then returns unerringly to the freshwater stream where it was born. There it spawns and dies. Its fingerlings migrate again to the sea, renewing a mysterious and fascinating cycle.

The mature salmon is a magnificent fish varying in size from 6 to 60 pounds, or even more. Vigorous and game, it is a spectacular jumper of rapids during its final journey to the spawning ground. It often migrates as far as 200 miles inland. There are several varieties of Pacific salmon — Chinook is perhaps the best known — and the meat varies in color from very pale pink to reddish. Eastern salmon is usually paler than the western salmon found in the markets, and some people contend that its flesh is not so firm.

I was brought up near Astoria, Oregon, the center of the Columbia River fishing industry, and salmon was a steady part of our family diet. We never tired of it. My father, who had been a "covered wagon child" during the pioneer days, used to tell us how the Indians smoked and cured salmon for their winter food — and when I was a child, I too saw them spearing and smoking the salmon. Their recipe was beautifully simple. Having speared the fish, they cleaned it, split it, and put it between the branches of a sapling, often spiraea wood. Then they tied the twigs so as to hold the salmon in a sort of cage of wood. This they hung over the fire and slowly cooked and smoked the fish at the same time. This was known to me, when I was small, as Indian "barbecued" salmon. I can recommend it highly. For sauce, try lemon butter.

For broiling or sautéing, you may buy salmon steaks sized according to the fish. I suggest you have steaks cut 1 to 1½ inches thick. Some places sell fillets of salmon cut from the tail. For baking or cooking in a court bouillon, the best choice is a center cut or a half or whole fish. In our family we used a baby's bath-tub for cooking any whole salmon that was beyond the size of our fish boiler. If you have a revolving split with your outdoor grill or in front of your fireplace, it is no trick to spit and roast the whole fish. In my opinion, a whole salmon revolving on a spit is a pretty wonderful sight.

Fresh Salmon

BROILED SALMON

Whether this is done over charcoal or in the broiler, the procedure is the same. The fish should be about 4 inches from the heating unit.

Brush the steaks or fillets well with oil and squirt with a little lemon juice. If you like herb flavors, you will find that rosemary, dill, or tarragon are all delicious when cooked with salmon. Rub in a little of the herbs before you oil the fish. Place the fish in an oiled broiling pan that has been preheated and broil according to the Canadian cooking theory (pages 9–10), basting the fish once and turning it halfway through the cooking time. Salt and pepper it and remove it to a hot platter. Serve with plenty of lemon, plain boiled potatoes, and a cucumber salad.

VARIATION

If you prefer a rich sauce with the already rich salmon, serve a Hollandaise (pages 25–26) or a Béarnaise (page 26).

SAUTÉED SALMON

Sauté your steaks in a mixture of butter and a small amount of oil. Because salmon is such an oily fish, not much lubrication is required. Flour the steaks lightly, brown on one side, and turn with a large spatula. Salt and pepper the fish and continue cooking until the fish is done, according to the Canadian cooking theory (page 10). Do not overcook. Sprinkle with chopped parsley and serve with lemon. Pour the pan juices over the fish if you wish.

This needs no sauce with it. It is rich, oily, and flavorful.

BAKED STUFFED SALMON

Choose any of the fish stuffings given in the section on stuffings. Salt the interior of the fish lightly and stuff it well. Use small metal skewers stuck through the edges to secure the salmon; lace with light twine. Place the fish in a lightly oiled pan and oil the surface of the skin. Bake at 450° according to the Canadian cooking theory (page 8).

You may bake a whole fish, half a fish, or a center cut. You can also bake salmon steaks and fillets (see page 8).

POACHED SALMON

You may poach the whole fish, half of it, or a small piece. Prepare a court bouillon and, if you are going to make a cold dish, add some extra fish bones and heads to make a rich broth. Wrap the fish in cheesecloth or thin cotton, leaving a length of the material protruding on either end to use as handles. Poach according to the Canadian cooking theory (page 12). Remove the fish and let it cool out of the court bouillon. Reduce the broth and strain.

SAUTÉED SALMON WITH CREAM

4 salmon steaks	⅓ cup sherry
Flour	1 cup heavy cream
4 tablespoons butter	Beurre manié (page 475)
Salt	Chopped parsley
Freshly ground black pepper	

Dust the steaks lightly with flour and sauté them in butter according to the Canadian cooking theory (page 10). Salt and pepper to taste. When the salmon is done remove it to a hot platter. Add the sherry to the pan and let it cook down for a minute or two. Add the cream and beurre manié and stir until nicely thickened. Add chopped parsley, taste for seasoning, and pour over the salmon.

SALMON SAUTÉ FLORENTINE

4 salmon steaks	3 cups finely chopped spinach, cooked
Flour	
4 tablespoons butter	1 clove garlic
Salt	1 teaspoon tarragon
Freshly ground black pepper	Lemon juice

Dip the steaks in flour and sauté them in butter according to the Canadian cooking theory (page 10). Season to taste. Serve them on a bed of spinach that has been flavored with garlic, tarragon, and lemon juice. Surround with slices of boiled potato browned and crisped in butter and mixed with sliced mushrooms.

SAUTÉED SALMON WITH CURRY SAUCE

½ cup finely chopped onions	2 tablespoons curry powder
6 tablespoons butter	Salt
4 salmon steaks or fillets	Freshly ground black pepper
Flour	1 cup sour cream

Sauté the chopped onions in 2 tablespoons of butter until just soft. Remove them from the pan and add the remaining butter to the pan. Dust the salmon with the flour mixed with about 2 teaspoons of the curry powder. Season with salt and pepper. Sauté the steaks very quickly according to the Canadian cooking theory (page 10). Remove to a hot platter. Return the onions to the pan and reheat. Add the rest of the curry powder and blend well. Gradually stir in the sour cream and heat but do not boil. Check seasoning. Pour sauce over the salmon and serve with rice.

SALMON SAUTÉ WITH MUSHROOM PUREE

½ pound mushrooms, finely
  chopped
8 tablespoons butter
Salt
Freshly ground black pepper

2 cups sauce velouté (page 21)
4 salmon steaks
Flour
8 anchovy fillets
Lemon slices

Sauté the mushrooms in 4 tablespoons of butter until they are thoroughly cooked and almost a puree. Salt and pepper to taste and combine with the sauce velouté. Dust the salmon steaks with flour and sauté in the remaining butter according to the Canadian cooking theory (page 10). Serve with the sauce poured around the fish. Garnish with anchovy fillets and slices of lemon.

BREADED SALMON STEAK NIÇOISE

4 salmon steaks
2 eggs, beaten
Bread crumbs
⅓ cup olive oil
Salt
Freshly ground black pepper

Anchovy fillets
Lemon slices
1 cup tomato sauce
1 clove garlic
Ripe olives

Dip the salmon steaks in the beaten eggs and roll well in bread crumbs. Sauté them quickly in the olive oil according to the Canadian cooking theory (page 10). Salt and pepper to taste and arrange them on a hot platter topped with anchovy fillets and lemon slices. Serve with a hot tomato sauce flavored with garlic and garnished with ripe olives.

NOTE: If the paste is too thick, thin it with red wine.

PLANKED SALMON

For this spectacular dish, you will want a whole salmon weighing anywhere from 3 to 12 pounds. (It would be wise to consider the size of your plank in choosing your fish.) Clean and wash the fish as for baking, being sure to leave the head intact. This will give you a juicier, more flavorful dish and also a handsomer one.

Oil the plank well and place it in a cold oven. Bring the heat up to 400°. Remove the plank and arrange the fish on it. Brush it well with butter, and salt and pepper to taste. Return the plank with the fish to the oven and bake according to the Canadian cooking theory (page 8). Shortly before the fish is done, remove the plank from the oven. Using a pastry tube, pipe a border of duchess potatoes to decorate the edge of the plank. Then pipe strips of the potatoes from this border to the fish in the center, like the spokes of a wheel, leaving spaces between to be filled with other vegetables. Brush the potatoes with butter, return the plank to the oven and continue baking until the fish is done and the potatoes browned.

When the fish is done, fill the spaces between the potatoes with any vegetables you choose: small grilled tomatoes, tiny cooked green peas, tiny onions steamed in butter and glazed, bundles of cooked French green beans. Garnish the fish with rings of green pepper and lemon slices. Whisk to the table with a flourish and serve with any sauce you prefer.

SALMON TARTARE

1 medium onion, chopped
2 to 3 cloves garlic, chopped
2½ to 3 pounds of coarsely chopped
   bone-free salmon
Salt
Freshly ground black pepper

1 tablespoon lemon juice
1 tablespoon Dijon mustard
Chopped parsley
Chopped dill
2 tablespoons brandy

Mix the onion and the garlic well with the salmon. Flavor to taste with salt, pepper, lemon juice, mustard, parsley, a small amount of dill, and the brandy. Taste for seasoning and add whatever you feel is lacking. Pile the mixture into an attractive serving dish, garnish it with some greens, and chill before serving.

BAKED SALMON, OREGON FASHION

4 to 6 pounds salmon
Salt
Lemon
2 green peppers, seeded and
   cut in fine strips
2 large onions, thinly sliced
4 large tomatoes, peeled and
   sliced

3 to 6 sprigs parsley
Salt
Freshly ground black pepper
4 tablespoons olive oil
4 strips salt pork
2 cups tomatoes (cooked
   or canned)

Wash the fish and rub it with salt and lemon. Stuff it with the green peppers, onions, tomatoes, and parsley. Salt and pepper lightly. Place the fish in a lightly oiled baking pan and top with slices of salt pork. Surround it with tomatoes and bake in a 450° oven according to the Canadian cooking theory (page 8), basting occasionally with the pan juices. Remove the fish to a hot platter, blend the pan juices, and taste for seasoning. Serve the sauce separately. Plain boiled potatoes and French peas are excellent with this dish.

NOTE: If you like, add chopped garlic and red wine to the tomatoes to make a more flavorful sauce.

BAKED SALMON SCANDINAVIAN

1½ pounds fillet of whitefish
  or sole *or* haddock
3 eggs
1 cup cream
1 teaspoon salt
1 tablespoon chopped fresh
  dill

½ cup crumbs
6 to 8 pounds salmon
4 tablespoons olive oil
4 slices salt pork
Sauce velouté (page 21)
Chopped fresh dill
Parsley

Put the whitefish through the fine blade of the grinder twice or chop in the food processor. Pound it in a mortar or work it over with a wooden spoon, mixing in the eggs and cream until the whole is well blended and smooth. Work in the salt, dill, and the crumbs. Stuff the salmon with this mixture and either sew it up or secure it with skewers and twine. Place the fish on an oiled baking pan and top with salt pork strips. Bake in a 450° oven according to the Canadian cooking theory (page 8). Serve with a sauce velouté seasoned with chopped fresh dill and parsley.

BAKED SALMON SLICES IN SOUR CREAM

2 salmon steaks (2 inches
  thick)
1 teaspoon salt
2 cups sour cream
1 onion, finely chopped

1 tablespoon lemon juice
1 tablespoon chopped fresh
  dill *or* tarragon, *or* 1
  teaspoon dried tarragon
Parsley

Arrange the steaks in a baking dish and salt lightly. Mix all the other ingredients except the parsley with the sour cream and pour it over the fish. Bake at 450° for about 20 minutes. Sprinkle with chopped parsley and serve with crisp shoestring potatoes.

BAKED SALMON SLICES WITH
MUSHROOMS AND SEAFOOD

2 salmon steaks, 1½ inches thick	Salt
Oil	Freshly ground black pepper
½ pound mushrooms, sliced	Fennel *or* tarragon
4 tablespoons butter	1 teaspoon salt
½ pound shrimp, finely chopped	1 pint sour cream

Brush the salmon well with oil and place one steak on the bottom of a baking dish. Sauté the mushrooms in butter until just soft, add the chopped shrimp, and let the mixture cook for 1 minute. Spread it on the steak in the pan, salt and pepper to taste, and top with the second steak. Mix the herbs and 1 teaspoon of salt with the sour cream and pour it over the fish. Bake 20 minutes at 450°.

BRAISED SALMON BURGUNDIAN

2 medium onions, thinly sliced	6 to 8 pounds salmon
2 stalks celery, cut in strips	1 quart (or more) red wine
1 carrot, cut in thin strips	1 teaspoon thyme
3 sprigs parsley	1 bay leaf
1 leek, cut in strips	18 small white onions
8 tablespoons butter	3 tablespoons butter
Salt	1 pound mushrooms

Place the sliced onions, celery, carrot, parsley, and leek in the bottom of a large fish cooker or braising pan with 5 tablespoons of the butter and let it cook over medium heat until wilted down. Salt the salmon inside and out and place it on this bed of vegetables. Add red wine to half the height of the fish and add the thyme and bay leaf. Let just come to a boil. Cover the fish with a piece of cooking parchment and place it in a 425° oven for 10 minutes per inch thickness, according to the Canadian cooking theory (page 11). Meanwhile, brown the onions in the remaining 3 tablespoons butter and let them cook through in a covered pan. Sauté the mushrooms lightly and season to taste.

Baste the fish in the oven from time to time. When it is cooked, arrange it on a hot platter and surround it with the onions and mushrooms. Strain the sauce, and if you wish it thickened, add beurre manié (page 475). Taste for seasoning and serve it separately. Plain boiled potatoes go well with this dish.

BRAISED SALMON IN WHITE WINE

Red Wine is an important ingredient in the previous recipe. Is there really much difference when you use white wine? Definitely yes. The whole principle is different, the trimmings are different, and so is the flavor.

Finely cut onions, celery, carrot, leek, parsley (see previous recipe)	White wine
	½ pound mushrooms
	1 pound shrimp
Butter	1 cup cream *or* Hollandaise
5 to 7 pounds of salmon	sauce (pages 25–26)
Fish stuffing (pages 39–41)	Beurre manié (page 475)

Prepare the vegetables and smother them in butter as in the preceding recipe. Stuff the fish with the fish stuffing and sew it or secure with skewers and twine. Place it on the bed of vegetables and add white wine to half the height of the fish. Bring it to a boil, cover the fish with parchment paper and place in a 350° oven. Cook according to the Canadian cooking theory for braising (page 11), basting the fish often.

Sauté the mushrooms in butter. About 5 minutes before the fish is done, add the shrimp to the pan juices. At the end of the cooking time, remove the fish to a hot platter and surround it with the shrimp and mushrooms. Strain the sauce and reduce it to 1 cup. Add the cream and thicken with beurre manié. If you prefer, you may serve this with Hollandaise sauce.

BRAISED SALMON À L'AMÉRICAINE

Here we are back to an old friend, sauce à l'Américaine (page 28), which, except for Hollandaise, is probably the greatest fish sauce in the world.

Prepare one recipe of shrimp à l'Américaine (see page 456) and let it stand for an hour or so. Meanwhile prepare braised salmon in white wine as in the preceding recipe. When the salmon is cooked, remove it to a hot platter and surround it with the shrimp à l'Américaine. This dish is sometimes served with the Hollandaise sauce or the white wine sauce from the pan juices, but to my taste it actually doesn't need anything in addition to the sauce à l'Américaine.

Be sure to serve rice with this.

PAPRIKA SALMON

1 tablespoon paprika	6 tablespoons butter
Flour	½ cup white wine
4 salmon steaks	1½ cups sour cream
Salt	

Mix a little paprika with the flour and dip the salmon steaks in the mixture. Sauté them quickly in butter according to the Canadian cooking theory (page 10). Season with salt. Remove the steaks to a hot platter. Add the wine to the pan, stir it around to mix well, and let it cook down to ¼ cup. Add the sour cream and additional paprika, blending it well, and heat through, but do not let it boil. Taste for seasoning and pour over the salmon steaks. Serve with rice.

NEW ENGLAND BOILED SALMON IN EGG SAUCE

There is a tradition in classic New England cuisine that the Fourth of July opens the season for eating new potatoes, new peas, and summer salmon. The new potatoes must be the small ones, cooked in boiling water until just tender, then drenched with butter, salt, pepper, and a fine sprinkling of chopped parsley. The peas are smothered in wet lettuce leaves, with a large lump of butter, and cooked just long enough to make them tender without dulling their brilliant green. The salmon:

4 to 6 pounds salmon   1 bay leaf
Salt   2 slices lemon
3 peppercorns

Egg Sauce

2 cups sauce béchamel (page 23)   2 hard-cooked eggs

Garnish

Lemon slices   Parsley

Wash the salmon and wrap it in a piece of cheesecloth or folded strip of foil, leaving the ends long enough so that you can easily lift it in and out of the pan. Heat 2 to 3 quarts of water mixed with salt and the other seasonings. Bring it to the boiling point and let it boil for 15 minutes. Reduce the heat until the water is barely simmering, add the salmon, and simmer it for 15 to 20 minutes. It generally takes 6 to 8 minutes per pound. Do not overcook it or it will be mushy.

Serve the salmon with egg sauce made by mixing coarsely chopped hard-cooked eggs with the sauce béchamel. If you like it that way, make your béchamel with some of the fish stock. Garnish the platter with lemon slices and parsley.

POACHED SALMON WITH VARIOUS SAUCES

Poach any salmon, from 1 pound to an entire fish, in any of the court bouillons listed on pages 18–20, allowing 10 minutes cooking time per inch of thickness. Serve poached salmon with:

1. Hollandaise sauce (pages 25–26)
2. Sauce Béarnaise (page 26)
3. Béchamel or velouté made with fish stock (pages 21, 23)
4. Egg and parsley sauce (page 23)
5. Sauce rémoulade (page 35)
6. Sauce gribiche (pages 36–37)
7. Duxelles (page 27)
8. Lobster sauce (page 21)
9. Oyster sauce (page 21)

Plain boiled potatoes, with butter and parsley, and peas are customary with salmon. I also like a puree of spinach or a puree of spinach mixed with sorrel.

COULIBIAC OF SALMON

This roll of salmon, a Russian dish, is one of the most unusual I have encountered. It is wonderful for buffet services, for it slices well and is easy to eat with a fork. With spinach or a salad it is a meal in itself.

Begin by preparing a brioche dough for the crust:

Brioche Commune

4 to 5 cups all-purpose flour, sifted
1 package active dry yeast dissolved in ½ cup warm water, 105° to 110°
1 tablespoon sugar
4 eggs
1 tablespoon salt
¾ cup butter, softened to the same consistency as the dough

Combine 1 cup flour, the dissolved yeast, and the sugar to make a soft dough, adding 1 or 2 tablespoons water if needed. Knead on a lightly floured board and form into a ball. Cut a cross in the top of the ball, transfer to a warm bowl, and cover with a towel. Allow to rise in a warm draft-free place for about 1 hour.

In a large mixing bowl or the bowl of an electric mixer with a dough hook, combine the remaining 3 cups flour, the eggs, and salt. Mix with a wooden spatula or spoon or mix at low speed in the electric mixer for 3 minutes or until thoroughly blended. Scrape the sides with a rubber spatula once during the process. Next, work in the butter, 1 or 2 tablespoons at a time, being certain each piece is completely blended before adding more.

When the yeast mixture is doubled in bulk, remove from the bowl and combine with the second dough mixture. Mix thoroughly with the hands, a wooden spatula, or in a mixer with a dough hook. Scrape down the sides of the bowl, cover with a towel, and set to rise in a warm, draft-free place until doubled in bulk. When the dough has risen, punch it down with your fist. Cover the bowl with aluminum foil and refrigerate several hours or overnight before using. The dough will rise again slowly under refrigeration and the texture will become more solid and workable. When ready to use, punch down again and roll out on a heavily floured board.

Crêpes

⅞ cup all-purpose flour
⅛ teaspoon salt
3 eggs

2 tablespoons melted butter
1½ cups milk

Sift the flour and salt into a bowl. Add the eggs, one at a time, mixing well after each addition until there are no lumps. Add the melted butter. Gradually stir in the milk and mix until the batter is the consistency of thin cream (you may not need all the milk, so add it slowly). Let the batter rest before using.

Make the crêpes in a heated 8-inch crêpe pan (this makes 6-inch crêpes). Put the pan over medium-high heat and, when hot, brush with a little melted butter. Pour a little of the batter into the pan, tilting and rotating it so the batter coats the surface evenly. Pour any excess back into the bowl. Cook the crêpe until lightly browned on one side; turn and lightly brown the other side. Keep warm on a plate until ready to use.

Coulibiac

4 or 5 fillets salmon, about 12 inches long
1 pound white fish (sole, haddock, etc.)

12 ounces melted butter
3 tablespoons chopped parsley
1 recipe Brioche Commune
12 to 14 unsweetened crêpes

Poach the salmon in salt water, allowing 10 minutes per inch of measured thickness. Poach the white fish separately, following the same timing. Drain and chop the white fish, then mix in 8 ounces melted butter and parsley. Set this farce aside.

Remove the brioche dough from the refrigerator, punch down, and roll out into a large rectangle. Melt the remaining 4 ounces butter. Put a layer of crêpes on the dough, then some of the farce, melted butter, another layer of crêpes and more farce, and more melted butter. Arrange the salmon fillets in the center and cover with crêpes. Roll up and decorate the top (roll each end 1 inch over the filling and then the sides meeting and overlapping slightly). Place seam side down on a greased baking sheet. Allow to stand for 25 minutes to rise slightly. Brush with egg wash and bake in a 375° oven for 45 minutes. Serve the coulibiac with melted butter.

SALMON PIE

2 pounds salmon cut in cubes
Salt
Freshly ground black pepper
Paprika
½ pound shrimp
2 tablespoons finely chopped onion

3 tablespoons chopped parsley
¼ cup sherry *or* Madeira
2 cups sauce velouté (page 21)
Rich pie crust
Beaten egg yolk

You can use either fillets or a large piece of salmon for this recipe. Remove the bones and skin, cut into cubes, and dust with salt, pepper, and paprika. Place the fish, shrimp, onion, and parsley in a casserole. Combine the sherry or Madeira with the sauce and pour over the fish mixture. Put a support in the center to hold up the crust, or else build the fish up in the center and pour the sauce around it. Cover with a rich pastry. (It is wise to roll it out about 1 hour ahead and chill it in the refrigerator.) Cut little leaves and decorations from the leftover pastry and decorate the crust. Brush well with beaten egg yolk and bake in a 450° oven for 15 minutes. Reduce the heat to 375° and cook for another 10 to 15 minutes or until the top is nicely browned.

SALMON SOUFFLÉ

4 tablespoons butter	Juice of half a lemon
3 tablespoons flour	6 eggs, separated
¾ cup milk	Pinch of fresh dill *or* ½
Salt	teaspoon tarragon
1 cup flaked cooked salmon	

Make a heavy cream sauce with the butter, flour, and milk. Season to taste. Add the salmon, lemon juice, and the dill or tarragon and let it cool for a few minutes. Gradually add 5 of the 6 egg yolks, slightly beaten. Beat the egg whites until stiff and fold them into the mixture. Pour into a buttered soufflé dish. Bake at 375° for 35 to 45 minutes or until lightly browned. Serve with a Hollandaise sauce (pages 25–26). (Use the extra egg yolk in making the sauce.)

Canned Salmon – Hot Dishes

Following are some recipes particularly suited to canned salmon as well as to cooked fresh salmon.

QUICK SALMON CURRY

1 onion, finely chopped	1 cup flaked salmon
3 tablespoons butter	1½ tablespoons curry powder

1¼ cups sauce béchamel (page 23)

Heavy cream *or* vermouth *or* white wine

Sauté the onion in butter until lightly browned. Add the salmon, curry powder, and béchamel, and blend well. Heat to the boiling point. If the mixture is too thick, add several tablespoons of cream or vermouth or white wine. Serve with rice and chutney.

SCALLOPED SALMON

1 can (16 ounces) salmon
2 tablespoons lemon juice
2 tablespoons chopped onion
1½ cups coarse cracker crumbs
½ cup melted butter

½ teaspoon salt
½ teaspoon freshly ground black pepper
1 cup milk *or* other liquid

Combine the salmon, lemon juice, and onion. Blend the crumbs, butter, and seasonings. Pile in alternate layers in a buttered baking dish and add just enough milk (or fish broth or tomato juice) to moisten the crumbs. Dot with butter and bake in a 350° oven for about 30 minutes or until nicely browned.

VARIATIONS

1. To the salmon and lemon juice, add ½ cup finely diced celery, ½ cup finely diced onion, ½ cup finely chopped parsley, and 1 teaspoon freshly ground pepper. Mix with cracker crumbs, butter, and salt, and add just enough milk to moisten. Pile in a casserole and dot with butter.

2. To the salmon, add ½ cup finely diced onion, 1 clove garlic, grated, ¼ cup finely diced green pepper, and 1 tablespoon chili powder. For liquid use ½ cup chili sauce diluted with 2 tablespoons Worcestershire sauce, a dash of Tabasco, and 2 tablespoons sherry or red wine. Proceed as above.

3. With the basic mixture include layers of peeled, sliced tomatoes sprinkled with chopped garlic and parsley. Add tomato juice with a dash of cayenne. Top the casserole with anchovies

and dot with butter. Poke large ripe olives into the crumbs after 25 minutes of baking.

4. Mix the salmon with the crumbs and ½ cup each of finely diced celery, onion, and parsley. Add 12 to 14 mushroom caps, 3 chopped hard-cooked eggs, 3 tablespoons sherry, and salt to taste. Moisten with milk, top with buttered crumbs, and sprinkle with grated Parmesan cheese.

5. Brown eggplant slices in butter. Alternate layers of the eggplant, the salmon mixture, the crumbs, and sliced, peeled tomatoes. Top with buttered crumbs and moisten with tomato juice. Sprinkle with grated Parmesan cheese.

SALMON CUTLETS

1 can (16 ounces) salmon	Flour
2 cups creamy mashed potatoes	1 egg, beaten
1 tablespoon grated onion	Bread crumbs
1½ teaspoons salt	Fat for frying
1 teaspoon paprika	

Bone, flake, and mash the salmon. Combine it with the potatoes and seasonings and form into cutlets. Chill. Roll the cutlets in flour, dip in beaten egg, and roll in crumbs. Chill for one hour. Fry in deep fat heated to 390°. Serve with egg sauce (page 23) or Hollandaise sauce (pages 25–26).

KEDGEREE

Kedgeree (or cadgery) may be made with either fresh cooked salmon or canned or smoked salmon.*

2 cups cooked rice	4 hard-cooked eggs, sliced
1 pound salmon, flaked	¼ cup chopped parsley

* This dish is often made with other fish, such as cod, haddock, or finnan haddie.

1½ cups sauce béchamel (page   1 or 2 tablespoons curry powder
  23)

Place alternate layers of rice, fish, eggs, parsley, and béchamel
(which has been mixed with the curry powder) in the top of a
double boiler or in a mold. Place over hot water and heat
thoroughly.

You may wish to serve additional béchamel with curry as a
sauce.

VARIATION

Omit the curry and use tomato sauce spiced with chili powder.
Or instead of the béchamel use heavy cream — enough to moisten
the mixture.

SALMON MOUSSE

See halibut mousse, page 129.

Smoked Salmon – Hot Dishes

SMOKED SALMON À LA BERNARD

4 to 6 medium potatoes, peeled   Butter
  and quartered   Freshly ground black pepper
1 small onion, sliced   Chopped parsley
1 pound smoked salmon

Barely cover the potatoes and onions with unsalted water and
boil until just turning tender. Place the salmon on top and continue cooking until the potatoes are soft and the salmon is heated
through. Serve in bowls with the broth from the bottom of the
pan, a dab of butter, and a grind of fresh pepper. Sprinkle with
chopped parsley.

SMOKED SALMON ROLLS

½ recipe flaky pastry	Finely chopped green onion
6 to 8 ounces thinly sliced	Freshly ground black pepper
smoked salmon	Beaten egg

Prepare the pastry and roll out into a 9-inch circle. Cover the top with strips of the salmon and add seasonings. Cut the circle into wedge-shaped pieces and roll each one tightly, beginning at the outside edge. Brush the rolls with beaten egg and bake at 425° for about 15 minutes. Serve hot with cocktails.

Cold Salmon Dishes

GRAVAD LAX (SWEDISH MARINATED SALMON)

4 to 5 pounds salmon, dressed	1 tablespoon coarsely ground
weight, bone removed	black pepper
⅔ cup salt	Bit of saltpeter
½ cup sugar	Fresh dill

Cut the salmon into two even pieces. Combine the salt, sugar, pepper, and saltpeter* together and rub the salmon well with this mixture. Line the bottom of a deep pan or casserole with dill branches, place a piece of salmon on them skin side down, sprinkle the top with the spices, and add more dill sprigs. Place the second piece of salmon on this, skin side up. Put a board and a weight on top and place it in the refrigerator for 24 hours or more.

This dish is not cooked. The action of the spices and seasonings gives it an unusual texture and a remarkably good flavor. It is excellent sliced thin and served with black bread as a cocktail snack, or it is a pleasant addition to a luncheon plate of cold meat and salad.

* Saltpeter is no longer available commercially, but may be obtained on prescription from your local pharmacist. It is not essential to this recipe, but if obtainable should be used.

Gravad Lax is traditionally served with a mustard sauce, made by combining 4 tablespoons dark, highly seasoned, prepared mustard with 1 teaspoon powdered mustard, 3 tablespoons sugar, 2 tablespoons white wine vinegar, and ⅓ cup olive or vegetable oil. Combine all the above ingredients well, and mix with 3 tablespoons of fresh chopped dill.

Another delicious way to serve Gravad Lax is to slice it very thin and broil it with the skin attached.

COLD POACHED SALMON

The ultimate in summer dining is cold salmon. New York restaurants proudly advertise it, especially as the "season's first." It is a spectacular dish for a buffet supper.

Poach the salmon in a highly spiced court bouillon (page 19). It is wise to use a cheesecloth or cotton wrapper for the fish so that you can lift it from the boiler without breaking it.* When the fish is done remove it from the bouillon and set the bouillon aside to cool. While the fish is cooling, carefully remove the skin and trim the fish so that it looks inviting. If you are serving a whole fish, you may want to leave the head and tail on it. This gives it a classical appearance. Arrange your fish on a large platter and garnish with sliced cucumbers, tiny or sliced tomatoes, greens — parsley or masses of watercress — and thin slices of lemon with scalloped edges or cut into any fancy shapes you wish.

Serve the salmon with any of these sauces:

1. Mayonnaise (page 34)
2. Rémoulade (page 35)
3. Vinaigrette (page 36)
4. Gribiche (pages 36–37)
5. Verte (page 34)
6. Tartar (pages 35–36)

Cucumber salad is the traditional accompaniment, and a salad of string beans in vinaigrette sauce garnished with tiny artichoke hearts is another excellent addition.

* There are long fish boilers which are especially adapted to this form of cookery. If you do much fish cooking they are a fine addition to your kitchen.

Elizabeth David serves a walnut and horseradish sauce with cold poached salmon that is excellent. To make the sauce for 3 or 4 people, use 2 ounces of skinned walnuts. Skin the walnuts, by putting boiling water over them and rubbing off the skins as soon as the walnuts are cool enough to handle. Chop them finely. Stir very lightly into ½ cup heavy cream and add 2 tablespoons freshly grated horseradish, 1 teaspoon sugar, a little salt, and the juice of ½ lemon.

VARIATIONS

1. Salmon steaks may be poached in court bouillon and chilled and served in the same way. They make an attractive platter if they are of fairly even size. Naturally they take much less cooking time than a large piece of fish.

2. Spiced salmon is another fine cold dish. After poaching the fish, reduce the court bouillon to half its volume. Flavor to taste with vinegar, herbs, and seasonings; pour this over the salmon and let it stand for 24 hours. Drain and serve with a mayonnaise. The pickle should be highly spiced and quite well laced with vinegar.

SAUMON FROID AU CHAMBERTIN

Whole salmon with head	3 envelopes gelatin
Red wine court bouillon	Salt
(page 19) (6 cups clarified	Freshly ground black pepper
bouillon)	

Prepare about 4 quarts or more of red wine court bouillon, using heads and bones of fish. (The amount you will need depends on the size of the salmon.) Wrap the fish in cheesecloth or place it on a rack and poach it according to the Canadian cooking theory (page 12). Remove the fish carefully to a large board or platter and let it cool. Take off the skin, cutting sharply at the tail and stripping it up to the head.

Reduce the bouillon to about 2 quarts. Clarify it with the white of an egg and the shell (see page 18) and strain it through a linen napkin. Dissolve the gelatin in ¾ cup of cold water and prepare an aspic, using 6 cups of the hot bouillon stirred into the gelatin.

While the aspic is cooling, prepare the garnishes:

1 cup cooked small peas	15 hard-cooked eggs
1 cup finely cut, cooked snap beans	Salt
1 cup finely diced, cooked carrots	Freshly ground black pepper
1 cup finely diced, cooked potatoes	Chopped ripe olives
Mayonnaise (page 34)	Cucumbers, sliced
Small tomatoes	Lemons, sliced
Ripe olives	

Mix the cooked vegetables with enough mayonnaise to bind them stiffly. Peel and scoop out the tomatoes and stuff them with the vegetable salad. Brush the tops with a thin layer of the aspic and top each one with a ripe olive. Cut the eggs in half horizontally and remove the yolks. Mash and mix with salt, pepper, chopped ripe olives, and mayonnaise. Heap this mixture into the whites, or pipe it through a pastry tube. Glaze the tops with aspic. Brush the salmon with aspic, giving it a thick coating. It is sometimes better to give it a first heavy coating, then let it set thoroughly, and give it another coating. Decorate the fish with thin cucumber slices, lemon slices, and quarters of ripe olives and hard-cooked egg yolk.

You may arrange the platter as elaborately as you wish, for this is a showpiece. Surround the salmon with the stuffed tomatoes and the stuffed eggs. Serve with either mayonnaise or sauce verte (page 34).

SALMON CUTLETS IN ASPIC

6 salmon steaks	Hard-cooked eggs
White wine court bouillon	Cucumber
(pages 19–20)	2 envelopes gelatin
Fresh tarragon leaves, if	
available	

Poach the salmon steaks in the bouillon according to the Canadian cooking theory (page 12). Remove them to a dry towel or absorbent paper and take off the skin. Arrange the steaks on a deep platter or in individual serving dishes. Decorate them with tarragon leaves and hard-cooked eggs, or any other garnish you may prefer.

Prepare an aspic by dissolving the gelatin in ½ cup of cold water and combining it with 4 cups of hot clarified bouillon. Allow it to cool. When it is partly congealed, brush the decorated salmon slices with this mixture and place them in the refrigerator to chill. When the glaze is firm, pour enough of the rest of the gelatin mixture over the slices to cover them. Chill until ready to serve. Serve with a mayonnaise or sauce verte (page 34).

MOLDED SALMON LOAF

4 salmon steaks
White wine court bouillon (pages 19–20) (2 cups clarified)
1 egg white and shell
1 envelope gelatin
12 stuffed olives
3 hard-cooked eggs
1 medium onion, thinly sliced
1 cucumber, seeded and cubed
2 pimientos cut in strips
Mayonnaise
Greens

Cook the salmon steaks in court bouillon according to the Canadian cooking theory (page 12). Cool them and cut them into small cubes. Reduce the bouillon to 2 cups, clarify it with the egg white and shell (page 18), and strain it through a napkin. Dissolve the gelatin in ¼ cup of cold water or broth and combine it with the hot bouillon. Let it cool until it starts to set.

Pour a thin layer of the gelatin mixture into a bread pan or small mold and put it in the refrigerator to solidify. Arrange sliced olives, halved hard-cooked eggs, and onion rings on the bottom of the mold. Toss the salmon cubes with the cubed cucumber, the pimiento, and more onion rings and arrange this mixture in the mold. Cover with the remaining gelatin and chill in the refrigerator. Unmold on a bed of greens and serve with either a mayonnaise or a sauce verte (page 34).

SALMON STEAKS PARISIENNE

4 thick salmon steaks (about 2
   inches, center cuts)
White wine court bouillon
   (pages 19–20) (3½ cups clarified)

1 egg white and shell
2 envelopes gelatin
Sauce verte (page 34)
Asparagus tips
Hard-cooked eggs

Poach the salmon in the court bouillon according to the Canadian cooking theory (page 12). Remove to cool. Cook the bouillon down to about 4 cups. Clarify it with the egg white and shell (page 18) and strain through a napkin. Dissolve the gelatin in ½ cup of cold water or bouillon and add the rest of the broth. Let it cool until almost set.

Remove the skin from the salmon steaks. When the jelly is almost set, combine 1 cup of it with 1½ cups of sauce verte. Give the salmon steaks a liberal coating of this mixture. Spread the jellied bouillon on the bottom of a rather deep platter, arrange the salmon on top of this, and decorate with asparagus tips and hard-cooked eggs. Serve with additional sauce verte.

Cold Canned Salmon

Canned salmon comes in various grades. Some very choice cuts are put up in cans, but there are also some very inferior grades. Because of the requirements of federal law, you can usually judge the quality from the labels. Good grades of salmon may be served in one piece, chilled, with a mayonnaise and cucumber salad. Garnish it any way you choose. Be sure to remove the skin, which is often unsightly.

Here are several salad recipes suitable for either canned or freshly cooked salmon.

SALMON MAYONNAISE

2 cups cold, flaked salmon
Mixed greens
Mayonnaise

Cucumber *or* cooked peas in
vinaigrette sauce (page 36)

Arrange the salmon on a bed of greens. Top with mayonnaise
and decorate with sliced cucumbers or cold cooked peas that
have marinated in a vinaigrette sauce. Serve with additional
mayonnaise.

SALMON CELERY SALAD

2 cups cold, flaked salmon
1 cup finely diced celery
Mayonnaise

Greens
¼ cup chopped parsley
Hard-cooked eggs

Combine the salmon and celery and bind them with mayonnaise. Heap the mixture on a bed of greens, sprinkle liberally
with chopped parsley, and decorate with sliced or quartered
hard-cooked eggs.

SALMON SALAD BOATS

6 cucumbers
Greens
1½ cup cold flaked salmon
½ cup finely diced celery

1 cup cooked peas
½ cup chopped green onion
2 hard-cooked eggs, chopped
Mayonnaise

Halve the cucumbers the long way, remove the seeds, and
make the cucumbers into boats. Arrange them on beds of greens.
Combine all the other ingredients, binding them together with
mayonnaise; fill the cucumbers with this mixture.

VARIATION
Use tomatoes or avocado halves for the boats.

Cold Dishes with Smoked Salmon

SMOKED SALMON CORNUCOPIAS

Roll perfect slices of smoked salmon into small cornucopias and secure them with toothpicks. Fill them with a mixture of cream cheese combined with freshly grated horseradish. Serve as an hors d'oeuvre.

CANAPÉ DANOIS

This is merely a round or square of fried toast with a layer of smoked salmon topped with a thin slice of ham and decorated with olives. Serve it as a first course with a little horseradish sauce (horseradish mixed with sour cream).

SMOKED SALMON APPETIZERS

The finest quality of smoked salmon has practically no salt content and has a very delicate flavor. It is expensive, but worth it. Serve thin — very thin — shavings of this fish delicacy, and allow several to each portion. The usual and certainly the best accompaniments are freshly ground black pepper, capers, and thin slices of Spanish or red Italian onion in an olive oil and lemon dressing. Pumpernickel or rye bread and butter sandwiches go with this.

SMOKED SALMON SANDWICHES

These may be used for luncheon or supper sandwiches or cut into small bits to serve with cocktails. Smoked salmon calls for rye or pumpernickel or a heavy whole wheat bread. It also needs plenty of butter — preferably unsalted. Try these combinations:

1. Smoked salmon, coarse black pepper.
2. Smoked salmon, cream cheese, sliced onion.
3. Smoked salmon, onion, ham.
4. Smoked salmon, cream cheese, sliced egg, sliced onion.

SMOKED SALMON QUICHE

PASTRY

1¾ cups flour
8 tablespoons butter
1 egg yolk
2 tablespoons ice water
¼ teaspoon salt
1 tablespoon lemon juice

FILLING

8 ounces cream cheese
5 eggs, slightly beaten

1 cup heavy cream
½ teaspoon Dijon mustard
Salt
Freshly ground black pepper
Cayenne pepper
1 tablespoon grated lemon rind
½ cup minced onion
Butter
¼ pound smoked salmon

To make pastry: Work the flour and butter together until it forms small granules. Then add the egg yolk, salt, and lemon juice. With tightly cupped hands, work the dough into a mass, pulling in any crumbs in the bottom of the bowl. Place on a lightly floured board, break off some small pieces — about 2 to 3 tablespoons each — and, with the heel of your hand, push each one across the board to flatten it. With the aid of a baker's scraper or spatula, pull them together. Continue this process, called the *fraisage,* until all the dough has been flattened, then form into a ball and wrap in wax paper or foil and chill well before using.

To make pastry in a food processor: Place the flour, salt, and butter in the beaker. Process for 10 seconds. Add the lemon juice and egg yolk and process, pouring in enough water to form a ball on the top of the blades. Remove pastry and chill.

Roll out the pastry and line a 9-inch pie pan. Cover the inside of the shell with foil, weight down with rice or beans, and bake in a 425° oven for 12 minutes; remove beans and foil and bake a few minutes longer, to bake the center. Brush the bottom of the shell with beaten egg and put in the oven for a minute or two to set the glaze.

Filling. Soften the cream cheese and mix with slightly beaten eggs and heavy cream. Add the mustard, salt, pepper, cayenne, and lemon rind. Sauté the onions in a little butter until soft. Chop the smoked salmon into coarse pieces, approximately ¼-to-½-inch squares, and add to the softened onion, stirring until the salmon just barely warms through. Drain the butter from the onion and salmon mixture into the cream mixture and mix thoroughly. Arrange the onion and salmon in the pastry shell. Pour the cream mixture over and bake in a 350° oven for 30 to 35 minutes, or until the quiche tests done when a knife inserted in the center comes out clean.

Other Salmon Dishes

SALT SALMON AND SALMON BELLY

Both these preserved parts of salmon, as well as salmon tips, are very salty. Soak them for several hours or overnight before cooking. They are all primarily breakfast or luncheon dishes. Steam or poach them according to the Canadian cooking theory (page 12) and serve with a sauce béchamel (page 23) to which you have added chopped parsley and chopped hard-cooked eggs.

SALMON CHEEKS

These tiny delicacies — they are about the size of a fifty-cent piece — are hard to come by. If you live near the canneries or in the salmon district, possibly you can get some. To my taste, the cheeks are the very best part of the fish. They should be lightly dipped in flour and sautéed in butter. Serve them with lemon and finely chopped parsley.

Cheeks are often kippered and put in tins or glasses for cocktail tidbits. They are remarkably good.

KIPPERED SALMON

Kippered salmon is fish that has been cooked while it was being smoked. It has a pleasant flavor and is a most attractive luncheon dish with salad or it may be heated for a breakfast or supper. Flaked and mixed with horseradish, chopped fresh dill, and sour cream, it makes a wonderful spread for sandwiches or canapés.

SALMON ROE

The roe of salmon, like that of similar fish, is a delicacy of which many people are very fond. Try it sautéed or poached. Salmon roe is also used and cured, in various grades, as red caviar. (See shad roe, pages 222–224.)

Sand Dabs

Unfortunately this delightful morsel is not available outside the state of California. I can think of no other fish that is so delicately, subtly flavored.

BROILED SAND DABS

To broil these delicate fish, anoint them well with butter and cook quickly. The meat must not harden or dry out or the perfect texture will be destroyed. Season to taste and serve with a delicate sauce.

SAUTÉED SAND DABS

To my taste, the best way a sand dab can be cooked is sauté meunière (page 10).

BAKED SAND DABS

Helen Evans Brown says in her *West Coast Cook Book* that sand dabs are excellent cooked in parchment, as follows:

Cut heart-shaped pieces of cooking parchment big enough to hold filleted, skinned pieces of sand dab. Butter the paper well and place a fillet on each piece of parchment, a little to one side. Season with salt and freshly ground black pepper. Add a thin slice of ham, 2 or 3 mushroom caps that have been lightly cooked in butter, and a sprinkling of chives and parsley. Fold the parchment over and crimp the edges together. Bake at 425° according to the Canadian cooking theory (page 8), adding 5 minutes for the paper.

Sardines

No doubt there are many children — and possibly some adults — who think that sardines are caught in cans. The fresh fish are available, also, and may be prepared in a variety of ways. For myself, I prefer them tinned.

Actually, there is no one fish named "sardine." The term refers to any tiny fish with weak bones that can be preserved in oil. They are probably called sardines because they were first prepared in this manner on the island of Sardinia. In the Mediterranean and in the English Channel the pilchard is used for sardines. The Norwegian sardine is the brisling or sprat. Our East Coast variety is an infant alewife or herring, while the West Coast version, as in the Mediterranean, is the pilchard.

The sardines of Maine and California would be tops if the packers seasoned them well and used good oil. Since this is not the case, I recommend the fine Portuguese, whole, and skinned and boned. Try also the smaller Norwegian fish.

Sardines are the perfect emergency food. If your shelves are stocked with these, and good canned salmon and tuna, you need never worry about feeding the unexpected guest.

Fresh Sardines

Either the pilchard of the West or the infant alewife or herring of the East cooks well and makes a tasty dish.

GRILLED SARDINES

Estimate 4 to 5 sardines per person. Remove the heads, brush with oil, and broil 5 minutes. Add salt and pepper and serve at once with lemon wedges.

SAUTÉED SARDINES

Split and bone the fish. Dip them in milk and crumbs and sauté them in butter very quickly until nicely browned on both sides. Serve with a tartar sauce (pages 35–36), a lemon-flavored vinaigrette sauce (page 36), or a mustard sauce (page 23).

FRIED SARDINES

Wash and clean the fish. Dip them in flour, in beaten egg, and then in corn meal or crumbs. Fry in deep hot fat according to the Canadian cooking theory (page 11). Remove to absorbent paper and season to taste. Serve with tartar sauce or tomato sauce. Fried parsley (page 253) as an accompaniment is a "must."

BAKED SARDINES

Bone the fish or not, as you choose. Arrange the sardines in a buttered baking dish or pan and top with finely cut shallots or green onions (about 4 to a fish). Season to taste, dot with butter, and barely cover with white wine. Bake at 425° according to the Canadian cooking theory (page 8).

Serve with plain boiled potatoes and grilled tomatoes.

SARDINES IN ESCABECHE

This recipe is suitable for any small fish. It makes an outstanding first course or luncheon dish.

36 fresh sardines
⅔ cup olive oil
Flour
Salt
Freshly ground black pepper
2 small carrots, thinly sliced
1 medium onion, thinly sliced
1 clove garlic, minced
1 bay leaf

1 teaspoon freshly ground black pepper
½ teaspoon thyme
¾ cup chopped parsley
½ cup wine vinegar
⅔ cup water
Pimiento
Green pepper

Clean the sardines but leave their heads and tails intact. Heat the oil in a skillet. Dust the fish with flour and salt and pepper them to taste. Sauté them in the oil just long enough to brown. Remove to a hot dish.

Add the carrots and onions to the oil and let them cook until almost tender. Add the garlic, bay leaf, pepper, thyme, and parsley. Pour the vinegar and water over this and bring it to a boil. Add the sardines and simmer for about 5 minutes. Let the fish cool in the sauce and chill thoroughly before serving. Decorate with strips of pimiento and green pepper.

Serve with a cucumber salad for contrast.

Canned Sardines

Few simple meals are tastier than a can of fine sardines, lemon, good bread and sweet butter, and a glass of chilled white wine or beer. But here are some suggestions for "dolling up" the tinned variety.

GRILLED SARDINES

Carefully remove the fish from the can. (There is a permanent key for sardine cans that has a good lifter as part of the gadget.) Arrange the sardines in a shallow pan or rack and pour the oil over them. Run them under the broiler flame just long enough to heat through. Serve on pieces of fried toast with lemon wedges.

This makes a good fish course as well as a good luncheon or supper dish.

VARIATIONS

1. Sprinkle the sardines with a little curry powder and chopped parsley and give them a squeeze of lemon juice. Grill them and serve them on toast with chutney.

2. Arrange sardines on a baking sheet, sprinkle with lemon juice and grated Gruyère or Swiss cheese. Broil until the cheese melts. Serve on fried toast.

3. Grill sardines with curry powder and serve on a bed of scrambled eggs.

4. Arrange grilled sardines on fried toast. Cover with a sauce Mornay (page 22) and run under the broiler flame for a minute or two.

SARDINE PUFFS

1 can skinned and boned sardines	1 teaspoon freshly ground black pepper
2 tablespoons onion juice	2 egg whites, stiffly beaten
⅔ cup grated Gruyère *or* Cheddar cheese	Bread

Mash the sardines with a fork. Add the onion juice, cheese, and pepper and blend thoroughly. Fold in the egg whites. Toast slices of bread on one side. Spread the sardine mixture on the untoasted side and place under the broiler or in a 450° oven. Cook until they puff and brown lightly, or about 4 minutes. Serve as a first course or as a cocktail snack.

SARDINE TURNOVERS

Sardines	Grated onion
Pastry *or* puff paste	Chopped parsley
Lemon juice	Beaten egg yolk

Roll pastry or puff paste out thin and cut into circles large enough to accommodate a whole sardine with some room to spare. Place a sardine to one side of each circle. Sprinkle with lemon juice, a bit of onion, and the parsley. Fold the pastry over and crimp the edges. Brush the top with beaten egg yolk. Bake at 450° until the pastry is puffed and brown — about 12 to 15 minutes. Serve hot with cocktails or as a first course for luncheon or dinner.

SUMMER SUPPER IN A HURRY

For a perfect summer meal prepared in a rush, open 1 or 2 cans of fine sardines, a can of solid-pack tuna, and perhaps a can of crabmeat or the frozen lobster meat that comes in cans. Arrange these delicacies on a large platter with hard-cooked eggs, wedges of tomato, and plenty of sweet onions sliced to transparent thinness. Accompany this with a bowl of mayonnaise, some good pumpernickel bread, and sweet butter. Serve chilled white wine or beer.

This same dish may be served to a large group as a first course at dinner if you plan to follow it with a rather light meat course.

SARDINE SALAD

Arrange a bed of greens and make a sunburst of sardines in the center. Garnish with halved hard-cooked eggs, onion rings, pimiento strips, and capers. Serve with a bowl of mayonnaise.

For 2 servings, use 1 large can of sardines, 4 eggs, and 1 onion.

For 6 servings, use 3 cans of sardines, 12 eggs, and 2 large onions.

NORWEGIAN SARDINE APPETIZER

2 pounds cream cheese
⅓ cup lemon juice
3 to 4 cans sardines, mashed well
Salt

Freshly ground black pepper
Paprika
Onion juice

This is strictly a spread and a wonderful one.

Mash the cream cheese well with a fork. Beat in the lemon juice, bit by bit, and then beat in the sardines. Season with salt, pepper, and paprika, and blend the mixture thoroughly. (If you are going to eat it all during one sitting, add a little onion juice; if you plan to keep some, omit the onion to avoid a stale taste.)

Spoon the mixture into a well-oiled mold and chill thoroughly. Unmold on a large plate and surround with pumpernickel fingers and crackers. Let people do their own spreading.

This is a favorite dish of mine for parties. I vary the seasonings, but the basic flavors must be sardine and lemon.

Sculpin

This is a bony fish with a large meaty head. Although it is common in Atlantic waters, it does not seem to be well known in the eastern area of the country. On the Pacific Coast, however, some sculpin is sold commercially in California markets, usually whole. I am sure that if you try it you will find it an excellent food fish.

Sea Bass

This popular game fish is a member of a large family of fishes that includes the groupers and the jewfish. Varieties are caught on both coasts, and the Atlantic sea bass is commercially important in the Middle Atlantic region.

The sea bass usually sold in Eastern markets lurk around sunken ships and pilings just offshore, a habit that makes trawl-fishing difficult. As a result, some of the commercial catch is taken in fishpots.

Market sizes range from about ½ pound to 5 pounds, and the fish is sometimes cut into steaks or fillets. Cooked and on the table, sea bass clearly resembles its relatives. It can be prepared in any of the ways suggested for striped bass.

(See also California black sea bass.)

SEA BASS ITALIAN

Butter
⅔ cup each of finely cut onion, carrot, celery
Several sprigs of parsley
Spring of thyme
1 bay leaf
2 cloves garlic
1 teaspoon salt

1 teaspoon freshly ground black pepper
1½ cups red wine
½ cup water
1 whole sea bass
3 tablespoons butter
3 tablespoons flour
Juice of 1 lemon

Butter a good-sized saucepan or Dutch oven. Add all the vegetables and herbs, salt, pepper, wine, and water. Bring it to a boil. Place the cleaned fish on the bed of vegetables, cover the pan, and simmer according to the Canadian cooking theory for braising (page 17).

While the fish is cooking, melt the butter in a pan and blend in the flour. Remove the fish to a hot platter, strain the bouillon, and add it gradually to the mixed butter and flour. Stir until thickened. Taste for seasoning, add the juice of a lemon, and serve with the fish. Baked rice and asparagus are good with this dish. Also a bottle of rosé wine.

SAUTÉED SEA BASS

Small sea bass are delicious when sautéed and served with a tartar sauce (pages 35–36) or a rémoulade (page 35). I shall always remember a hot summer day when we sat down to a platter heaped with them — they had been caught that morning and were as delectable as any fish could be.

Clean the sea bass, roll in flour, dip in beaten egg, and then in dry bread crumbs. Sauté quickly in butter or olive oil, browning well on both sides. Salt and pepper to taste. Serve crisp and hot with your favorite sauce. Boiled potatoes and grilled tomatoes are ideal accompaniments.

SEA BASS FILLETS PACIFIC

Sea bass caught on the Pacific Coast are larger than the Eastern variety and are more often sold as fillets.

Marinate 2 good-sized fillets in lemon or lime juice for an hour. Dip them in flour, again in the lemon or lime juice, and roll them in sesame seeds. Sauté them in olive oil according to the Canadian cooking theory (page 10). Season to taste with salt and pepper. Serve with lemon butter (page 31).

SEA BASS AMANDINE

Split a good-sized sea bass and rub it well with butter. Sprinkle with sliced blanched almonds and salt and pepper. Place in an oiled baking dish or pan and bake at 450° according to the Canadian cooking theory (page 8). Baste during the cooking with the butter in the pan.

HELEN EVANS BROWN'S BROILED SEA BASS SESAME

1 sea bass (3 or 4 pounds)
2 cloves garlic
1 tablespoon salt
2 tablespoons soy sauce
2 ounces whiskey *or* brandy

2 tablespoons lemon juice
½ cup butter, melted
1 cup or more of sesame seeds
Slivers of ginger (if desired)

Split the fish and remove the backbone. Grind the garlic very fine or pound it in a mortar with the salt. Or you may crush it and mix it in a bowl with a heavy wooden spoon. Rub this mixture on the fish and let it stand for at least 1 hour — 2 or 3 will make it much better. Prepare a basting sauce with the soy sauce (use more than 2 tablespoons if you like the flavor), the whiskey or brandy, the lemon juice, and melted butter. Paint the fish with this mixture before and during the broiling process. This dish is much better if charcoal-broiled; in this case you should place it in a hinged broiler so that it can be turned. If you broil it in the oven, cook it skin side down.

Broil according to the Canadian cooking theory (pages 9–10). Near the end of the cooking time, sprinkle heavily with sesame seeds and continue broiling until the seeds are well toasted. Serve on a hot platter with wedges of lemon or lime.

Slivers of ginger (fresh or preserved) may be added to the basting sauce if you like the zest they give.

Sea Trout

Among the fish that bear this name are the California corbina, the white sea trout, the spotted weakfish or spotted sea trout, and the weakfish or gray sea trout. The weakfish is sought along the Middle Atlantic Coast by both anglers and commercial fishermen. Its name implies no lack of strength, but tenderness of flesh.

All sea trout like warm weather. At times they venture north, and when they are caught in unusually low temperatures, their flavor and texture are badly affected.

Since they are small, sea trout are usually sold whole, although you may find some fillets cut from larger fish.

SEA TROUT SAUTÉ MEUNIÈRE

Follow directions on page 10.

BROILED SEA TROUT

Clean and split the fish, sprinkle with seasonings, and broil according to the Canadian cooking theory (pages 9–10).

VARIATION
Follow directions for bass flambé, page 267.

SEA TROUT BROILED OUTDOORS

Broil a whole sea trout over charcoal, basting it with a white wine and butter sauce. When almost done, brush well with a spicy barbecue sauce (page 30) and let the fish glaze. Serve with additional barbecue sauce.

SEA TROUT SAUTÉED WITH ALMONDS

See directions for sauté amandine, page 216.

PAN-FRIED SEA TROUT

Dip small whole fish or fillets in flour, then in beaten egg, and roll in any of the following: buttered crumbs, corn meal, cracker crumbs, sesame seeds, crumbs mixed with chopped nuts, or corn-flakes. Pan fry quickly in butter or oil according to the Canadian cooking theory (page 10). Serve with lemon or sauce rémoulade (page 35).

SEA TROUT SAUTÉED WITH TARRAGON

Sea trout	¼ cup chopped parsley
Flour	¼ cup chopped tarragon
Butter	½ cup white wine

Use either fillets or whole sea trout. Clean the fish and flour lightly. Sauté in butter according to the Canadian cooking theory (page 10). Season to taste and remove to a hot platter. Add the chopped parsley and tarragon to the pan. Add the wine and let it cook down for 1 minute. Pour this over the fish. Serve with boiled potatoes and sautéed mushrooms.

BAKED SEA TROUT

Follow the directions for striped bass, page 269.

BAKED SEA TROUT SCANDINAVIAN

2 small sea trout	Sour cream
Parsley sprigs	Salt
Fresh dill	Capers
Butter	Paprika

Clean and stuff the sea trout with parsley sprigs and fresh dill. Sprinkle with salt. Arrange them on an oiled baking dish, dot them with butter, and bake at 425° according to the Canadian cooking theory (page 8). Near the end of the cooking time, cover the fish with sour cream that has been seasoned with chopped dill and salt. Return to the oven to finish cooking the fish and heat the cream thoroughly.

Sprinkle with capers and a dash of paprika.

Shad

This great gastronomic delight is native to Europe and to our Atlantic Coast. In the 1870s it was transplanted to the Pacific Coast, where it has flourished ever since. The shad is in season from early January, when the first of the southern catch arrives, until May, when the northernmost supply is at its height.

Shad has such an intricate bone structure that boned fillets are most desirable for general use. A stuffed baked shad, however, offers so much pure eating joy that the task of extracting all the bones is worth the effort. There was a time when people felt that shad should be slowly cooked for hours to dissolve the bones. If you care to eat fish that has been overcooked and is tasteless, you may try it.

BROILED SHAD

Unless you are an expert, don't try to bone shad for broiling. It is a tedious job that requires skill. Either use the boned fillets or a split shad. In my opinion, it is wiser to leave the skin on the fillets. Place the fish skin side down, and broil according to the Canadian cooking theory (pages 9–10), turning once during the broiling. Serve with parsley butter (page 33).

SAUTÉED SHAD

Roll boned shad in flour and proceed as for sauté meunière (page 10). Serve with lemon wedges or tartar sauce (pages 35–36).

VARIATION

Dip pieces of shad in flour, then in beaten egg and in rolled bread crumbs. Sauté in butter or oil until nicely browned. Serve with lemon butter (page 31) or rémoulade (page 35).

BAKED SHAD

Split a shad or buy a whole boned shad. Place it on a flat oiled baking dish or pan. Dot with butter, and salt and pepper to taste. Bake at 450° according to the Canadian cooking theory (page 8). Baste several times during the cooking process. Serve with herb butter (page 33) or lemon butter (page 31).

BAKED STUFFED SHAD

1 split, boned shad	½ teaspoon thyme
2 large onions, sliced	2 tablespoons finely chopped
4 tablespoons butter	celery leaves
1 cup bread crumbs	1 teaspoon salt
¼ cup finely chopped parsley	1 egg, well beaten

Sauté the onions in the butter until they are soft. Add the other ingredients and mix well. Stuff a split, boned shad with this mixture and sew it up or secure it with string. Place it in an oiled baking dish or pan and bake at 450° according to the Canadian cooking theory (page 8). Serve it with boiled parsley potatoes and fresh green peas. The fish needs no sauce, but if you must have one, use Hollandaise (pages 25–26) or tartar sauce (pages 35–36).

VARIATIONS

1. Sauté 1 sliced onion in butter until just soft. Add ½ pound chopped mushrooms and cook for 5 minutes. Season to taste and mix with ¼ cup chopped parsley and ½ cup crumbs. Stuff the fish and sew it or tie it with string. Cover the fish with rashers of bacon and bake as above. Serve with a sauce duxelles (page 27).

2. Sauté 2 sliced onions in butter until soft. Add I clove garlic, 1 green pepper, and 4 ripe tomatoes, all chopped. Season and mix well. Stuff the fish with this and sew or tie securely. Place it on an oiled baking dish, dot with butter, season with salt and pepper, and pour 1 cup of white wine over it. Bake as above, basting often. Use the juices in the pan and additional wine to make a white wine sauce (page 24).

3. Split a shad and place it in the following marinade: 1 cup olive oil, 2 cloves crushed garlic, 1 sliced onion, 1 bay leaf, 1 teaspoon salt, 1 teaspoon freshly ground black pepper, ¼ cup lemon juice, and enough white wine to cover. Let it stand for 12 hours. Prepare a stuffing with the following: 1 small chopped onion sautéed in 4 tablespoons fat, 1 cup dry bread crumbs, salt, pepper, ¼ cup chopped parsley, ½ cup sliced, toasted almonds, and enough of the marinade to moisten. Mix this thoroughly and stuff the fish with it. Place it on an oiled pan or baking dish and

bake as above. Heat the marinade separately and use as a basting sauce. Serve with the pan juices.

NOTE: In France, shad is often served with sorrel — more commonly known in this country, where it grows wild, as "sour grass." To some extent sorrel is cultivated here as a vegetable. It is delicious in soups; or it may be cooked in the same way as spinach; or it may be combined with spinach and made into a puree.

If you like the taste of sorrel, try stuffing a shad with a sorrel puree, or baking a shad on a bed of the puree. In France, shad stuffed with sorrel puree is often baked for seven hours, something we do not recommend.

SHAD BAKED IN CREAM

Split a shad and place it on an oiled baking dish. Dot with butter and sprinkle with salt and pepper. Bake at 450° according to the Canadian cooking theory (page 8). Add ¾ cup heavy cream for the last 5 minutes of baking time. Serve with plenty of chopped parsley and the pan juices.

Shad Roe

This is one of our finest treats. Strangely enough, it is practically unknown in France, where the shad is greatly appreciated, and it is not done well in England. It seems to be a dish that has but two extremes — wonderful and horrible. The mistreatment of roe may almost always be attributed to overcooking. It should never be dry, never tasteless.

Roe are usually sold by the pair. They are apt to be expensive

except at the end of the season, when they become plentiful. I
believe that the only way to cook shad roe is as follows:

SMOTHERED SHAD ROE

For 2 pairs of roe, melt 6 ounces butter — 12 tablespoons — in a
covered skillet. When the butter is melted and warm, but not
hot, dip the roe in it and arrange them in the pan. Cover and
simmer over a low flame for about 12 to 15 minutes, turning
once. Season to taste with salt, pepper, and chopped parsley.
Serve with lemon wedges and the butter from the pan. Accompany this dish with crisp bacon and boiled potatoes. This is a
dinner that deserves to be enhanced by a good bottle of Chablis
or a fine Meursault.

BROILED SHAD ROE

Personally, I think that to parboil and then broil shad roe is to
make it unfit for human consumption. If you must broil it, do so
without parboiling. Brush it well with butter and baste often
during the process. Even then, it tends to become dry and uninteresting.

SHAD ROE SOUFFLÉ

2 pairs shade roe	4 tablespoons flour
Salt	¾ cup milk
1 tablespoon lemon juice	Freshly ground black pepper
2 tablespoons melted butter	4 egg yolks, slightly beaten
4 tablespoons butter (for sauce)	6 egg whites, beaten stiff

Poach the shad roe in boiling salted water according to the
Canadian cooking theory (page 12). Remove, and when cool

enough to handle break up into small bits. Add the lemon juice and melted butter. Prepare a thick white sauce: Melt the 4 table-spoons of butter, blend in the flour, and add a little of the water in which the shad roe was cooked and about ¾ cup of milk. Stir until thick and smooth. Season to taste and cool slightly.

For the soufflé, add the egg yolks to the white sauce. Mix the shad roe through it. Beat the egg whites until stiff and fold these into the mixture. Pour it into a buttered soufflé mold and bake at 375° for 30 to 40 minutes, *or* until the soufflé is puffy and brown. Serve with lemon butter (page 31) or shrimp sauce (page 21).

SHAD ROE EN PAPILLOTTE

Partially cook 6 rashers of bacon. Cut 6 pieces of cooking parchment in heart shapes — about 9 by 11 inches — and butter them. Place a piece of shad roe on one side of each piece of parchment. Brush well with softened butter; season to taste with salt, pepper, and chopped parsley. Top with a rasher of bacon. Fold the parchment over this and crimp the edges together, making an airtight package. Bake on a buttered pan at 450° according to the Canadian cooking theory (page 8), adding 5 minutes for the paper.

CANNED SHAD ROE

This is excellent when sautéed quickly in butter. It is also delicious when made into a quiche or sieved first and then baked into a soufflé.

Sheepshead

The sheepshead, a relative of the porgy, abounds in Florida, Gulf, and California waters. It is no relative of the freshwater sheepshead (page 333), which belongs to the croaker family.

The smaller sheepshead are the ones usually found in Southern markets. Occasionally a 20-to-25-pounder is available. Sheepshead are sold either whole or filleted.

BROILED SHEEPSHEAD

Either the whole sheepshead or the fillets may be broiled. Follow directions for broiling on pages 9–10. Serve with lemon, lemon butter, or parsley butter (pages 31, 33).

SAUTÉED SHEEPSHEAD

For sautéing the whole fish or the fillets, see the directions for sauté meunière (page 10) or for sauté à l'Anglaise (page 142). Serve with lemon butter (page 31), lemon quarters, or sauce rémoulade (page 35).

BAKED SHEEPSHEAD

Clean and split the fish. Dot with butter, season with salt and freshly ground black pepper, and sprinkle with parsley. Place on an oiled baking dish or pan and bake at 425° according to the Canadian cooking theory (page 8).

BAKED STUFFED WHOLE SHEEPSHEAD OR FILLETS

Prepare your favorite fish stuffing (pages 39–41). Clean a whole fish, stuff it, and tie it securely. If you are using fillets, spread them with the stuffing, roll, and tie securely. Dot with butter, sprinkle with salt and pepper, and bake at 425° according to the Canadian cooking theory (page 8). Baste frequently with the juices in the pan.

Skate

Abundant on both coasts, the skate, or *raie* as it is called in France, is regarded by most people as something odd and uneatable that floats in on the tide. Children are fascinated by them and dogs like to roll on top of them, apparently preferring them to any other type of dead fish. The fact is that, despite its strange look, the skate is good eating. Especially on the East Coast, it is beginning to be more popular.

The wings are the part generally used for cooking. The flesh is very gelatinous and the flavor is delicate and distinctive. I have eaten it since I was a child, in both English and French versions. If you have never tried it, you owe it to yourself to make the experiment.

In eating skate, you do not cut through the meat as you do with other fish. You scrape along the wings with your knife and fork. This gives you the full benefit of the long strips of delicious flesh.

SKATE BEURRE NOIR

This is the best-known fashion of serving skate. If you buy large wings, cut them into serving-sized pieces. If you buy the small ones, cook them whole.

Prepare a court bouillon of vinegar, salt, and water. Poach the wings in the bouillon according to the Canadian cooking theory (page 12) and drain them thoroughly. Place them in a serving dish. Melt and brown butter; add a little wine vinegar and plenty of capers. Pour this over the fish.

SKATE WITH TOMATO SAUCE

Prepare skate wings as above. Serve with sautéed onions and a rich tomato sauce (page 23).

COLD SKATE RÉMOULADE

Prepare skate wings in court bouillon, using white wine (pages 19–20). Remove to a deep platter. Let the bouillon cook down to half its volume and pour it over the fish. Cool and chill in the refrigerator. Serve with sauce vinaigrette (page 36) or rémoulade (page 35).

VARIATION
The meat of the skate may be scraped from the bones and used

in a salad combined with finely chopped celery and onion. Moisten with mayonnaise and serve on a bed of greens.

You will find that this dish is a welcome change from the usual fish salad.

Smelt

Columbia River smelt, which are related to Eastern smelt, are the best I have tasted. They are fat, rich, and mildly flavored. Their oil content is so high that Indians used to dry them in large quantities and then burn them for light, a practice that led to their being known as "candlefish."

During my childhood the smelt run in the Columbia River and its tributaries resembled an orgy. The word that the fish were running attracted thousands of people, many of whom had never baited a hook. The smelt were so abundant that the channel of a small stream would glisten with the silver of their bodies. I have watched entire families — men, women, and children — dragging the fish from the water with nets, bird cages, gunny sacks, and even old dresses knotted together. The squirming fish were dumped into boxes, and the sight of so many smelt and so much waste was far from appetizing. For a long time I disliked the fish and only in recent years have I become fond of them.

The smelt is sometimes called the "king" of the small fishes. Its relationship to the salmon gives it a distinctive flavor and good texture. Sometimes the smelt is excessively oily, or it may absorb unpleasant flavors of the river. When this happens, the only thing to do is discard the fish.

In New England, as on the Pacific Coast, the smelt is a migrating saltwater fish. The Great Lakes smelt is a transplant from New England. It has flourished in fresh water, but has retained the migratory habits of its marine ancestors. During the spawning seasons, it runs up the streams and rivers of the Great Lakes region. In all locations, coastal and inland, the spawning season of the smelt is variable, and a run may last a week or so.

Most people like smelt cooked crisp in butter or oil, and some people like them crisp enough to eat the bones. As a matter of personal preference I recommend boning the fish.

BROILED SMELT

Split and clean the smelt. Brush them well with butter, dip in cream, and roll in crumbs until they are well coated. Broil over charcoal, basting with butter during the broiling process. (You may skewer them, if you wish, and make your task easier.) Salt and pepper to taste.

SAUTÉED SMELT

Split and clean the smelt and bone them if you wish. However, it is a simple job to do this after they are cooked — just remove the head and backbone at one time.

Dip the fish in flour and sauté them quickly in butter or oil. Season to taste and serve with tartar sauce (pages 35–36) or sauce rémoulade (page 35).

VARIATIONS

1. Split the smelt at the back and remove the bone. Dip the fish in beaten egg and then in finely rolled crumbs. Sauté quickly in butter, browning well on both sides. Season to taste and serve with tartar sauce.

2. Bone the smelt as above and then marinate them in lemon or lime juice for 1 hour. Roll them in flour and sauté in olive oil very quickly. Season to taste and serve with lemon or lime butter (pages 31–32).

3. Split the smelt at the back and remove the bone. Dip the fish in beaten egg and then in finely rolled crumbs. Sauté in but-

ter and add ½ cup buttered, toasted almonds to the pan. Season to taste.

4. Dip the fish in milk and roll in seasoned corn meal. Sauté in butter or olive oil. Serve with a tomato sauce (page 23).

5. Split the fish and remove the bones. Spread with mustard, dip in crumbs, and sprinkle with dry mustard, salt, and cayenne. Sauté in butter or oil and serve with a sauce diable (page 29).

FRIED SMELT

You may bone the fish, or not, before frying. Heat fat in your deep fryer to 375°. Dip the smelt in crumbs, then in beaten egg, then in crumbs again. Fry according to the Canadian cooking theory (page 11). Drain, season to taste, and serve with tartar sauce (pages 35–36) or sauce rémoulade (page 35). Always serve fried parsley (page 253) with smelt.

VARIATIONS

En Brochette. Skewer the smelt S-shape by running the skewer through the head, then through the middle, and then through the tail. Or you may make loops of them by running the skewer just through the heads and tails. Dip the skewered fish in flour, then in beaten egg, and roll in crumbs. Fry as above.

Curried. Mix 1 cup or more of corn meal with 1 teaspoon salt and 1½ tablespoons curry powder. Beat 2 eggs very light and add 1 teaspoon freshly ground pepper and 1 teaspoon curry powder. Dip the smelt in flour, then in the beaten egg, and roll in the seasoned corn meal. Fry as above. Serve with rice heavily laced with curry. Chutney goes well with this.

Rolled. Split and bone the smelt and lay them out flat. Place an anchovy fillet on each fish, sprinkle with a little salt and pepper and some chopped parsley. Roll them up and fasten on brochettes. Dip in flour, then in beaten egg, and roll in crumbs. Fry as above. Serve with anchovy butter (page 32).

Piquant. Clean the smelt but do not bone them. Dip them in flour, then in beaten egg, and roll them in crumbs mixed with finely chopped garlic, salt, and cayenne. Fry as above and serve with a tomato sauce (page 23).

BAKED SMELT AU GRATIN

Oil	Freshly ground black pepper
Chopped onion, carrot, and	Butter
celery	White wine
Smelt	Buttered crumbs
Salt	Grated Parmesan cheese

Oil a large flat baking dish or pan. Cover the bottom with the chopped vegetables. Clean the smelt and arrange them on top. Sprinkle with salt and pepper and dot with butter. Add enough wine to the pan to half cover the fish. Bake at 425° according to the Canadian cooking theory (page 8). Remove the pan from the oven; sprinkle the top with buttered crumbs and grated Parmesan cheese. Run under the broiler for a few minutes.

Cold Smelt

BAKED SPICED SMELT

We often used to have this dish when the smelt run was on. It was a great favorite at our home. The fish should be very cold, and are delicious accompanied by potato salad, pickled beets, and rye bread. Have beer to drink with it, too.

36 to 48 smelt	2 bay leaves
2 large onions, thinly sliced	8 peppercorns
2 cloves garlic, chopped	5 lemon slices
2 carrots, grated or chopped	½ cup olive oil

½ cup wine vinegar
1 tablespoon salt
1 tablespoon of allspice, cloves,
    and cinnamon bark mixed

1 teaspoon paprika
2 cups water
1 cup white wine

Clean and arrange the fish in a large baking dish. Combine all the other ingredients and bring to a boil. Simmer for 15 minutes. Pour this sauce over the fish and bake at 425° according to the Canadian cooking theory (page 8). Let the smelt cool in the pickle and serve chilled.

SMELT ORIENTAL

This is another delicious cold dish. It may be used as hors d'oeuvre or part of a buffet supper.

36 smelt
Olive oil
Salt
Freshly ground black pepper
Paprika

3 cups tomato sauce
4 cloves garlic, finely chopped
Juice of 2 lemons
3 tablespoons chopped parsley

Clean the fish, dip them in olive oil, and arrange on an oiled baking dish. Brush again with oil and sprinkle with salt, pepper, and paprika.

Mix the tomato sauce with the garlic, lemon juice, and parsley. Cover the smelt with this mixture and bake at 425° according to the Canadian cooking theory (page 8). Let the fish cool in the sauce. Serve very cold and garnish with lemon slices, chopped parsley, and hard-cooked egg.

Sole and the Flounder Family

There is no genuine sole in American waters, but more fish called sole are served in our restaurants than any other kind. We tend to apply the name "sole" to any white fish that comes in fillets, with the result that the average diner has only the haziest idea of what fish he is eating. Generally, he is eating one of the abundant members of the flounder family — the dab, the gray sole, the yellowtail, the winter flounder, the lemon sole.

In Eastern cities you can easily obtain true Channel sole imported from England, Belgium, the Netherlands, and Denmark. It comes frozen, of course, and demands a fine price. Its texture is quite different from that of the so-called American sole.

In the fish markets of seaboard towns, a great percentage of the flounders and sole are sold in fillets, and even greater quantities are sold as frozen fillets all over the country. However, the fish is also often sold whole. The most common American flounder is a flat fish, darkish gray on top and white on the bottom, with its two eyes on top.

Any of these recipes will fit any type of flounder and will be just as appropriate to the true Channel or Dover sole. It is difficult to tell you just how much to buy since fillets vary so much in size, as does the whole fish. If you figure on about a half pound per person, you will always have plenty. Some people contend that a pound of fish will serve three, but I find this skimpy. In the following recipes for fillets, I have counted on one large fillet per person.

GRILLED SOLE

This, naturally, is the simplest way to prepare a whole sole or fillets. A charcoal fire is perfection, but gas or electricity does nearly as well. Give it a good bath of melted butter or oil. Broil about 3 inches from the flame according to the Canadian cooking theory (pages 9–10). Baste it with butter or oil while it is cooking. Salt and pepper before removing from the grill.

Serve the broiled sole with some of the pan drippings, or with lemon or lemon butter. If you prefer a sauce, serve Hollandaise (pages 25–26), Béarnaise (page 26), tomato (page 23), or mustard (page 23). Anchovy butter (page 32), parsley butter (page 33), and caviar butter (page 32) are also all excellent with the grilled fillets.

If you want to save yourself the work of cleaning a broiling pan, line it with metal foil before you put in your fish.

VARIATIONS

1. Cook the grilled fish in the oven at 425° according to the Canadian cooking theory (page 8). Then brush it with butter and crumbs and run under the broiler to brown nicely.

2. Serve the grilled sole with steamed clams and mussels.

SAUTÉED SOLE

When you sauté either the whole fish or the fillets, you have a choice of many interesting ways to garnish and sauce the fish.

SOLE MEUNIÈRE

Dredge the fish or fillets well with flour. Sauté quickly in butter or oil according to the Canadian cooking theory (page 10). Turn once during the cooking process and salt and pepper to taste. Remove to a hot platter; add the butter from the pan and a goodly sprinkling of lemon juice and chopped parsley. This simple method of preparation seems to bring out the true flavor of the fish about as well as any other way.

VARIATIONS

1. After dishing onto the hot platter, sauce with some beurre noisette (page 31) and garnish with lemon slices.

2. Add anchovy butter and lemon and garnish with strips of anchovy.

3. Peel, seed, and chop ½ pound very ripe tomatoes. Let them cook down in 4 tablespoons butter until they are a paste. Season with a little grated garlic, 1 teaspoon salt, and 1½ tablespoons curry powder. Add ½ cup white wine and allow the mixture to simmer for ½ hour. Pour over the sautéed sole.

4. Sauté slices of eggplant or summer squash until golden brown. Season well with salt and freshly ground black pepper. Place sautéed sole on these slices, surround with freshly steamed rice, and serve with a tomato sauce (page 23).

SOLE À LA TSAROVITZ

3 cups mashed potatoes	Salt
3 egg yolks	6 tablespoons butter
1 teaspoon paprika	4 large fillets of sole
1 tablespoon each of chopped parsley, chives, chervil	

SAUCE

1 tablespoon chopped shallot *or* green onion	½ cup tomato paste
½ cup white wine *or* dry vermouth	Beurre manié (page 475)
	Salt
	Freshly ground black pepper

Combine the potatoes with the egg yolks and the seasonings. Beat them well, form into thin flat cakes, and cook them in butter on a griddle or in a frying pan until they are nicely browned on both sides. Sauté the fillets as in the preceding recipe. Top the potato cakes with the sautéed fish and serve with the sauce.

Sauce. Add the shallot to the pan in which the fish was sautéed and let it cook for a few minutes. Add the white wine, swirl it around a bit, then add the tomato paste and blend well. Add the beurre manié and stir until it is nicely blended and thick. Taste for seasoning and pour over the fish.

VARIATION
Instead of the tomato sauce, garnish the fillets with sautéed mushroom caps and serve with a Hollandaise sauce (pages 25–26).

FILLETS À LA CECILY

6 fillets of sole	Butter *or* oil
1 cup sauce duxelles (page 28)	2 cups cooked, buttered spinach
Flour	Grated Parmesan cheese
1 egg	Beurre noisette (page 31)
Bread crumbs	Lemon slices

Choose long fillets for this dish. Spread each one well with the duxelles and fold over once. Dip in flour, beaten egg, and crumbs, and sauté in butter or oil according to the Canadian cooking theory (page 10). Arrange the fillets on a bed of cooked, buttered spinach, sprinkle with grated cheese, and run under the broiler for a minute to brown on top. Serve with beurre noisette poured over the fish and a garnish of lemon slices.

SOLE GAVARNI

5 or 6 green and red peppers	Salt
Olive oil	Freshly ground black pepper
1 pound mushrooms, sliced	6 fillets of sole
1 clove garlic	Flour
4 tablespoons butter	6 tablespoons butter

Cut the peppers into thin strips and sauté in olive oil until just soft. In another pan, sauté the mushrooms and garlic in butter; salt and pepper to taste. Dredge the fillets in flour and sauté in butter according to the Canadian cooking theory (page 10). When the fish is cooked, serve it on a bed of the mushrooms topped with the sautéed peppers.

SOLE À L'INDIENNE

1 onion, chopped	4 fillets cut in small pieces
Butter *or* oil	Flour
1 cup rice	6 tablespoons olive oil
1 tablespoon curry powder	Curry sauce (pages 22, 29)
Broth	

Sauté the onion in butter or oil until tender, add the rice, and brown quickly. Add the curry powder and enough boiling broth (or water) to rise 1 inch above the rice. Bake in a 350° oven until the rice is tender and the liquid absorbed, adding more liquid if it cooks away too quickly.

Dredge the fillets with flour and sauté them in olive oil until nicely browned and just cooked through.

Prepare a curry sauce with 1½ cups of sauce béchamel flavored to taste with curry powder. Unmold the rice, arrange the sole around it, and cover with the curry sauce.

Thin French-fried onions are excellent with this dish.

SOLE À LA PIEMONTESE

4 cups water	1 tablespoon lemon juice
1 cup corn meal	6 fillets of sole
1½ teaspoons salt	Flour
4 tablespoons butter	6 tablespoons butter *or* oil
4 tablespoons grated cheese	Parsley
2 cups cooked chopped spinach	½ cup white wine
1 teaspoon tarragon	½ cup tomato paste

Prepare a polenta by bringing to a boil 3 cups of water and stir in the corn meal and 1 teaspoon of the salt, which has been mixed with 1 cup of cold water. Stir until thickened, add the butter and cheese and let it cook over hot water for 1½ hours.

Cook the spinach; chop and season it with tarragon, the remaining ½ teaspoon salt, and the lemon juice.

Flour the fillets and sauté them in butter or oil according to the Canadian cooking theory (page 10). Pour the polenta on the bottom of an oval serving dish, top with the spinach, and cover with the fillets. Sprinkle with chopped parsley. Make a sauce by adding the wine and tomato paste to the pan juices, blending them well. Pour this over the fish.

FILLETS WITH PILAF, ITALIAN

6 large fillets of sole	18 mushroom caps
Flour	Butter
Rice pilaf *or* rice ring	Salt
6 tomatoes	Freshly ground black pepper
6 zucchini *or* summer squash	Tartar sauce (pages 35–36)

Cut the fillets into small julienne strips and roll in flour.

Prepare a rice pilaf or rice ring according to your own recipe. Sauté the vegetables in butter until they are nicely browned and just cooked through. Salt and pepper to taste. Sauté the sole strips very quickly in butter and season to taste.

Set the pilaf or ring in the center of a platter, decorate it with the strips of fish and surround it with the sautéed vegetables. Serve with a tartar sauce.

VARIATION

Mix a great quantity of chopped parsley and tiny cooked peas with the rice.

This is a delightful dish for a buffet supper since the entire meal is right there on the platter. You can vary the vegetables as you wish.

GINGER-FRIED FLOUNDER

Make the following batter:

3 eggs
3 tablespoons cornstarch
1 tablespoon grated ginger
   (fresh *or* preserved)

2 tablespoons soy sauce
3 tablespoons chopped green
   onion
3 tablespoons sherry

Mix thoroughly. Cut 6 fillets of flounder in strips, dip in the batter, and fry in shallow or deep fat.

FILLETS CASSIS

1 tablespoon finely chopped basil
1 cup thick tomato sauce
Freshly ground black pepper
6 fillets of sole
Flour
2 eggs, beaten
Crumbs

Butter *or* oil
Salt
8 ounces spaghetti
6 tablespoons butter
1 cup grated Cheddar *or*
   Gruyère cheese
Chopped parsley

Mix the basil and the tomato sauce and add the pepper. Spread each fillet well with this mixture and fold over. Dip the fillets in flour, in beaten egg, and in crumbs, and sauté in butter (or oil) according to the Canadian cooking theory (page 10). (Be careful when you turn them not to drip the tomato filling all over the pan.) Salt them to taste. When they are nicely browned and cooked through, serve them on a bed of sphaghetti that has been boiled, drained, and mixed with the butter and grated cheese.

You may serve this with a tomato sauce if you wish, but I think it needs nothing more than a little parsley and some more pepper.

NOTE: For a change, when you mix your spaghetti and cheese, sauté it in butter until it is lightly browned. Turn it with the aid of spatulas, brown the other side, and turn it out on a serving dish with the brown showing. This is a fine treat.

FILLETS PAYSANNE

½ pound mushrooms, coarsely
    chopped
8 tablespoons butter
8 tablespoons olive oil
½ cup shredded almonds
6 sour *or* dill pickles
¼ cup capers

Salt
Freshly ground black pepper
6 fillets of sole
Paprika
Flour
Chopped parsley

Cook the mushrooms in the 4 tablespoons each of the butter and olive oil. Add the almonds, blanched and cut into small pieces. When slightly browned add the pickles and capers and season to taste.

Sprinkle the fillets with paprika and dredge in flour. Sauté in the remaining butter and oil according to the Canadian cooking theory (page 10), and salt and pepper to taste. Arrange the fish on a platter and cover with the mushroom and almond mixture. Combine the juices of the two pans and pour over the fish. Sprinkle with chopped parsley.

FILLETS OF SOLE ST. JACQUES

4 fillets of sole
Flour
6 tablespoons butter
Salt
Freshly ground black pepper

½ pound scallops, finely
    chopped
2 cloves garlic
Chopped parsley
Sauce Béarnaise (page 26)

Cut the fillets into small strips, approximately 3 inches long by ¾ to 1 inch wide. Roll them in flour and sauté in butter according to the Canadian cooking theory (page 10) just long enough to color them. These small pieces are very easy to overcook, so be careful. Salt and pepper to taste.

Roll the scallops in flour and sauté in butter. Add the garlic and parsley and season to taste.

Heap the scallops in the center of a hot platter and arrange the fillets around the edge. Or arrange the fillets in individual shells and use the scallops for topping. Sprinkle with chopped parsley and serve with a sauce Béarnaise.

POACHED SOLE, FILLETS AND WHOLE FISH

Poaching is usually done in one of the court bouillons — preferably those with white wine, for most of the appropriate sauces include white wine broth. Occasionally a recipe calls for a red wine sauce, and some use vermouth. In some cases the fillets are poached in undiluted white wine with the addition of flavoring agents.

Sole — or fish of the flounder family, as the case may be — requires very little poaching to make it palatable and juicy. The delicate flesh is very fragile and should be watched carefully. There is no danger of overcooking if you follow the Canadian cooking theory (page 12).

ESCABECHE OF FLOUNDER

2 pounds fillets *or* steaks
Lemon *or* lime juice for dipping
Flour
Butter
1 clove garlic
3 tablespoons lemon *or* lime juice
⅓ cup orange juice
⅓ cup olive oil
¼ cup minced green onions
Dash of Tabasco *or* cayenne pepper
Salt to taste
Ripe olives
Quartered limes *or* lemons

Dip the fish in lemon or lime juice, rub with flour, and sauté in butter until golden brown according to the Canadian cooking theory (page 10). Arrange in a dish (about 2 inches deep) in a symmetrical fashion. Remove any skin and bone, if it is steak.

Make a sauce by crushing the garlic and adding the lemon or lime juice, orange juice, olive oil, minced onions, Tabasco or cayenne, and salt to taste. Pour this over the fish, and let it stand in the refrigerator for 24 hours or more. To serve as a first course or one of the dishes at a buffet supper, garnish with ripe olives and quartered limes or lemons.

NOTE: You may add fresh coriander (sometimes called Chinese parsley) to the sauce. Also try ground cumin seed or toasted coriander seeds.

SOLE WITH SHRIMP SAUCE

2 medium-sized soles *or*
 flounders
White wine court bouillon
 (pages 19–20)

2 pounds shrimp, cleaned
2 cups sauce velouté (page 21),
 prepared with the broth
Grated Parmesan cheese

Poach the soles or flounders in the court bouillon according to the Canadian cooking theory (page 12). Four minutes before the fish is done, add the shrimp. When they are done, place the fish on a hot serving dish or gratin dish.

Select the 12 largest and best-looking shrimp and set them aside to use as a garnish. Chop the rest of the shrimp very fine or put them through a food chopper, using the finest blade. While you are doing this, let the bouillon reduce to 1½ cups. Strain it and correct the seasoning. Prepare 2 cups of sauce velouté, using the bouillon as a base, and when it is smooth and thick add the chopped shrimp. Pour the sauce over the fish, garnish with whole shrimp, sprinkle with grated Parmesan cheese, and brown quickly under the broiler.

NOTE: You may prepare this dish with fillets instead of whole fish.

FILLETS OF SOLE BENEDICTINE

Brandade de morue (page 100)
White wine court bouillon
 (pages 19–20)

6 fillets of sole
Chopped parsley

This has a delightful combination of flavors and is a wonderful dish for a buffet party. It's so good, in fact, that it's worth keeping secret as a "specialty of the house."

Prepare a brandade de morue. Poach the fillets in a simple court bouillon. When done, arrange them on top of the brandade and sprinkle with chopped parsley. To serve, surround the fish with grilled whole tomatoes or sautéed zucchini.

FILLETS OF SOLE CLOVISSE

6 fillets of sole
White wine court bouillon
  (pages 19–20)
2 cans (7 ounces each) minced
  clams

Sauce velouté (page 21)
12 mushroom caps
Chopped parsley

Poach the fillets in the court bouillon according to the Canadian cooking theory (page 12). Remove them to a baking or gratin dish. Add the juice from the clams to the court bouillon and let it reduce to 1½ cups of liquid. Prepare 2 cups of sauce velouté, using the broth as a base. When it is thick, add the minced clams and taste for seasoning. Pour the sauce over the fillets and garnish with sautéed mushroom caps and chopped parsley. Run the dish under the broiler just long enough to brown lightly.

NOTE: Naturally, you may use fresh minced clams for this dish. If you do, use several whole poached clams as a garnish.

FILLETS OF SOLE CASANOVA

1 pound mushrooms
2 cups shredded celery root
Salt
Freshly ground black pepper
2 teaspoons curry powder
Butter

Garlic
6 fillets of sole
Beurre manié (page 475)
1 cup cream
Grated Parmesan cheese

Chop the mushroom stems, combine them with the celery root, cover with cold water, and bring to a boil. Add seasoning and simmer until the celery root is tender. Add the curry powder.

Sauté the mushroom caps in butter with just a touch of garlic. Season to taste.

Following the Canadian cooking theory (page 12), poach the fillets in the curry broth with the celery root and mushroom stems. When they are done, place them in a gratin or baking dish and top with the celery root. Thicken the curry broth with beurre manié, add the cream gradually, and stir until smooth and well blended. Taste for seasoning and pour over the fish. Surround with the sautéed mushroom caps, sprinkle with the grated cheese, and brown quickly under the broiler.

FILLETS OF SOLE CREOLE

6 fillets of sole
Court bouillon (page 18)
1½ cups sauce velouté (page 21)
3 large tomatoes, peeled and
  diced

2 medium onions, thinly sliced
½ pound mushrooms, sliced
6 tablespoons butter
Chopped parsley

Poach the fillets in court bouillon according to the Canadian cooking theory (page 12) and remove to a hot gratin or serving dish. Reduce the bouillon to 1 cup and strain. Using it as a base, prepare 1½ cups of sauce velouté.

Sauté the vegetables in butter until lightly browned but not mushy. Season to taste. Top the fillets with the vegetable mixture, cover with the sauce, sprinkle with chopped parsley, and run under the broiler for a few minutes.

FILLETS OF SOLE NIÇOISE

2 cloves garlic, chopped
4 tablespoons olive oil
1½ cups tomato sauce
12 anchovy fillets
6 fillets of sole

2 cups tomato juice
¼ cup vermouth *or* red wine
1 teaspoon basil
18 ripe olives
Chopped parsley

Sauté the garlic in olive oil; add the tomato sauce and 6 of the anchovy fillets, chopped. Season to taste.

Poach the sole fillets in the tomato juice and the vermouth (or wine) flavored with the basil, following the Canadian cooking theory (page 12). Remove the fish to a hot platter and reduce the liquid to 1 cup very quickly. Combine it with the tomato sauce and allow it to cook down and blend nicely. Taste for seasoning and pour over the fish. Garnish with the 6 remaining anchovy fillets and the olives. Sprinkle with chopped parsley.

SOLE AU VERMOUTH

6 fillets of sole
1¼ cups dry vermouth
4 egg yolks

½ cup butter
3 tablespoons cream
Salt

Poach the fillets in just enough dry vermouth to cover them according to the Canadian cooking theory (page 12). Remove them to a flat baking or gratin dish. Reduce the cooking liquid over a brisk flame until it is practically a glaze.

Put the egg yolks and the butter cut into small pieces into the top of a double boiler. Cook over hot water and beat with a wire whisk or electric beater until thickened and smooth. Add the cream and the reduced cooking liquid, and salt to taste. Take care that the water never boils, or you will have scrambled eggs instead of a smooth sauce. Pour the sauce over the fillets and run under the broiler to glaze.

NOTE: The many herbs and flavorings in the vermouth make extra seasonings unnecessary in this dish.

FILLETS OF SOLE MARGUERY

This is one of the most famous recipes for sole, having been created in the old Restaurant Marguery in Paris. It is not a difficult dish, and the combination of flavors makes it remarkably good.

6 fillets of sole	36 mussels
White wine	Sauce au vin blanc (page 23)
24 shrimp	

Poach the fillets in enough white wine to cover them according to the Canadian cooking theory (page 12). Remove to a baking dish. Shell and clean the shrimp and poach in the same wine for 3 minutes. Keep hot. Steam the mussels until they open (page 416) and extract the meat. Reduce the white wine and prepare the sauce. Cover the fillets with the sauce, surround them with the shrimp and mussels, and run under the broiler for a minute to glaze.

FILLETS OF SOLE DUXELLES

6 fillets of sole	Salt
White wine	Freshly ground black pepper
Sauce duxelles (page 27)	1/4 cup port wine
18 small mushroom caps	Chopped parsley
4 tablespoons butter	

Poach the fillets in white wine to cover as in the preceding recipe. Remove to a flat baking or gratin dish. Reduce the wine and make the sauce duxelles. Sauté the mushrooms lightly in butter and season to taste. Remove to a hot plate and keep hot. Rinse the pan in which the mushrooms were cooked with the port and pour it over the fish. Cover with the sauce, top with the sautéed mushroom caps, and run under the broiler to glaze. Sprinkle with chopped parsley.

FILLETS OF SOLE WITH LOBSTER

2 lobsters (1½ pounds each)	Sauce béchamel (page 23)
Salt	¼ cup cognac *or* whiskey
4 fillets of sole (about equal size)	½ cup heavy cream
White wine	Grated Parmesan cheese

Cook the lobsters in boiling salted water for about 8 to 10 minutes. When cool enough to handle, split them and remove all the meat from the bodies and claws. The pieces of claw meat should be removed carefully so as to keep them perfect. Set them aside and chop or grind the rest of the lobster meat very fine.

Poach the fillets of sole in white wine according to the Canadian cooking theory (page 12). Remove them to a piece of absorbent paper or cloth. Reduce the wine to half and use it as a base for preparing 2 or 3 cups of béchamel. Combine the chopped lobster meat and the sauce béchamel, add the cognac or whiskey, and gradually stir in the heavy cream. Continue stirring until the mixture is thoroughly blended and heated through. Line each half lobster shell with a little of the sauce. Place a fillet in each half shell, cover with additional sauce, top with a piece of claw meat, sprinkle with cheese, and glaze under the broiler.

FILLETS OF SOLE MORNAY

6 fillets of sole	Sauce Mornay (page 22)
White wine *or* vermouth	Grated Parmesan cheese

Poach the fillets in white wine or vermouth, according to the Canadian cooking theory (page 12); when they are done put them in a flat baking or gratin dish. Reduce the wine by half and add it to the sauce Mornay. Pour this over the fish, sprinkle with grated cheese, and run under the broiler to glaze.

FILLETS IN SHELLS

6 croustades
Butter
6 fillets
White wine
8 ounces noodles (green *or* white)
Salt
Butter

Garlic
Freshly ground black pepper
½ cup grated Swiss Emmer-
    thaler *or* Swiss Gruyère cheese
Sauce Mornay (page 22)
Grated Parmesan cheese

Prepare 6 croustades from large loaves of bread by trimming the crusts and hollowing out the loaves. The croustades should be about 6 inches long and 4 inches wide and fairly deep — 3 inches at least. Toast them, butter them well, and keep hot.

Next, poach 6 fillets that you have folded in half in white wine according to the Canadian cooking theory (page 12).

Third, cook the noodles in boiling salted water until just tender. Drain them and sauté lightly in butter with a touch of garlic and some coarsely ground pepper. Add the grated cheese.

Fourth, prepare a sauce Mornay and add the reduced wine broth to the sauce.

Fifth, fill the croustades with the noodle mixture, top each one with a folded fillet and cover with sauce Mornay. Sprinkle with grated Parmesan cheese and glaze for a minute under the broiler.

This, with a green vegetable such as green beans, with plenty of butter, and a salad, makes a remarkably good supper for a large group of people. It takes a little extra trouble to prepare, but it is attractive and the individual loaves make it convenient to serve. A white wine, dry and flinty — such as a fine Chablis — is excellent with it.

FILLETS IN BLANKETS

4 fillets of sole
White wine *or* vermouth
Sauce Mornay (page 22)
2 cups cooked spinach

Salt
Butter
4 individual omelets
Chopped parsley

Poach the fillets in white wine or vermouth according to the Canadian cooking theory (page 12), and keep them hot in a warm oven or over low heat. Use the liquid to make a sauce Mornay. Cook the spinach and flavor with salt and butter.

Prepare omelets according to your favorite recipe. When they are ready to roll, add to each a bit of the sauce, a little spinach, and a fillet. Then roll and top with more spinach and sauce. Sprinkle with the parsley.

SOLE MIRABEAU

This is the original version of the fillets in blankets. It is simple to make although it sounds involved.

6 fillets of sole	6 eggs
White wine *or* vermouth	Salt
2 cups sauce Mornay (page 22)	Freshly ground black pepper
2 cups cooked, buttered spinach, *en branche*	6 tablespoons butter

Fold the fillets in half and poach them according to the Canadian cooking theory (page 12) in enough white wine or vermouth to cover. Remove them from the broth and keep warm. Reduce the cooking liquid and add it to the sauce Mornay.

Prepare a large soufflé omelet with 6 eggs. Beat the yolks and whites separately, and fold the whites into the yolks. Season and cook in a skillet in which you have melted 6 tablespoons of butter. While it is cooking, make a soufflé mixture:

4 tablespoons butter	3 egg yolks
4 tablespoons flour	4 egg whites
½ cup milk	Salt
½ to ¾ cup grated Parmesan cheese	Freshly ground black pepper

Melt the butter, blend in the flour, and add the milk and grated cheese. Cool slightly, season to taste, and add the slightly beaten egg yolks; then fold in the stiffly beaten whites.

When the soufflé omelet is deep and puffy, slide it onto a large baking dish, and with a sharp knife and a spatula remove the center part. Cover the bottom with a layer of the sauce Mornay. Then add a layer of spinach, then the fillets, and cover the entire top with a thin layer of the soufflé and Parmesan cheese mixture. Bake for about 10 minutes in a 425° oven until the soufflé mixture is puffy and lightly browned. Serve with additional sauce Mornay.

OMELET STUFFED WITH SOLE

Here is a quick version of the recipes above. For each serving make two small plain omelets. Place an omelet on each dish, top with a fillet of sole which has been poached in court bouillon, cover this with the second omelet, and over all pour a good cheese sauce (page 23).

FILLETS OF SOLE BONNE FEMME

Butter	1 cup white wine
2 shallots, finely chopped	Beurre manié (page 475)
¼ pound mushrooms, chopped	Lemon juice
4 fillets of sole	Salt
Chopped parsley	Freshly ground black pepper

Melt enough butter in a large sauté pan to oil the bottom well. Add the shallots and half the mushrooms, place the fillets on top, and cover with the rest of the mushrooms. Season to taste and sprinkle with a little chopped parsley. Add the wine and poach according to the Canadian cooking theory (page 12), basting often. Remove the fish to a serving dish. The liquid should have reduced to less than half its original volume. If not, cook it rapidly until it is reduced. Thicken with a little beurre manié, add a few drops of lemon juice, and taste for seasoning. Pour over the fillets and sprinkle the top with chopped parsley.

FILLET OF SOLE DUGLÉRÉ

The French chef Dugléré invented this now classic dish in the nineteenth century.

2 Dover soles, about 1¼ pounds each
4 tablespoons butter
½ small clove garlic
Salt
Freshly ground black pepper
2 to 3 shallots, finely chopped
4 large tomatoes, peeled, seeded, and chopped
½ cup of fish stock

½ cup of dry white wine
1 cup of heavy cream
Beurre manié (page 475)
1 teaspoon chopped fresh tarragon
1 egg yolk
Lemon juice
Tabasco
Chopped parsley

Fillet the sole, keeping the bones and skins for making a fish stock. Rub an ovenproof dish with 1 tablespoon of the butter, greasing the bottom completely. Cut the garlic and rub it lightly around the dish. Carefully dry the sole with a clean cloth. Arrange the fillets in a single layer in the dish; season with salt and pepper.

Sprinkle the shallots over the fish and top with the tomatoes. Strain the stock and wine and pour it over the fish; cover the dish with a buttered piece of parchment paper. On the top of the stove bring the pan to a simmer, then lower the heat. Poach the sole gently according to the Canadian cooking theory (page 12).

Carefully lift the fillets out, strain and cool them. Bring the cooking liquid, with the shallots and tomatoes, to the boil and reduce by at least a third. Take the pan from the heat and stir in the cream. Add small bits of the beurre manié and whisk until completely absorbed. You should have a medium-thick sauce. Add the tarragon. Melt the remaining butter and beat with the egg yolk. Blend this into the cream sauce, heat just to thicken slightly, and combine. Correct seasonings.

Just before serving, arrange the sole fillets on a large flat tray and sprinkle them with a little lemon juice. Stir a few drops of Tabasco into the sauce. Coat the fillets with the sauce and sprinkle with parsley.

FILLETS OF SOLE WITH SCALLOPS MORNAY

4 fillets of sole   Sauce Mornay (page 22)
½ pound scallops   Paprika
White wine   Toast points

Poach the fillets and the scallops in white wine according to the Canadian cooking theory (page 12) and season to taste. Remove from the liquid and keep hot. Reduce the wine broth and use it to make the sauce Mornay, which should be well seasoned. Place the fillets in a flat baking dish. Add the scallops to the sauce and pour it over the fish. Run under the broiler to glaze, sprinkle with paprika, and serve garnished with fried toast points.

DEEP-FRIED SOLE

Fillets of sole should be fried at a temperature of 375° according to the Canadian cooking theory (page 11). If you overcook it, you will have a dish that resembles sawdust and that has no more flavor than the breading materials. It is much more difficult to fry fish well than to grill or poach it.

Fish fillets for frying should be dredged with flour, dipped in a mixture of well-beaten eggs and milk, then rolled in crumbs or corn meal until they are thoroughly covered. Then they should be carefully lowered into the hot fat. When cooked, drain on absorbent paper. Salt and pepper.

For the average frying you will want 2 eggs beaten with about ¾ cup of milk. Corn meal is exceedingly popular with many people as a covering for fish because of the added flavor it gives. Others use cracker crumbs, bread crumbs, prepared cereals, and various mixes for pancakes and foodstuffs. But whatever you use, be sure the pieces of fish are thoroughly covered.

FRIED FILLET OF SOLE

Follow the directions above and serve with a tartar sauce (pages 35–36), sauce Béarnaise (page 26), or with lemon wedges.

JULIENNE OF SOLE

These are also called goujons* of sole. Cut the fillets into small strips and fry as you do whole fillets. These make a most unusual appearance on a platter — the small strips, golden brown, piled high, with a garnish of parsley and a bowl of sauce. They taste wonderful, too. Serve them with cocktails and have a bowl of tartar sauce (pages 35–36) at hand for dunking. Pass plenty of paper napkins.

VARIATIONS

1. Serve fried fillets with French-fried parsley and a good tomato sauce (page 23). French-fried parsley is simple: Merely dip a bunch of parsley into the hot fat and fry for about 2 minutes, or until crisp. The flavor is unforgettably good.

2. Serve fried fillets on a bed of onions fried in butter until soft. Make a sauce by frying 1 chopped onion and ½ pound of chopped mushrooms in plenty of butter. Add 4 chopped dill or sour pickles, some chopped parsley, and a good slug of lemon juice. Heat this well, season to taste, and pour over the fillets on the bed of onions. Sprinkle with paprika.

3. Fry julienne of sole and arrange on a mound of rice. Serve with a sauce made with 1½ cups of sauce velouté (page 21) flavored with 1 tablespoon of curry powder and 3 tablespoons of chutney. Top with grated coconut.

* From *goujon,* a tiny freshwater fish popular in France.

ROLLED FILLETS

Spread fillets with anchovy butter (page 32) or herb butter (page 33), roll, and fasten with toothpicks. Roll in flour, dip in a beaten egg and milk mixture, roll well in crumbs, and fry according to the directions above.

STUFFED SAUTÉED FILLETS

4 fillets of sole
Fish forcemeat (page 41)
Flour
2 eggs, beaten
½ cup milk
Crumbs *or* corn meal
6 tablespoons butter

3 ounces sherry
4 tablespoons tomato paste
1 cup sauce béchamel (page 23)
Salt
Freshly ground black pepper
6 grilled tomatoes

Spread the fillets with forcemeat, roll, and secure with toothpicks. Dust with flour, dip in beaten egg and milk, and roll well in crumbs or corn meal. Sauté the rolls in butter according to the Canadian cooking theory (page 10). Remove to a hot platter. Rinse the pan well with sherry, add the tomato paste and the béchamel, blend thoroughly, and let it come to a boil. Taste for seasoning. Surround the fillets with grilled tomatoes and serve the sauce separately.

STUFFED FILLETS

4 fillets of sole
Fish forcemeat (page 41)
Mirepoix (carrots, onions, celery)
4 tablespoons butter
White wine

1 cup cream
Beurre manié (page 475)
Salt
Freshly ground black pepper
1½ cups mashed potatoes
2 eggs

Spread the fillets with the forcemeat, roll them, and secure with toothpicks. Chop the vegetables very fine and steam them in butter until soft. Add the fillets and enough white wine to cover the bottom of the pan. Poach the fish, basting with the wine, according to the Canadian cooking theory (page 12). Remove them to a hot plate. Strain the cooking liquid, add the cream, and return it to the stove to cook down for a few minutes. Thicken slightly with beurre manié. Season to taste.

Mix the seasoned mashed potatoes with the eggs and blend well. Arrange small rosettes of the potatoes (piped through a pastry tube, using the large rosette end) on a serving dish. Place the fillets in the center and cover with the sauce. Dust with paprika and run under the broiler to brown the potatoes and the sauce.

HERBED ROLLED FILLETS

1½ cups finely chopped mush-
    rooms
4 tablespoons butter
Salt
Freshly ground black pepper
½ cup chopped chives
½ cup chopped parsley
½ cup chopped onion
6 to 8 fillets of sole, depending
    on size

Flour
2 eggs beaten with ¾ cup of
    milk
Crumbs
Butter
2 tablespoons flour
1 cup (about) white wine
1 cup cream
Grated Parmesan cheese

Sauté the mushrooms in 4 tablespoons butter until well cooked. Add the chives, parsley, and onion, and season to taste. When thoroughly blended and cooked, remove from the heat and spread the mixture on the fillets. Roll the fillets and secure with toothpicks. Dip each fillet in flour, then in beaten egg and milk, and roll in crumbs. Sauté in butter according to the Canadian cooking theory (page 10). Remove to a hot platter. Add the 2 tablespoons flour to the pan and mix well with the juices. Add the wine and cook to reduce the liquid a bit. Add the cream and stir until well blended and thickened. Pour the sauce around the fillets, sprinkle with grated Parmesan cheese, and run under the broiler to glaze.

ROLLED FILLETS WITH SHRIMP SAUCE

Fish forcemeat (page 41)
Tarragon
8 fillets of sole
½ pound shrimp
White wine

Sauce béchamel (page 23)
Salt
Freshly ground black pepper
Grated Parmesan cheese

Prepare a fish forcemeat and flavor it heavily with tarragon. Spread each fillet with the forcemeat, roll, and secure with toothpicks. Poach the fillets and the shelled and cleaned shrimp in white wine, according to the Canadian cooking theory (page 12), basting often so as to cook evenly. Remove the cooked fish to a hot serving dish. Remove the shrimp and chop very fine. Prepare a sauce béchamel, using the reduced cooking liquid as a base. Salt and pepper to taste and add additional tarragon. Add the chopped shrimp and pour over the fillets. Sprinkle with grated Parmesan cheese and run under the broiler to glaze for a minute or two.

FILLETS STUFFED WITH SALMON

½ pound salmon
2 eggs
½ cup chopped parsley
Salt
Freshly ground black pepper
6 fillets of sole

White wine
1½ cups sauce velouté (page 21)
12 mushroom caps
6 artichoke hearts
Butter
Sautéed potatoes

Grind the salmon and mix with the eggs and parsley until it is smooth and pasty. Season to taste and spread on the fillets. Roll and secure with toothpicks. Poach the fillets in white wine, basting well, according to the Canadian cooking theory (page 12). Remove the fillets to a baking dish. Prepare a sauce velouté, using the cooking liquid. Sauté the mushrooms and artichoke hearts in butter and season to taste. Pour the sauce over the fish, surround with the artichoke hearts, top with the mushrooms, and garnish with sautéed potatoes.

ROLLED FILLETS OF SOLE NIÇOISE

8 fillets of sole	½ pound shrimp, shelled and
Chopped parsley	deveined
Chopped shallots *or* green onions	24 clams
Anchovy fillets	Sauce velouté (page 21)
Court bouillon (page 18)	Grated Parmesan cheese

Sprinkle the fillets heavily with the parsley and green onions or shallots. Lay several anchovy fillets on each one. Roll and secure with toothpicks. Measure the diameter, and poach in a court bouillon according to the Canadian cooking theory (page 12). About 3 minutes before the fillets are done add the shrimp to the bouillon. Remove the fillets to a hot platter.

Steam the clams until they open (page 358). Take the meat from the shells. Prepare a sauce velouté (1¼ cups), using the reduced court bouillon as a base. Add the clams and shrimp to the sauce and pour over the fillets. Sprinkle with the cheese and glaze under the broiler for a few minutes.

TOAD IN THE HOLE

6 large Idaho potatoes	2 eggs, beaten with ¾ cup of
6 fillets of sole	milk
Fines herbes	Bread crumbs
Salt	6 tablespoons butter, or more
Freshly ground black pepper	½ cup cream
Flour	2 egg yolks
	1 teaspoon paprika

Bake the potatoes. Sprinkle the fillets with the herbs and season to taste. Roll and secure with toothpicks. Dip in flour, then in the egg mixture, and roll in the crumbs. Measure the diameter of the rolls and sauté in butter according to the Canadian cooking theory (page 10).

When the potatoes are baked, cut the tops off and scoop out most of the pulp. Mash and whip with the butter, cream, egg yolks, salt, pepper, and paprika. Place a fillet in each potato, surround with the whipped potato and put the potato shell back on. Serve any leftover potato filling in a separate dish.

Cold Fillets

COLD JELLIED FILLETS WITH FINES HERBES

8 fillets of sole
1½ cups chopped herbs (dill, parsley, chives, tarragon)
Salt
Freshly ground black pepper
White wine court bouillon (pages 19–20)

Egg white
2 envelopes gelatin
1½ cups mayonnaise
Black olives
4 cups (or more) potato salad
Hard-cooked eggs

Spread the fillets well with the herbs and sprinkle with salt and pepper. Roll and secure with toothpicks. Poach in court bouillon according to the Canadian cooking theory (page 12). Be very careful not to overcook. Remove the toothpicks.

Let the bouillon cook down to a little less than a quart — about 3 cups. Strain and clarify with egg white (page 18). Melt the gelatin in ½ cup of water; when it is thoroughly dissolved combine with the boiling bouillon. Let it cool until it is thick and syrupy. Combine 1 cup of the jelly with 1 cup of mayonnaise and taste for seasoning. Mask the fillets with this mixture and chill well until firm. Decorate with slices of ripe olives and brush with another coat of the jelly. Chill.

Arrange a bed of highly seasoned potato salad on a platter. Make a row or circle of the glazed fillets on top and decorate with hard-cooked eggs and olives. Serve with additional mayonnaise.

JELLIED FILLETS OF SOLE NIÇOISE

4 hard-cooked eggs, chopped
12 to 15 anchovy fillets, chopped
½ cup chopped parsley
1½ cups chopped onion
8 fillets of sole
White wine court bouillon
  (pages 19–20)
Egg white
2 envelopes gelatin

1 cup tomato sauce
1 teaspoon basil
Sliced hard-cooked eggs
Olives
Greens
Onion rings
French dressing
Tomato mayonnaise

Combine the eggs, and anchovy fillets, parsley, and onion. Spread each fillet with this mixture and fold over. Poach in court bouillon according to the Canadian cooking theory (page 12). Remove with a spatula, being careful that you do not break the fish. Reduce the liquid to about 3 cups, strain, and clarify with egg white (page 18). Melt the gelatin in ½ cup of cold water and combine with the boiling bouillon. Chill until thick and syrupy, but not set.

Cover each cooked fillet with a highly seasoned tomato sauce to which you have added the basil. Decorate with slices of hard-cooked egg and sliced olives. Cover with some of the jelly and chill. When set, brush again with jelly and chill.

Arrange a bed of greens on a platter and place the fillets on top. Decorate with onion rings that have been marinated in a French dressing. Garnish with hard-cooked egg slices and serve with tomato mayonnaise.

VARIATION

Prepare the fillets of sole as above but omit the greens. Make a rice salad by combining 3 cups cold cooked rice, 1 cup chopped cooked shrimp, ½ cup each of chopped onion, green pepper, and parsley, and salt and pepper to taste. Make a sauce vinaigrette (page 36) and add chopped pickles and herbs. Pour this over the rice mixture. Arrange the rice salad on a platter, and place the fillets on top in the shape of a fan. Put rows of chopped jellied bouillon between the fillets. Garnish with sliced pickles and hard-cooked eggs. This is an easy but spectacular dish for a supper party.

JELLIED FILLETS WITH TARRAGON

8 fillets of sole
Fish forcemeat (page 41)
Fresh tarragon leaves
White wine court bouillon
 (pages 19–20)
Egg white
2 envelopes gelatin

3 to 4 cups salade Russe (page
 372)
Green mayonnaise
Small tomatoes
Sliced cucumbers
Sauce verte (page 34)

Spread the fillets with the highly seasoned forcemeat and tarragon leaves. Roll and secure with toothpicks. Poach in court bouillon according to the Canadian cooking theory (page 12). Chill. Reduce the bouillon, strain, and clarify with egg white (page 18). Melt the gelatin in ½ cup of cold water and combine with the boiling bouillon. Cool until thick but not solid. Pour the jelly into eight small molds or one large mold and place in the refrigerator to chill until a thin layer has formed on the bottom and sides. Pour off the rest of the jelly and arrange the fillets, topped with additional tarragon leaves, in the mold. Pour the rest of the jelly over this and chill until firm. Arrange the molds of fillets on a platter with a mound of salade Russe in the center. Surround with tiny tomatoes and cucumber slices. Serve with sauce verte.

WHEEL OF SOLES

This is another spectacular buffet dish. The fillets are arranged in the form of a wheel around a mound of salade Orientale and coated with a mayonnaise colée.

12 fillets of sole
Court bouillon (page 18)
Egg white
2 envelopes gelatin
2 cups mayonnaise (and a little
 extra)

Chopped parsley
Hard-cooked eggs
Chopped onion
Chili sauce

Salade Orientale

5 cups cold cooked rice
12 chopped anchovies
½ cup chopped parsley
1 cup chopped green onion

½ cup chopped pimiento
Sauce vinaigrette (page 36)
  mixed with ¼ cup chili sauce

Trim the fillets until they are of equal size and are each pointed at one end. Poach them in court bouillon according to the Canadian cooking theory (page 12). With a spatula (or with a pair of them) remove the fish carefully to a platter to cool. Reduce the bouillon to 3 cups, strain, and clarify with egg white (page 18). Dissolve the gelatin in ½ cup of cold water and add to the boiling bouillon. Cool. When it is syrupy, combine 2 cups of the jelly with an equal amount of thick mayonnaise. Chill.

Combine the ingredients for the salade Orientale and chill. When ready to serve, mound the salad in the center of a large serving platter, arrange the fillets in the form of a wheel, and spoon the mayonnaise colée (jellied mayonnaise) over them. Sprinkle the fillets heavily with chopped parsley.

Halve each hard-cooked egg horizontally and remove the yolk. Mash it and mix with a little mayonnaise, some chopped parsley, chopped onions, and a dash of chili sauce. Fill the egg whites with this mixture piped through a pastry tube. Decorate the platter with the stuffed eggs in the center and between the fillets.

No additional dressing is needed for this dish, but you may serve a bowl of mayonnaise with it if you wish.

Spanish Mackerel

The ichthyologist Mitchell, writing in 1815 in his *Fishes of New York,* gave the Spanish mackerel this brief but favorable biography: "A fine and beautiful fish; comes in July."

The Spanish mackerel is a handsome wanderer. It loves the warm seas of the south, and in the summer it migrates to the cool northern waters. Then it heads south again before cold weather sets in. Smart fish.

A fine sport, Spanish mackerel gives a good battle. It is vigorous and sometimes grows to 50 to 75 pounds in weight. In the markets, however, the average weight of the fish sold is about 2 pounds, and it usually comes whole. It is readily bought in the Atlantic Coast area, but unfortunately is rare along the Pacific Coast.

BROILED SPANISH MACKEREL

The Spanish mackerel either split or filleted makes a magnificent dish when broiled and served with lemon butter (page 31), tartar sauce (pages 35–36), or any of the favorite fish sauces (see pages 21–38).

SAUTÉED SPANISH MACKEREL

Sauté fillets of Spanish mackerel or small whole fish according to directions for sauté meunière, page 10.

BAKED SPANISH MACKEREL

This fish is particularly adapted to baking, either plain or stuffed. It varies in size from 1 to 4 pounds. If you have a large number to serve, you may need to plan on baking 2 mackerel.

Place the fish on an oiled pan or baking dish, dot with butter, and season with salt and freshly ground black pepper. Bake at 450° according to the Canadian cooking theory (page 8). Baste frequently.

Serve with parsley butter (page 33), lemon butter (page 31), maître d'hôtel butter (page 31), or tomato sauce (page 23).

BAKED STUFFED SPANISH MACKEREL I

Choose 4 mackerel small enough for individual portions. Make the following mixture:

½ cup soft bread crumbs	1 cup sliced green olives
1 tablespoon grated onion	¼ cup melted butter

Combine the ingredients, stuff the fish, and sew them up securely. Place them on an oiled sheet or pan and surround them with 1½ cups of ripe olives (the dried Italian or green ones are best). Brush the fish lavishly with olive oil and sprinkle with pepper. Bake at 450° according to the Canadian cooking theory (page 8). Serve with the olive garnish, steamed potatoes, and a cucumber salad.

BAKED STUFFED SPANISH MACKEREL II

6 tablespoons butter	1 teaspoon freshly ground
½ cup finely chopped green	black pepper
onions or scallions	½ cup fine bread crumbs
¼ cup parsley	1 large Spanish mackerel (or 2
½ teaspoon salt	medium-sized mackerel)

Blend the butter, herbs, salt, and pepper and gradually work in the crumbs. Stuff the mackerel and sew up securely. Place the fish in an oiled baking dish or pan, dot with butter, and sprinkle with salt and pepper. Bake at 425° according to the Canadian cooking theory (page 8). Serve with parslied potatoes and a tomato and cucumber salad. This will serve four people.

BAKED STUFFED SPANISH MACKEREL III

1 clove garlic, chopped
1 medium onion, chopped
2 green peppers, chopped
6 tablespoons oil or fat
4 large tomatoes, peeled,
   seeded, and chopped
½ cup crumbs

8 anchovy fillets, chopped
1 teaspoon coarsely ground
   black pepper
1 teaspoon fennel seeds
2 tablespoons capers
1 large Spanish mackerel

Sauté the garlic, onion, and green pepper in the oil until soft. Add the tomatoes and let them cook down for about 20 minutes. Add the rest of the ingredients, mix well, and stuff a good-sized fish. Sew it securely. Place the fish in a well-oiled baking dish and brush with olive oil. Bake at 425° according to the Canadian cooking theory (page 8), basting frequently. Serve with a tomato sauce (page 23).

Spot

This is an Atlantic Coast member of the croaker family and, like its relatives, can play little tunes with the aid of its air bladder. Spot is not well known and is rarely found in the markets at this time. This is regrettable, since it is an attractive fish.

Prepare spot according to the directions for sea trout or butterfish.

Squid

Also called poulpe, inkfish, and cuttlefish, this elongated ten-armed cousin of the octopus was once a "poor man's" dish, and was eaten only by the Italians, Spaniards, and the Orientals. Squid is now becoming "chic" and it is served in the most elegant restaurants.

The Spaniards and Italians like the squid stewed in its own ink, and so do I. But for most dishes you should slit the belly and remove the bone, which, incidentally, has a number of commercial uses — canary food, for one thing. Wash the squid well under running cold water.

FRIED SQUID I

Cut the tentacles into small pieces, dust them with flour, and dip in beaten egg and crumbs or in batter. Fry quickly in oil heated to 375°. Drain on absorbent paper and salt and pepper to taste. Serve with tartar (pages 35–36) or mustard sauce (page 23).

These are excellent as part of a "mixed fry" in the Italian style. Use a selection of small bits of fish, all fried and served with a highly seasoned sauce.

FRIED SQUID II

Cut the tentacles into small pieces and dust well with flour. Sauté in plenty of olive oil. It's wise to cover the pan, for the small pieces of squid may fly out and hit you in the face. Salt and pepper well and serve with puree of spinach lightly flavored with garlic.

BAKED SQUID

Clean the squid and soak it in milk for an hour. Roll it well in buttered bread crumbs and arrange it in an oiled pan or baking dish. Season with salt and freshly ground black pepper and dot with butter. Bake at 500° for 12 minutes. Serve with a sauce diable (page 29), tartar sauce (pages 35–36), or tomato sauce (page 23).

Striped Bass

Striped bass, known below the Mason-Dixon Line as rockfish, is a great favorite with anglers on both coasts and an important commercial fish on the East Coast.* Though not yet a household food in the same sense as mackerel and cod, its popularity is growing. Occasionally you may see an exceptionally large striped bass in your market, but on the average the fish runs from 15 to 18 inches long. Some is sold filleted, some frozen.

BROILED STRIPED BASS

Either fillets or the whole split fish may be broiled according to the recipes on pages 9–10. Serve with lemon butter (page 31) or

---

* In California, however, striped bass is a game fish and is not available commercially.

Hollandaise sauce (pages 25–26), cucumber sauce with sour cream (page 37), tartar sauce (pages 35–36), oyster sauce (page 21), or lobster sauce (page 21).

VARIATIONS

1. Flambé. Broil a whole striped bass. When it is done, arrange it on a large metal platter on a bed of dried fennel or thyme. Top with a mixture of dried herbs — fennel, thyme, parsley. Add cognac and ignite. Let the herbs burn down so that their flavors permeate the whole fish. You may vary the dried herbs as you wish, but fennel and thyme seem to me to be the perfect combination.

2. Split a whole striped bass and remove the backbone. Oil the broiler pan well and place the fish on it, skin side down. Oil the fish well, and broil it according to the Canadian cooking theory (pages 9–10). Halfway through the cooking time, cover it with paper-thin slices of lemon, salt, and pepper to taste and continue broiling until done. Remove the lemon slices and add herb butter (page 33).

STUFFED STRIPED BASS I

Split a whole striped bass and remove the backbone. Stuff it with thin slices of onion, tomato, green pepper, and plenty of chopped parsley. Salt and pepper to taste; add some fresh or dried tarragon to taste and dot heavily with butter. Sew the fish together or secure with skewers and twine. Flour it lightly, butter it well, and season to taste. Place it in an oiled baking dish and add 1 cup of red wine. Bake at 425° according to the Canadian cooking theory (page 8). Baste with the wine while it is cooking. Serve with a tomato sauce well flavored with the wine and some garlic.

STUFFED STRIPED BASS II

Prepare a stuffing mixture of the following:

1 pound crabmeat
¼ cup chopped chives *or* green
   onion
¼ cup chopped parsley
4 tablespoons melted butter

3 tablespoons chopped celery
½ cup crumbs
¼ cup heavy cream
Salt
Freshly ground black pepper

Stuff the fish and sew it up or fasten it with skewers and twine. Oil and season it and place it on an oiled baking dish or pan. Bake at 425° according to the Canadian cooking theory (page 8). Serve with a sauce rémoulade (page 35) that you have mixed with ½ cup of crabmeat.

STUFFED STRIPED BASS III

2 slices salt pork, cut in small
   pieces
4 tablespoons butter
½ cup finely chopped onion
¼ cup finely chopped celery
¼ cup finely chopped green
   pepper
½ cup finely rolled crumbs

1 teaspoon fennel *or* thyme
½ cup toasted chopped
   almonds
Striped bass
Salt
Freshly ground black pepper
Bacon strips

Cook the salt pork in the butter. Add the onion, celery, and green pepper. Sauté until just soft. Mix in the crumbs, fennel or thyme, and toasted chopped almonds (the canned ones are excellent). Stuff the fish and sew it up or fasten it with skewers and twine. Season to taste, place in an oiled baking dish, and top with strips of bacon. Bake at 425° according to the Canadian cooking theory (page 8). Serve with a tomato sauce (page 23) or a cucumber and sour cream sauce (page 37).

STUFFED STRIPED BASS IV

Prepare an omelet fines herbes with 4 or 5 eggs and a mixture of herbs. Stuff the fish with the omelet and sew it up. Make a bed of sliced shallots or green onions on the bottom of an oiled baking dish or pan. Add enough white wine to cover halfway. Place the fish on top; oil and season it to taste. Bake at 425° according to the Canadian cooking theory (page 8), basting often. Remove the fish to a hot platter and strain the liquid in the pan. Reduce quickly to 1½ cups. Correct the seasoning and add ½ cup of heavy cream mixed with 2 or 3 egg yolks. Stir until the sauce is thickened, being careful that it does not boil. Serve with the fish.

BAKED STRIPED BASS

Split a whole fish and place it on an oiled baking pan or dish. Dot with butter and salt and pepper to taste. Bake at 425° according to the Canadian cooking theory (page 8). Serve with parsley butter (page 33).

STRIPED BASS SAUTÉ

You may sauté either a small whole striped bass or the fillets. Follow directions for sauté meunière (page 10). The fish may be served in this manner with any of the following sauces:

1. Tomato sauce (page 23)
2. Sauce Provençale (pages 30–31)
3. Sauce duxelles (page 27)

STRIPED BASS EN PAPILLOTE

First, see the instructions on page 162 for cutting and folding parchment paper for baking.

1 striped bass, filleted, *or* 2 pounds fillets
White wine sauce (page 24)
¼ cup chopped mushrooms, sautéed

¼ cup chopped shallots, sautéed
½ cup finely chopped cooked shrimp
Truffles *or* mushroom caps

Cut a striped bass into fillets or buy the fillets. Cut these into portions small enough to fit a piece of parchment 8 by 11 inches. Prepare the white wine sauce and add to it the mushrooms, shallots, and shrimp. When the sauce is cool, spread it over half of each piece of paper. Place a piece of fillet on top of the sauce and top each fillet with another spoonful of sauce and a slice of truffle or a mushroom cap. Fold the paper over and crimp it securely.

Bake at 425° according to the Canadian cooking theory (page 8), adding 5 minutes for the paper. Serve at once in the paper. When you pierce the paper to get at the fish, a mouthwatering odor pours out — one reason why this method of serving fish is so delightful.

POACHED STRIPED BASS

Poach a striped bass in boiling salted water or in a court bouillon (pages 18–20) and serve it with any of the following sauces:

1. Hollandaise sauce (pages 25–26)
2. Sauce mousseline (page 26)
3. Shrimp sauce (page 21)
4. Lobster sauce (page 21)
5. Oyster sauce (page 21)
6. Sauce velouté (page 21)
7. Parsley sauce (page 23)

STRIPED BASS CURRY

Poach 2 pounds of filleted striped bass in boiling salted water according to the Canadian cooking theory (page 12). Remove and cool. Prepare a curry sauce (pages 22, 29). Flake the fish and mix it with the sauce. Heat thoroughly. Serve in a ring of saffron rice and pass chutney, chopped toasted almonds, chopped hard-cooked eggs, sliced cucumbers, and thinly sliced bananas in a vinaigrette sauce. The secret of this dish is to be sure not to over-cook the fish. It is wonderful for a buffet dinner.

COLD STRIPED BASS

Cold striped bass, which must resembles the French fish *loup de mer,* or *bar,* has become one of the most popular dishes in the great French restaurants in New York. It is often served as a main course in the spring, summer, and fall, and equally fre-quently as an hors d'oeuvre.

Poach the fish according to the Canadian cooking theory (page 12) and remove from the bouillon. Cool. Serve with a sauce grib-iche (pages 36–37), mayonnaise (page 34), or mustard sauce (page 23), and a wilted cucumber salad. With a chilled white wine, bread, and butter, it makes a superb luncheon or dinner dish. It is sometimes served with a garnish of lump crabmeat and the same sauce, giving it added luxury and glamour. Certainly it is one of the two or three greatest fish on the East Coast of the United States.

STRIPED BASS SALAD

Poach 3 pounds of striped bass fillets in boiling salted water according to the Canadian cooking theory (page 12). Dice the cooked fillets or flake with a fork. Combine with 1 cup of finely chopped celery and 1 cup of mayonnaise or Russian dressing.

Arrange on a bed of watercress. Decorate with additional mayonnaise, quartered hard-cooked eggs, strips of pimiento, green pepper, and ripe olives.

Sturgeon

This fine fish used to be plentiful on the West Coast, in the Great Lakes, and in some Eastern rivers. Now it is scarce indeed. Fishing for sturgeon is prohibited by law in many states, and you will rarely see a freshly caught specimen in the market. Its scarcity is a pity, for besides being delicious in itself, the American sturgeon is a source of excellent caviar.

Of all varieties, including the giants of the Columbia and Sacramento rivers, none compares in flavor and texture to the lake sturgeon. A considerable amount of smoked sturgeon is sold throughout the country. It is very expensive, but when you buy it you may console yourself with the thought that you are paying for a great delicacy.

BRAISED STURGEON

1 large onion, finely chopped
2 carrots, finely chopped
2 stalks of celery, finely chopped
4 sprigs of parsley, finely chopped
A pinch of thyme
Salt
Freshly ground black pepper
9 tablespoons butter

A few mushroom stems *or* peelings
1½ cups white wine
5-to-6-pound piece of sturgeon
3 tablespoons butter
2 tablespoons freshly grated horseradish
1 teaspoon sugar
2 tablespoons vinegar

Combine the onion, carrots, celery, parsley, thyme, salt and pepper to taste, and sauté in 6 tablespoons of the butter until soft. Transfer to a large braising pan or Dutch oven. Add the pan juices, the mushroom stems or peelings, and the wine. On a rack over this arrange the sturgeon and steam it in a 350° oven for about 1 hour. The container — braising pan or Dutch oven — must be sealed tightly. When the fish is cooked remove it to a hot platter and baste with the liquid from the pan.

Now, put the pan juices and the vegetables through a food mill, a fine sieve, or a food processor. Add 3 tablespoons of butter, the horseradish, and the sugar dissolved in the vinegar. Blend thoroughly, taste for seasoning, and pour over the fish. Serve with wild rice and mushrooms.

STURGEON SCANDINAVIAN

5-pound cut of sturgeon	Beurre manié (page 475)
Anchovy fillets	1 tablespoon anchovy paste
Bacon	¼ cup finely chopped sour
White wine court bouillon	pickles
(pages 19–20)	

Bone the sturgeon and replace the bone with anchovy fillets and pieces of bacon. Tie the fish securely.

Prepare the bouillon and soak the fish in it for 2 hours. Bring it to a boil. Remove all to a 425° oven and bake according to the Canadian cooking theory (page 8). Put the fish on a hot platter. Strain the sauce, reduce by two-thirds, and thicken with beurre manié. Add the anchovy paste and the pickles. Pour the sauce over the fish.

STURGEON STEAK SAUTÉ MEUNIÈRE

Dip sturgeon steaks in flour and season them with salt and freshly ground black pepper. For every 2 pounds of steak, melt 4 tablespoons of butter in a large skillet. Sauté the steaks gently according to the Canadian cooking theory (page 10), browning them nicely on both sides. Baste with butter during the process. Remove the fish to a hot platter and pour the butter over it. Sprinkle with chopped parsley and serve with lemon wedges and Béarnaise sauce (page 26).

BRAISED STURGEON, SWEET AND SOUR

4-pound piece of sturgeon	Salt
Larding pork	Freshly ground black pepper
3 onions, sliced thin	Bouquet garni: leek, stalk of
3 carrots, sliced thin	celery, bay leaf, thyme
2 cups white wine	

SAUCE

¼ cup vinegar	Green onions, sliced thin
½ cup brown sugar	Green peppers, sliced thin
3 tablespoons cornstarch	Pineapple chunks
Soy sauce	

Skin the sturgeon and tie it with pieces of larding pork. Place it on a rack in a braising pan or Dutch oven over the onions and carrots. Add the wine, salt and pepper to taste, and the bouquet garni. Cover and cook in a 425° oven according to the Canadian cooking theory (page 11). Remove the fish to a hot platter and make the sauce.

Sauce. Put the pan juices through a food mill or fine sieve. Return to the heat, add the vinegar, brown sugar, and the cornstarch mixed with a little of the broth. Stir until thickened. Season with soy sauce. Add the green onions, green peppers, and chunks of pineapple. Cook them just until well glazed. Pour over the fish.

Rice is a must with this dish.

COULIBIAC OF STURGEON

See coulibiac of salmon, pages 189–191.

STURGEON STEAKS WITH CREAM

2-inch-thick steaks	½ cup heavy cream
Salt pork *or* bacon	Beurre manié (page 475)
Finely chopped onion	Salt
2 cups white wine	Freshly ground black pepper
Butter	Cognac

Skin the steaks and tie them with salt pork or bacon. Arrange them on a bed of finely chopped onion in a gratin dish or baking pan and pour the wine over them. Butter the steaks well and cover the pan with a piece of buttered paper. Bake at 425° according to the Canadian cooking theory (page 8). Remove the fish to a hot platter. Add heavy cream to the pan juices and boil for five minutes to reduce. Put the sauce through a food mill or fine sieve and thicken if necessary with beurre manié. Taste for seasoning. Add a dash of cognac and pour over the fish.

My choice of accompaniment for this dish is wild rice or a rice pilaf baked in the oven with strong consommé. For salad, cucumbers in a sweet-sour sauce are ideal.

Caviar

True caviar, which is always gray, is the roe of the sturgeon and is one of the most expensive foods in the world.* The best-quality sturgeon caviar is priced at about $100 a pound. The gray roe of the whitefish and the red caviar, which comes from the salmon, are less expensive, but could never be called cheap.

Nowadays the finest caviar comes from Iran and the Soviet Union. Its quality is judged by the largeness of the eggs — the sevruga and the sterlet are regarded as the finest of all. Another

---

* Since the original writing of this book, caviar has become increasingly costly and, regrettably, has thus moved further and further from our purses.

test of quality is the amount of salt. The less salt, the better the caviar.

In the past, really excellent caviar came from the Great Lakes region and from the mouth of the Columbia River, but the present output is very small as a result of years of wholesale slaughter of sturgeon.

TO SERVE CAVIAR

Caviar is the perfect hors d'oeuvre. If you have the finest with practically no salt in it, store it at around 28° until you are ready to use it. About 2 ounces, or 2 good-sized spoonfuls, are considered an ample serving. My contention is that there is no better way to serve it than straight, with nothing save perhaps a little lemon juice, and some toast or dark bread.

Serve it in a glass bowl placed in another bowl full of chopped ice. Or, if you prefer, use a silver bowl. On very elaborate occasions caviar is sometimes served in ice carved into the figure of a swan or some other design. There are even special caviar bowls on the market for those who can afford to serve this great delicacy often.

The drink usually associated with caviar is vodka, straight, although many people prefer champagne. This is entirely a matter of personal taste.

If you wish to embellish the caviar serving there are certain accompaniments that are considered *de rigeur*. Besides the usual lemon, they include chopped hard-cooked egg — yolks and whites chopped separately; chopped raw onion; sour cream. Any or all of these are good, but I am definitely of the opinion that they are not needed unless the roe is exceedingly salty.

The perfect after-theater supper, or the perfect celebration of any special event, is certainly as much fresh caviar as you can afford along with toast, sweet butter, and champagne.

CAVIAR CANAPÉS

To serve caviar as canapés: Arrange a bowl of the roe surrounded by small bowls of chopped onions, chopped egg —
whites and yolks separate; quarters of lemon, and sour cream.
Have plenty of hot toast fingers, and let the guests spread their
own canapés. Or arrange fingers of toast topped with caviar on a
platter along with small dishes of the condiments, and pass the
platter. Be certain the canapés are fresh. There is no dish less
interesting than tired flabby dabs of food on cold, dank toast.

BLINIS WITH CAVIAR

This is one of the most popular hot hors d'oeuvres in Europe.
It should be made with the true caviar and served with sour
cream. Often, however, you will find it served with the red caviar
or herring.

1 package yeast	3 egg yolks
¾ cup milk	½ teaspoon salt
1 teaspoon sugar	⅓ cup cream, whipped
2 cups flour	3 egg whites, stiffly beaten
½ cup butter	

Dissolve the yeast in ¼ cup of the warm milk. Add the sugar.
Add the remaining ½ cup of lukewarm milk and the flour. Make
a paste of this, cover, and put in a warm place to rise until it is
doubled in bulk.

Cream together the butter, egg yolks, and salt. Combine this
with the sponge when it is risen, and beat thoroughly. Let it
rise again for 1 hour. Finally add the whipped cream and the
egg whites and let rise again for 15 minutes. Bake into small pancakes about 3 inches in diameter in a buttered pan or griddle.

Serve the cakes very hot with melted butter, caviar, and sour
cream. From 3 to 6 pancakes will make a serving.

CAVIAR OMELET

This is sheer luxury, but exceedingly delicious luxury. Prepare an omelet in your usual fashion. Fold in about 2 tablespoons of chilled caviar and serve with a dollop of sour cream on top.

TO SERVE RED CAVIAR

Red caviar, or salmon roe, is not so delicate as the caviar of the sturgeon, but it is excellent in appetizers. It may be used for canapés with chopped onion, sour cream, and chopped egg. Or make this dip of red caviar:

RED CAVIAR DIP

1 pint sour cream	1 teaspoon freshly ground
¼ cup cream *or* milk	black pepper
1½ cups red caviar	1 tablespoon lemon juice
1 small onion, grated	Chopped hard-cooked egg

Dilute the sour cream with cream or milk. Add the caviar, onion, pepper, and lemon juice. Heap in a bowl and sprinkle the top with the hard-cooked egg. Serve with raw vegetables, toast, or bread sticks.

RED CAVIAR CHEESE

Cream ½ pound cream cheese. When it is light and fluffy, add ½ cup red caviar, 1 tablespoon grated onion, and 1 teaspoon freshly ground black pepper. Season to taste with lemon juice and beat thoroughly with a fork. Serve with crackers or toast.

CAVIAR EGGS

This is a delightful hors d'oeuvre. For 6 servings:

6 hard-cooked eggs	1 tablespoon chopped parsley
6 tablespoons caviar (red *or* black)	1 tablespoon mayonnaise *or* sour cream
1 tablespoon chopped chives *or* green onion	1 teaspoon freshly ground black pepper

Shell the eggs, cut them in halves, and remove the yolks. Mash these well and combine with the remaining ingredients. When it is thoroughly whipped together, heap it into the whites with a spoon, or pipe it in, using the rosette end of a pastry tube.

For a first course, serve 2 halves per person. Arrange them on greens and pass a Russian dressing. Or double the recipe and serve it as a salad course with watercress, Russian dressing, and crisp French bread.

Surf Perch and Sea Perch

Sometimes called striped or blue perch, the surf perch is a small Pacific fish. I like it cooked simply and served with a good sauce, such as an olive sauce or a sweet-sour sauce.

The sea perch of the Atlantic is sometimes sold as frozen fillets, which can be cooked according to the recipes for ocean perch (pages 154–159). New England anglers, fishing off the rocks, often catch sea perch. It is a very bony fish to cook whole; however, it may be prepared in the same ways as the Pacific surf perch.

BROILED SURF PERCH

Broil the fish whole, following the directions on pages 9–10.

SAUTÉED SURF PERCH

Follow the directions for sautéing, page 10.

Swordfish

This continues to hold its place among the most popular fish marketed in the United States. Swordfish is caught on both the Atlantic and Pacific coasts and in most coastal waters around the world. For years we have imported it in large quantities, sometimes bringing in more poundage than is caught in American waters. Swordfish is a fine game fish and is eagerly sought by anglers.

The meat of the fish is firm, oily, and well flavored. It is sold mainly in steaks, sometimes in fillets. Usually it is served broiled with a variety of sauces, but it is also often baked or sautéed. The flesh tends to be dry if not basted often.

BROILED SWORDFISH

Swordfish steaks are large and will usually serve several people. The size of the steak — it can be cut from ½ to 2 inches thick — will depend on the number of servings you wish.

Brush the fish well with butter or oil and place it on an oiled rack about 2 inches from the flame. Broil according to the Canadian cooking theory (pages 9–10), basting with more butter or oil during the cooking process, and turning once. Be careful not to let the flesh become too dry.

Season to taste with salt and freshly ground black pepper and serve with lemon wedges, lemon butter, tarragon butter, parsley butter, or beurre noisette (pages 31–33). Excellent accompaniments are sautéed potatoes and a tart salad, such as celery in French dressing made with plenty of dry mustard. Cold broiled swordfish, served with a mayonnaise, is a great delicacy.

VARIATIONS

1. Baste the fish with a mixture of melted butter, white wine, and dried or fresh tarragon.

2. Marinate the fish for 1 hour in a mixture of lemon juice, chopped onion, olive oil, and basil. Baste with this sauce while broiling. Season and serve with crisp julienne potatoes and slices of raw onion and cucumber in vinaigrette sauce (page 36).

PLANKED SWORDFISH STEAKS

This is a festive dish for a dinner party.

Select 1 or 2 large steaks — about 5 to 6 pounds — for 6 people. Broil them as above, but remove them just before they are done. Arrange them on a hot hickory or oak plank and surround with a border of duchess potatoes and vegetables, as follows:

Mash or puree 8 large boiled or baked potatoes. Season to taste with salt and freshly ground pepper; add ¼ pound butter and the yolks of 3 eggs beaten with a little cream. The potatoes must be stiff enough to force through a pastry tube. Using the large rosette end of the tube, make a border of the potatoes around the edge of the plank. Then make strips, like spokes, of the potatoes running from the fish in the center out to the potato border. Fill the spaces between the spokes with green peas, julienne beets, tiny grilled tomatoes, and snap beans.

Sprinkle the top of the whole plank with paprika, dot with butter, season with salt and pepper, and run it under the broiler flame to brown slightly. Sprinkle with chopped parsley.

A sweet-sour cucumber salad is delicious with this, and needless to say, the addition of some good chilled white wine will make this dinner party one your guests will never forget.

BARBECUED SWORDFISH STEAK

This is an outstanding fish dish when cooked over charcoal and basted with a good tart sauce. But it's almost as good cooked indoors as outdoors.

Use your own special barbecue sauce, or try this one:

Barbecue Sauce

½ cup soy sauce
2 cloves garlic, chopped
4 tablespoons tomato sauce *or* catsup
2 tablespoons lemon juice
¼ cup chopped parsley

1 teaspoon finely powdered oregano
½ cup orange juice
1 teaspoon freshly ground black pepper

Mix the ingredients together and soak the swordfish steak in it for 2 hours before cooking. Brush or baste the fish with the sauce during the broiling. Serve with braised kidney beans, a hearty salad of greens, tomatoes, and onion rings, and a red wine.

SWORDFISH STEAK WITH PEPPER

2-inch-thick steak
Flour
2 teaspoons freshly ground black pepper

Oil
Butter
Salt
¼ cup white wine *or* sherry

Dredge the steak with flour and grind the pepper onto the surface. Press the pepper into the flesh of the fish with the heel of your hand. Brush with oil and sauté in 5 tablespoons of butter according to the Canadian cooking theory (page 10). Turn once during the cooking. Salt to taste and remove the steak to a hot platter. Add a little more butter to the pan and the wine. Swirl it around and pour it over the fish. Serve with lemon quarters, plain boiled new potatoes, and beets dressed with sour cream and dill.

VARIATION

Swordfish Steak with Rosemary. Follow the recipe above, but substitute dried or fresh rosemary for the pepper. The rosemary gives a rare and unusual flavor to the fish.

BAKED SWORDFISH STEAK

2 steaks, 1 inch thick	Salt
Flour	Freshly ground black pepper
Oil	1 cup white wine
Fresh dill	1 cup cream
Sliced onions	3 egg yolks
Butter	

Dust the steaks with flour and brush with oil. Place one in the bottom of a well-oiled baking dish. Spread it with a layer of dill and then a layer of onion slices. Dot with butter and season with salt and pepper. Top with the second steak, and dot this with butter and seasonings. Pour ½ cup of the wine into the pan and bake at 425° according to the Canadian cooking theory (page 8). Baste the fish several times during the cooking.

Remove the fish to a hot platter. Add the remaining ½ cup wine to the pan, bring it to a boil, and gradually stir in the cream mixed with the egg yolks. Stir until well thickened and smooth. Pour the sauce over the fish.

BAKED SWORDFISH WITH MUSHROOMS

2 steaks, 1 inch thick
Butter
Crumbs
3 cans of "broiled in butter" chopped mushrooms
2 tablespoons chopped shallots *or* onions

Salt
Freshly ground black pepper
½ cup white wine
1 cup cream
Beurre manié (page 475)

Place one steak in the bottom of an oiled baking dish. Spread the steak with butter and top with crumbs. Open 2 cans of chopped mushrooms and drain, saving the juice. Spread the mushrooms over the steak. Add the shallots or onions, salt and pepper to taste, and dot with butter. Top with the second steak, dot this with butter and season with salt and pepper. Add the wine to the mushroom liquid and pour over the fish. Bake at 425° according to the Canadian cooking theory (page 8), basting with the pan juices.

Remove the fish to a hot platter. Open the third can of mushrooms and add them to the pan juices. Add 1 cup of cream and thicken with beurre manié. Taste for seasoning and pour over the fish. Serve with crisp sautéed potatoes and braised endive. A chilled rosé is the perfect complement.

BAKED SWORDFISH CASTILIAN

4 green peppers, shredded
Olive oil
Salt
Freshly ground black pepper
1 teaspoon lemon juice
3 medium onions, chopped
3 cloves garlic, chopped

2 cups stewed *or* canned tomatoes
1 teaspoon oregano
1 tablespoon chili powder
2 tablespoons chopped parsley
Fresh coriander *or* cilantro
1 thick swordfish steak
Butter

Sauté the peppers in the oil, season to taste, and add the lemon juice. Sauté the onion and garlic in oil. Add the tomatoes, oregano, chili powder, parsley, and coriander (or cilantro, if available). Simmer for 25 minutes.

Place the steak in an oiled baking dish. Dot it with butter and season with salt and pepper. Bake at 425° according to the Canadian cooking theory (page 8). Pour the sauce over the fish, top it with the green peppers, and return it to the oven for 5 minutes to blend thoroughly. Serve with rice and sautéed eggplant.

Tautog (Blackfish)

This is a good game fish that is well known to sportsmen on the North and Middle Atlantic Coast. In New England it is known as tautog; elsewhere it is called blackfish, or sometimes black porgy or saltwater chub. It is usually caught near shore, since it is a fish that likes rocks and ledges. It is also fond of snooping around piers and old wrecks.

The tautog, or blackfish, is taken commercially from Cape Cod to Delaware Bay. The average fish weighs 2 to 3 pounds and is 12 to 18 inches long. The flesh is white, juicy, and has a pleasant flavor.

SAUTÉED TAUTOG

Clean and split the fish and sauté according to the directions on page 10.

BROILED TAUTOG

Broil according to the directions on pages 9–10.

BAKED TAUTOG

Bake tautog as you would striped bass (see page 269).

Tuna and Related Fish

This is a fish that I think is better canned than fresh. There are many varieties of tuna on both coasts, and all are robust game fish. The albacore, which has the true white meat, is the one used for the finest pack tunafish and for the most delicate dishes. The others are not so white, varying in color from a sort of amber to a purply red. Bonito is an important Pacific member of the family, all members of which are related to the mackerel.

Small tuna weigh 10 to 15 pounds, large ones up to 600 pounds. The fish is sold whole, in steaks, and in fillets.

Some smoked tuna is found here and there on the market, but other varieties of smoked fish are more popular.

Fresh Tuna

GRILLED TUNA WITH VARIOUS SAUCES

Marinate 1-inch-thick tuna steaks in olive oil flavored with garlic and lemon juice. Soak the fish for 1 hour before cooking. Grill the steaks over charcoal or in the broiler, basting well with additional oil. Cook according to the Canadian cooking theory (page 9), turning once. Season the steaks with salt and freshly ground black pepper, remove them to a hot platter, and serve with any of the following sauces; Hollandaise (pages 25–26), Béarnaise (page 26), lobster (page 21), shrimp (page 21), lemon butter (page 31), or parsley butter (page 33).

VARIATION

Marinate the fish in your favorite barbecue sauce and brush it with the sauce while it is grilling. Serve with sautéed potatoes and plenty of garlic bread to dunk into the sauce.

TUNA SAUTÉ AMANDINE

4 pounds tuna steaks	Salt
½ pound almonds	Freshly ground black pepper
6 tablespoons butter	2 tablespoons chopped parsley
Flour	Lemon wedges

Use 1-inch-thick tuna steaks. Blanch and sliver the almonds, or open a can of the chopped buttered almonds. Melt the butter, flour the fish lightly, and brown quickly in the butter. Salt and pepper them to taste. When you have turned the steaks, add the almonds and chopped parsley. Total cooking time will be 10 minutes per inch thickness. Add more butter to the pan if necessary. Remove the fish to a hot platter, pour the almonds and butter over the top, and surround with lemon wedges.

Serve with plain boiled potatoes.

SAUTÉED ALBACORE WITH TARRAGON AND WHITE WINE

1 albacore steak	1 teaspoon dried, *or* 1 table-
4 tablespoons butter	spoon fresh, tarragon
⅔ cup dry white wine	

Choose a good-sized albacore steak — about 1 inch thick or thicker. Melt the butter in a skillet, add the steak, and brown lightly on both sides according to the Canadian cooking theory (page 10), over fairly brisk heat. Add the white wine in which you have soaked the tarragon while the steak is browning. Let the wine cook down rapidly and spoon it over the fish. Remove the fish to a hot platter and pour the wine sauce over it.

Serve with tiny new potatoes smothered in butter and small glazed onions.

FRIED FINGERS OF TUNA

These are delicious for a luncheon dish. If you have the patience to cut the fingers very small, you can serve them as an appetizer with a good dunk sauce.

Cut tuna steaks into small fingers about 3 inches long and ½ inch through. Marinate these in oil for 1 hour. Dip them in flour, then in beaten eggs, and roll them in crumbs or corn meal. Fry in deep hot fat heated to 375°. They will take 5 minutes according to the Canadian cooking theory (page 11). Drain on absorbent paper, season with salt and pepper, and serve with tartar sauce (pages 35–36), sauce rémoulade (page 35), or sauce diable (page 29).

VARIATIONS

1. Mix grated Parmesan cheese and a good deal of chili powder in with the crumbs. Roll the fish in this, fry, and serve with a hot Mexican sauce.

2. Mix the crumbs well with sesame seeds. Roll the fish in this, fry, and serve with sauce diable.

3. Roll the fish in sesame seeds alone, fry, and serve with a sweet-sour sauce.

HELEN EVANS BROWN'S BAKED ALBACORE

4 pounds albacore steaks *or* fillets	½ cup olive oil
1 large onion, chopped	1 teaspoon salt
1 green pepper, chopped	1 teaspoon freshly ground black pepper
4 or 5 stalks of celery, chopped	1 teaspoon oregano
6 sprigs of parsley, chopped	1 cup red wine
1 large clove garlic, chopped	1 No. 2½ can of tomatoes

Sauté the onion, pepper, celery, parsley, and garlic in the olive oil. Season with salt, pepper, and oregano and add the wine and tomatoes.

Place the fish on a well-oiled baking dish and pour the sauce over it. Bake at 450° according to the Canadian cooking theory (page 8). Baste frequently during the cooking.

Serve it in the dish in which it was baked and pass plenty of sourdough bread with garlic butter or — if you live on the East Coast — garlic bread.

MARINATED ALBACORE

2 cups red wine	1 heaping teaspoonful of dried basil *or* several leaves of the fresh basil
2 cloves garlic, chopped	
1 or 2 leeks, cleaned and chopped	
1 or 2 stalks of celery, chopped	4-pound piece of albacore *or* other tuna
1 carrot, thinly sliced	4 tablespoons butter
1 teaspoon salt	Beurre manié (page 475)

Make a marinade of the wine, vegetables, and seasonings. Soak the fish in this for 6 hours. Remove the fish and strain it. Melt the butter in a skillet, add the vegetables from the marinade, and cook until they are just soft.

Oil a baking dish, place the vegetables on the bottom, and top with the fish. Dot it with butter and pour the wine around it. Bake at 450° according to the Canadian cooking theory (page 8), basting often during the cooking process. Remove the fish to a hot platter. Force the sauce through a fine sieve, return it to the stove, and thicken with beurre manié. Taste for seasoning.

POACHED TUNA WITH VARIOUS SAUCES

Since albacore has the lightest meat, it is, of course, the best of the various tunas for poaching.

Poach a 3- or 4-pound piece of tuna in court bouillon (page 18) according to the Canadian cooking theory (page 12). Serve with sauce Béarnaise (page 27) or oyster sauce (page 21).

COLD POACHED TUNA

Serve the poached fish cold with a good olive oil mayonnaise, sauce rémoulade (page 25), or Russian dressing (page 35).

Canned Tunafish

The finest canned tuna is the albacore, or all white meat solid pack. Tuna flakes, tuna hunks, and tuna bits in cans are excellent for salads and other dishes in which the fish must be cut up.

CANNED TUNA AS HORS D'OEUVRE

I think one of the finest first courses or luncheon dishes is a good can of tuna with some capers, some homemade mayonnaise, and crisp French bread and butter.

TUNA AS A COCKTAIL SPREAD

1 No. 1 can of tuna, mashed
½ cup capers
2 tablespoons mayonnaise

1 teaspoon paprika
2 tablespoons onion juice
3 egg whites, stiffly beaten

Blend all ingredients. Spread on fingers of toast and place under the broiler flame until lightly browned and puffy.

CURRY OF TUNAFISH

1 large onion, chopped
1 unpeeled apple, chopped
2 cloves garlic, chopped
6 tablespoons oil *or* butter
1½ tablespoons curry powder

½ cup water
1 cup tomato sauce
Salt
½ cup white wine
1½ cups canned tuna

Sauté the onion, apple, and garlic in oil or butter. Add the curry powder and blend well. Add the water and let it cook down. Gradually stir in the tomato sauce and blend thoroughly. Taste for seasoning. Stir in the wine and add the tunafish. Heat thoroughly. Serve with rice, chutney, French-fried onions, and chopped hard-cooked egg.

TUNAFISH PLATE

For each serving, arrange a bed of shredded greens topped with 1 small can of solid pack tuna broken into pieces. Garnish with paper-thin slices of onion, sliced hard-cooked egg, and capers. Serve mayonnaise separately.

TUNAFISH SAUCE FOR SPAGHETTI

This is an authentic Italian recipe. It is simple, but delicious.

¼ pound dried mushrooms	1 teaspoon basil
3 cloves garlic, chopped	Salt
¼ cup olive oil	Freshly ground black pepper
1½ cups tomato sauce	½ can of tuna, drained
	Chopped parsley

Soak the mushrooms in water for 2 hours. Sauté the garlic in olive oil for a few minutes. Add the tomatoes and simmer until thick. Add the mushrooms and basil, season to taste with salt and pepper, and add the tuna. Cook for 10 minutes. Serve over spaghetti or other pasta, and top with more pepper and chopped parsley.

SCALLOPED TUNAFISH

1½ cups cracker crumbs	1 teaspoon salt
1 cup celery, chopped fine	1 teaspoon freshly ground black
1 cup onion, chopped fine	pepper
2 cloves garlic, chopped fine	1½ cups tuna bits
1 green pepper, chopped fine	½ cup butter
½ cup parsley, chopped	2 eggs, lightly beaten

Use rather coarse cracker crumbs. Combine them with the chopped vegetables, seasonings, and tuna. Add the butter and eggs. Blend well and pour into a buttered casserole. Dot the top with butter and bake at 375° for 25 or 30 minutes.

TUNAFISH OMELET

Use ½ cup of flaked tuna for each omelet. Heat the fish in a little olive oil or butter, and season with onion juice and freshly ground black pepper. Make omelets according to your usual method and fold the hot tunafish into them. Garnish with chopped parsley, or parsley and chives mixed.

SALADE NIÇOISE

This will make a salad for 3 or 4 people or a first course for 6 people.

Arrange greens on a large platter. Open 2 cans of solid pack tunafish and place it in the center of the platter. Around the edge arrange fillets of anchovies (about 3 2-ounce cans), 6 small or 3 large tomatoes cut in wedges, onion rings, 6 hard-cooked eggs quartered, and strips of green pepper and pimiento. Garnish with chopped parsley and ripe olives and serve with sauce vinaigrette (page 36) or sauce gribiche (pages 36–37).

VARIATION

Sometimes sliced cooked potatoes and cooked green beans are added.

TUNA SALAD SUPREME

This will make a salad for 6 people.

Grate 2 heads of raw celery root. Add 2 7-ounce cans tunafish, 2 chopped hard-cooked eggs, 6 chopped green onions, and blend with a vinaigrette sauce (page 36) to which you have added 1 tablespoon prepared mustard, 1 teaspoon chopped parsley, and 1 teaspoon tarragon. Serve on endive spears or chicory. Garnish with ripe olives and pimiento strips.

OLD-FASHIONED TUNA SALAD

Combine 1½ cups tuna bits with ½ cup finely chopped celery, 8 chopped green onions, 2 tablespoons capers, and enough mayonnaise to bind the salad. Serve in a nest of romaine or lettuce. Garnish with mayonnaise, ripe olives, tomato wedges, and sliced hard-cooked eggs.

TUNA SALAD BUFFET PLATE

Make a good French potato salad: Pour white wine and olive oil over hot sliced potatoes; add slivered almonds, chopped chives, onions, and parsley; add a dash of vinegar and chill it well.

Make a Russian salad with finely cut cooked vegetables: peas, carrots, string beans, and potatoes bound together with mayonnaise.

Arrange greens on a long platter. In the center place a smoked whitefish, the tuna from 3 large cans, skinless and boneless sardines from 3 cans. Spoon the French potato salad and the Russian salad around the fish. Garnish with paper-thin slices of onion, quartered hard-cooked eggs, and wedges of tomato. Serve with a bowl of mayonnaise and a dish of fresh horseradish mixed with sour cream and dill.

Hard Swedish bread and a bottle of chilled white wine will make this a summer buffet of exceptional flavors.

Whitebait

These minnowlike fish are much discussed. Some experts say they are a mixture of various infant fish, while others claim they are a definite species. Who knows, who cares, and what can we do about it? They are wonderful eating.

When you sample whitebait for the first time, you may find it disconcerting to have a whole plateful of eyes staring up at you. I did. This initial reaction soon passes, and they become one of your favorite delicacies. They are often served with tiny oyster crabs, and when offered in this fashion at a smart restaurant they are definitely on the expensive side.

SAUTÉED WHITEBAIT

Use 1 to 1½ pounds of whitebait for 4 servings. Soak them in ice water for an hour or two. Drain them on a towel and roll in corn meal. Sauté them very quickly in olive oil, shaking the pan often to move the fish around, and shifting them carefully with a wooden spoon. Salt and pepper to taste and serve with a rémoulade (page 35) or tartar sauce (pages 35–36).

VARIATIONS
1. Serve with sautéed oyster crabs as a garnish.
2. Dust with flour instead of corn meal.

FRIED WHITEBAIT

Prepare whitebait as above and fry in deep fat heated to 375°. The fish will take about 15 seconds to cook — at the most a half minute. Drain on absorbent paper and season to taste.

VARIATION
Let the fish cook until very crisp. Sprinkle with a little cayenne and dry mustard and squeeze lemon juice over them.

WHITEBAIT PANCAKES

Wash and dry a pound of whitebait. Mix with the following:

3 eggs, lightly beaten
¼ cup chopped parsley
1 clove garlic, finely chopped
⅓ cup grated Parmesan cheese

1 teaspoon sweet basil
Salt
Freshly ground black pepper

Add enough flour to hold the fish and egg mixture together —
about 1 cup. Form into small cakes. Dust them lightly with flour
and fry in olive oil until browned on both sides. Serve with a
rémoulade (page 35) or tartar sauce (pages 35–36).

WHITEBAIT ITALIAN

1½ pounds whitebait
Corn meal
Olive oil
2 teaspoons grated onion
1 teaspoon salt

1 tablespoon paprika
4 eggs
4 tablespoons cream
½ cup grated Parmesan cheese

Wash the whitebait and roll them in corn meal. Sauté in olive
oil until just barely cooked through. Remove fish to an ovenproof serving platter or baking dish. Sprinkle over it the onion,
salt, and paprika. Beat the eggs well and add the cream and
cheese. Gently pour over the whitebait. Run under the broiler
for 3 or 4 minutes to set the eggs.

Whiting

Whiting, or silver hake, are caught off the coast of New England,
New York, and New Jersey, and as far south as Virginia. They

are most plentiful in the spring and the fall. The frozen product is shipped throughout the country and has a ready market, especially in "fish 'n' chips" shops.

The flesh is white and delicately flavored. It adapts well to nearly all forms of preparation. The average whiting is about 12 to 14 inches long, but occasionally one may reach 24 inches and weigh as much as 8 pounds. One small whiting is usually considered a portion.

GRILLED WHITING

Have small whiting — one per portion — split and dressed. Sprinkle with salt and freshly ground black pepper, brush with melted butter or oil, and grill about 4 inches from a medium flame according to the Canadian cooking theory for broiling (page 9). Baste often with butter or oil. Serve sprinkled with chopped parsley.

VARIATIONS
1. Serve with Hollandaise sauce (pages 25–26) or sauce Béarnaise (page 26).
2. Sprinkle the split whiting heavily with sesame seeds.
3. Grill as above, sprinkle with fried crumbs, and serve with lemon wedges.
4. Mix together ½ cup oil, ½ cup chopped parsley, 1 tablespoon paprika, and 1 teaspoon salt. Baste the fish with this mixture while it is cooking.

WHITING SAUTÉ MEUNIÈRE

Choose 1 small whiting per person and have it dressed. Cook according to directions for sauté meunière, page 10.

FRIED WHITING

The usual method is to remove the backbone from the whiting before frying in deep fat. Dip the fish in flour, then in beaten egg and milk, then roll well in crumbs or corn meal. Fry in fat heated to 375° according to the Canadian cooking theory (page 11). Drain on absorbent paper and season to taste. Serve with tartar sauce (page 36) or lemon wedges.

VARIATIONS

1. Mediterranean. Sauté 6 green peppers, cut in strips, in 6 tablespoons of olive oil until just tender. Season to taste; add 1 teaspoon of wine vinegar and swirl it around the pan. Deep-fry 4 whiting according to the directions above. Arrange them on a bed of the peppers and serve with rice pilaf and a tomato sauce.
2. Serve the fried fish with sautéed onion rings and fried parsley (page 253).
3. Serve the fried fish on a bed of eggplant slices that have been dipped in flour and sautéed in olive oil until nicely browned. Garnish with sautéed green peppers and grilled tomatoes. This combination of flavors is delicious.

POACHED WHITING

Poach whiting in boiling salted water according to the Canadian cooking theory (page 12). Be very careful not to overcook. Serve it with:

1. Melted butter, lemon, boiled potatoes, parsley.
2. Hollandaise sauce (pages 25–26), boiled potatoes, parsley.
3. Tomato sauce (page 23), sautéed potatoes.
4. Black butter (page 31), capers, lemon juice.

STUFFED ROLLED WHITING

6 whiting fillets
Fish forcemeat (page 41)
1½ cups sauce velouté (page 21)
Lemon juice

½ pound mushrooms
4 tablespoons butter
¼ cup chopped parsley

Stuff the fillets with the forcemeat, roll and pin with tooth-picks. Poach them in boiling salted water according to the Canadian cooking theory (page 12). Arrange them on a hot platter, cover with sauce velouté flavored with a little lemon juice, surround with mushroom caps sautéed in butter, and sprinkle with parsley.

WHITING CREOLE

2 tablespoons butter
1 onion, chopped
½ cup chopped celery
½ cup chopped green pepper
½ cup chopped pimiento
3 cups canned tomatoes

1 tablespoon cornstarch
2 tablespoons water
Salt
Freshly ground black pepper
Chopped parsley
6 small whiting

Melt the butter, add the onion, and let it brown lightly. Add the celery, pepper, and pimiento and sauté for a few minutes. Add the tomatoes; bring it to a boil and simmer for 1 hour. Mix the cornstarch and water, add it to the sauce and stir until thickened. Season to taste and add parsley. Put the fish in the sauce and let them cook according to the Canadian cooking theory for braising (page 11).

Yellowtail

The Pacific Coast yellowtail is a juicy fish with a rather heavy texture, but with a really pleasant flavor. It is a good game fish, always plentiful in the spring and early summer.

Yellowtail is sold in the markets whole, or as fillets or steaks.

BROILED YELLOWTAIL

For broiling, select steaks 1½ to 2 inches thick. It is a good idea to marinate them before broiling. Try a marinade of olive or peanut oil and white wine or sherry. Soak the steaks for 1 hour, and baste them with this sauce during the broiling process. Follow the Canadian cooking theory for broiling (pages 9–10). Serve with lemon butter (page 31), parsley butter (page 33), anchovy butter (page 32), or a dill sauce (page 23).

BAKED YELLOWTAIL

Yellowtail steaks	Chopped parsley
Salt	Chopped chives *or* green onions
Freshly ground black pepper	Butter
Chopped tarragon	1 cup white wine

Arrange the steaks in an oiled baking dish. Season to taste with salt and pepper. Sprinkle with chopped tarragon, parsley, and chives or green onions. Dot with butter and add the wine to the pan. Bake at 425° according to the Canadian cooking theory (page 8). Baste with the pan juices during the cooking process. Serve with tarragon butter mixed with the juices from the pan.

Freshwater Fish

Bass

The name "bass" means different things to different people. When you think of catching or eating a bass, the way you picture the fish in your mind depends upon where you live or possibly upon the memory of your youthful experiences as an angler.

Bass is usually described by a qualifying word, such as small-mouthed, large-mouthed, spotted, striped, black, white, rock, and calico, not to mention many local names, or to reckon with the fact that some of the qualifying terms apply to the same fish or to other fishes that are not bass at all. To add to the confusion, there are some marine fishes called bass.

To simplify the matter of freshwater bass, I shall make only these generalizations: Bass are members of a large voracious family of fishes that includes the sunfish and the crappie; most bass are good game fishes; they are abundant, widely distributed, and well adapted to pond culture.

The small-mouthed bass, a lively game fish, is found in the streams and lakes of the northern and central states. It weighs from 3 to 4 pounds. The spotted bass, somewhat smaller, inhabits the same general area.

The large-mouthed bass, sometimes called a black crappie, prevails in the central and southern states. Less lively than its small-mouthed relative, it usually weighs about 3 pounds but has been known to attain very impressive weights.

The rock bass, sometimes called red-eyed or goggle-eyed, is a common game fish in the Great Lakes region, Mississippi Valley, and in eastern and southern states. It is thick-bodied, meaty, and averages about 10 inches in length. It likes shadowy spots and is actually not much of a fighter.

BROILED BASS

Small whole bass or larger ones split can be broiled and served with lemon butter (page 31), tartar sauce (pages 35–36), or any of the favorite fish sauces. Follow the directions for broiling on pages 9–10).

PAN-FRIED BASS

Small bass may be pan-fried as you would crappies (see page 322).

BAKED BASS

Clean and wash the bass, place it on an oiled baking dish, dot with butter, and season with salt and pepper. Bake at 450° according to the Canadian cooking theory (page 8). Baste the fish frequently during the cooking process.

Serve with parsley butter (page 33), lemon butter (page 31), or with your favorite fish sauce.

Bluegill Sunfish

Most states prohibit commercial fishing of the bluegill sunfish, reserving it for the benefit of sportsmen. It is a delightful pond fish, highly prolific, and has been artificially propagated over a wide area. The flesh is firm, flaky, and of good flavor. A bluegill rarely weighs over 1 pound, but it is game for its size and fairly amusing as a sport fish.

Occasionally you may hear anglers refer to the bluegill and to other sunfishes as "bream," a name that is also applied sometimes to such unrelated saltwater fishes as ocean perch or rosefish, and to porgy or scup. At any rate, the bluegill sunfish and any fresh-water fish called bream may be cooked by following the recipes for crappies (page 322).

Bowfin

The bowfin is a prehistoric holdover. It sometimes breathes air, a faculty it developed in the Devonian period when severe droughts made life tough for fish. In fact, it is claimed that when droughts occur in the South, live bowfins can go underground and breathe air.

The bowfin is practically never prepared fresh. It needs much careful attention and skilled cookery. Smoked bowfin is superb. It should be approached with a good appetite.

Buffalo Fish

There are different varieties of this fish in the Middle West — the common buffalo, sometimes called the redmouth and the big-mouth; the round or prairie buffalo, also called the rooter; and the small-mouthed buffalo.

This fish is less bony than the carp and has an excellent flavor. Many people prefer it to carp, feeling that the somewhat musty taste of the latter is unpleasant.

A great deal of smoked buffalo fish is available in the East and

Middle West. It is more delicate than smoked carp and a delicious change in the smoked fish field.

You may prepare buffalo fish in the same way you prepare carp.

Burbot

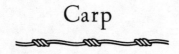

The burbot is the one freshwater member of the cod family. It has a slight beard and fins that resemble those of the cusk. Burbot liver oil is one of the most valuable sources of vitamin A, and the fish itself is fine eating. It is found in northern waters.

Prepare burbot in any of the ways suggested for cod or haddock.

Carp

This fish has a splendid literary background. There are many references to it in fables and stories, and its long history includes an Asiatic origin followed by plantings in Europe and America. American carp have been known to weigh as much as 60 pounds, and I have seen even larger ones in Europe. I remember especially a magnificent carp that I saw fished out of a pond on an estate in France. After it had been cooked and wonderfully decorated, it was placed on a plank. It was so large that it took two maids, carrying it between them, to bring it to us.

Carp are sometimes transported to market in tanks. Some are sold filleted, and pieces are occasionally available, but the usual thing is to find the carp whole. It is a very scaly fish and should be carefully prepared. Some people object to its rather muddy flavor. This can be overcome by the seasoning and by bleeding the fish completely before cleaning it.

CARP FILLET, SPENCER METHOD

Mary Evelene Spencer, who was a government food expert many years ago, developed a form of fish cookery that has been known since as the Spencer Method. Any fillets may be cooked this way, but I think that it applies particularly well to the carp. The following recipe is for four people.

Cut 4 fillets of carp into serving portions. Fill a shallow pan with salted milk and a large flat plate with dry bread crumbs. Dip the fillets into the milk and then into the crumbs, being sure that the crumbs cover both sides of the fish. Lay the fillets on a well-buttered baking sheet and pour 3 tablespoons of melted butter or bacon fat on each one. Heat the oven to 550° and place the pan near the top of the oven. Bake for 10 to 12 minutes. Remove the fillets to a hot platter and serve with quarters of lemon or tartar sauce (pages 35–36).

This method is intended to achieve a fine crust on the outside and tender moist fish inside. You'll find it is amazingly good.

OVEN-BRAISED CARP FILLETS PROVENÇALE

2 medium onions, coarsely chopped	1 teaspoon salt
Oil	1 teaspoon freshly ground black pepper
4 carp fillets	1 cup red wine
Flour	Tomato sauce (about 1 cup)
2 cloves garlic, chopped	18 to 20 ripe olives
½ cup chopped parsley	Steamed rice
Dried thyme	

Place the onions on a well-oiled baking pan. Dip the fillets in flour and arrange them on the onions. Sprinkle with the garlic, parsley, thyme, salt, and pepper. Add the wine, and then drizzle olive oil all over the fish. Top each fillet with 3 tablespoons of tomato sauce. Bake at 425° according to the Canadian cooking theory (page 8), basting often with the wine in the pan. Remove to a hot serving platter. Blend the sauce in the pan with 3 or 4 more tablespoons of tomato sauce and add the ripe olives. Pour the sauce around the fish and serve with steamed rice.

CARPE AU BLEU

The small fish are sometimes cooked like trout, in a vinegar and water bouillon. Serve them with melted butter, sauce gribiche (pages 36–37), or vinaigrette (page 36) and a boiled potato.

ALSATIAN CARP WITH SAUERKRAUT

4 pounds sauerkraut	Flour
4 cloves garlic	Butter *or* bacon fat
1 tablespoon coarsely ground black pepper	Grated Gruyère *or* Cheddar cheese
4 cups beer	Sour cream
4 carp fillets	Buttered crumbs

Steam the sauerkraut mixed with the garlic, black pepper, and beer for 4 to 6 hours in a covered dish over low heat.

Flour the fillets and sauté them in butter or bacon fat according to the Canadian cooking theory (page 10).

Arrange a layer of the sauerkraut in the bottom of a well-buttered baking dish, then add a layer of grated cheese, then a layer of the fish covered with sour cream; repeat these layers and top with a layer of the kraut. Add 2 cups of beer or liquid from the sauerkraut, sprinkle with grated cheese and buttered crumbs. Dot with butter and bake at 350° for 30 minutes.

BAKED CARP, HUNGARIAN STYLE

4-pound carp	2 large onions, thinly sliced
Salt	4 to 6 tablespoons fat
Freshly ground black pepper	Oil
Paprika	Sour cream

Clean and prepare the carp for baking. Season the inside with the salt, pepper, and 1 tablespoon of paprika.

Sauté the onions in fat until they are just tender but not colored. Spread them on the bottom of a well-oiled baking dish and place the carp on top. Brush the fish with oil, sprinkle heavily with paprika, cover with sour cream, and sprinkle again with paprika. Bake at 450° according to the Canadian cooking theory (page 8).

Serve with buttered noodles mixed with poppy seeds and sprinkled with a little grated cheese.

BRAISED CARP MEXICAN

4-to-6-pound carp	½ cup chicken broth *or*
2 medium onions, chopped	white wine
2 cloves garlic, chopped	Salt
5 tablespoons olive oil	Sesame seeds
2 tablespoons chili powder	Chopped buttered almonds

Clean, scale, and split the fish and remove the backbone.

Sauté the onions and garlic in the oil until soft and lightly colored. Add the chili powder and the broth or wine, salt to taste, and blend well.

Place the fish on a well-oiled baking dish or pan, spread the chili-onion mixture over the flesh of the fish, and brush with oil. Bake at 425° according to the Canadian cooking theory (page 8). Sprinkle with sesame seeds and the chopped almonds. Run under the broiler for 3 or 4 minutes to brown the seeds and nuts. Serve with cornmeal mush crisply fried with salt pork or bacon.

CARPE DE CAHORS

This is a delicious recipe from my friend Madame Pannetrat.

3-pound carp	Salt
3-egg omelet fines herbes	Freshly ground black pepper
(parsley, chives, tarragon, or	1 cup white wine
your own choice)	1 cup cream
Chopped shallots *or* scallions	3 egg yolks

Clean and split the carp.

Prepare the omelet and roll it into the fish as stuffing. Sew up the carp and place it on a bed of chopped shallots or onions in a well-oiled baking dish. Salt and pepper the fish and add the wine. Bake at 425° according to the Canadian cooking theory (page 8). Remove the fish to a hot platter and take out the string or thread that you used to secure it. Strain the pan juices and force the onion through a fine sieve or a food processor. Reduce the juices slightly and add the cream mixed with the egg yolks; stir until thick but do not let it boil. Taste for seasoning and pour the sauce around the fish.

PÂTÉ CHAUD DE CARPE

This is an elaborate dish for a buffet party or a magnificent first course for a special dinner party at which you wish to display your prowess as a cook.

Puff paste	½ cup cream
4-pound carp	4 egg yolks
Salt	1 teaspoon rosemary
Freshly ground black pepper	⅓ cup mixed chopped herbs
1 medium onion, sliced	(chives, parsley, and the like)
1 carrot, sliced	1 cup dry bread crumbs
Parsley	4 tablespoons butter
2 cups white wine	

Prepare puff paste from any good recipe.

Clean the carp and place it on a well-oiled baking dish. Salt and pepper to taste and add the onion, carrot, a few sprigs of parsley, and the wine. Bake at 425° according to the Canadian cooking theory (page 8), basting frequently. When the fish is cool enough to handle, remove the bones and the skin and add them to the liquid in the pan. Reduce the liquid to 1 cup. Strain and return to the stove. Add the cream mixed with the egg yolks and cook over low heat, being sure it does not boil, until the sauce is thickened.

Mix the rosemary, herbs, bread crumbs, and blend in the butter.

Roll out the puff paste and cover the bottom of a round pan or pie plate with a layer of the paste. Add the crumbs and herb mixture. Sprinkle with salt and pepper. Add the fish, cut into good-sized pieces, and top these with the sauce. Cover all with a crust of puff paste. Cut 2 vents in the top and bake at 450° for 12 minutes. Reduce the heat to 350° and continue baking until the paste is nicely browned and cooked through.

Cut into wedges or squares and serve very hot.

CARPE À LA CHAMBORD

This is a simplification of one of the most elaborate dishes in all cookery. Over the years many variations of it have been created, but this I feel is the best.

Fish forcemeat (page 41)
4-to-6-pound carp
Salt pork
2 medium onions, finely chopped
3 carrots, finely chopped

3 stalks of celery, finely
  chopped
4 tablespoons butter
Red wine and water *or* fish
  broth
Beurre manié (page 475)

Prepare the forcemeat.

Clean and scale the carp and stuff it with the forcemeat. Sew it up securely and cover it with strips of salt pork, tying them well around the fish.

Cook the onions, carrots, and celery in the butter for 8 minutes. Place in the bottom of a well-buttered fish cooker or Dutch oven and put the fish on top. Now pour in a mixture of red wine and fish broth or water — ⅔ wine to ⅓ water or broth. Fill up to two-thirds the thickness of the fish. Cover and bake at 425° according to the Canadian cooking theory (page 8). Remove the fish to a hot platter dressed either with a bed of rice or a croustade that is large enough to be a base for the whole fish.

Reduce the sauce, strain it through a fine sieve, and check for seasoning. Thicken it with a little beurre manié. Serve the sauce separately.

Garnish the fish generously with cooked mushroom caps; quenelles, if you feel like taking the trouble to make them; truffles, if available; or crawfish. This is a classic dish and will win you a round of applause when it reaches the table.

MARINATED CARP

3-to-4-pound carp
1 large onion, chopped
¼ cup chopped parsley
1 piece of chopped fresh ginger
   or 1½ teaspoons powdered
3 tablespoons oil
Salt

Freshly ground black pepper
⅔ cup white wine
Beurre manié (page 475)
2 egg yolks
4 tablespoons cream
1 tablespoon lemon juice

Clean the carp and place it in a steamer or fish boiler. Add the onion, parsley, ginger, and oil to the fish. Cover and let it stand for 3 hours. Turn the fish from time to time.

Add salt and pepper to taste and the wine, and poach the fish according to the Canadian cooking theory (page 12). When it is done, remove it to a serving dish. Thicken the sauce with beurre manié. Stir in the egg yolks mixed with the cream and blend well, but do not let it boil. At the last minute, stir in the lemon juice. Pour the sauce over the fish and serve with Lyonnaise potatoes heavily laced with parsley.

COLD CARP WITH VARIOUS SAUCES

Serve poached carp cold with:

1. Mayonnaise (page 34)
2. Sauce rémoulade (page 35)
3. Sauce verte (page 34)

Garnish cold carp with cucumbers, tomatoes, salade Russe, olives, truffles, greens. Or, if you like, you may put the cold carp in an aspic (see salmon in aspic, pages 198–201).

SWEET AND SOUR CARP, JEWISH FASHION

This is one of the oldest recipes for carp. Sometimes it is made without the addition of the vinegar and raisins, but it is almost invariably served cold.

4-to-5-pound carp	1 bay leaf
⅔ cup olive oil	Pinch of thyme
3 or 4 shallots, chopped	2 cloves garlic, crushed
2 large onions, chopped	¾ cup olive oil
4 tablespoons flour	2 tablespoons chopped parsley
1 pint white wine	½ cup seedless raisins
1 pint water	½ cup currants *or* sultana
1 teaspoon salt	raisins
Few grains cayenne pepper	⅓ cup wine vinegar
Bit of nutmeg	2 tablespoons brown sugar

Cut the carp into 2-inch slices. Heat the ⅔ cup of olive oil in a large skillet or deep Dutch oven. Add the shallots and onions to the oil. When they are soft add the flour and blend thoroughly. Gradually stir in the wine and water; continue stirring until thickened. Add the salt, cayenne, and nutmeg. Bring to a boil; then add the pieces of fish, the bay leaf, thyme, and garlic. Simmer according to the Canadian cooking theory for braising (page 11). Remove the carp and arrange it on a long deep serving dish.

Now reduce the sauce over a medium flame to a third of its volume. With a whisk or electric mixer at medium speed or in a blender beat in the ¾ cup of olive oil as you would if making mayonnaise. When thoroughly blended, add the parsley, raisins, currants, vinegar, and sugar. Pour over the carp and chill thoroughly.

POACHED CARP WITH VARIOUS SAUCES

Poach whole carp in court bouillon (page 18). Serve with:

1. White wine sauce (page 23)
2. Hollandaise sauce (pages 25–26)
3. Sauce duxelles (page 27)
4. Shrimp sauce (page 21)
5. Lobster sauce (page 21)
6. Sauce Béarnaise (page 26)

POTTED CARP

This is an old Central European dish that has a flavor entirely different from that of most fish dishes.

4 carrots, thinly sliced	Flour
8 gingersnaps	Salt
½ cup sherry	Freshly ground black pepper
4 carp fillets	Butter

Blanch the carrots until they are just tender. Soak the gingersnaps in the wine. Butter a large skillet that can be covered. Dip the fillets in flour and arrange them in the pan. Salt and pepper lightly, top with the carrots and their cooking water, and the sherry-gingersnap mixture. Cover, bring to a boil, and simmer according to the Canadian cooking theory for braising (page 11). Serve with steamed rice and a crisp green salad.

GEFILTE FISH

5 to 6 medium-large onions
4 pounds fish (buffalo, whitefish, carp, pike, or a mixture), including heads and bones
Salt
Freshly ground black pepper

1 bay leaf
4 to 5 eggs
1½ slices bread (soaked in water)
5 to 6 carrots

Chop 2 of the onions very coarsely, place them in a large pot, add the fish heads and bones, water to cover, and bring to a boil. Add 1 or 2 tablespoons salt and simmer this to make fish stock while you prepare the fish. Grind the cleaned and skinned fish with the rest of the onions. Mix them together, chop them in a large bowl, pound them in a mortar, or put them through the food processor until they are thoroughly blended. Salt and pepper to taste. Beat the eggs slightly and add to the mixture gradually. Add the bread, which has been soaked for an hour or so, and pound again until thoroughly smooth.

Scrape the carrots and cut them into rather thick slices. Strain the broth and bring to a boil. Shape the fish mixture into egg-sized balls and drop them, with the carrot slices, into the boiling broth. If the broth has cooked down too much, add a bit more water. Simmer for 1 to 1½ hours. Cool in broth. Remove the fish balls and strain the broth. Clarify it with egg whites and shells (page 18), if you wish. Chill the broth and fish overnight in the refrigerator. Serve garnished with a slice of carrot and the jellied broth as a sauce. Grated horseradish and beet salad go well with this dish.

SMOKED CARP

Smoked carp is served a great deal as an appetizer, as a luncheon dish, or with salad. It has a rather nice texture, though not so delicious as smoked sturgeon or so delicate as smoked whitefish.

Catfish

Even though you may never have eaten catfish, you most certainly know someone who has. Commercially, over 10,000,000 pounds are consumed each year, and many millions more are carried home by individual anglers. Despite the impressive quantities, catfish remains an inland dish. It is rarely sold in coast markets.

Common sorts of catfish are the channel cat, blue cat, spotted or fiddler cat, yellow or goujon, and the differently designed bullhead or horned pout. These vary in size from 1 to 50 pounds or more, but none equals the European catfish, which, in full sail, may weigh over 400 pounds.

For flavor, the best American catfish is the spotted or fiddler cat, which runs around 5 pounds and is found everywhere in the Mississippi Valley — as far south as Mexico and as far north as the Great Lakes. Catfish must be skinned before cooking. Draw a sharp knife around the fish just in back of the gills and strip off the skin by hand or with tweezers.

Catfish are oily and lend themselves to many different forms of cookery. They are sold whole or skinned and dressed.

SAUTÉED CATFISH

Small-sized catfish may be sautéed as for sauté meunière (page 10).

PAN-FRIED CATFISH

Use either the whole fish or pieces of fish. It is customary to use lard or oil for frying in this manner — which actually is not pan-frying, but semi-deep-frying. Dip the fish in milk, then in crumbs or corn meal. Cook rapidly in the skillet in fat about 1 inch deep. Season to taste.

FRIED CATFISH

Deep-fried catfish is probably the most usual method of preparation. Use either the whole fish or pieces of fish.

Heat the fat in your deep fryer to 375°. Beat 2 eggs lightly. Roll out bread or zwieback crumbs or use corn meal. Dip the fish in flour, then in beaten egg, and roll in the crumbs. Fry according to the Canadian cooking theory (page 11). Drain and season to taste. Serve with tartar sauce (pages 35–36), rémoulade (page 35) or mustard sauce (page 23).

POACHED CATFISH

Catfish may be poached in salted boiling water or in a court bouillon (page 18). Serve it with lemon butter (page 31) or with Hollandaise (pages 25–26), Béarnaise (page 26), or lobster sauce (page 21).

It may be served cold with mayonnaise (page 34) or rémoulade (page 35).

CATFISH HEAD SOUP

This is a great favorite in the South.

2 or 3 good-sized catfish heads	A few sprigs of parsley
1 onion stuck with 1 clove	6 cups water
1 carrot	1 tablespoon salt
1 leek	½ teaspoon thyme

Wash the catfish heads well and let the tap water run over them. Place them in a saucepan with the onion stuck with a clove, the carrot, leek, and parsley. Add the water and bring it to a boil. Add the salt and thyme and simmer for 45 to 60 minutes. Remove the heads and take the meat from the bones. You may use this in the soup or serve it the next day in a soufflé or creamed fish dish — any of your favorite ways of using leftover fish.

Strain the broth and taste for seasoning. Serve any of the following ways:

1. Add 1 cup of finely chopped carrots and string beans cooked for 12 minutes in boiling salted water.

2. Add ½ cup of finely broken noodles. Cook these in the broth for 12 minutes.

3. Add the meat from the catfish heads and chopped parsley and grated cheese.

4. Prepare a recipe of fish forcemeat (page 41) and drop small balls of it into the boiling broth. Let them poach for 15 minutes, or until the tiny dumplings are cooked through.

NOTE: Catfish may be used in any of the fish stews or in bouillabaisse (pages 42–43).

Chub

The varieties of chub, which is a member of the whitefish family, are known mainly for their excellence as smoked fish. The fish resembles whitefish, of course, but is smaller and thinner. The flesh is extremely soft.

Prepare chub as you would whitefish.

Crappies

Crappies are seldom taken commercially because of state prohibitions. An excellent pan fish, they are caught frequently by sportsmen. They propagate readily, and in sections where fish is scarce they are sometimes planted in ponds and used for individual family consumption.

The crappie is a small fish, seldom weighing more than a pound or exceeding a foot in length. The white crappie, also known as the chinquapin or white perch, is found in New England and down the Mississippi Valley. The black crappie, also known as the strawberry bass, is found in almost the same section.

BROILED CRAPPIES

The usual portion is one crappie to a person. Oil the fish well, or brush it with melted butter, and broil according to the directions on pages 9–10.

CRAPPIES SAUTÉ MEUNIÈRE

See directions on page 10.

PAN-FRIED CRAPPIES

When pan-frying crappies, it is probably better to remove the heads and tails of the fish. Clean them well, run the fins, and wash thoroughly. Dip them in flour, then in milk, and roll them in crumbs or corn meal. Sauté in butter, oil, or bacon fat according to the Canadian cooking theory (page 10). Serve with tartar sauce (pages 35–36) or lemon wedges.

Lake Herring

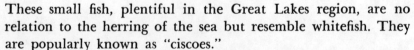

These small fish, plentiful in the Great Lakes region, are no relation to the herring of the sea but resemble whitefish. They are popularly known as "ciscoes."

Some of the lake herring catch is sold salted, and much of it is smoked. The smoked fish is exceedingly good; the texture is delicate. Altogether, lake herring is deservedly popular and is one of the most important freshwater catches.

Lake herring sold fresh in the market average ½ to 1 pound.

Any of the recipes for small trout (pages 336–344) and smelt (pages 229–232) can be followed in preparing them.

Pike and Pickerel

Among the well-known varieties of pike are the common pike, the pickerel, and, most of all, the huge muskellunge. All varieties are popular as sport fish.

The pike is a fierce and voracious fish, even devouring small waterfowl and mammals, and it puts up a strong fight when hooked. Like many fish popular with anglers, it has special local names: lake pickerel, grass pike, jack pike, great northern pike. It is abundant from New York to the mouth of the Ohio River and thence northward to Alaska. Some varieties of pike often weigh up to 25 pounds, but the average market weight is 1½ pounds to 10 pounds.

Eastern pickerel, called chain pickerel in the North and jack pickerel in the South, is well known to anglers east of the Alleghenies. It can grow to 8 pounds, but the average size is a 22-inch fish weighing 2 to 3 pounds.

There are innumerable ways of cooking pike, but it has often seemed to me that not enough care is taken to bring out its fine flavor and texture.

BROILED PIKE

You may broil either the steaks, the fillets, or the boned and split whole fish. Pike is a lean fish, however, and I do not believe broiling is the best method of preparing it. If you do broil it, be sure to lubricate it well during the cooking with butter or oil. Follow the general rules for broiling on pages 9–10. Serve with

maître d'hôtel butter, lemon butter, or parsley butter (pages 31–
33).

BAKED STUFFED PIKE

2 cups cracker crumbs	1 teaspoon salt
½ cup chopped celery	Heavy dash of cayenne pepper
½ cup chopped onion	1 teaspoon dry mustard
¼ cup chopped green pepper	½ cup melted butter
½ cup crabmeat	5-to-6-pound pike
3 eggs	Strips of salt pork

Make a stuffing of the crumbs, chopped vegetables, crabmeat,
eggs, seasonings, and melted butter. Clean the fish and stuff it
with this mixture. Sew it up and place on an oiled baking dish
or pan. Top with strips of salt pork and bake at 425° according
to the Canadian cooking theory (page 8).

Serve with a crabmeat sauce (page 21), saffron rice, and
cooked chopped spinach seasoned with garlic, nutmeg, and
butter.

BRAISED STUFFED PIKE

5-pound pike	3 eggs
½ cup chopped onion	4 tablespoons melted butter
4 tablespoons butter	Strips of salt pork
½ pound smoked ham, ground	White wine
2 cups dry bread crumbs	Beurre manié (page 475)
½ cup chopped parsley	2 egg yolks, slightly beaten
½ teaspoon thyme	Lemon juice
1 teaspoon salt	Parsley
1 teaspoon freshly ground black pepper	

Clean the fish and prepare for stuffing. Sauté the chopped onions
in 4 tablespoons of butter until soft. Combine with the ham,
crumbs, parsley, thyme, salt, pepper, eggs, and the melted butter.

Stuff the fish with this mixture and sew it up. Place it in a shallow baking pan with enough white wine to cover the bottom of the pan well. Top the fish with strips of salt pork and bake at 425° according to the Canadian cooking theory (page 8). Baste occasionally, and cover the pan after the first 15 minutes of cooking. When the fish is done, remove the salt pork and arrange the stuffed pike on a platter.

Strain the pan juices and thicken with beurre manié. Stir in the egg yolks and continue stirring until well blended. Do not let the sauce boil. Check for seasoning; add a dash of lemon juice and plenty of chopped parsley. Pour the sauce over the fish.

QUENELLES DE BROCHET I

These have been great favorites in France for many years. They are not simple to make, and they must be done properly or they are not good.

1 cup boiling milk	¼ teaspoon nutmeg
3 cups soft bread crumbs	1 cup creamed butter
1 pound of pike	2 eggs
1 teaspoon salt	4 or 5 egg yolks
1 grind fresh black pepper	

Pour the boiling milk over the bread crumbs and let the crumbs stand until the milk is entirely absorbed. Mix them well with a wooden spoon until they are practically a paste. Place this over the lowest flame on your stove and dry it out, working it all the time with the wooden spoon. Spread it out on a flat pan and let it cool thoroughly.

Put the pike through the fine grinder twice or chop in the food processor. Then work it in a mortar, or put it in a heavy bowl and work it with a wooden spoon. Add the salt, pepper, and nutmeg and blend thoroughly. Turn it out on a board, combine it with a crumb mixture, and mix well with your hands. Return it to the mortar or bowl, add the creamed butter, and continue blending until it is smooth and thoroughly mixed. Gradually work in the eggs and additional egg yolks. Put the mixture through a fine sieve or a food mill and work it again with a wooden spoon until it has a smooth and silky texture.

Form into flat oval cakes about the size of an egg or a little larger and arrange them in a buttered skillet so that they barely touch one another. Cover them with boiling salted water and poach gently for about 10 minutes. Remove the cooked quenelles to absorbent paper. Serve them with a rich cream sauce (page 23), shrimp sauce (page 21), lobster sauce (page 21), sauce Mornay (page 22), or Hollandaise (pages 25–26).

VARIATIONS

1. Arrange the quenelles on a bed of spinach, top with sauce Mornay, sprinkle with grated cheese, and run under the broiler for a few minutes.

2. Prepare a white wine sauce (page 23). Add small sautéed onions, sautéed mushrooms, and chopped parsley. Add the quenelles to the sauce and heat thoroughly.

QUENELLES DE BROCHET II

This recipe for quenelles may be a little simpler than the one above.

½ cup hot water	6 ounces kidney fat, finely
¾ cup butter	chopped
½ cup flour	Salt
¼ teaspoon salt	Freshly ground black pepper
2 eggs	Nutmeg
1 pound of pike	3 egg whites
	½ cup heavy cream

Put the hot water and ¼ cup of the butter in saucepan. When the butter is melted and the water boiling, add the flour and salt sifted together and stir with a wooden spoon until the mixture leaves the sides of the pan and forms a ball in the middle. Remove from the heat and continue beating with the spoon, or use an electric beater. Cool for 10 minutes. Add the eggs, one at a time, and continue beating until the mixture is waxy and smooth. Cool.

Put the fish through the fine grinder several times, pound it in a mortar, or use a food processor. Work it well in a heavy bowl with a wooden spoon. Gradually add the kidney fat and the pâte à choux (the butter, flour, and egg mixture that you prepared). Season with salt, pepper, and nutmeg. Work in the egg whites, the remaining ½ cup butter, and the cream. Work the mixture thoroughly until it is smooth and satiny. Chill for 24 hours.

Form into small oval cakes and poach as in the preceding recipe. Serve with a rich sauce and garnish with fried toast.

PIKE PUDDING OR MOLD

1 pound pike fillets	3 egg yolks
1 cup heavy béchamel sauce	Salt
(page 23)	Freshly ground black pepper
1 egg	

Grind the fish very fine. Then pound it in a mortar or give it a second grinding. Beat it with a wooden spoon until it forms a paste. Blend in the béchamel. Gradually work in the egg and the extra yolks. Force the mixture through a fine sieve or a food mill. Season it to taste and pour it into a well-buttered earthenware casserole with straight sides. (A copper or glass oven dish with fairly straight sides will do.)

Place the casserole in a pan of hot water and bake at 350° for 25 to 30 minutes, or until just set. Unmold on a hot platter and surround with shrimp sauce (page 21) or sauce Béarnaise (page 26). Garnish with cooked shrimp and sprigs of parsley.

MOUSSE OF PIKE

See halibut mousse, page 129.

POACHED PIKE

Pike lends itself to poaching even better than most fish. It can be poached whole or in 3-to-4-pound pieces. Wrap the fish in cheese-cloth, poach in a white wine court bouillon (pages 19–20) according to the Canadian cooking theory (page 12). Serve it with Hollandaise (pages 25–26), Béarnaise (page 26), duxelles (page 27), or shrimp sauce (page 21), or with anchovy (page 32) or lemon butter (page 31).

VARIATIONS

1. Prepare a court bouillon as follows:

Chop fine 8 to 10 shallots or 12 green onions, 2 cloves garlic, 1 leek, 2 or 3 carrots and plenty of parsley; add 1 tablespoon salt, 1 teaspoon freshly ground pepper, 1 bay leaf, and a heaping spoonful of thyme. Cover with white wine and let stand for 3 hours. Put it on the stove and slowly bring it to a boil. Add the fish and poach according to the Canadian cooking theory (page 12). Remove the fish to a hot platter.

Strain the bouillon through a fine sieve or food mill. Reduce it quickly to 2 cups. Add 1 cup of heavy cream and 4 or 5 egg yolks. Stir well until thickened, being careful that the mixture does not boil. Cream 4 to 5 tablespoons of butter with a little flour and add it to the sauce. Stir until smooth, taste for seasoning, and pour over the fish.

Serve with plain boiled potatoes and follow with a dish of braised celery topped with bits of marrow poached in boiling salted water.

2. Poach pike in simmering salted water with the addition of plenty of fresh dill, parsley, and an onion stuck with 2 cloves. When the fish is cooked, remove it to a hot platter. Make a sauce velouté (page 21) with some of the broth, season it with chopped fresh dill, parsley, and 1 tablespoon of lemon juice. Pour the sauce over the fish.

COLD PIKE WITH VARIOUS SAUCES

Cold pike is one of the most delicate and flavorful of the white fish. A delightful supper dish in summer is a whole cold pike garnished with cucumbers, tomatoes, salade Russe, stuffed eggs flavored with anchovy and sardines, and olives.

To prepare the fish, poach it in a court bouillon (page 18) according to the Canadian cooking theory (page 12). Chill it, and when cool skin it, leaving the head and tail intact. You may make an aspic of the broth, if you wish, and mask the fish with it. Or simply place the cold poached pike on a platter of greens and garnish to suit your own taste. Serve it with a well-flavored olive oil mayonnaise (page 34), sauce verte (page 34), or sauce rémoulade (page 35).

If you wish to be really elaborate, you may make an aspic of the court bouillon (pages 18–19). Combine some of the aspic with mayonnaise (page 34) and cover the fish with this. Chill until set, then mask with aspic and chill again. Decorate with truffles, pickled mushrooms, capers — anything you like. For suggestions for decorating fish in aspic, see page 131.

IZAAK WALTON'S RECIPE FOR ROASTING A PIKE
from THE COMPLEAT ANGLER

Mr. Walton's comment on this recipe for roasting pike is ample proof that he enjoyed the cooked results of his angling as much as the angling itself. He wrote: "This dish of meat is too good for any but anglers, or very honest men; and I trust you will prove both, and therefore I have trusted you with this secret."

Here is the recipe:

"First, open your pike at the gills, and if need be, cut also a little slit towards the belly; out of these take his guts and keep his liver, which you are to shred very small with thyme, sweet marjoram, and a little winter-savory; to these put some pickled oysters, and some anchovies, two or three, both these last whole (for the anchovies will melt, and the oysters should not); to these you must add also a pound of sweet butter, which you are to mix with the herbs which are shred, and let them all be well salted (if the pike be more than a yard long, then you may put into these herbs more than a pound, or if he be less, then less butter will suffice): these being thus mixed with a blade or two of mace, must be put into the pike's belly, and then his belly so sewed up as to keep all the butter in his belly, if it be possible, if not, then as much of it as you possibly can; but take not off the scales: then you are to thrust the spit through his mouth out at his tail; and then take four, or five, or six split sticks or very thin laths, and a convenient quantity of tape or filleting: these laths are to be tied round about the pike's body from his head to his tail, and the tape tied somewhat thick to prevent his breaking or falling off from the spit: let him be roasted very leisurely, and often basted with claret wine and anchovies and butter mixed together, and also with what moisture falls from him into the pan: when you have roasted him sufficiently, you are to hold under him (when you unwind or cut the tape that ties him) such a dish as you purpose to eat him out of; and let him fall into it with the sauce that is roasted in his belly; and by this means the pike will be kept unbroken and complete: then, to the sauce which was within, and also that sauce in the pan, you are to add a fit quantity of the best butter, and to squeeze the juice of three or four oranges: lastly, you may either put into the pike with the oysters two cloves of garlick, and take it out whole, when the pike is cut off the spit; or to give the sauce a *haut-gout* let the dish (into which you let the pike fall) be rubbed with it: the using or not using of this garlick is left to your discretion."

Pike Perch

In spite of the name, pike perches are not related to pike. They are, rather, members of the same family as the yellow perch. There are three well-known varieties: blue pike perch, yellow pike perch — also called wall-eyed pike — and sauger or sand pike. These are excellent food fishes with firm white flesh.

Yellow pike perch are found plentifully in streams along the Middle Atlantic seaboard, westward to the Mississippi Valley, and north through the Great Lakes region to Hudson Bay. There is a large commercial catch each year, and sizable amount is caught and cooked by sportsmen. The sauger is found farther west in the Missouri Valley region. The blue pike perch likes deep water and is caught mainly in the Great Lakes.

Most of the perch caught are small fish weighing around 1 to 1½ pounds, although occasionally larger ones are marketed. A large proportion of the commercial catch is filleted, but the fish are also sold whole.

PIKE PERCH SAUTÉ MEUNIÈRE

The fish may be cleaned and split or, if small enough, they may be sautéed whole. Follow directions for sauté meunière, page 10. Fillets may be treated in the same manner.

VARIATIONS

1. After removing the fish to a hot platter, add blanched almonds to the pan and toss them about until they brown. Pour the almonds and the pan juices over the fish and serve with lemon wedges.

2. Sauté mushroom slices with the fish.

3. Add chopped parsley and white wine to the pan juices, bring to a boil, and pour over the fish.

PAN-FRIED PIKE PERCH

Follow directions for pan-frying crappies, page 322.

OVEN-FRIED FILLETS OF PIKE PERCH

Follow directions for oven-frying fillets of whitefish, pages 345–346.

BAKED PIKE PERCH

Clean and wash the fish. Oil a large flat baking dish and cover the bottom with chopped green onions. Arrange the fish on top, dot them with butter and sprinkle with salt and freshly ground pepper. Add enough white wine to cover the bottom of the pan. Bake at 425° according to the Canadian cooking theory (page 8). Baste during the cooking process, and add more wine and butter if needed.

VARIATION

Just before the fish are done, sprinkle the top with bread crumbs and grated Parmesan cheese.

Sheepshead

The sheepshead is the only freshwater relative of the drums and the croakers — the fish that are heard as well as seen. They love to play tunes, and you may hear their entertaining music on still nights.

The flesh of the sheepshead is white, lean, and tender, with an excellent flavor. You will find sheepshead on the market in the Middle West and the South, whole and filleted. They come in sizes from 1 to 12 pounds, though some sheepshead have been known to weigh 60 pounds.

Cook sheepshead as you would drum, croaker, or weakfish.

Suckers

When I was about eight years old, my neighborhood contemporaries were always running off on fishing excursions and coming home with suckers — and I was never much impressed. I still think the sucker is a dull fish, a sort of underwater vacuum cleaner. It is plentiful, however, in country streams and many people enjoy eating it. In fact, there is a good commercial market for suckers.

The sucker is not a fat fish, and needs the lift of a good sauce to make it palatable.

BROILED SUCKER

Suckers must be lubricated well with oil or butter before broiling. Follow the general directions on pages 9–10. Serve with lemon butter (page 31) or anchovy butter (page 32).

PAN-FRIED SUCKER

Small-sized suckers may be pan-fried whole. Clean them and soak for about ½ hour in milk with salt and freshly ground black pepper added. Roll them in crumbs and sauté in butter or bacon fat according to the Canadian cooking theory (page 10). Serve with a tartar sauce (pages 35–36) or rémoulade (page 35).

BRAISED SUCKER

2 large onions, chopped	4 pounds of sucker
2 cloves garlic, chopped	Salt
6 tablespoons olive oil	Freshly ground black pepper
1 tablespoon chili powder	Oregano
2 cups tomato paste *or* strained canned tomatoes	

Sauté the onions and garlic in the olive oil. Add the chili powder and tomato paste. Place the fish on a well-oiled baking dish or pan; season to taste with salt, pepper, and oregano. Cover with the sauce and bake at 450° according to the Canadian cooking theory (page 8).

POACHED SUCKER

Poach suckers in a court bouillon (page 18) according to the Canadian cooking theory (page 12). Serve them with a Hollandaise sauce (pages 25–26), or with a shrimp or lobster sauce (page 21), or with sauce velouté (page 21) made with the reduced court bouillon.

COLD POACHED SUCKER

Mask the cold poached sucker in mayonnaise (page 34) or rémoulade (page 35). This is a nice change for a hot summer day when the neighborhood fisherman brings you part of his catch.

Trout

Trout is the glamour fish. They are beautiful, they are perfectly meated, and in many places they are scarce.

Since I am not an ichthyologist, I am not going into a discussion of all the different varieties of trout. I recommend all of them indiscriminately. I do remember particularly, however, a mess of tiny mountain trout caught in a cold Oregon stream, cooked with bacon over a campfire, and served up for breakfast less than an hour after they have been taken from the water. The combined flavors of wood smoke, bacon, and delicate trout cannot be duplicated in a modern kitchen by even the most experienced chef. But if outdoor simplicity can work miracles with trout, so can sophistication. I recall with drooling tastebuds the incomparable *truite en chemise* at the station restaurant in the Gare de l'Est in Paris.

The recipes here are for the small trout — mountain trout, Dolly Vardens, small-sized brook or speckled trout, all those running from 8 to 12 inches. These are usually served whole with head and tail intact. Simply wash and clean them. As for the amount of trout per serving, that depends on individual taste.

Certainly at least one per person, and of the smaller fish, two or three. But suit yourselves.

If the trout you intend to cook is one of the larger varieties, try the salmon recipes (pages 178–192). You'll find that they apply perfectly.

TROUT SAUTÉ MEUNIÈRE

This, of course, is the classic preparation for trout. See directions for sauté meunière, page 10.

VARIATION

Sauté the trout, and just before removing it from the pan add ½ to 1 cup of heavy cream. Let it come to a boil and cook for 2 minutes. Remove the trout to a hot platter. Correct the seasoning, reduce the cream a bit, and pour it over the fish. Sprinkle with chopped parsley.

TROUT AMANDINE, IN THE MANNER OF RESTAURANT CASENAVE IN PARIS

½ pound shelled almonds   Salt
6 tablespoons butter   Freshly ground black pepper
4 trout   Chopped parsley
Flour

Blanch the almonds. Leave half of them whole and cut the rest into slivers. Melt the butter in a skillet. Dip the trout in flour, and when the butter is bubbly but not burning add the trout and almonds. Spoon the nuts around in the butter so that they will brown well. Cook according to the Canadian cooking theory (page 10), turning the trout once. Salt and pepper to taste. Remove the trout to a hot platter and sprinkle with chopped parsley. Pour the golden-colored almonds and the butter from the pan over the fish. With this serve new potatoes in their jackets, and some lemon butter (page 31) or lemon wedges.

BROOK TROUT, OUTDOORS METHOD

If you catch trout early and can have them for breakfast that same morning, you are the most fortunate of people. To cook 6 trout:

Try out 6 to 12 rashers of bacon, depending on your appetite. When the bacon is crisp, remove it to a paper or plate. Dip the trout in flour or corn meal and sauté them quickly in the bacon fat. Do not add salt until the fish are cooked and you have tasted them; the bacon fat may add enough seasoning. Serve the trout with the bacon rashers and toast made over the fire. Steaming campfire coffee is a must, of course.

TRUITE EN CHEMISE

This delightful way to serve trout and other small fish will always bring cheers from your guests. For 6 people:

½ pound mushrooms, finely chopped
4 tablespoons butter
Salt
Freshly ground black pepper
3 tablespoons flour

4 tablespoons heavy cream
6 crêpes, made without sugar
6 trout, sauté meunière (page 10)
Browned butter
Lemon juice

Sauté the mushrooms in the butter until they are soft and well cooked. Sprinkle with the salt, pepper, and flour. Add the cream and stir until the mixture is thick.

Prepare the crêpes without sugar according to the recipe on page 190. They should be about 6 inches in diameter, well browned, thin and tender.

Sauté the trout meunière according to the directions on page

10. Spread each pancake with the mushroom mixture, place a trout on top of this, and roll up the pancake so that the head sticks out one end and the tail the other. Arrange these rolls in a baking dish — an oval one is perfect. Cover with a little browned butter and lemon juice. Heat for just a moment or two in the oven and serve. Delicious with a good green salad and a brittle white wine.

TROUT À L'ANGLAISE

12 trout	Salt
4 tablespoons butter	Freshly ground black pepper
3 tablespoons olive oil	2 eggs, lightly beaten
Flour	2 cups crumbs, crushed

Clean and wash the trout. Heat the butter and olive oil in a large skillet. Dust the trout with flour, sprinkle with salt and pepper, dip in the egg, and then in the crumbs. Sauté quickly in the hot fat according to the Canadian cooking theory (page 10). Remove to a hot platter and serve with a tartar sauce (pages 35–36), sauce diable (page 29), or rémoulade (page 35). Boiled potatoes and peas seem to be a good but rather homely accompaniment.

VARIATION

French-Fried Trout. Prepare the fish as above, but fry it according to the Canadian cooking theory (page 11). Serve with tartar sauce (pages 35–36) or rémoulade (page 35).

CHARCOAL-BROILED TROUT

I have had all sorts of trout broiled over coals: wrapped in wet newspapers; wrapped in clay (and they were not too bad this way); and held over the coals after being impaled on a stick — which works very well if you do it right.

I really feel, however, that there are only two ways of doing the job and doing it well.

I. Clean the trout, dip them in flour, and then in melted butter. Salt and pepper them and arrange securely in a wire grill. Grill over hot coals according to the Canadian cooking theory (page 9). Brush with butter during the cooking (a good-sized pastry brush or a small paintbrush is excellent for doing this). The trout should have a nice crispy coating — be careful not to overcook them. Serve with potatoes sautéed over or baked under the fire and cole slaw.

II. Arrange the trout in an S-shape on long skewers, or make rings of the fish by running the skewers through the head and tail. Dip these in flour, then in melted butter, and sprinkle with salt and pepper. Broil them over the coals as above, brushing with butter during the process. Serve with lemon or lime wedges and melted butter or with a Hollandaise sauce (pages 25–26).

TROUT EN PAPILLOTES

For 6 people:

6 trout	Freshly ground black pepper
Butter	Oil
Salt	

FILLING

2 carrots, finely chopped	2 stalks celery, finely chopped
2 small white onions, finely chopped	4 to 6 tablespoons butter
	Salt
2 shallots or green onions, finely chopped	Freshly ground black pepper

Prepare the filling by sautéing the vegetables in the butter until soft. Salt and pepper to taste.

Split and clean the trout and stuff each one with a little of the mixture. Dot with butter, and place about 3 inches from the broiler flame. Broil for 6 minutes. Salt and pepper the fish when you remove them.

Have ready 6 heart-shaped pieces of cooking parchment large enough for the trout. Place a fish on each piece of parchment, near one edge. Fold the rest of the paper over the fish and crimp the edges together so that the fish is sealed in. Oil the paper. Place these on a buttered baking sheet and bake at 425° according to the Canadian cooking theory (page 8), adding an additional five minutes for the paper.

VERY DRESSY STUFFED TROUT

This is a spectacular dish for special occasions.

12 good-sized trout
3 large onions, chopped
½ pound (2 sticks) butter plus
  6 tablespoons

2 cups dry white wine
1 cup very heavy béchamel
  (page 23)

FILLING

2 medium onions, chopped
Butter
Salt
Freshly ground black pepper
½ pound raw white-meated fish

2 egg yolks, lightly beaten
3 egg whites
Chopped tarragon
Chopped parsley

Clean the fish and prepare them for stuffing. Leave the heads intact.

Filling. Sauté the onions in butter until they are soft and golden. Salt them lightly. Grind the white-meated fish several times; salt and pepper it to taste. Add it to the onions and blend the two together with a wooden spoon. Add the egg yolks and egg whites and season with tarragon and parsley. Stuff the fish with this mixture.

Sauté the onions in the 6 tablespoons of butter until soft. Force them through a sieve or food mill. Cover the bottom of a baking dish with this puree and arrange the trout on top. Dot with butter, add the wine, and bake at 450° according to the Canadian cooking theory (page 8).

Remove the fish to a hot platter. Force the sauce through a

sieve or food mill and combine it with the béchamel and the remaining butter. Blend thoroughly and pour over the fish. Sprinkle with chopped parsley. Serve with julienne potatoes and a good green salad.

TROUT SMOTHERED IN MUSHROOMS

8 trout
1 pound mushrooms, finely chopped
6 tablespoons butter
1 clove garlic, minced
1 teaspoon salt
1 teaspoon freshly ground black pepper

1½ cups and 2 tablespoons heavy cream
Butter
Beurre manić (page 475)
Fried toast
Parsley

Clean and wash the trout. Sauté the mushrooms in butter until they are soft. Season with the garlic, salt, and pepper. Add the 2 tablespoons of cream and let it cook down.

Arrange the trout on a well-oiled baking dish and top with the mushrooms. Dot with butter and bake at 425° according to the Canadian cooking theory (page 8). Remove to a hot platter. Add the remaining cream to the pan, heat, and blend thoroughly. Add the beurre manié and stir until nicely thickened. Taste for seasoning and pour over the trout. Garnish the platter with pieces of fried toast heavily sprinkled with chopped parsley.

TRUITE AU BLEU

This, I am told, was originally an outdoor meal, and the trout were cooked as soon as caught. In fact, they are supposed to be alive, or practically alive, when they are plunged into the boiling acidulated water. Many restaurants have tanks of trout so that they can pull them out and pop them into the cauldron on order.

Prepare a court bouillon of 3 parts water to 1 part vinegar. Add 6 peppercorns, a part of a bay leaf, and 1 teaspoon of salt to each quart of liquid. Bring this to a boil. Plunge in the trout and poach them according to the Canadian cooking theory (page 12). Serve them hot with melted butter and boiled potatoes, or chill and serve cold with mayonnaise.

The vinegar in the water turns the skin of the fish a vivid metallic blue, hence the name.

POACHED TROUT

Trout are delicious if they are poached lightly in a court bouillon (page 18) according to the Canadian cooking theory (page 12). It is better to poach them in a flat dish so that they are barely covered. It is difficult to remove them from a deep pan. Serve the poached trout with beurre noisette (page 31), shrimp sauce (page 21), sauce Béarnaise (page 26), or Hollandaise sauce (pages 25–26).

COLD TROUT IN JELLY

6 trout
White wine court bouillon
  (pages 19–20)
White of egg and eggshells
1½ envelopes gelatin

⅓ cup water
Green onion or leeks or chives
  or tarragon leaves
Hard-cooked eggs

Poach the trout in the bouillon as above and remove them to a platter. Reduce the bouillon to 3 cups and clarify with the lightly beaten egg white and shells (page 18). Strain. Soak the gelatin in the water and combine it with the boiling broth. Chill until it is thick and syrupy.

The fish may be decorated as elaborately as you choose. Or you may prefer to serve them plain, simply masked with the jelly. If you want a spectacular dish, remove about half of the skin from the chilled, cooked trout. Then make a flower design on the flesh. Use the green stems of onions, leeks, or chives or green tarragon leaves, and make tiny flowers cut out of hard-cooked egg.

Pour enough of the jelly over the decorated (or plain) trout to mask it thoroughly. Put the platter with the fish and a bowl of the rest of the jelly in the refrigerator to chill. Just before serving, chop the rest of the jelly very fine and garnish the fish platter with it. Serve with mayonnaise (page 34) or rémoulade (page 35).

VARIATION

Reduce the broth to 1 cup. Soften 1 envelope of gelatin with 1 cup red wine or port; add to the broth. Boil a few minutes to dissolve the gelatin.

COLD TROUT WITH DILL SAUCE

Poach 6 or 8 trout in court bouillon (page 18) according to the Canadian cooking theory (page 12). Chill thoroughly. Remove part of the skin from the top of the trout, leaving the heads and tails intact. Sprinkle with finely chopped dill, parsley, and chives. Arrange alternate slices of cucumber and hard-cooked egg on each fish. Serve with a sour cream sauce made with 1½ cups sour cream, 1 tablespoon fresh dill, 1 teaspoon grated onion, 1 teaspoon dry mustard, and ½ cup finely chopped hard-cooked egg. Season to taste with salt and freshly ground black pepper.

PICKLED TROUT

1 bottle white wine	1 teaspoon tarragon leaves
6 peppercorns	Pinch of thyme
1 carrot, thinly sliced	1 teaspoon salt
4 small white onions	1 teaspoon freshly ground black
2 cloves	pepper
1 bay leaf	¼ cup wine vinegar

12 trout
½ cup olive oil

12 thin lemon slices
1 medium onion, thinly sliced

Prepare a court bouillon with the wine, peppercorns, carrot, small onions (two with cloves stuck in them), bay leaf, tarragon, thyme, salt, pepper, and vinegar. Bring it to a boil and let it boil for 15 minutes. Add the trout and poach according to the Canadian cooking theory (page 12). Remove the fish to a serving dish.

Add the olive oil, lemon slices, and onion to the broth. Reduce it to 1 cup and, when cool, pour it over the trout. Chill for 24 hours before serving.

These may be served with their own marinade for the sauce, or with mayonnaise. A salad of cucumbers, tomatoes stuffed with cucumbers, or salade Russe are good additions.

SMOKED TROUT

This is a rare treat if you can come by it. Skin the trout, cut it into long fillets, and serve with lemon for a truly distinctive hors d'oeuvre.

Whitefish

One of the most important freshwater food fishes, whitefish comes from the Great Lakes, from small lakes in many sections of the country, and from very far north in Canada. The supply has been noticeably reduced by overfishing and also by the activity of an eel called the lamprey, which attaches itself to the fish and chews off the flesh. The Fish and Wildlife Service of the government is now dealing effectively with this problem.

Whitefish available in the markets weighs from 2 to 6 pounds and is sold whole or in fillets. Smoked whitefish is sold widely in the East and Middle West as well.

Whitefish roe can be lightly salted and made into a caviar that is excellent if well prepared. There used to be a great deal of this in the markets, and you may find it today from time to time.

BROILED WHITEFISH

You may broil either the fillets or the whole fish, split or round. Follow the directions for broiling, pages 9–10.

Serve with lemon butter (page 31), maître d'hôtel butter (page 31), or parsley butter (page 33).

WHITEFISH SAUTÉ MEUNIÈRE

The small fish may be sautéed whole, or you may use fillets. Follow directions for sauté meunière, page 10.

VARIATIONS

1. Sprinkle the fish heavily with sesame seeds after sautéing and put them in a hot oven or under the broiler flame to brown the seeds.

2. Add buttered almonds, chopped or slivered, to the pan while the fish are cooking.

3. Add small mushroom caps while the fish are cooking.

OVEN-FRIED FILLETS OF WHITEFISH

Soak the fillets in salted milk for 1 hour. Roll them in crumbs and arrange on a well-oiled baking dish. Pour melted butter over them and bake at 450° according to the Canadian cooking theory (page 8).

Serve with a tartar sauce (pages 35–36), sauce gribiche (pages 36–37), or with lemon (page 31) or parsley butter (page 33).

BAKED WHITEFISH

Clean a 4- or 5-pound whitefish. Rub with oil, butter, or fat and season with salt and freshly ground pepper. Place it in a well-oiled baking dish and bake at 450° according to the Canadian cooking theory (page 8). Baste frequently during the cooking. Serve with parsley potatoes and grilled tomatoes.

BAKED STUFFED WHITEFISH

Prepare the fish for stuffing. Leave the head and tail on. Prepare a stuffing (pages 39–41), stuff the fish, and sew it up. Place it on a well-oiled baking dish, strip it with bacon or dot it with butter, and sprinkle with salt. Bake at 450° according to the Canadian cooking theory (page 8). Transfer the fish to a hot platter with the aid of two spatulas.

Serve with lemon wedges, lemon butter (page 31), or anchovy butter (page 32). Accompany the stuffed fish with boiled new potatoes heavily sprinkled with parsley and tiny green peas cooked with a little onion.

VARIATIONS

1. Make a fish forecmeat (page 41) to use as stuffing. Sew up the whitefish. Chop 8 to 10 shallots or small green onions and place them in the bottom of a well-oiled baking dish. Top these with the fish, dot it with butter, sprinkle with salt and pepper, and pour 1½ cups of white wine over all. Bake as above, basting frequently. Remove the fish to a hot platter.

Force the pan juices through a sieve or mix in a blender. Add ½ cup heavy cream mixed with 2 egg yolks. Stir over medium heat until the mixture thickens slightly, but do not let it boil.

Taste for seasoning and pour over the fish. Serve with rice and a spinach puree.

2. Sauté slices of Spanish onion in butter until soft but not colored. Stuff the whitefish with slices of the onion alternated with sliced, peeled tomato, thinly sliced mushrooms, and chopped parsley. Salt and pepper to taste and dot with butter. Sew up the fish and place it on a well-oiled baking dish. Brush it with oil, sprinkle it with salt and pepper, and bake as above. Serve with a tomato sauce and buttered noodles or macaroni.

HELEN EVANS BROWN'S CHINESE STEAMED WHITEFISH

This is cooked in the typical Chinese manner. The fish is stuffed and arranged on the dish in which it is to be served. Then the dish is set on a rack over hot water, a lid is clamped on tightly, and the fish steams until it is done. If you want the fish to be really handsome, arrange it in an S-shape with the split, stuffed side underneath. You can secure it with the aid of a long skewer. Here is the recipe:

1 cup ground Virginia ham
¾ cup sherry
¼ cup plus 1 tablespoon soy
  sauce
2 tablespoons grated ginger

6 minced green onions
½ cup chopped water chestnuts
3- or 4-pound whitefish
¼ cup of water

Prepare a stuffing with the ham, ¼ cup of the sherry, 1 tablespoon of the soy sauce, the ginger, onions, and water chestnuts. Stuff the fish and sew it, or secure it with skewers or toothpicks. Arrange it on the serving dish and place the dish on a rack in a large steamer. Pour over the fish the remaining ¼ cup soy sauce and ½ cup sherry, and the water. Pour hot water in the bottom of the steamer, being careful not to get any in the serving dish. Cover the steamer tightly and steam until the fish is tender — about 25 minutes.

Serve with rice.

POACHED WHITEFISH

This delicate fish takes very well to poaching. Be careful not to overcook it, and remove it from the boiler very gently. The old method of wrapping fish in cheesecloth is excellent; it's a good idea to leave long ends of the cloth that you can use as handles when you lift the fish. Of course, a real fish boiler with a rack solves the problem.

Poach the fish in a court bouillon (page 18) or in a mixture of milk and water — perfect with this type of fish. Follow the Canadian cooking theory for poaching on page 12.

There is a wide variety of sauces to use with poached white-fish. Personally, I like an oyster or shrimp sauce (page 21), but Hollandaise (pages 25–26) and Béarnaise (page 26) go well with it, too. Serve plain boiled potatoes and a puree of spinach mixed with a little grated garlic, grated Parmesan cheese, and butter.

COLD WHITEFISH

A whole poached whitefish that has been chilled makes a very good buffet dish or a good dish for any summer meal. Or you may serve it as a first course at dinner, followed by game or a red meat. This combination gives you a chance to serve a nice contrast of wines.

Garnish the whitefish with cucumbers in sour cream and dill and hard-cooked eggs stuffed with caviar in the yolks. If you use the fish as a luncheon dish, serve a real French potato salad made with a white wine and olive oil dressing, with the addition of a few slivered almonds and onion. An outstanding dressing for cold poached whitefish served as a salad or hors d'oeuvre course is mayonnaise mixed with lemon juice, finely chopped hard-cooked egg, caviar, grated onion, and just a touch of sherry or Madeira.

SMOKED WHITEFISH

Smoked whitefish is one of the greatest fish delicacies. The meat, being delicate and fat, lends itself to the smoking process as readily as sturgeon, salmon, or eel. I enjoy it served with cocktails or as a first course.

To serve with cocktails: Remove the skin and arrange the whole fish, with head and tail intact, on a bed of watercress. Garnish with wedges of lemon and have several fish knives available. On another plate arrange some buttered strips of pumpernickel and let people help themselves. If you want to do something especially fancy, accompany this with a bowl of caviar and some finely chopped onions.

To serve as a first course: Place a section of smoked whitefish on a bed of watercress. Garnish with a lemon wedge, some chopped onion and parsley. Thin sandwiches of buttered pumpernickel are a must.

SUNDAY BREAKFAST SPECIAL

Friends of mine serve a Sunday breakfast that is a delight. Their handsome oval table is dominated by a huge platter of smoked whitefish, smoked salmon, and smoked sturgeon with thinly sliced Bermuda onion and lemon wedges. When the guests are seated, a big dish of fluffy scrambled eggs is brought in, steaming hot, and hot rolls and toasted bagels are passed. This is a superb combination of flavors.

WHITEFISH ROE

The fresh roe of whitefish is very good when sautéed or poached. See directions for cooking shad roe, pages 222–224.

Yellow Perch

Many people think that the yellow perch is one of the best flavored of freshwater fishes. A small greenish-golden fish easily obtainable in markets in the Middle West, it is caught commercially in rather large quantities in the Great Lakes, and anglers take it in unrecorded quantities from lakes, streams, and ponds of the interior. It has been transplanted successfully to lakes in the Far West.

The yellow perch seems to flourish best in lakes. It likes shallow water and the company of its kind. Seldom exceeding 12 inches in length or 1 pound in weight, it is a relative of the sauger and pike perches and can be cooked in the same way. See pages 331–332.

Shellfish

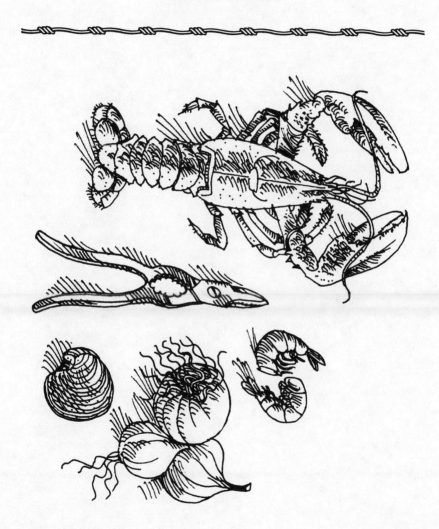

Abalone

This univalve, native to the waters of California, has been popular for many years among the Chinese-Americans of the Far West, who dried and canned it in large quantities. Now that other Americans have learned to appreciate it, the supply is very small. No fresh abalone can be purchased outside California, but small amounts of canned abalone, including some imported from Mexico, are available in certain Eastern shops.

The fresh abalone meat needs tenderizing before cooking. Most of that bought in California markets is ready to use; if it has not been tenderized, you must soften the meat by pounding with a mallet. Never overcook abalone. It will be tough and disappointing.

ABALONE SAUTÉ

Have the abalone sliced thin and tenderized. Melt butter in a skillet and cook the fish for 45 to 55 seconds, turning once. Salt and pepper to taste.

NOTE: Please remember that the Canadian cooking theory does not apply when cooking shellfish, mollusks, or crustaceans.

BREADED ABALONE

Bread slices of abalone in flour, then dip them in eggs beaten with water, and roll them in crumbs. Sauté in butter as in the recipe above.

FRIED ABALONE

Slice and tenderize abalone and cut into thin strips. Heat fat or oil in a deep fryer to 375°. Dip the pieces of abalone into beer batter for frying (page 99) and fry until delicately browned. Salt and pepper to taste.

ABALONE CHOWDER

This is made in the same way you make clam chowder (pages 55–57) except that the abalone is cooked in chicken broth until tender and then ground. The ground abalone is added to the potatoes while they are cooking.

STUFFED ABALONE

From Helen Evans Brown's *West Coast Cook Book*.

For each serving:

1 lobster tail, sliced	Butter
2 tablespoons crabmeat	1 abalone steak
3 or 4 shrimp	Sauce béchamel (page 23)

Sauté the lobster tail, crabmeat, and shrimp in butter for 2 or 3 minutes. Sauté the abalone steaks lightly for about 45 seconds, or even less. Brush the cooked steak with sauce béchamel flavored with sherry. Dip the shellfish in the sauce and place on top of the abalone. Roll each steak and fasten with a toothpick. Brush with more sauce and run under the broiler to brown lightly.

CANNED ABALONE, CHINESE STYLE

4 or 5 large Chinese black
 mushrooms
1 cup chicken stock
1-pound can of abalone
5 water chestnuts, sliced

4 green onions, split and cut
 into 1-inch lengths
½ cup sliced celery
1 tablespoon soy sauce
1 tablespoon sherry
2 tablespoons cornstarch

Soak the mushrooms in water for 2 or 3 hours, then cut them into strips. In a cup of chicken stock with the juice from the canned abalone, simmer the water chestnuts, the onions, and the celery. After 5 minutes, add the sliced abalone, soy sauce, and sherry. Mix the cornstarch with 2 tablespoons of water and stir it in. Stir until the sauce is thickened. Serve with rice.

This will serve 4 to 10 people, depending on whether it's a Chinese or American meal.

Clams

We in America are fonder of clams than are the people of other nations. And fortunately for us, our shoreline is well supplied with them.

Clams come in a variety that is often confusing to the inlander. Two main species make up the bulk of East Coast clamming — the soft or long-necked clam (*Mya arenaria*) and the hard or little-necked clam (*Venus mercenaria*). Many New Englanders will assure you that the soft clam is the only "real" or "true" clam. The exclusiveness of this claim may possibly be attributed to the fact that *Mya* is abundant north of Cape Cod but scarce to the south. New Englanders refer to the hard clam by its Indian name, quahog, while other Easterners more often call it the "littleneck" or "round clam." The species begins to be abundant south of the Cape, is especially plentiful on the North Carolina and Florida shores, and occurs all the way to Texas.

The Pacific Coast has some thirty varieties of clams, dominated by the razor clam, the famous Pismo clam, and the large mud clam. There is also that odd, gargantuan member of the clam family called the geoduck, goeduck, or gweduc (pronounced *gooey-duck*). It has an excellent flavor but, sad to say, is not generally obtainable in the markets.

Like the razor clam, New England's soft clam is a tide-flat dweller with a long tubelike siphon. It is a deep burrower and is taken by digging. The hard or littlenecked variety generally lives in deeper water, is not so active in its burrowing, and is taken by long-handled rakes or tongs and by dredging.

In my opinion, the razor clam — correctly prepared — is unsurpassed in flavor and texture. When I was a child and living near the Oregon coast, I used to dig them by the bucketful in the early morning when the tide was out. My mother sautéed them in butter, cooked them as delicately light fritters, or made them into magnificent chowder. You may now buy the Pacific Coast razor clam, minced, in cans. The canned variety is fine for soups and soufflés and for the clam appetizer that is so widely popular these days.

In the East, the distinct flavor of the hard clam or quahog makes it the preferred ingredient in Boston clam chowder and in that entirely dissimilar soup — not so highly regarded by connoisseurs — Manhattan clam chowder. Several regional varieties of clams are popular on the half shell, but perhaps the best known is the "cherrystone," which is actually a small quahog. Clams served on the half shell must be very cold. Care should be taken when they are opened that no drop of the wonderful juice is lost, and anyone who does not drink the juice from the shells is losing half the enjoyment of eating clams. Raw clams are usually served with cocktail sauce, which in my opinion really ruins their delicate flavor. I prefer lemon juice and a little freshly ground pepper or horseradish. Others insist that lime juice is far better with clams than lemon.

CLAM APPETIZERS

1 clove garlic, mashed	Sour cream
7-ounce can minced clams	Parsley
¼ pound cream cheese	

Mix the garlic with the clams, cream cheese, and enough sour cream to thin it down for dunking. Taste for seasoning and add chopped parsley.

This makes an excellent dunk for crisp raw vegetables. It is also good with bread sticks or very small corn sticks.

VARIATIONS

1. Try a spread instead of a dunk. Drain the clams and work them into the cream cheese. Then add just enough of the clam juice to make a smooth spread. Flavor with a little grated onion, salt, and pepper.

2. Drain the clams and mix with cottage cheese and a dash of Worcestershire sauce.

3. Drain the clams, mix with sour cream, a tablespoon of chopped fresh dill, a tablespoon of chopped parsley, a little onion juice, and salt and pepper. You may add some cream cheese to this to make a stiffer paste, if you prefer.

4. Mince tiny white pickled onions and combine with cream cheese and minced clams, drained. Salt and pepper to taste.

CLAM CHOWDER

See pages 55–57.

CLAM SOUP

This may be made with any type of clam. It is best, to my taste, with either littlenecks (known as quahogs in New England) or razor clams.

2 cups milk	Salt
1 cup minced clams	Freshly ground black pepper
2 egg yolks	3 tablespoons butter
½ cup heavy cream	Paprika

Scald the milk. Grind the clams and save their liquor. Beat the egg yolks with the cream, stir them into the clams and clam juice, and add to the hot milk. Continue stirring over low heat until the clams are just heated through and the cream and egg yolks well blended in. Correct the seasoning and serve in small bowls with a lump of butter and a dash of paprika added at the last minute.

STEAMED CLAMS

For this popular dish, figure an average of 20 clams per person. You may increase or decrease this amount according to the appetites of the diners. Place the clams, which have been thoroughly scrubbed, in a large kettle with ½ inch of salt water at the bottom. Cover the kettle tightly and steam just until the clams open. This should take from 6 to 10 minutes. Discard any clams that do not open. Serve at once with large bowls of melted butter and cups of the broth. (Taste the broth for seasoning.)

STEAMED CLAMS À LA MARINIÈRE

This recipe is usually used for preparing mussels, but clams may be prepared in any way that you cook mussels.

6 to 7 dozen clams
1 large onion, chopped
Parsley
Thyme
Bay leaf

1 cup (approximatey) white
   wine
6 tablespoons butter
Freshly ground black pepper

Scrub the clams well and put them in a large kettle with the onion, parsley, thyme, and bay leaf. Add the wine and 4 tablespoons of the butter; grind a little pepper over all. Cover tightly and steam until the clams open. Discard any that do not open. Remove the clams to a large serving dish or to individual serving dishes. Put the sauce through a fine sieve, taste it for seasoning, and reheat, adding the remaining 2 tablespoons butter and a little chopped parsley. Pour this sauce over the clams.

VARIATIONS

1. Some people like 2 or 3 cloves of garlic chopped and added to the mixture in the pan.

2. If you like a thicker sauce, stir a half cup of sauce velouté (page 21) into the broth after it has been strained.

STEAMED CLAMS ON TOAST

2 dozen steamed clams (page
   358)
4 slices bread
½ cup butter

2 cloves garlic, finely chopped
4 tablespoons chopped parsley
Lemon wedges

Remove the steamed clams from their shells. Check the broth for salt. Toast the bread and trim the crusts. Melt the butter with the garlic and parsley, and proceed as in the recipe for steamed clams à la marinière. Arrange the clams on the hot toast, pour some of the sauce over them, and serve at once with additional sauce and lemon wedges.

STUFFED CLAMS

24 steamed clams (page 358)
1 tablespoon each chopped
  onion, parsley, tarragon
½ cup buttered crumbs
¼ cup thick béchamel (page 23)

1 tablespoon sherry
Salt
Freshly ground black pepper
Cayenne pepper

Remove the steamed clams from their shells. Chop very fine and combine with the seasonings, crumbs, and just enough béchamel sauce to bind them. Add the sherry, salt, pepper, and a few grains of cayenne. Fill the clam shells with this mixture, dot with butter and crumbs, and brown very quickly under the broiler.

NOTE: For certain clam, oyster, and other seafood dishes in the shell, it is a good idea to have some inexpensive pie plates or cake pans which you can fill with rock salt. Heat the pan filled with salt, and place the clams in their shells on the hot salt. Then return the pans to the oven or under the broiler. Serve the food right in the salt-filled pans. The salt retains the heat and keeps the seafood hot.

VARIATIONS

1. Steam clams as for clams marinière. Reduce the liquid to ⅓ cup. Add ⅓ cup heavy sauce velouté (page 21). Season with cayenne and chopped parsley. Add chopped clams and stuff the mixture into the shells. Top with buttered crumbs and small cubes of bacon. Bake at 400° until the bacon is crisp.

2. Use 24 clams on the half shell. Sprinkle with chopped chives, parsley, and garlic. Top with bacon. Bake in a 425° oven until the bacon is crisp.

3. Top 24 clams on the half shell with a lump of anchovy butter, made by creaming together ½ cup butter with 2 or 3 teaspoons finely chopped anchovies and 1 teaspoon finely chopped onion. Sprinkle with buttered crumbs and broil for 3 or 4 minutes.

4. Use 24 clams on the half shell. Combine 1 cup bread crumbs with the clam liquor, ⅓ cup white wine, 1 tablespoon each chopped onion, parsley, and green pepper. Salt and pepper to taste. Cover the clams with this mixture, pour melted butter

over it, and sprinkle with grated Parmesan cheese. Bake at 400°
until nicely browned.

CLAM HASH

During the summer months when we lived at the shore near the
mouth of the Columbia River, we used to feast almost daily on
clams, and we ate them in many different ways. Clam hash was
one of the favorites, and although it was never made the same
way twice, it always tasted ambrosial. This is an approximation
of it:

6 tablespoons butter	Freshly ground black pepper
1 tablespoon finely minced onion	Nutmeg
	4 egg yolks
1½ cups finely diced cooked potatoes	4 tablespoons grated Parmesan cheese
1½ to 2 cups minced clams	6 tablespoons heavy cream
Salt	

Melt the butter in a heavy skillet and cook the onion until it is
just transparent. Add the finely diced potatoes and the clams
and press them down with a spatula. Salt and pepper lightly and
add a few flecks of nutmeg. Let the hash cook for about 10 minutes over medium heat and stir with a fork or spatula, mixing in
some of the crust which forms on the bottom. Press down again.
Beat the egg yolks well; combine with the grated cheese and
cream. Pour this over the hash very gently, and cover tightly for
a few minutes until the egg is set.

CLAM FRITTERS

2 eggs, separated	1 cup cracker crumbs *or* toasted bread crumbs
1 cup minced clams (fresh *or* canned	1 teaspoon salt

½ teaspoon freshly ground
  black pepper
Few grains cayenne pepper

Milk *or* clam juice
Butter *or* oil

Beat the egg yolks until light and lemon-colored. Gradually add the clams, crumbs, and seasonings. Add enough liquid — clam juice or milk — to make a rather heavy batter. Fold in the stiffly beaten egg whites. Drop the batter by spoonfuls into hot butter or oil and sauté 3 or 4 minutes, turning once.

VARIATIONS

1. Beat 2 eggs until light. Add 1 cup mixed milk and clam juice, and ¾ cup flour sifted with 1 teaspoon baking powder. Stir in 1 cup minced clams and season with salt and pepper. Drop by spoonfuls into hot butter or oil and sauté for 4 or 5 minutes, turning once.

2. Beat 2 eggs, stir in 2 cups minced clams, ⅔ cup bread crumbs that have been browned in butter, ½ teaspoon salt, ½ teaspoon paprika, and 2 tablespoons chopped parsley. With your hands, form the mixture into cakes — round, cutlet-shaped, or oval. Roll these in flour and crumbs and sauté them in butter or oil over medium heat until nicely browned. Serve with lemon wedges.

Or you may deep-fry them for 4 or 5 minutes in fat heated to 365°. Drain on absorbent paper.

CLAM SOUFFLÉ

3 tablespoons butter
3 tablespoons flour
½ cup clam juice
½ cup cream
⅔ cup minced clams
4 egg yolks

2 tablespoons chopped parsley
Salt
Freshly ground black pepper
Nutmeg
6 egg whites

Melt the butter in a saucepan; add the flour and brown lightly. Stir in the clam juice and the cream and continue stirring until the mixture thickens. Add the minced clams and remove from the stove. Cool slightly. Beat the egg yolks into this mixture, one by one; add the chopped parsley and the seasonings. Beat the egg whites until stiff and fold them in. Pour into a well-buttered soufflé dish. Bake at 375° for 30 to 35 minutes, according to the state of runniness you prefer in a soufflé.

To be really elegant, serve this soufflé with a sauce mousseline (page 26).

SCALLOPED CLAMS

½ cup butter
½ cup toasted bread crumbs
1 cup cracker crumbs
Salt
Freshly ground black pepper
Paprika

2 cups minced clams
2 tablespoons finely minced onion
2 tablespoons finely minced parsley
⅓ cup cream

Melt the butter and mix it with the bread and cracker crumbs. Add salt and pepper to taste and a dash of paprika. Set aside ⅓ cup of this mixture for the top of the casserole. With the rest mix the clams, onion, and parsley. Pour it into a well-buttered baking dish and top with the remaining crumb mixture. Dot with additional butter and pour the cream over all. Bake in a 375° oven for 20 to 25 minutes.

CLAM PIE

2 quarts clams in shells
2 cups white wine
1 carrot
1 onion
1 bay leaf
1 teaspoon freshly ground black pepper
2 cups sauce velouté (page 21)

1 pound mushrooms
5 tablespoons butter
Salt
Freshly ground black pepper
3 tablespoons sherry *or* Madeira
1 recipe of rich pastry
Beaten egg yolk

Steam the clams in the white wine with the carrot, onion, bay leaf, and pepper (see page 358). Remove from the shells. Prepare a sauce velouté, using some of the clam broth (see page 21). Sauté the mushrooms in butter; season to taste with salt and pepper. Combine the mushrooms, clams, and the sauce and add the sherry or Madeira. Taste for seasoning. Cool thoroughly. Pour into a deep baking dish and top with pie crust rolled ¼ inch thick. Decorate with leaves cut out of additional crust, brush with beaten egg yolk mixed with a little water, and bake at 450° for 15 minutes. Reduce the heat to 350° and bake until nicely browned, about 20 minutes.

CLAM QUICHE

Pastry for 1 pie crust	Salt
4 strips of bacon	Freshly ground black pepper
2 tablespoons minced onion	Nutmeg
4 eggs	1 cup minced clams, drained
1½ cups clam juice and cream, mixed	

Line a 9-inch pie tin with the pastry and chill in the refrigerator for several hours. Sauté the bacon until crisp and drain on absorbent paper. Sauté the onion in the bacon fat until just soft. Beat the eggs, combine with the liquid, and add seasonings to taste. Remove the pie shell from the refrigerator. Sprinkle crumbled bacon and the onion on the bottom; then add the clams. Pour the custard mixture over all. Bake in a 450° oven for 10 minutes. Reduce the heat to 350° and continue baking until a knife inserted in the center comes out clean. Serve hot.

VARIATION

You may sprinkle the tart with grated Parmesan cheese before baking it.

CLAMS WITH RICE, SPANISH STYLE

1 medium onion, finely chopped	Salt
1 clove garlic, finely chopped	Freshly ground black pepper
1 slice smoked ham, shredded	Pinch of saffron
1 cup cooked tomatoes	18 to 20 small clams
1 pint clam broth (fresh *or* canned)	1 cup washed rice

Combine the onion, garlic, ham, tomatoes, and the clam broth and simmer for 20 minutes. Season to taste and add the saffron. Wash the clams, scrubbing them well. Arrange them in a large casserole with the rice. Pour the hot sauce over this and bake in a 350° oven until the rice is cooked and the liquid nearly all absorbed.

CLAM PAN ROASTS

In reality, pan roasts are nothing more nor less than sautés, a most delicate and delicious way to serve clams. There seem to be endless variations on this theme, and I include only the few that are my favorites. For a plain pan roast:

¼ pound butter	Paprika
1 pint drained clams	Buttered toast
Salt	Chopped parsley
Freshly ground black pepper	

Melt the butter in a skillet or chafing dish. Add the drained whole clams from which you have trimmed the tough littlenecks. Cook them just long enough to heat through and plump up. Season to taste with salt, pepper, and paprika, and serve on rounds of toast, buttered (or on fried toast), and top with parsley.

VARIATIONS

1. Add a spoonful of Worcestershire sauce and a dash of Dijon mustard to the pan when the clams are cooked.

2. Add finely chopped chives, fennel, parsley, or tarragon to the clams as they cook.

3. Add ½ cup white wine or champagne to the pan and let it cook for just a minute after the clams have puffed.

4. Add butter, ⅓ cup sherry, ⅓ cup chili sauce, and a little grated onion. Cook the clams in this mixture and serve them on garlic fried toast with the sauce poured over.

5. Chop 1 small green pepper and 1 onion very fine and sauté them in ⅔ cup butter until soft. Add the clams and cook until they are plump and heated through. Salt and pepper to taste and add a few grains of cayenne. Serve on toast.

CLAMS SAUTÉ

Clams should be dipped in flour or beaten egg and crumbs and then sautéed in plenty of butter.

1. *Razor clams.* Clean the clams, and either use whole or only the tender digging foot — if clams are plentiful. Dip in flour, or in egg and crumbs, and sauté quickly in plenty of butter. Salt and pepper to taste and serve with lemon wedges.

2. *Soft clams.* Clean and dip in flour, or egg and crumbs, and sauté lightly until delicately browned. Add chopped parsley and lemon juice, salt, and freshly ground black pepper.

3. *Littleneck clams.* The procedure is the same as for soft clams.

BATTER-FRIED CLAMS

2 eggs, separated	1 tablespoon lemon juice
1 tablespoon olive oil	About 2 cups of small clams
1 cup sifted flour	Fat *or* oil heated to 365°
⅓ teaspoon salt	Salt
½ cup milk	Freshly ground black pepper

Beat the egg yolks until light and lemon-colored. Beat in the olive oil, flour, salt, milk, and lemon juice. Beat the egg whites until stiff and fold them in. Add the clams. Let stand for 2 hours. Drop by spoonfuls into hot fat and pan-fry 4 or 5 minutes or until golden brown. Drain on absorbent paper and salt and pepper to taste.

VARIATION

Substitute 1 tablespoon of brandy or whiskey for the lemon juice.

GREEN NOODLES WITH CLAMS

1 quart clams in shell	½ cup chopped parsley (Italian,
1 medium onion	if possible)
1 stalk of celery	1½ tablespoons chopped basil
1 carrot	Salt
1 cup white wine *or* vermouth	Freshly ground black pepper
½ cup olive oil	8 ounces green noodles
3 cloves garlic, finely chopped	(white will do)

Wash the clams well. Cut the onion, celery, and carrot into fine strips, and put them in a large kettle. Add the wine and the clams. Cover tightly and steam until the clams open. Remove the clams from their shells and strain the broth. Heat the olive oil and the garlic; add the parsley, basil, salt, and pepper to taste. Reduce the clam broth by half, add it to the olive oil mixture, and let it come to a boil. Taste for seasoning. Add the clams, chopped.

Cook the noodles and drain. Pour the clam mixture over the noodles.

VARIATION

Combine the clam mixture with ½ cup of tomato sauce and cook until well blended. Thin with a dash of white wine or vermouth. Serve the same way.

SPAGHETTI WITH CLAM SAUCE

Use the preceding recipe but substitute spaghetti for the noodles.

Conch

This southern shellfish has a fine flavor, but its toughness presents the same problem as the Pacific Coast abalone. There are several ways to tenderize it. One is to pound it with a sharp-edged instrument, or as the average housewife does, with the edge of a plate. Another way is to parboil it and then pound until the flesh is tender. Still another method, followed by Sloppy Louie, the famous New York fish dealer and restaurateur, is to immerse live conch in boiling water. As soon as the live conch (pronounced *konk,* by the way) is affected by the heat and retreats into its shell, take it from the water, drain, and shell it. It must be shelled at almost the instant it releases its muscles or it will still require beating or parboiling.

CONCH FRITTERS

6 conchs
½ cup chopped onion
½ cup chopped tomato
  (peeled and seeded)
2 cloves garlic, chopped

1 teaspoon salt
1 cup rolled cracker crumbs
¼ cup chopped parsley
3 eggs, separated

Grind the conch meat and combine it with the onion, tomato, garlic, salt, parsley, crumbs, and the yolks of the eggs beaten lightly. Beat the egg whites until stiff. If the batter seems stiff thin it with cream, then fold in the egg whites. Drop the mixture by spoonfuls on a well-buttered pan or griddle. Cook until nicely browned and turn to brown the other side. Serve with lemon butter (page 31).

STEWED CONCH

4 conchs	1 teaspoon basil, or more
2 onions, chopped	1 teaspoon salt
3 cloves garlic, chopped	2 cups tomato sauce
6 tablespoons olive oil	1 cup red wine

Tenderize the conchs. Sauté the onions and garlic in oil. Add the basil, salt, tomato sauce, and wine and simmer for 30 minutes. Dilute the sauce with a little more wine if it gets too thick. Add the conch and cook just until it heats through and is tender. Taste for seasoning and serve on rice.

FRIED CONCH

For 4 people, tenderize 4 conchs. Cut them into thin slices. Dip them in flour, then into beaten egg, and roll in crumbs or corn meal.

Heat the fat in your deep fryer to 375°; and fry the strips of conch for about 3 minutes or until nicely browned and crisp on the edges. Remove to absorbent paper and season to taste. Serve with tartar sauce (pages 35–36).

Crab

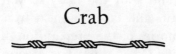

Crab is second to shrimp as the shellfish most preferred by

Americans, and the supply is varied and fairly abundant. The magnificently flavored Pacific Coast crab — the Dungeness — is now brought frozen to the East. The giant king crab is flown fresh from Alaska and is also shipped frozen. Crab caught in the Gulf and in the North and South Atlantic is sent in refrigerated tins to all parts of the East and far inland. In addition, the famous stone crabs from Florida often appear in our markets, and quantities of soft-shelled crabs are shipped all over the East.

There is general misunderstanding about soft-shelled crabs. They are not a distinct soft-shelled species — they are the same blue crabs (*Callinecte sapidus*) found all along the Atlantic Coast. It is the habit of the crab to shed its shell many times before maturity, and the soft-shelled crab is one caught just as it has shed one shell and before it has grown a new and larger one.

On the Pacific Coast, most crabs are sold whole and freshly cooked. In the East, with the exception of the soft-shelled, crab is usually sold already cleaned and shelled in 1- or ½-pound tins. There are many different grades of this crabmeat on the Eastern market. The larger, choice lump crabmeat is hard to find in retail shops, for most of it is bought by the better restaurants and clubs. But various other qualities are generally available. Some markets carry the leg meat, which has excellent flavor and is delicious for salads and for deviled crab. The giant crab legs (from claw tip to claw tip, these gargantuan crustaceans sometimes measure almost 9 feet across) are sent from Alaska frozen and ready to broil.

Crabmeat is expensive; however, there is no waste, and a pound will serve 4 people well.

If you are cooking live crabs — which is unlikely unless you go crabbing — boil them in sea water or in a mild court bouillon, allowing 8 minutes for each pound of crab. When the crab is cool, remove its back and the spongy parts under the shell. Then remove the apron and split the body so you can take out the meat. Crack the claws and take the meat from them.

I have vivid memories of the preparation of the crabs that we caught on the Pacific Coast when I was young. The system followed by my mother and most of our neighbors was to remove the back and clean the crab before plunging it into the boiling sea water. Supposedly the flavor was much better if the crab were cleaned first. These crabs — the Dungeness variety — were cooled and then used for many special dishes. My favorite was, and still is, a feast of cracked crab and mayonnaise freshly made with good olive oil, flavored with lemon juice, mustard, salt, pepper, and a touch of tarragon. With good bread and butter and a bottle of chilled white wine, this is the absolute ultimate for a summer luncheon.

CRABMEAT VINAIGRETTE

Arrange 1 pound of crabmeat (either Dungeness or blue crab) on romaine or lettuce. Cover with the vinaigrette sauce (page 36) and sprinkle with fresh or dried tarragon.

CRABMEAT COCKTAIL OR CRABMEAT AS A FIRST COURSE

Most restaurants insist on smothering crab with a hot tomato sauce that kills its elegant flavor. If more of them would only learn to send you a choice of different sauces for crabmeat, I'm sure the dining-out public would be pleased. Here are a few suggestions.

1. Serve fine lump or leg crabmeat on a bed of watercress or romaine. Top with a sauce rémoulade (page 35).

2. Arrange crabmeat on a bed of shredded Boston or leaf lettuce and serve with a Russian dressing. Garnish with hard-cooked egg slices.

3. Serve large lump crabmeat — or the choicest Dungeness crab legs — garnished with paper-thin slices of peeled tomato and very thinly sliced onions. Pass a bowl of well-flavored olive oil mayonnaise and capers.

CRAB LEGS PALACE COURT

This is one of the most famous first course specialties in the country. It has been one of the outstanding dishes at the Palace Hotel in San Francisco for generations. It was a favorite at the old Wednesday luncheons and is truly an American classic.

Start with a bed of shredded lettuce — preferably leaf or Boston lettuce. Then add a large artichoke heart filled with salade Russe (a mixture of cooked tiny peas, finely diced cooked carrot, finely cut cooked snap beans, and diced cooked potatoes bound together with mayonnaise). Arrange 5 or 6 large crab legs on the salade Russe and top with a Thousand Island dressing or a Russian dressing. Surround the base of the artichoke with finely chopped hard-cooked egg and garnish with strips of green pepper or pimiento.

CRAB LOUIS

This is another dish that comes from the Pacific Coast. The late Helen Evans Brown said it was served at Solari's in San Francisco in 1914. If I'm not mistaken, the father of the late West Coast writer Richard L. Neuberger served it in his Bohemian Restaurant in Portland, Oregon, at that time, too. At any rate, the old Bohemian served the finest Louis I have ever eaten.

It is very easy to make this superb dish. Begin with a bed of finely shredded lettuce. Heap plenty of crabmeat on top and garnish with quartered hard-cooked eggs and quartered tomatoes. Pour a Louis dressing (page 36) over all.

AVOCADO STUFFED WITH CRABMEAT

This is a very popular first course in Florida and in the West. My favorite sauce for this is made with ½ cup good mayonnaise, ½ cup stiffly whipped cream, ⅓ cup chili sauce, and 1 tablespoon grated onion. Mix the sauce with the crabmeat and stuff the avocado.

SAUTÉED CRAB WITH ALMONDS

7 tablespoons butter	Salt
1 pound crabmeat	Freshly ground black pepper
⅔ cup almonds, blanched and split in half	⅓ cup heavy cream
	3 tablespoons chopped parsley

Melt 4 tablespoons of the butter in a skillet over medium heat, add the crabmeat, and toss lightly until it is delicately browned. While this is cooking, sauté the almonds in the remaining 3 tablespoons butter over a rather brisk flame until they brown lightly. Salt and pepper to taste and add to the crabmeat. Finally add the cream and parsley, increase the heat, and let it cook up and boil for 2 minutes. Serve on rice or rounds of fried toast.

VARIATIONS

1. Add 3 tablespoons sherry just before serving.
2. Omit the almonds and add 3 tablespoons chives or finely chopped green onion. Cook these with the crab and then add 3 tablespoons tomato sauce or chili sauce to the pan before adding the cream.
3. Add ½ cup cream and 1 tablespoon curry powder to the crabmeat and serve on rice with crisp French-fried onions.
4. Combine the crab with ½ pound mushrooms that have been sautéed in 6 tablespoons butter and flavored with lemon juice. Add ⅓ cup cream and let it cook down for 3 or 4 minutes.
5. This variation is called *Crabmeat Marseillaise*. To the sautéed crabmeat add an equal amount of mussels that have been opened (see mussels, page 416) and removed from their shells. Add 1 cup of heavy cream and let it cook down slightly.

POLLY HAMBLET'S DEVILED CRAB
(DEVILED CRAB I)

This is the recipe for the deviled crab that I ate as a child. It was the first one I ever tasted and has been my favorite ever since. Originally I had it made with Dungeness crab, but many times since I have had it made with blue crabs and even with king crab. It never fails to please me.

1 pound crabmeat	1 teaspoon dry mustard
1½ cups rolled cracker crumbs	½ teaspoon salt
¾ cup finely diced celery	Few grains cayenne pepper
¾ cup chopped onion	2 tablespoons chopped parsley
½ cup butter, melted	1 tablespoon chopped green
¼ cup milk	pepper

Combine the crabmeat with the crumbs, celery, and onion and moisten with the butter and milk. Season with the mustard, salt, cayenne, parsley, and green pepper. Mix thoroughly, pile into shells or a casserole, and bake in a 350° oven for about ½ hour.

DEVILED CRAB II

The average deviled crab in New York is made with a cream sauce base. It has other seasonings, but the creaminess is the dominant quality.

1 pound crabmeat	2 tablespoons chopped parsley
2 cups sauce velouté (page 21)	2 tablespoons finely chopped
2 egg yolks, lightly beaten	green pepper
1 teaspoon dry mustard	Buttered crumbs
Few grains cayenne pepper	

Combine the crabmeat, the sauce, egg yolks, and the flavorings. Heap into individual shells or ramekins or a large baking dish. Dust with buttered crumbs and brown quickly in a 425° oven.

1. Add 3 tablespoons sherry to the mixture before putting it in the shells.

2. Add 2 tablespoons grated onion to the sauce before adding the crabmeat.

DEVILED CRAB III

½ cup red wine	2 tablespoons chopped green
1 tablespoon chili sauce	pepper
1 teaspoon dry mustard	4 tablespoons butter
1 tablespoon Worcestershire	4 tablespoons chopped parsley
sauce	1 pound crabmeat
Dash of Tabasco	Salt
6 tablespoons finely chopped	Buttered crumbs
onion	

Combine the wine and the seasonings and heat thoroughly for 3 or 4 minutes. Cook the onion and green pepper in the butter for 2 minutes. Add the parsley and combine with the sauce and the crabmeat. Salt to taste, pile into shells, top with buttered crumbs, and dot with butter. Bake at 425° just long enough to brown.

CRABMEAT IN CREAM

Add 1 pound of crabmeat to 1 cup of béchamel (page 23) or sauce velouté (page 21). Serve on toast, in patty shells, or in croustades.

VARIATIONS

1. Add ¼ cup sherry or Madeira to the sauce.

2. Use half crabmeat and half shrimp, clams, or mussels. Add 4 tablespoons sherry or Madeira to the mixture.

3. Combine ¾ pound crabmeat with ½ pound sliced sautéed mushrooms. Add to the sauce and flavor with 3 tablespoons brandy or whiskey.

4. This variation is called *Hongroise*. Add 1 tablespoon of Hungarian paprika to the sauce.

5. *Indienne.* Add 2 tablespoons grated onion and 1 tablespoon curry powder to the sauce. Serve on rice with a garnish of toasted almonds and crisp French-fried onions.

6. Pile creamed crab in a baking dish or in individual ramekins. Sprinkle with finely chopped almonds and crumbs and dot with butter. Brown quickly in a 425° oven.

CRABMEAT MORNAY

Combine 1 pound crabmeat with 1¾ to 2 cups sauce Mornay (page 22). Serve with croustades or in ramekins.

VARIATIONS

1. Heap the crabmeat Mornay in shells or ramekins and top with grated cheese and buttered toasted crumbs. Run under the broiler for a few minutes to brown.

2. *Florentine.* Cover the bottom of a casserole with finely chopped cooked spinach. Top with crabmeat and cover with sauce Mornay. Sprinkle with paprika and buttered crumbs and brown quickly under the broiler or in a hot oven.

3. Poach some small oysters in their own liquor and a little white wine until the edges curl. In a baking dish arrange a layer of crabmeat and then a layer of the oysters. Top with sauce Mornay, sprinkle with crumbs and grated cheese, and brown quickly under the broiler.

4. Stuff large mushroom caps with crabmeat and arrange in a flat baking dish. Top each mushroom with sauce Mornay and sprinkle with crumbs. Brown quickly under the broiler or bake in a 450° oven for 10 or 12 minutes.

5. Heat the crabmeat in 3 tablespoons butter. Add 1 tablespoon grated horseradish, 1 teaspoon dry mustard, 4 tablespoons chopped parsley, and 2 tablespoons grated onion. Arrange in the bottom of a baking dish and top with sauce Mornay. Sprinkle with buttered crumbs and brown quickly under the broiler.

CRABMEAT SOUFFLÉ

3 tablespoons butter	Nutmeg
1 tablespoon grated onion	Juice of ½ lemon
4 tablespoons flour	1½ cups crabmeat
¾ cup milk	4 egg yolks, slightly beaten
Salt	6 egg whites
Freshly ground black pepper	

Melt the butter in a heavy saucepan, add the onion, and cook for 2 or 3 minutes. Add the flour and mix well. Gradually stir in the milk until the mixture has thickened. Season to taste with the salt, pepper, nutmeg, and lemon juice. Remove from the heat, add the crabmeat, and stir in the egg yolks. Beat the egg whites until stiff. Fold in one half of them and blend well. Then fold in the second half very lightly. Pour into a buttered soufflé dish and bake in a 375° oven for 35 to 45 minutes or until the soufflé is light and puffy.

Serve with a sauce Mornay (page 22) or a sauce béchamel (page 23) with a little crabmeat and 4 tablespoons sherry added.

CRAB CAKES

This famous Southern dish has changed a great deal from the early days, possibly because we have lost much of the quality and distinction of the good regional cooking of the eighteenth and nineteenth centuries. It is my personal opinion that these popular cakes, considered great delicacies in Maryland, are a bit on the heavy side. But they have a great public.

4 tablespoons butter	1 teaspoon salt
1 medium onion, chopped	1 teaspoon dry mustard
1 cup bread crumbs	4 tablespoons chopped parsley
1 pound crabmeat	Heavy cream
3 eggs, beaten	Flour

Melt the butter in a skillet and cook the onion until just transparent. Add the crumbs and blend well. Mix with the crabmeat, eggs, and seasonings. Add just enough cream to bind the mixture together. Shape into large flat cakes. Roll each cake in flour and fry in butter or oil until nicely browned on both sides and cooked through. Serve with tartar sauce (pages 35–36) or lemon butter (page 31).

PILAF DE CRABE

This is a recipe from a small Martiniquaise restaurant in Paris that specializes in all the dishes of the Indies.

6 strips of bacon, finely cut	1 pound crabmeat
2 medium onions, finely chopped	1/3 cup dark rum
1 clove garlic, finely chopped	1 cup white wine
1/2 pound smoked ham, cut in thin strips	1 tablespoon chopped parsley
3 tablespoons tomato paste	Pinch of sugar
	1/4 cup heavy cream

Let the bacon try out in a large skillet. Add the onions and garlic and allow them to just color. Add the ham and heat through. Add the tomato paste and crabmeat; pour the rum over this and ignite. When it has flamed, add the wine, parsley, and sugar and let it all simmer for 15 minutes. Finally stir in the heavy cream. Serve with a rice pilaf.

CRAB À L'AMÉRICAINE

If live crabs are available in your part of the country, use them in this recipe and eat the crab from the shell, cracking the claws at the table. If you cannot get crab in the shell, follow the note at the end of the recipe. First, the sauce:

Sauce Américaine

3 tablespoons butter	3 tablespoons chopped parsley
1 small onion, finely chopped	1 tablespoon fresh *or* 1 teaspoon
6 shallots *or* green onions,	dried tarragon
finely chopped	1½ teaspoons thyme
5 large or 8 medium tomatoes,	½ bay leaf
peeled, seeded, and chopped	Salt
1 clove garlic, chopped	4 tablespoons tomato paste

Melt the butter in a skillet, add the onions, and let them cook for a few minutes but do not let them brown. Add the shallots, tomatoes, garlic, and seasonings and salt to taste. Let this all simmer for 1 hour or until well blended and thick. Add the tomato paste. Now, for the rest of the recipe:

3 Dungeness crabs *or* 6 rather	1½ cups white wine
small blue crabs	¼ cup cognac *or* whiskey
½ cup olive oil	Few grains cayenne pepper

Wash the crabs and remove their backs. Crack the claws, and cut the crabs in half with a sharp knife. Heat the olive oil in a large kettle, add the pieces of crab and sear quickly, turning with a wooden spoon and fork so that the flesh of the crab comes into contact with the hot oil. Add the white wine, brandy, and sauce and let it all simmer for 20 or 25 minutes. Add the cayenne, and taste for seasoning. Serve with a rice pilaf and plenty of large paper napkins or biblike aprons. This is not a dainty dish to eat and you must use your fingers.

NOTE: If you are making this dish with crabmeat already taken from the shell, prepare the sauce in the same way. Then sauté the crabmeat — 1½ pounds — in the olive oil for 3 minutes. Add the brandy or whiskey and the wine. Combine with the sauce and cook up for just a few minutes before serving.

CRABMEAT AND RICE

1½ cups rice	3 tablespoons grated onion
1 pound crabmeat	2 finely chopped pimientos
1 cup cooked green peas	Salt
6 tablespoons butter	Freshly ground black pepper
½ cup finely chopped parsley	Grated Parmesan cheese

Cook the rice in your usual way. When it is drained and fluffy add the crabmeat, peas, butter, and flavorings. Season to taste and toss lightly until well mixed. Place in a casserole or copper baking dish, sprinkle liberally with grated cheese, dot with butter, and heat in a 425° oven for 10 minutes — or until it is thoroughly heated through. Serve with a tomato sauce, if you wish, although I prefer mine plain.

CRABMEAT CREOLE

2 small onions, thinly sliced	½ cup white wine
¼ cup olive oil	1 clove garlic, crushed
1 large *or* 2 small green peppers, finely shredded	3 tablespoons tomato paste
4 tomatoes, peeled and chopped	Salt
1 stalk celery, finely chopped	Freshly ground black pepper
	1 pound crabmeat

Sauté the onions in the olive oil until just soft but not browned. Add the peppers, tomatoes, and celery. Cover and simmer for 25 to 30 minutes or until the vegetables are soft and well blended. Add the garlic, tomato paste, and salt and pepper to taste. Finally add the crabmeat and cook until it is thoroughly heated. Serve with rice.

CRABMEAT QUICHE

Pastry for a 9-inch shell	1 tablespoon finely chopped
Egg white	celery

2 tablespoons finely chopped
  parsley
¼ cup white wine *or* 2 tablespoons sherry *or* dry vermouth
About 1½ cups crabmeat

Salt
Freshly ground black pepper
5 eggs
1½ cups milk
Paprika

Line a 9-inch pie plate with a rich pastry and chill it for at least
1 hour. Brush the bottom of the crust with white of egg. Fill it
with a mixture of the celery, parsley, wine, crabmeat, and seasonings. Mix the eggs and milk together thoroughly and pour over
the crabmeat mixture. Sprinkle lightly with paprika and bake at
450° for 10 minutes. Reduce the heat to 350° and continue baking until the custard is set, about 20 minutes. Serve as a first
course or as the main course at luncheon.

Soft-Shelled Crab

The smaller the soft-shelled crab and the earlier it is caught
in the molting process, the tenderer and the better flavored it
will be. Usually soft-shelled crab is bought already cleaned at
the market, but here is the process in case you must do it yourself. With the aid of a small sharp-pointed knife, fold back the
covering at the points of the back, and remove all the spongy
bits you find there. Turn the crab over and remove the small
apron on the front.

Two or three soft-shelled crabs are usually ample for one portion. There are, of course, some people with hearty appetites
who can eat a dozen at a sitting.

SOFT-SHELLED CRABS MEUNIÈRE

8 to 12 soft-shelled crabs,
  cleaned
Flour
6 to 8 tablespoons butter
Salt

Freshly ground black pepper
6 or more tablespoons chopped
  parsley
Lemon slices

Dip the crabs in flour and cook them in hot butter until they are delicately browned and crisp on the edges. Salt and pepper to taste. Add chopped parsley and transfer to a hot platter. Pour the pan juices over the crabs and serve with lemon slices.

VARIATIONS

Sautéed Crabs Amandine. Add ½ cup of blanched sliced almonds to the pan with the crabs and cook them until they are lightly browned. Pour over the crabs.

Soft-shelled Crabs in Cream. After removing the sautéed crabs to a platter add 3 tablespoons flour to the pan and stir until lightly browned. Add 1½ cups heavy cream and stir until thickened and well blended. Add 4 tablespoons Madeira or sherry. Taste for seasoning. Pour the cream sauce over the crabs and serve with fried toast.

SAUTÉED CRABS GRENOBLOISE

Dust 8 to 12 soft-shelled crabs with flour. Sauté, 3 or 4 crabs at a time, in 3 tablespoons of butter and 3 tablespoons of oil, until nicely browned, adding more butter and oil if needed. Remove the crabs to a warm platter and add to the pan the juice of one lemon, ⅓ cup capers, ⅓ cup chopped parsley, and ⅓ cup chopped chives (optional). Swirl sauce in pan, adding a tablespoon or two of butter if you wish, and pour sauce over the crabs. Garnish with paper-thin slices of lemon and serve immediately.

BROILED SOFT-SHELLED CRABS

12 Soft-shelled crabs, cleaned	½ cup chopped parsley
Flour	2 teaspoons paprika
½ cup butter or more	1 teaspoon salt

Dust the crabs lightly with flour. Arrange them on a broiling rack or in a flat broiling dish. Cream the butter with the seasonings. Dot the crabs liberally with the butter mixture and broil about 3 inches from the heat, basting often and turning once during the cooking. These will take from 5 to 8 minutes to cook, depending upon their size. Serve with the pan juices poured over them.

FRIED SOFT-SHELLED CRABS

Heat fat for frying in your French fryer to 375°. Dip cleaned crabs in flour, then in beaten egg, and then in dry crumbs (bread or cracker). Fry for 4 or 5 minutes or until nicely browned. Remove to absorbent paper and salt and pepper to taste. Serve with tartar sauce (pages 35–36) or sauce rémoulade (page 35).

SOFT-SHELLED CRABS À L'AMÉRICAINE

Prepare a sauce à l'Américaine (page 28). Sauté the crabs in olive oil with a finely chopped clove of garlic. Add the sauce and let it all simmer for about 10 minutes. Serve with rice.

King Crab or Alaska Crab

These giant land crabs were known before World War II as Japanese crabs, and great quantities of them were shipped into this country in cans. It was excellent canned crab for creamed dishes, soups, and curries. Now it is a product of Alaska — the fishing beds having come under our supervision since World War II. This delectable and expensive delicacy is obtainable frozen — usually precooked in its shell — and also as cleaned crabmeat. One of the giant center claws is a generous portion. In my opinion it is as fine as any crabmeat I have ever tasted.

KING CRAB SALAD

Cut the meat into good-sized lumps and combine with mayonnaise. Garnish with chopped hard-cooked eggs and capers. Serve on a bed of greens.

BROILED KING CRAB LEGS

Remove just enough of the tough shell of each leg so that you can baste the meat inside freely. You should also consider the diner and allow enough room for him to get in with knife and fork. Brush the meat well with butter and broil over charcoal or under the broiler just long enough to heat it through. (Remember these crabs are precooked.) Baste during the cooking with melted butter and lemon juice or dry sherry. Take care that you do not overcook. Serve with additional melted butter.

CRAB LEGS RÉMOULADE OR MAYONNAISE

Serve the crab legs in the shell after you have thoroughly thawed them. Pass the rémoulade (page 35) or mayonnaise (page 34) and lemon wedges.

KING CRAB À L'AMÉRICAINE

Leave the meat in the shells, but cut each shell in half and sauté very quickly in olive oil. Combine with sauce à l'Américaine (page 28) and serve as you do lobster à l'Américaine.

KING CRAB NEWBURG

See lobster Newburg, pages 396–397.

KING CRAB THERMIDOR

See lobster thermidor, page 398.

KING CRAB SOUFFLÉ

See crabmeat soufflé, page 377.

Stone Crabs

This delicacy is found mainly in the South around Key West, Miami, and Palm Beach. Only the large claws are used.

STONE CRAB LEGS BEURRE NOIR

Cook the crabs in a court bouillon (page 18) for 20 minutes. Remove the large claws and serve them, 2 to 4 to a person, with beurre noir and wedges of lemon. (For beurre noir, see page 31.) Save the other parts of the crab for salad or for:

CRABMEAT SAUTÉ FLORIDA

Pick the meat from the crab and sauté 2 cups of it in ¼ pound butter, tossing it lightly. Salt and pepper to taste and add 4 tablespoons lime juice and ¼ cup chopped parsley. Serve on fried toast.

VARIATION

Add 4 tablespoons sherry or Madeira.

Crawfish or Crayfish

These are the beloved écrevisses of the French. They are rare in Eastern markets but sold in large quantities in Portland, Seattle, New Orleans, and in Wisconsin and Minnesota.

As a young boy, I often fished for crawfish in the Necanicum River in Oregon, using a piece of liver on a string. Later, I also enjoyed great plates of them, along with many glasses of beer, at Jake's Crawfish Parlor in Portland. Jake's crawfish were cooked to perfection in a spiced court bouillon. Years afterward, in more sophisticated days, I ate the fabulous and famed *gratin d'écrevisses* in the great restaurants of France. I have eaten them, too, at the Swedish festivals in August when crawfish are the special dish, accompanied, of course, by aquavit and beer.

In some parts of the country you will find crawfish in the markets the year round. In other areas you must check with your local fish dealer to find when they will be available.

It is hard to tell you just how many crawfish will make a serving. One person can easily eat 10 to 12, but some people may want more than a dozen.

ÉCREVISSES BORDELAISE

24 to 36 crawfish
2 carrots, cut in julienne strips
2 onions, cut in julienne strips
2 stalks celery, cut in julienne strips
4 or 5 tablespoons butter

Salt   2 cups white wine
Freshly ground black pepper   1½ cups tomato sauce

Wash the crawfish well. It is wise to tear off the tiny wing in the center of the tail. This loosens and brings with it the small black intestine.

Prepare a mirepoix: Melt the butter in a large kettle and cook the vegetables in it until they are wilted. Salt and pepper to taste, add the wine, and let it cook for a few minutes. Add the crawfish and cook them just long enough to color their shells — about 5 minutes. Add the tomato sauce. Bring it up to a boil and let it blend with the other seasonings. Taste for seasoning, and pour into a big tureen or bowl. Serve with plenty of saffron rice and a good stout salad of greens.

GRATIN D'ÉCREVISSES

36 crawfish   Duchess potatoes, *or* rice *or* a
Court bouillon *or* salted water   croustade
½ cup creamed butter   Grated Gruyère *or* Parmesan
Sauce velouté (page 21)   cheese

Clean the crawfish (or not, as you prefer) and cook in a court bouillon (page 18) or in salted water. When they are cool enough to handle, remove the meat from the tails, and any meat from the bodies. Keep several of the shells for garnish. Grind the rest of the shells, or pound them in a mortar. Blend them with the creamed butter and force the mixture through a fine sieve.

Prepare a sauce velouté. Stir the crawfish butter into the sauce to color it and give it flavor. Add the crawfish meat and cook just long enough to heat it through.

Pour the crawfish mixture on a flameproof serving dish and surround it with a border of Duchess potatoes or rice. Or pour it into a large croustade, which you have made by hollowing out a loaf of bread and toasting it in the oven. Sprinkle the top with the grated cheese and decorate it with the whole shells. Run the dish under the broiler just long enough to melt the cheese and glaze the top.

COLD CRAWFISH, SPICED

Wash and clean the crawfish, being sure to pull off the tiny wing in the center of the tail. Cook them in a spicy court bouillon (page 18) for about 5 minutes — no more. Cool the crawfish in the court bouillon and let them stand in it for several hours. Serve cold with bread and butter — preferably rye bread — and either beer or a dry white wine, well chilled.

CRAWFISH RÉMOULADE

This is one of my favorites as a first course.

To serve 4 people, cook 36 crawfish in a court bouillon (page 18) and let them cool. When cool enough to handle, remove the meat from the tails. Chill it. To serve, arrange the crawfish meat on a bed of greens and accompany with a well-seasoned sauce rémoulade (page 35).

Lobster

Like Europeans, we are blessed with two types of shellfish called lobster. The "homard," or lobster with claws, comes from the northern waters around Maine and Nova Scotia. The spiny, or rock, lobster is caught in southern waters, but is only a distant relative of the homard. Both varieties are superb eating, and the homard, especially, is one of the great delicacies of the sea.

The northern European homard is very much like ours, and their Mediterranean langouste resembles our rock lobster, although, to my taste, the Mediterranean variety has much sweeter meat. European lobster is not sold in our markets, but frozen rock lobster tails shipped from South Africa are now generally available and are very popular.

Our native lobsters can be bought whole and already boiled in most markets — or as cooked lobster meat in frozen tins. If you prefer to cook your own, as most people do, you buy a live lobster. Never cook a dead one. The larger the lobster the more likely it is to be tough. The small lobster is the true delicacy.

Some people object to plunging a lobster into boiling water or bouillon while it is still alive. Don't let this process affect your appetite. Lobsters are most insensitive creatures. Killing them in hot water is almost instantaneous and certainly as merciful as any other method. True, they wriggle. It would be helpful if more American fish dealers would adopt the French custom of trussing the beasts with string when they sell them. This makes the task of popping the lobster into the pot much simpler.

The easiest way to prepare lobster is to boil it. It can be served hot with melted butter and lemon juice, or cold with mayonnaise or any other cold sauce.

BOILED LOBSTER

For a 1-to-1½-pound lobster use 3 quarts of water and about 3 tablespoons of salt. Or you may use ocean water. Bring the water to a rolling boil. Grab the lobster from behind the head and plunge it into the water. Cover and let it simmer for 5 minutes for the first pound, and 3 minutes more for each additional pound. Remove the lobster from the water and place it on its back. Using a large heavy knife and a hammer or mallet, split it in half from end to end starting at the head. Remove the stomach and intestinal vein.

Do not discard the green liver, or tomalley. It is delicious. In female lobsters you may find a pinkish red deposit — the roe —

often called lobster coral. This is one of the choicest bits and can be eaten with the lobster or used in sauce.

The claws should be cracked with a nutcracker so the meat can be easily extracted at the table.

BROILED LIVE LOBSTER

This is one of the favorite dishes in the United States. Personally, I think it is rather dull and, unless superbly done with a wood or charcoal fire, not worth the money. However, here is the method.

Use a 1½- or 2-pound lobster for each person. You can ask your fish dealer to split and clean the lobster. To do it yourself, first kill the lobster by inserting a sharp knife between the body and tail shells; this cuts the spinal cord. Then place the lobster on its back, and with a heavy sharp knife and mallet, split it. Cut right through the back shell separating the two halves. Remove the stomach and the intestinal vein that you will find running down the tail section close to the back. Leave the liver, which is the grayish-looking meat in the body cavity (it turns green after cooking). Butter each half lobster well. Have bowls of melted butter handy. You will need it during the cooking process and will serve it with the lobsters later. Preheat your broiler for 10 minutes.

Place your lobster halves on the broiler rack, flesh side to the heat, and broil until they are cooked through. Baste frequently with the melted butter. The cooking time should be about 12 to 15 minutes. Salt and pepper to taste and serve on very hot plates with plenty of melted butter and lemon wedges. Shoestring or French-fried potatoes are the accepted accompaniment.

LOBSTER À L'AMÉRICAINE

This is probably the most famous of all lobster dishes. It has been called by many names and was originally lobster Proven-çale, a dish native to the south of France where the people have used tomatoes in sauces for generations. It has also been called *homard armoricaine* by those who thought the dish originated in Armorique. It is now generally conceded that the first lobster à l'Américaine, as we now know it, was prepared at the restaurant of Noel-Peters in the Passage de Prince in Paris — not a favorite spot today, but once exceedingly fashionable.

3 pounds lobster
½ cup olive oil
3 tablespoons butter
1 small onion, finely chopped
6 shallots, finely chopped
1 clove garlic, peeled and
  chopped
6 ripe tomatoes, peeled, seeded,
  and chopped
3 tablespoons chopped parsley

1 tablespoon chopped fresh, *or*
  1 teaspoon dried, tarragon
1½ teaspoons thyme
½ bay leaf
1½ cups white wine
3 tablespoons tomato paste
Cayenne pepper
Salt
¼ cup cognac

Wash the lobster(s) well. With a very sharp heavy knife cut medallions of the tail, cutting through the markings in the tail. Cut the body in half, clean it, and save the liver and coral, if any, for the sauce. Remove the claws.

Heat the olive oil and add the pieces of lobster. Toss them around in the oil until the shells have turned red and the meat is seared. Remove the meat and shells to a hot platter. Add the butter to the pan with the olive oil and sauté the onions and shallots until lightly colored. Add the garlic, tomatoes, herbs, and white wine and let it simmer for 30 minutes. Add the tomato paste and season to taste. Pour the cognac over the lobster pieces and ignite. Then put them in the sauce, cover, and simmer for about 20 minutes. At the last, stir in the liver and lobster coral.

Serve with a rice pilaf.

NOTE: The meat of the lobster may be removed from the shells before adding it to the sauce. If you do this, be sure to put the shells in for the added flavor they give to the sauce. Personally,

I feel that taking lobster meat from the shell before serving makes no sense unless it is going into a tart, or soufflé, or some other form of preparation that actually requires it.

CHAUSSON OF LOBSTER À L'AMÉRICAINE

1 pound puff paste
Lobster à l'Américaine (see
   preceding recipe)
Beaten egg

Heavy cream
Butter
Chopped parsley

A chausson is a large turnover made of puff paste. Use your favorite recipe for the paste and chill it for 2 hours. Then roll it out in a circle about ⅓ inch thick. Spread the center with lobster à l'Américaine (without the shells) and save some of the sauce. Now, fold one part of the circle two-thirds of the way over the lobster mixture. Take the other end of the pastry and pull that over the first fold. Now you should have two thicknesses of pastry over the center part. Seal the edges with a little cold water, brush the pastry well with beaten egg, and put it in a 450° oven. Bake for 10 minutes and reduce the heat to 350°. Continue baking until the pastry is cooked — about 30 to 35 minutes.

Serve the chausson in slices with the remaining sauce, which you have heated with a little heavy cream and a good pat of butter. Garnish with chopped parsley.

LOBSTER OMELET

Sauté lobster meat lightly in butter with a little chopped onion and parsley. Fold the mixture into individual omelets and garnish with broiled mushroom caps.

LOBSTER FRA DIAVOLO

This is the Italian version of lobster à l'Américaine. In fact, it might even be the original. The following recipe will serve two people.

2 lobsters (1 to 1½ pounds each)
6 tablespoons olive oil
4 sprigs of parsley
1 teaspoon thyme *or* oregano
1 small onion, finely chopped
1 clove garlic, finely chopped
Pinch of cloves
Pinch of mace
Salt
Freshly ground black pepper
2 cups cooked tomatoes
¼ cup brandy

Split the live lobsters and cook them in hot olive oil until the color has turned. Continue cooking gently for about 10 minutes. Add the seasonings, herbs, and tomatoes. Cover and cook for about 15 minutes, stirring often. Arrange a ring of rice on a serving dish. Put the lobster halves in the center and pour the sauce over them. Add the brandy and blaze just before serving.

CIVET OF LOBSTER

This is really still another version of lobster à l'Américaine.

1 lobster (about 2 pounds)
2 tablespoons butter
2 medium onions, chopped
2 cloves garlic, chopped
4 or 5 ripe tomatoes, peeled, seeded, and chopped
½ teaspoon thyme
½ teaspoon tarragon
2 tablespoons chopped parsley
Salt
Freshly ground black pepper
3 tablespoons olive oil
½ cup white wine
¼ cup cognac *or* whiskey
Liver and intestines of the lobster

Cut the lobster in small pieces as for lobster à l'Américaine. Remove the claws. Reserve the liver and intestines. Butter a shallow skillet or saucepan. Put the onions, garlic, and tomatoes with the herbs in the saucepan. Place the pieces of lobster on this bed of vegetables, salt and pepper to taste, and brush well with olive oil. Add the wine and cognac, cover, and bring to a boil. Let it boil vigorously for about 2 minutes. Remove the pieces of lobster to a hot platter. Add the liver, intestines, liquid, and a little more parsley to the saucepan and let it cook down for a few minutes. Taste for seasoning and pour the sauce over the pieces of lobster. Serve with rice.

LOBSTER FRANCO-AMERICAN

This, too, is a version of lobster à l'Américaine.

2 lobsters (about 2 pounds each)
⅓ cup olive oil
2 medium onions, finely chopped
2 cloves garlic, finely chopped
1 cup tomato sauce

¼ cup plus 2 tablespoons cognac
2 tablespoons meat glaze
⅓ cup sherry *or* Madeira
2 tablespoons chopped pimiento

Plunge the lobsters into boiling water for 1 minute to kill them. Cut them in half, and save the liquid and liver and intestines. Put the olive oil in a large ovenproof pan and heat over a flame. Add the onions, garlic, and lobster halves and season to taste. Add the tomato sauce and let it cook with the other ingredients for 4 minutes. Pour ¼ cup of the cognac into the pan, cover it, and place it in a 400° oven for approximately 18 minutes. Remove the lobsters to a hot platter and keep warm.

Strain the sauce through a fine sieve. Reheat it, add the liver, intestines, and liquid from the lobsters, the meat glaze, the sherry or Madeira, the remaining 2 tablespoons of cognac, and the pimiento. Pour the sauce over the lobster.

LOBSTER AU GRATIN

3 cups cooked lobster meat
6 tablespoons butter
¼ cup cognac

¼ cup white wine
½ cup heavy cream
Hollandaise sauce (pages 25–26)

Sauté the lobster in butter just long enough to heat it. Add the cognac and ignite. Add the white wine and cream and cook for 5 minutes. Pour into a casserole, top with Hollandaise sauce, and run under the broiler long enough to glaze. Serve with rice.

LOBSTER IN CREAM

This is very delicate and flavorful.

2 lobsters (1 to 1½ pounds each)	Paprika
6 tablespoons butter	⅓ cup sherry
Salt	Cream to cover
Freshly ground black pepper	Beurre manié (page 475)

Cut the lobsters as for lobster à l'Américaine. Melt the butter in a large skillet, add the lobster, and let it just color. Season to taste, add the sherry, and let it cook down a little. Add just enough hot cream to cover the lobster, clap on a lid, and let it simmer for 20 minutes. Remove the pieces of lobster, take the meat from the shells and put it in a serving dish. Thicken the sauce with beurre manié and taste for seasoning. Pour the sauce over the lobster. This may be served in patty shells or croustades or with rice or toast points.

VARIATIONS

Lobster in Cream, Mornay. When the lobster is cooked and removed from the cream, add 1 cup of grated cheese (Gruyère or Cheddar) and a few grains of cayenne to the sauce. Stir until the cheese is well blended and the sauce thickened. Place the lobster meat in an ovenproof dish, pour the sauce over this, and top with more grated cheese and a sprinkling of bread crumbs. Brown under the broiler.

Lobster Curry. While the lobster is cooking in the cream, sauté 3 tablespoons chopped onion in 3 tablespoons butter. When the onions are soft, add 3 tablespoons flour and 1 tablespoon curry powder. Blend well and add ½ cup white wine. Add the cream and continue stirring until the sauce is thickened. Arrange the lobster meat in a serving dish and pour the curry sauce over it. Serve with rice.

Lobster Hungarian. Add 1 tablespoon paprika to the sauce just before pouring it over the lobster meat.

LOBSTER NEWBURG, FRENCH VERSION

Although lobster Newburg has appeared in many French books, including Montagne and Salles's, it is definitely an American dish. It was originally named for a man named Wenburg, not Newburg, so the story goes.

There are two different theories about the preparation of a Newburg. The French is a little more deft than the American, so I give it first.

1 lobster (2 to 3 pounds)	¼ cup brandy *or* whiskey
2 tablespoons butter	1½ cups heavy cream
2 tablespoons olive oil	½ cup bouillon (fish *or* meat
Salt	stock)
Freshly ground black pepper	Beurre manié (page 475)
⅔ cup white wine	Cayenne pepper

Cut the lobster in sections. Heat the butter and oil and sear the lobster, seasoning it to taste while it is cooking. When the shell has turned red — in about 3 minutes — remove the lobster and add the white wine and spirits to the fat. Let this cook down to half its volume. Add the cream, lobster, and bouillon. Cover and simmer for 30 minutes. Remove the lobster and take the meat from the shell and arrange it on a serving dish. Let the sauce cook down a bit and thicken it with beurre manié. Add a dash of cayenne and taste for seasoning. Pour the sauce over the lobster and serve.

LOBSTER NEWBURG, AMERICAN VERSION

This is our version of Mr. Wenburg's dish.

1½ cups cooked lobster meat	3 egg yolks
4 tablespoons butter	Salt
¼ cup brandy	Freshly ground black pepper
1 cup heavy cream	

Cut the lobster meat into large pieces and sauté in butter for 5 minutes. Add the brandy and blaze. Mix the egg yolks and heavy cream together and heat in the upper part of a double boiler, stirring constantly until the mixture coats the spoon. Add the lobster and heat through, being careful not to let the mixture boil. Taste for seasoning. Serve in croustades or patty shells or on rice.

LOBSTER PHOCEENNE

Court bouillon (page 18)	3 shallots, chopped
1 lobster (about 2 pounds)	1 clove garlic, minced
¼ cup olive oil	1 green pepper, chopped
Salt	¾ cup rice
Freshly ground black pepper	Pinch of saffron

Prepare a strong court bouillon and let it reduce by half. Strain. Cut the live lobster in half and remove the intestinal tract. Heat the olive oil in a deep pot and add the lobster, salt, pepper, shallots, garlic, and green pepper. Toss the lobster in the oil to redden it; add the rice and saffron. Pour the court bouillon over all, cover tightly, and bring to a boil. Reduce the heat and let it cook very slowly for about 20 minutes or until the rice is done. Serve the lobster on a bed of the rice.

STUFFED LOBSTER DROUANT

4 small lobsters	1 tablespoon dry mustard
Butter	Cayenne pepper
2½ cups sauce béchamel (page 23)	1 cup grated Gruyère cheese

Split the live lobsters and remove the intestinal tract. Butter them lightly and broil for 12 to 15 minutes, depending on their size. When cooked, remove the lobster meat from the shells and keep it hot.

Season the sauce béchamel with the mustard and cayenne. Spread a thin layer of sauce in the empty lobster shells, add pieces of the lobster meat cut in thin slices and cover these with additional sauce. Sprinkle the top with grated cheese. Place in a 400° oven until heated through.

LOBSTER THERMIDOR

This dish was first served at the famous Café de Paris in Paris. It was created by Monsieur Tony Girod and this is the original recipe.

1 lobster (about 2 pounds)	1 tablespoon chopped tarragon
Salt	*or* chervil and tarragon
Freshly ground black pepper	1 cup sauce béchamel (page 23)
⅔ cup olive oil	¾ cup heavy cream, mixed with
⅔ cup white wine	2 egg yolks
⅔ cup bouillon (fish *or* meat	1 teaspoon dry mustard
stock)	Grated Parmesan cheese
1 tablespoon chopped shallot *or*	Melted butter
green onion	

Split the live lobster in half. Sprinkle with salt and pepper and brush with olive oil. Bake it in a 425° oven for approximately 18 minutes. Baste during the cooking with additional olive oil. When the lobster is cool enough to handle, remove the meat from the body and claws and dice it. Combine the wine, broth, and herbs and cook until it is reduced to practically a glaze. Add this to the sauce béchamel and stir in the cream mixed with the egg yolks. Allow this to heat without boiling. Add the mustard and taste for seasoning. When it is well thickened, add the lobster meat and heat through. Fill the lobster shells with this mixture, sprinkle with the grated cheese, brush with the butter, and brown in a 375° oven.

VARIATIONS

1. The American version of this recipe omits the mustard and tarragon and adds sautéed mushrooms and a little sherry.

2. Here is a quick version. Make a cream sauce and flavor it with sherry and plenty of mustard. Arrange frozen lobster meat in an ovenproof dish, add the sauce, sprinkle with grated cheese, and brown in the oven.

HOMARD AUX AROMATES

4 lobsters (about 1½ pounds each)
White wine court bouillon (pages 19–20; add thyme, bay leaf, parsley, peppercorns, and coriander)

4 tablespoons heavy cream
Beurre manié (page 475)
1 cup Hollandaise sauce (pages 25–26)
Fresh tarragon

This dish is a favorite in France and there are a number of recipes for it. I give two that I regard as distinctive, each in its own way. This recipe will serve 4 people.

Poach the lobsters in the court bouillon. When they are cool enough to handle remove the meat from the bodies and claws. Reduce the court bouillon to 1½ cups of liquid, strain, and add the cream and beurre manié. Stir until thickened and add the Hollandaise sauce. Arrange the lobster shells on a serving dish, fill them with the lobster meat, and cover with the sauce. Sprinkle generously with chopped tarragon.

VARIATION

Prepare 2 cups of sauce velouté (page 21) using bouillon, white wine, and cream in equal parts. Add chopped parsley, chervil, tarragon, and fennel and stir in 2 egg yolks. Taste for seasoning. Arrange the lobster shells filled with lobster meat on a hot platter and cover with the sauce.

DEVILED LOBSTER

4 small lobsters
4 tablespoons butter
1 medium onion, finely chopped
1 clove garlic, finely chopped
2 green peppers, finely chopped
2 stalks celery, finely chopped

Salt
Freshly ground black pepper
Mustard
Cayenne pepper
2 cups bread crumbs
Butter

Cook the lobsters in salted water. When cool enough to handle, split them and remove the meat. Dice it and mix it with the liver and lobster coral, if there is any.

Melt the butter in a skillet and sauté the vegetables. When they are tender, season them to taste and combine them with half the bread crumbs and the lobster meat. Season highly with salt, pepper, mustard, and cayenne and fill the lobster shells with this mixture. Dot with butter and sprinkle with the rest of the crumbs. Bake in a 400° oven for 15 to 20 minutes or until nicely browned.

BAKED LOBSTER ITALIAN

1 lobster (about 2 pounds)
3 tablespoons olive oil
1 clove garlic, minced
Fines herbes (parsley, basil,
  oregano)

6 tablespoons butter
½ cup bread crumbs
Salt
Freshly ground black pepper
Grated Parmesan cheese

Split the lobster and remove the intestinal tract. Brush with olive oil. Sauté the garlic and herbs for 3 minutes in 3 tablespoons of the butter and mix with the bread crumbs. Spread this paste over the lobster halves, salt and pepper to taste, and dot with the remaining 3 tablespoons butter. Bake in a 400° oven for about 20 minutes. Sprinkle with the cheese and run under the broiler to brown.

SAUTÉED LOBSTER WITH CURRY

¼ pound butter
½ cup shredded blanched
  almonds
2 tablespoons grated onion *or*
  shallot
1 pound cooked lobster meat
  (frozen is excellent), cut into
  scallops

1 tablespoon chopped parsley
2 teaspoons curry powder
½ cup heavy cream
Salt
Freshly ground black pepper

Melt the butter in a large skillet and add the almonds and onion
(or shallot). Cook for 3 or 4 minutes. Add the lobster and toss
lightly. Add the parsley and curry and blend in the cream. Let it
just come to a boil and simmer for 3 minutes. Taste for seasoning and serve on fried toast rounds.

LOBSTER NORTH AFRICAN

To be authentic this dish should be made with langouste, but
it can be prepared with any kind of lobster. This recipe will serve
two people.

1 large lobster
2 green peppers, cut in julienne
  strips
9 tablespoons olive oil
1 cup tomato sauce
⅓ cup white wine
Salt
Freshly ground black pepper

1 medium onion, chopped
1 small eggplant, peeled and
  diced
1 cup cooked rice
Cayenne pepper
Oregano
¼ cup brandy *or* whiskey

Cook the lobster in salt water for about 10 to 12 minutes, or
until done. When cool enough to handle, remove the tail and cut
it in half, cut the body in half and remove the claws. Take the
meat from the claws.

    Sauté the green peppers in 3 tablespoons of the olive oil until
they are soft. Then add the tomato sauce and wine and season
with salt and pepper. Let it cook down for several minutes. Add

the two sections of the tail and the meat from the claws and let it heat through. Remove from the fire but keep warm.

Sauté the onion in the remaining 6 tablespoons olive oil until soft. Add the eggplant. Sauté until it is soft and slightly colored. Mix this with the rice and season well with salt, pepper, cayenne, and oregano. Heap this on the two halves of the body of the lobster and top with the two halves of the lobster tail.

Add the brandy (or whiskey) to the tomato sauce, and cook it down for several minutes. Pour the sauce over the lobster halves and serve with additional rice.

SAUTÉED LOBSTER WITH TOMATOES

4 tablespoons butter	Freshly ground black pepper
4 tablespoons olive oil	Basil
1 cup chopped, seeded tomatoes	1 pound lobster meat, cut into
Salt	scallops

Heat the butter and olive oil and add the tomatoes. Salt and pepper to taste and add a touch of basil. Simmer until the tomatoes form a paste. Add the lobster, cut into scallops, and cook until it is heated through. Serve on fried toast.

LOBSTER CARDINAL

1 lobster (2 to 3 pounds)	½ cup heavy cream
½ pound shrimp	2 egg yolks
Court bouillon (page 18)	¼ cup brandy *or* whiskey
½ pound mushrooms, diced	Salt
3 or 4 truffles (optional), diced	Freshly ground black pepper
4 tablespoons butter	Grated Parmesan cheese
1 cup sauce béchamel (page 23)	Melted butter

Cook the lobster and the shrimp in court bouillon for about 10 to 12 minutes. When they are cool enough to handle, shell the shrimp and split the lobster in halves. Take the meat from the lobster tail and slice in even scallops. Remove the claws and take the meat from the body and claws and dice it. Sauté the mushrooms and truffles with the lobster (set the meat from the lobster tail aside) in a little butter for a few minutes.

Grind or chop the shrimp very fine and mix with the béchamel, cream, egg yolks, and liquor. Stir over low heat until thickened but do not let it boil. Taste for seasoning. Mix a little of the sauce with the mushrooms and lobster meat and arrange in the bottom of the lobster shells. Place the scallops of meat from the lobster tail on this bed of sauce, cover with more sauce, sprinkle with grated cheese, and brush with melted butter. Run it under the broiler for a few minutes to brown.

LOBSTER SAUTÉ FINES HERBES

¼ pound butter
1 pound lobster meat, cut into
    scallops
Salt
Freshly ground black pepper

¼ cup mixed chopped herbs
    (chives, parsley, tarragon, *or*
    your own choice)
¼ cup white wine

Melt the butter, add the lobster, and sauté, tossing lightly, until browned. Season to taste; add the herbs and the wine. Turn the pieces of lobster so they are thoroughly covered with the herbs and wine. Serve on fried toast.

LOBSTER SAUTÉ MEXICAN

3 sweet peppers, seeded and
    finely chopped
2 tablespoons chopped onion
⅓ cup olive oil
3 tomatoes, peeled, seeded, and
    chopped
½ cup white wine

2 teaspoons chili powder
Pinch of saffron
2 pimientos, finely cut
Salt
Freshly ground black pepper
1 pound lobster meat

Sauté the peppers and onion in the olive oil until soft. Add the tomatoes, wine, chili powder, saffron, and pimientos. Taste for seasoning. Cover and cook for 25 to 30 minutes over low heat. Add the lobster and cook for another 10 to 12 minutes. Serve with rice or polenta.

LOBSTER SAUTÉ LOUISIANA

1 clove garlic, chopped
3 green onions, chopped
1 green pepper, seeded and cut
   into strips
6 tablespoons butter
½ cup tomato sauce

Salt
Freshly ground black pepper
Cayenne pepper
¼ cup heavy cream
1 cup cooked lobster meat

Sauté the garlic, onions, and pepper in butter for 5 minutes; add the tomato sauce and let it cook down a bit. Season to taste, stir in the cream and blend well. Add the lobster meat and heat it through. Serve on fried toast.

MOUSSE OF LOBSTER

This mousse makes an excellent light luncheon main course with a Hollandaise sauce and an equally fine first course at dinner with a sauce mousseline. Considering the price of lobster and the optional truffles, should you use them, it has become something of an extravagance today. However, the mousse is beautifully light, tremendously delicate, and great fun to eat.

1 pound lobster meat
2 egg whites
Ice
Salt
Freshly ground black pepper
Paprika

2 cups heavy cream
Butter
24 mushroom caps
1 cup white wine
Hollandaise sauce (pages 25–26)

Grind the lobster meat through the fine blade of a meat grinder putting it through the grinder twice. Or you may pound it in a mortar. Gradually work in the egg whites with a wooden spoon. Next, put the mixture through a puree machine or a fine sieve. Place a bowl over cracked ice, place the mixture in the bowl and, with a wooden spoon, work in the salt, pepper, and paprika to taste and the cream, a tablespoon or two at a time.

If using a food processor, place the lobster meat and egg whites in the beaker, and process for 30 seconds. With the machine still processing, gradually pour the cream into the fish, and add the salt, pepper, and paprika to taste.

Butter a ring mold or charlotte mold and decorate it with slices of truffle, if you wish. Fill the mold ¾ full with the lobster mixture. Place in a pan of hot water and cook, either over low heat or in a moderate oven (350°), until set. This should take about 30 minutes. Unmold on a hot platter and decorate with mushrooms that have been poached briefly in the white wine. Serve with a Hollandaise sauce.

NOTE: Individual molds of the mousse may be made and served in the same way.

LOBSTER SOUFFLÉ

1 cup finely chopped lobster meat	Salt
½ cup court bouillon (page 18)	Freshly ground black pepper
3 tablespoons butter	Cayenne pepper
3 tablespoons flour	4 egg yolks
½ cup cream	6 egg whites

It is nice to prepare the lobster for this dish yourself. If you do, cook the live lobster in a court bouillon. When it is done, remove it from the bouillon and let the liquid cook down to ½ cup. Strain it and set it aside to use in the soufflé. After you have cleaned the lobster, be sure to chop the meat very fine; or put it through a food chopper, using the fine blade.

Melt the butter in a saucepan and add the flour. Cook over medium heat until it is golden and thoroughly blended. Gradually stir in the bouillon and cream, which you have mixed with the intestines of the lobster. Continue stirring until well thickened. Remove from the stove, season to taste, and add the lobster meat. Gradually beat in the egg yolks, one at a time. Beat the egg whites until stiff and fold them into the lobster mixture. Pour the mixture into a well-buttered soufflé mold and bake at 375° for 30 to 35 minutes. Serve plain or with a Hollandaise sauce (pages 25–26).

SOUFFLÉ OF LOBSTER PLAZA-ATHENÉE

1 live lobster (2 to 2½ pounds)
Salt
Freshly ground black pepper
Paprika
5 tablespoons butter
2 stalks celery, finely chopped
2 onions, finely chopped

2 carrots, finely chopped
2 ounces cognac
1 cup white wine
½ cup cream
5 or 6 egg yolks
½ cup sauce béchamel (page 23)
5 egg whites

Split the lobster in half and remove the intestines, liver, and coral. Season each half with salt, pepper, and paprika. Melt the butter in a deep saucepan and add the finely chopped vegetables. Put the lobster halves in the pan and let them cook until the shells redden. Add the cognac and blaze. Pour the wine in the pan and let it all cook for 15 minutes. Remove the lobster and, when cool enough to handle, take the meat from the body and claws and place it in a buttered casserole.

Add the cream and the lobster intestines, liver, and coral to the broth in the saucepan. Heat through for a few minutes and then remove from the heat and force it through a fine sieve. If the sauce needs thickening, add 2 to 3 of the egg yolks and cook gently but do not let it boil. Pour half of the sauce over the lobster meat.

Combine the remaining 3 egg yolks, beaten, with the sauce

béchamel. Beat the egg whites very stiff and fold them into the mixture. Pour this over the lobster and sauce in the casserole, place in a hot oven and let it cook 10 to 15 minutes or until it is puffy and delicately browned. Serve with the remaining sauce.

NEW ENGLAND LOBSTER STEW

2½ cups lobster meat
1 pint lobster bouillon
6 tablespoons butter
1 quart milk, scalded
2 egg yolks

1 cup cream
Salt
Freshly ground black pepper
Paprika

To get 2½ cups of lobster meat for this dish you will probably need to prepare 2 lobsters. Cook them in a court bouillon (page 18) for 10 to 12 minutes; when they are done, remove the meat from the shells. Reduce the bouillon to 1 pint.

Melt the butter in a large saucepan, add the lobster meat and toss it for several minutes to brown it lightly. Add the bouillon and the milk and let it heat through. Beat the egg yolks with the cream, stir them in, and continue stirring until the stew is very hot. Season to taste. Serve in bowls with a sprinkling of paprika.

Pilot crackers are the traditional accompaniment for this dish. Personally, I prefer plenty of good hot buttered toast.

COLD LOBSTER

Cold lobster is often served in the shell with a variety of different sauces. For hors d'oeuvres, a half lobster is an ample serving, but for a main course the usual portion is a whole lobster — unless it happens to be tremendous. Some of the very large langoustes popular on the Riviera will serve 3 to 4 people.

Serve cold lobster with any of the following sauces:

1. Mayonnaise (page 34)
2. Rémoulade (page 35)
3. Gribiche (pages 36–37)
4. Russian dressing (page 35)
5. Vinaigrette (page 36)

LOBSTER EN BELLEVUE, PARISIENNE

This is a classic French dish. You see it as often in France as you see cold decorated ham in America, and it is not really difficult if you are patient and clever with your hands. Lobster en Bellevue is an architectural triumph as well as a delicious morsel.

2 large lobsters
1½ quarts of aspic made from
 court bouillon (page 18)
Mayonnaise
6 hard-cooked eggs, halved
6 tomatoes, peeled

Lettuce
Bread
Russian salad
For decorating: truffles, olives,
 black and stuffed, parsley,
 chervil, tarragon

Cook the lobsters in the court bouillon. Depending on the size of the lobsters, you may need 2½ to 3 quarts of court bouillon. When they are cool enough to handle, carefully cut away the bottom part of each shell so that the back and tail remain in one perfect piece. Remove all the meat from the bodies of the lobsters and from the claws of one of them. Then gently loosen the meat in each tail and lift it out whole. Chill the lobster meat.

Prepare the aspic by clarifying the bouillon (which has been reduced first, if necessary) and adding gelatin, according to the recipe on pages 18–19. Mix 1 cup of the aspic with 1 cup of mayonnaise and chill. Chill half of the plain aspic.

Cut the meat from the lobster tails into even scallops. Combine the rest of the meat with mayonnaise and season to taste. Trim the eggs so they will stand. Hollow the tomatoes out and fill them with the lobster mixture. Cover the filled tomatoes and the eggs with the aspic and mayonnaise and dip each scallop of lobster meat in the same mixture, being sure it is thoroughly coated. Chill until firm.

Now you are ready for the decorating. If you use truffles, slice them. Then cut the sliced truffles and the black and stuffed olives into fancy shapes. (Pimientos can also be used.) Parsley, chervil, and tarragon can be used to fashion tiny leaves. Chop the plain aspic very fine to use as garnish. Decorate each lobster scallop, each egg and tomato with these garnishes. But make some definite plan for your decoration so that it all forms a pattern. Place your decoration on each piece, then brush with a little of the un-chilled jelly. Chill until it is firm and holds the decoration in place, then make a little border of some of the chopped aspic.

From a loaf of stale bread cut a cube about 4 or 5 inches square. Place this on a platter and cover with greens. Set the perfect lobster with the claws intact on the platter, resting the body on the bread cube. Stretch the tail across the bed of greens. If you have a decorative skewer, put one large perfect tomato or a small head of lettuce on the skewer and run it in between the lobster's eyes. Arrange the decorated scallops of lobster meat along the back of the lobster shell so that they overlap. Build them out fan-shaped at the bottom. Arrange the eggs and to-matoes around the shell and decorate the platter with additional chopped aspic.

Serve the dish with Russian salad and additional mayonnaise if you wish.

LOBSTER ASPIC

2 large lobsters
1 quart of aspic made from court bouillon (pages 18–19)

1 cup of mayonnaise
For decoration: olives, truffles, tarragon

Russian Salad

1 cup potatoes, diced
Mayonnaise mixed with aspic

½ cup each of finely cut green beans, carrots, peas

Cook the lobsters in court bouillon for 15 minutes. Remove and reduce the bouillon to 1 quart. Clarify and add gelatin for an aspic according to the recipe on pages 18–19.

When the lobster is cool enough to handle, remove the tails and claws. Cut the bodies in half and extract the meat. With a pair of sharp kitchen shears cut the shell of each tail so that the meat may be removed in one piece. Keep the claws whole for decoration. Slice the lobster meat from the tail into even scallops.

Pour the aspic into a mold (a ring mold, a decorative tail mold, or a flat mold — anything you choose) and place it in a large bowl filled with cracked ice. When the aspic has formed a thin film on the mold, gently pour off the rest of the jelly. Blend a little of this with mayonnaise and chill for several minutes.

On the aspic film in the mold make a decorative pattern with slices of truffle, stuffed olives, and black olives. You may cut these into fancy shapes if you wish and you may add slices of hard-cooked egg and pimiento. Arrange bits of tarragon in the decoration. Dip the scallops of lobster meat in the jellied mayonnaise and place them in the mold. If it is a ring mold overlap them in a circle; if it is a flat mold use a flat design. Pour the remaining jelly over all until the mold is full. Chill.

Russian salad. Cook the potatoes and vegetables until they are just tender. Combine them with mayonnaise that has been mixed with a little of the jelly. Taste for seasoning and chill.

When ready to serve, place a bed of greens on a large platter and unmold the aspic on this. Place the Russian salad in the center of a ring mold or around the edge of a flat mold. Decorate with the lobster claws. Serve with additional mayonnaise.

Lobster Salads

TRADITIONAL LOBSTER SALAD

To my mind, this simple traditional salad is far better than many more complicated combinations.

Greens (lettuce *or* romaine)   Hard-cooked eggs
2 cups diced lobster meat   Capers
Mayonnaise

Line a bowl with greens. Mix the lobster meat with mayonnaise and heap it in the bowl. Garnish with quartered hard-cooked eggs and capers.

VARIATION

Add 1 cup diced celery.

SALADE PARISIENNE

2 cups mixed cooked vegetables   Mayonnaise
2 cups lobster meat, diced   Greens
Salt   10 scallops of lobster meat
Freshly ground black pepper   Hard-cooked eggs
Onion juice

Cut the vegetables (green beans, carrots, potatoes, tiny French peas) very fine and cook in salted water until they are just tender. Drain and cool. Mix them with the lobster, season to taste with salt, pepper, and onion juice, and bind with mayonnaise. Line a bowl with greens and arrange the salad on top. Decorate with the scallops of lobster meat and slices of hard-cooked egg.

VARIATION

This salad may be jellied. Make an aspic. Combine a little of it with mayonnaise. Line a mold with some of the aspic, fill with the salad into which you have stirred the mayonnaise-aspic mixture. Cover with more aspic. Chill and serve with additional mayonnaise.

ENGLISH GARDEN PARTY SALAD

3 cups lobster meat, coarsely
  diced
1 cup sliced cucumbers, peeled,
  seeded, and thinly sliced

1 cup pickled mushroom caps
Mayonnaise
Greens
Asparagus tips

Combine the lobster, cucumber, and the mushroom caps with mayonnaise. Arrange a bed of greens on a platter and place the salad on top. Garnish with asparagus tips.

NOTE: If you cook your own lobster for this dish, you can use the claws as an added garnish.

LOBSTER SALAD RÉMOULADE

2 cups lobster meat, diced
1 cup shredded celery root
Rémoulade sauce (page 35)

Greens
Hard-cooked eggs

Combine lobster, celery root, and rémoulade. Arrange on a bed of greens and decorate with hard-cooked eggs.

COUPE D'AVOCADO À LA RITZ

½ cup lobster, diced
1 cup crabmeat
1 tablespoon tomato, peeled,
  seeded, and chopped
½ teaspoon each of chopped
  tarragon, chervil, chives
½ teaspoon salt

3 tablespoons mayonnaise
½ teaspoon Worcestershire
  sauce
1 tablespoon chili sauce
1 avocado, halved and pitted
Greens

Combine all the ingredients except the avocado and greens. Arrange beds of greens on two plates. Place an avocado half on each plate and fill with the salad mixture. Garnish with additional mayonnaise.

Mussels

The mussel is a rock-clinging mollusk with a rather soft, bluish-black shell that is slightly ribbed. It is one of the most abundant seafoods in America and one of the most neglected. In fact, so little attention has been paid to it that there is no accurate idea of the extent of the mussel beds around our shores. They are found in great profusion on both coasts, but on the Pacific Coast, where people have occasionally been poisoned by them, they are quarantined during the dangerous period and cannot be obtained.

It is interesting that in Europe mussels are so popular that the demand cannot be met from natural sources. For years they have been artificially propagated in enormous quantities.

The most common mussel dish known in this country is one served in nearly every French restaurant — moules marinière. It is often made incorrectly, but still people love it and order it over and over — dipping in with their fingers and lapping up the juice with great delight.

This is the most authentic recipe I know of for this really fine dish.

MUSSELS MARINIÈRE

The mussels must be washed and the beard — the gathering of vegetation on the shell — must be removed.

This recipe will serve 4 people.

1 large onion, chopped
2 or 3 sprigs of parsley
Pinch of thyme
2 quarts mussels, washed and
    bearded

6 or 7 tablespoons butter
Freshly ground black pepper
1 cup white wine
Chopped parsley
Salt (if needed)

Place the onion in the bottom of a saucepan with the parsley and thyme. Add the mussels, 3 or 4 tablespoons of the butter, and a good sprinkling of pepper. Pour over this the wine, cover the saucepan, and let it steam over a low flame. Steam just until the mussels open. (If by chance any of them do not open, remove them at once and throw them away.)

When the mussels are open, you may remove the empty half of the shell or not, as you prefer. Arrange them in a large tureen or bowl. Add the remaining 3 tablespoons butter and a handful of chopped parsley to the broth, taste for seasoning,* and pour it over the mussels. You'll need plenty of toasted French bread or toast with this dish to sop up the juice — and not a drop should be wasted.

VARIATIONS

1. Instead of the onion, use 3 cloves garlic, finely chopped, and substitute olive oil for the butter.

2. If you like a thick sauce, add a little beurre manié (page 475) and stir until smooth.

MUSSELS POULETTE

Prepare the mussels as for mussels marinière. Combine the broth with 1½ cups heavy white sauce and stir until thoroughly blended and thickened. Add a few tablespoons of essence of mushrooms or mushroom broth and the juice of a lemon. Remove the empty half of the shell from the cooked mussels and serve them with the sauce poured over them.

---

* Mussels, like clams, sometimes need no additional salt.

MUSSELS RAVIGOTE PASCAL

Steam the mussels as for mussels marinière. Remove the empty half of the shell and allow the mussels to chill. Add a spoonful of sauce rémoulade (page 35) to each mussel and serve as an hors d'oeuvre. Six to 8 mussels will make a serving.

MUSSEL SALAD

Prepare the mussels as for mussels marinière. Take the mussels out of the shells and marinate them in a well-seasoned vinaigrette sauce (page 36). Arrange them on a bed of shredded lettuce and mask with mayonnaise. Garnish with watercress, capers, and a good dash of paprika.

STUFFED MUSSELS

Prepare the mussels as for mussels marinière, reserving the broth. Remove the mussels from the shells, but keep the half shells. Chop the mussel meat coarsely and combine with the following stuffing.

4 tablespoons chopped onion	4 tablespoons chopped parsley
3 tablespoons chopped celery	1 cup toasted crumbs
1 tablespoon chopped green pepper	1 teaspoon dry mustard
	1 teaspoon salt
6 tablespoons butter	Few grains cayenne pepper

Sauté the onion, celery, and green pepper in the butter until just tender. Add the parsley, toasted crumbs, and seasonings. Add the chopped mussels and enough of the broth from the mussels to make a moist mixture. Heap this into the half shells and dot with butter. Heat in a 450° oven until lightly browned.

CURRIED MUSSELS

Prepare mussels as for mussels marinière. Remove the mussels from their shells and set aside while you prepare the sauce.

5 tablespoons butter	½ cup heavy cream
2 tablespoons chopped onion	1 tablespoon curry powder
1 clove garlic, chopped	1 teaspoon salt
4 tablespoons flour	Few grains of cayenne pepper
1 cup mussel broth	

Melt the butter in a large skillet and sauté the onion and garlic until just soft. Add the flour, mix well, and let it cook gently for a minute or two. Gradually stir in the mussel broth; continue stirring until the sauce is thickened. Add the cream slowly; add the seasonings and taste to be sure there is enough curry. Finally add the mussels and let them heat through. Serve with steamed rice, crisp fried onions, and chutney.

STEAMED MUSSELS

Place 2 quarts mussels with 1 cup water in a saucepan. Cover and steam over low heat until the mussels open. Taste the broth for salt. Serve the mussels with the broth and a little melted butter. This dish lacks the rich flavor of mussels steamed over white wine, but some people prefer this method.

MUSSELS CREOLE

Prepare 2 quarts of mussels as for mussels marinière. Remove the mussels from the shells and set aside while you prepare the sauce.

1 medium onion, finely chopped	4 tablespoons chopped green pepper
3 tablespoons butter	
3 tablespoons olive oil	⅔ cup tomato sauce
4 tablespoons chopped celery	1 cup mussel broth

1 clove garlic, chopped   Pinch of thyme
¼ cup chopped parsley

Sauté the onion in the butter and olive oil. Add the celery, pepper, tomato sauce, and broth and simmer for 30 minutes. Add more broth if the sauce gets too thick. Add the garlic, parsley, and thyme, and taste for seasoning. Finally add the mussels. Serve with steamed rice or risotto.

BARBECUED MUSSELS

2 quarts mussels, steamed as for   2 tablespoons whiskey
    mussels marinière   Salt (if needed)
4 tablespoons chili sauce   Beurre manié (page 475)
Few grains of cayenne pepper   Chopped parsley
1 clove garlic, finely chopped

Steam the mussels as for mussels marinière. Remove the empty half shell. Strain the broth, put it over high heat, and reduce it by half. Add the chili sauce, cayenne, garlic, and whiskey. Taste for salt and thicken with a little beurre manié. Pour over the mussels and sprinkle with chopped parsley. Serve with plenty of toasted French bread.

STUFFED MUSSELS PROVENÇALE

Prepare 2 quarts of mussels as for mussels marinière. Remove the empty half shell. Blend together:

6 finely chopped shallots *or*   ½ teaspoon freshly ground
    green onions   black pepper
2 cloves garlic, chopped   ½ pound butter
½ cup chopped parsley   1 egg yolk
1 teaspoon salt   ½ cup bread crumbs

When all this is well blended, spoon it into the shells containing the mussels. Sprinkle with additional crumbs. Arrange in a bak-

ing pan with a little white wine in the bottom. Bake in a 400°
oven until the sauce is melted and delicately browned.

MUSSELS IN CREAM

Wash and beard 2 quarts of mussels. Place them in a saucepan
with a finely chopped onion, a branch of celery, and a sprig of
parsley. Add 2 cups water, cover the pan, and steam until
the mussels open. Remove the mussels from the shells and keep
them warm.

Prepare 1½ cups of sauce béchamel (page 23), using some of
the mussel broth. Season well and add the mussels. Serve in patty
shells, over rice, or on mounds of mashed potatoes. Sprinkle with
paprika and chopped parsley.

MUSSEL FRITTERS

Prepare mussels as for mussels in cream. Heat fat or oil to 360°
for deep-fat frying. Prepare beer batter (page 99), dip each mussel into the batter, and fry in the hot fat for 3 to 5 minutes, or
until nicely browned. Serve with tartar sauce (pages 35–36).

SPAGHETTI WITH MUSSEL SAUCE

See spaghetti with clam sauce, page 368.

Oysters

Many gourmets, or so-called gourmets, tell you that to eat an oyster in any fashion except directly from the shell is to show ignorance of gastronomic tradition and the rules of good taste. This is nonsense. While there may be nothing quite so wonderful as a freshly opened oyster with just a squirt of lemon juice on it, still there are many delightful ways to eat these mollusks cooked.

The American oyster was a staple in the diet of our coast Indians, and the great piles of shells found in many areas along our shores are evidence of the magnitude of Indian appetites. And because the popularity of oysters has continued so strongly among those of us who have more recently taken over this continent, most of the natural oyster beds are gone. We must rely now on cultivated beds. Over 90 million pounds of oysters are consumed in this country every year, and that is quite a few oysters.

Even so, we are actually sissies when it comes to eating oysters. Our grandfathers ate them by the gross, not the dozen. It was once commonplace for people to eat several dozen just as a first course. Today, in most European cities, a dozen oysters are considered a portion, rather than the half dozen usually served here.

There is great variety in types of oysters. Those from separate beds in the same area, such as Long Island, have decidedly different flavors, as you can readily find out for yourself by a comparative tasting of them. They contain different quantities of salt* or have different degrees of coppery flavor. Some are fat and plump, others are thin and very flat. The tiny Olympia

---

* Since some oysters need no additional salt in preparation, I have not included salt in many of the recipes that follow. I feel that the individual should season to suit his own particular taste.

oyster of the Pacific Coast has a most distinctive flavor, as have certain Eastern oysters that have been transplanted to the Pacific. The Chincoteagues of Chesapeake Bay have their unique qualities. Then there are the Japanese oysters that have been planted along the Western coastline. These are giants — so large no one would dare try to eat them on the half shell.

But no matter what sort of oyster you select or how you choose to prepare it, you are eating great gourmet fare.

OYSTERS ON THE HALF SHELL

By far the most common way to serve oysters is raw. Unfortunately, someone who was certainly no oyster lover started serving what is now known far and wide as "cocktail sauce" — usually nothing more than a fantastic mixture of tomato sauce, chili sauce, horse-radish, and other condiments. This is my pet abomination. A sauce of this kind entirely destroys the delicate flavor of the oyster. A freshly opened oyster, served on the half shell in a bed of ice, needs only a little squirt of lemon juice, and perhaps some freshly ground pepper. The only tolerable variation is the addition of a dab of caviar. Some gourmets will allow sauce mignonette — a combination of pepper, vinegar, and a little shallot. Don't forget to drink the juice in the bottom of the shell — never waste it.

The usual portion is 6 oysters to a person. If they are medium-sized, serve 12. And you may figure that the average diner can eat 36 to 48 of the tiny Olympias. Always be sure that they are icy cold and serve them on ice so they will stay that way.

With all oyster dishes used as a first course, serve thin — paper-thin — slices of delicate rye or pumpernickel bread heavily buttered. A brisk dry white wine, such as a fine Chablis or a Pouilly Fuisse, is excellent with oysters. Some people prefer a light beer, and beer does do a wonderful job of complementing all seafoods and fish.

OYSTERS WITH COCKTAILS OR CHAMPAGNE

1. Several times in this country and many times in France I have been served oysters on the half shell with cocktails. Huge platters of them were passed and each guest helped himself.

2. Open-faced oyster sandwiches are another treat. Butter well some rounds of pumpernickel bread, spread with finely chopped onion, place a raw oyster on each, and top it with a dab of caviar. Superb!

3. Butter some pumpernickel rounds, spread lightly with anchovy paste, and top with a raw oyster. Delicious with cocktails.

4. Small oysters perfectly fried (see fried oysters, page 434) and served on fried toast rounds are wonderful hot tidbits with either cocktails or champagne. But they must be piping hot. You can spread the toast with anchovy paste before topping with the oyster if you wish.

5. Another unforgettable hot snack is creamed oysters in tiny patty shells. Make the shells yourself or order them from your favorite bakery. Use a rich Hollandaise (pages 25–26) or a curry sauce (pages 22, 29) for the oysters.

6. Any of the recipes for stuffed oysters (pages 40, 421–423) may be served with cocktails if you pass small plates and forks so your guests can manage this food easily.

HUÎTRES FARCIES CASENAVE

6 shallots (*or* green onions), finely chopped
½ cup chopped parsley
¼ cup chopped chervil
3 ounces butter

12 oysters on the half shell
Salt
Freshly ground black pepper
Rock salt

Mix the herbs and shallots or onions with the butter, and top each oyster with a spoonful of the mixture. Salt and pepper to taste and bake on a bed of rock salt in a 475° oven for 4 or 5 minutes, or until the oysters are just heated through.

These may be run under the broiler instead, but be careful not to overcook them.

OYSTERS ROCKEFELLER

There are as many recipes for this dish as there are for bread. This may not be the original recipe, but it makes a delicious treat. In the old days it was necessary to pound the ingredients for the sauce in a mortar — a very tiring job — but with today's electric mixers or a food processor, oysters Rockefeller is a simple treat to prepare.

¼ cup chopped shallots *or* green onions	2 cups watercress
¼ cup chopped celery	⅓ cup bread crumbs
1 teaspoon chopped chervil	⅓ cup Pernod *or* anisette
⅓ cup chopped fennel	Salt
⅓ cup chopped parsley	Freshly ground black pepper
½ pound butter	Cayenne pepper
	2 dozen oysters on the half shell

Sauté the onion, celery, and herbs in 3 tablespoons of the butter for 3 minutes. Add the watercress and just let it wilt. Put this mixture with the rest of the butter, the bread crumbs, and the Pernod or anisette in the blender. Season to taste with salt, pepper, and a few grains of cayenne. Blend for 1 minute. Put about 1 tablespoon of this on each oyster, place the oysters on beds of rock salt in individual containers, and dampen the salt slightly. Bake at 450° to 475° for about 4 minutes, or until the butter is melted and the oysters heated through.

NOTE: Tin pie plates are excellent for baking this dish.

OYSTERS KIRKPATRICK

There are as many versions of this as there are of the famous Rockefeller recipe. This is my choice:

24 oysters on the half shell
½ cup finely chopped onions *or* shallots
1 tablespoon chopped green pepper

3 tablespoons butter
⅔ cup tomato catsup
Chopped parsley
Bacon

Arrange oysters on the half shell on beds of rock salt. Sauté the onion and green pepper in the butter. Mix this with the catsup. Put a spoonful on each oyster, sprinkle with parsley, and top with a partially cooked piece of bacon. Place in a 450° oven just long enough to brown the bacon and heat the oysters.

VARIATIONS

1. Sprinkle grated cheese over the top, dot with butter, and top with the piece of bacon.

2. Simply spoon tomato catsup or chili sauce over the oysters and top with crumbs and the piece of bacon.

3. Cover the oysters with chopped green onion, tomato catsup, and top with pieces of partially cooked bacon. Bake in a 450° oven just long enough to brown the bacon and heat the oysters.

OYSTERS REMICK

36 oysters on the half shell
2 cups mayonnaise
4 tablespoons chili sauce
¼ teaspoon paprika
Few grains cayenne pepper
1 tablespoon prepared mustard

½ teaspoon salt
2 teaspoons lemon juice
2 tablespoons butter
½ cup bread crumbs
Bacon

Place the oysters on beds of rock salt. Mix the mayonnaise and the seasonings and spoon it over the oysters. Sprinkle with buttered crumbs and top with pieces of partially cooked bacon. Bake in a 450° oven for 4 or 5 minutes, then place under the broiler for 3 minutes — just until the edges curl.

OYSTERS AU GRATIN

Arrange oysters on the half shell on beds of rock salt. Add a dash of lemon juice to each oyster, cover with fine bread crumbs, a little melted butter, and a sprinkling of cayenne pepper. Bake in a 450° oven for a few minutes — just until the edges curl and the oysters are heated through. Sprinkle with chopped parsley just before you serve.

OYSTERS FLORENTINE

This is certainly a forerunner of the famous oysters Rockefeller, for it's a very old recipe — no one knows when it was introduced.

Poach oysters in their own liquor, with a little white wine added, just long enough for the edges to curl. Arrange oyster shells on a baking sheet and place a spoonful of chopped cooked spinach in each shell. Put an oyster on each spinach bed and top with sauce Mornay (page 22). Sprinkle with a little grated cheese and run under the broiler for a minute or two to melt the cheese and brown slightly.

OYSTERS BRETON

Remove the oysters from their shells and arrange the shells in a baking dish or pans filled with rock salt. In each shell put a spoonful of chopped lobster meat which has been heated in butter and cream. On top of this place an oyster and cover with a heavy béchamel (page 23) to which you have added more chopped lobster. Sprinkle with crumbs and brown under the broiler. Meanwhile sauté an equal number of oysters — dip them in egg and crumbs and brown quickly in butter. Just before serving top each oyster shell with a sautéed oyster and sprinkle with chopped parsley.

CURRIED OYSTERS

3 cups sauce béchamel (page 23)
12 shrimp, finely chopped
1 tablespoon curry powder

24 oysters on the half shell
Toasted bread crumbs

Prepare the sauce béchamel and add the shrimp and curry powder. Arrange the oysters on beds of rock salt and top each one with the sauce. Sprinkle with toasted crumbs and bake in a 475° oven for 4 or 5 minutes.

OYSTERS PAPRIKA

24 oysters on the half shell
3 medium onions, finely chopped
6 tablespoons butter
⅓ cup chopped mushrooms

1 cup sauce béchamel (page 23)
1 tablespoon, or more, paprika
Toasted bread crumbs

Arrange the oysters on beds of rock salt. Sauté the onion in the butter until tender, but not browned. Add the mushrooms and blend well. Prepare the béchamel and add 1 tablespoon or more paprika to color and flavor it. Combine with the onions and mushrooms. Spoon this over the oysters and sprinkle lightly with crumbs and paprika. Bake in a 475° oven for about 5 minutes or until the oysters are just cooked through.

CRUMBED OYSTERS

24 oysters on the half shell
1 cup toasted bread crumbs
8 tablespoons butter

Parsley
Chives

Arrange the oysters on beds of rock salt. Fry the bread crumbs in the butter until very crisp and brown. Top the oysters with the bread crumbs and sprinkle with chopped parsley and chives. Bake in a 475° oven for about 5 minutes or until the oysters curl at the edges.

OYSTERS CASINO

Here again, there are many versions of the recipe, so I include several. One thing on which everyone agrees is that oysters casino always contain green pepper and bacon.

24 oysters on the half shell	¼ cup finely chopped green
½ cup butter	pepper
⅓ cup finely chopped shallots	Lemon juice
¼ cup finely chopped parsley	Bacon, partially cooked

Arrange the oysters on beds of rock salt. Blend the butter, shallots, parsley, and green pepper. Spoon this over the oysters and add a dash of lemon juice to each one. Top with pieces of partially cooked bacon. Bake in a 450° oven until the bacon is brown and the oysters cooked through.

VARIATIONS

1. Try out ½ cup of finely chopped bacon. Add ⅓ cup finely chopped onion, ⅓. cup finely chopped green pepper, ¼ cup finely chopped celery, 1 teaspoon lemon juice, salt, pepper, Worcestershire sauce, and a few drops of Tabasco. Spoon this over the oysters, which have been placed on beds of rock salt. Bake in a 350° oven for 10 minutes.

2. Sprinkle the oysters with finely chopped green pepper and onion and top each one with a piece of bacon. Bake in a 450° oven until the bacon is done and the oysters cooked through.

OYSTER LOAF

There is an old story that oyster loaves were always "guilty conscience" presents or peace offerings. To take home an oyster loaf in New Orleans and certain other places meant that you had been misbehaving and were trying to get back into good graces. I can remember homes in my youth where oyster loaves were so constantly served that surely bad deeds must have been the regular rule.

1 loaf of bread, unsliced   Fried or sautéed oysters
Butter

For this dish, try to find a really good loaf of bread — difficult these days, I know, but try. The round Italian loaves will do, or the regular loaf-pan loaves. Cut about a ⅔-inch slice off the top of the loaf. Scoop out the interior, leaving a wall about ½ inch thick all around. Toast the loaf in a slow oven until it is nicely browned and then brush it well with butter. Fill it with hot fried oysters and put the cover on. To serve, slice with a sharp knife.

These may be made in individual sizes as well. French rolls — or, if you can find them, those rolls that are baked in miniature bread pans — are ideal for this.

I hate to mention it, but the traditional condiment with any oyster loaf is tomato catsup or chili sauce.

NOTE: Any other type of seafood may be substituted for the oysters in this recipe.

OYSTER FRITTERS

Drain the oysters well and roll them in flour. Preheat fat or oil to 380°. Dip the oysters in beer batter (page 99) and fry in the deep fat for about 2 minutes, or until browned and crisp. Drain on absorbent paper and salt and pepper to taste. Serve with a tartar sauce (pages 35–36) or rémoulade (page 35).

OYSTER CROUSTADES

Roll brioche dough ½ inch thick and cut it in small rounds. Place two oysters apiece on half of the rounds, sprinkle them with salt and freshly ground black pepper; add a dab of butter and some chopped parsley. Dampen the edges of the rounds. Cover each with another round of dough, press the edges together, and fry in deep fat, heated to 375°, until they have risen and browned. Turn once during the cooking. Serve with a tartar sauce (pages 35–36) or tomato sauce (page 23). For brioche dough, see pages 189–190.

VARIATION

Substitute rounds of roll or bread dough for the brioche.

OYSTER PAN ROAST

A pan roast is really oysters poached in butter — and they must have plenty of butter to be good. Personally, I think the tiny oysters of the Pacific Coast are far better for this dish than the larger ones.

1. Melt ½ cup butter (¼ pound) in a skillet. Add 1 pint drained oysters, salt, plenty of freshly ground pepper, a dash of cayenne pepper, and a good squirt of lemon or lime juice. When the oysters are plumped and puffy the pan roast is done. I like mine served on fried toast.

2. Proceed in the same way, adding 2 tablespoons catsup and 1 tablespoon Worcestershire sauce.

3. When the butter is melted, add ⅓ cup chopped shallots or green onions and ¼ cup chopped parsley. Add the drained oysters, a dash of red wine, and let it all boil up for 3 minutes.

4. Add 1 clove crushed garlic, 3 tablespoons tomato paste, and 1 teaspoon dry mustard to the butter. Then add the oysters and a dash of lemon juice.

5. Sauté ⅓ cup chopped shallots or green onions and ⅓ cup chopped green peppers in butter until tender. Add the drained oysters, salt, and freshly ground black pepper. A dash of vermouth or white wine makes this extra good.

DEVILS ON HORSEBACK

Wrap oysters individually in thin rashers of bacon and broil until the bacon is crisp. Turn once while cooking. (For added dash, you may, before cooking, marinate the oysters in white wine flavored with garlic and black pepper.)

ANGELS ON HORSEBACK

Sprinkle oysters with finely chopped onion and parsley and wrap in paper-thin strips of smoked ham. Broil for 5 to 8 minutes, turning once. Serve on buttered toast with Hollandaise sauce (pages 25–26).

OYSTERS EN BROCHETTE I

For each brochette:

4 oysters	3 to 4 mushroom caps
Lemon juice	1 long strip of bacon
Salt	Butter
Freshly ground black pepper	Parsley

Sprinkle the oysters with the lemon juice, salt, and pepper. At the end of the brochette place a mushroom cap. Next put the end of the bacon strip, then an oyster, then loop the bacon around the oyster onto the brochette again, add another mushroom, another oyster and continue until you have used four oysters. Brush with butter and broil over charcoal or under the broiler, turning several times. Sprinkle with chopped parsley and serve with lemon wedges.

OYSTERS EN BROCHETTE II

Alternate small cubes of beef tenderloin and oysters on a skewer. Brush well with butter and broil until the beef is delicately browned and the oysters cooked through. Salt and pepper to taste and brush with plenty of butter before serving.

OYSTERS EN BROCHETTE III

Alternate oysters, small tomatoes or chunks of tomato, mushrooms, and small cubes of cooked ham. Brush with butter and broil. Salt and pepper to taste and sprinkle with lemon juice.

CREAMED OYSTERS

1 pint sauce velouté (page 21)	3 tablespoons sherry *or* Madeira
Salt	1 pint oysters
Freshly ground black pepper	Patty shells *or* croustades

Make a sauce velouté, using some of the oyster liquor, and season well. Add the wine. Add the drained oysters and cook them just long enough to curl the edges. Serve on croustades or in patty shells that have been heated through.

VARIATION

If your baker makes a good puff paste, order a vol au vent, or make it yourself. Fill it with oysters in the sauce velouté and serve it with a salad of beets, hard-cooked eggs, and tender greens. Pass some crisp French bread and a cheese tray. This is an outstanding late evening supper. You can dramatize it by preparing the sauce in the chafing dish and filling the vol au vent at the table.

OYSTER PUREE

½ cup rice	4 tablespoons butter
1 quart bottled clam juice	18 oysters

Salt   1½ cups heavy cream
Freshly ground black pepper   ¼ cup cognac
¼ teaspoon Tabasco

Cook the rice in the clam juice until very soft. Add the butter. Force through a sieve, or puree in a blender. Finely chop 12 of the oysters, and swirl in a blender with their liquid. Add to the rice mixture. Season to taste with salt and pepper; add the Tabasco. Stir in the heavy cream. Heat just to the boiling point. Add the 6 whole oysters and heat just until they curl at the edges. Add the cognac and cook two minutes. Ladle into heated cups, putting a whole oyster in each cup. Garnish with chopped parsley and serve with crisp melba toast.

OYSTER OMELET

Prepare omelets in your usual fashion. Fold in oysters in velouté sauce or fried oysters. Serve with shoestring potatoes and a delicate white wine.

OYSTER CHOWDER

4 tablespoons butter   Sprig of thyme
3 tablespoons chopped onion   1 cup fish broth *or* white wine
¾ cup finely cut celery   2 cups diced potatoes
3 carrots, finely diced   1 quart milk
Salt   1 pint oysters
Freshly ground black pepper   ⅓ cup chopped parsley

Melt the butter in a saucepan and add the onion, celery, and carrots. Brown very quickly and salt and pepper to taste. Cover and let them cook for 5 to 8 minutes. Add the oyster liquor, the thyme, and the fish broth or white wine and bring to a boil. Add the potatoes; cover and simmer until the potatoes are tender. Add the milk and let it come just to the boiling point. Add the oysters and let them cook until the edges curl. Pour into bowls or a tureen and sprinkle liberally with chopped parsley.

OYSTER CLUB SANDWICH

This is a combination of fried oysters, bacon, tomato, lettuce, and mayonnaise on toasted white or rye bread. It's a very good dish late at night or for luncheon. This is a fine old recipe, almost traditional enough to be considered a classic.

SCALLOPED OYSTERS

This is a favorite old New England dish that has always had a place of honor at all functions — especially at holiday feasts — in that part of the country. It has never been popular with me but I can understand why many people like it.

Butter
1 cup freshly rolled saltine
    cracker crumbs
1 pint oysters
Salt

Freshly ground black pepper
Nutmeg
1/4 cup oyster liquor
4 tablespoons cream
1/2 cup buttered bread crumbs

Butter a baking dish and place a layer of cracker crumbs on the bottom. Place a layer of oysters over that and sprinkle with the salt, pepper, and a little nutmeg. Add 2 tablespoons of the oyster liquor, 2 tablespoons of the cream, and dot well with butter. Add a layer of cracker and bread crumbs mixed, then another layer of oysters, seasonings, and liquids. Dot with butter, cover with cracker crumbs, and top with bread crumbs. Add a little more cream, sprinkle with salt, pepper, and nutmeg, and dot with butter. Bake at 425° for approximately 40 minutes.

OYSTER STEW I

4 tablespoons or more butter	Salt
½ pint milk	Freshly ground black pepper
1 pint cream	Cayenne pepper
1½ pints oysters and liquor	

First of all heat the bowls. When they are hot, put a large piece of butter in each one and keep the bowls hot. Heat the milk, cream, and oyster liquor to the boiling point. Salt and pepper to taste and add a dash of cayenne. Add the oysters and let it come to the boiling point again. Ladle into the hot bowls. You may add a dash of paprika, if you like. I prefer my stew with hot crunchy French bread, although crackers are the traditional accompaniment.

This recipe makes four generous or six medium-sized servings.

OYSTER STEW II

4 tablespoons butter	Salt
1½ pints oysters	Freshly ground black pepper
1 quart milk *or* half cream and half milk	Paprika

Melt the butter, add the drained oysters and cook until the edges curl — about 3 minutes. Add the liquids, season to taste, and bring just to the boiling point. Serve with a dash of paprika. This will serve six people.

ZELMA SETON'S OYSTER STEW

1 cup milk	Freshly ground black pepper
3 cups cream	Tabasco
3 cups oysters, with their liquor	4 to 6 tablespoons butter
Salt	

Heat the milk and cream with the oyster liquor; add salt and pepper to taste and a dash or two of Tabasco. In a separate skillet melt the butter (be sure to have plenty). Take your oysters and toss them into the butter while it is bubbling. Shake the pan vigorously until the oysters just barely curl at the edges and have plumped. Don't overcook them, please. They should just heat through. When the milk and cream come to the boil, combine the delicately sautéed oysters with the liquid. Taste for seasoning, and serve in warm bowls with crisp buttered toast or a selection of crackers. Tossing the oysters in the butter first makes all the difference. The stew is much more flavorful.

FRIED OYSTERS

Among the most vivid gastronomical memories of my childhood are the visits we made to the home of friends who were in the oyster business. They had huge sacks of oysters sent to their beach home every week and when these arrived we knew we were in for many treats. The greatest treat of all would come after an early morning venture of clamming and crabbing followed by a dip in the surf. Then we would climb the sand dunes to the house with ravenous appetites, to be met by a wonderful aroma — a mixture of melting butter and coffee gently simmering. In the kitchen there would be a magnificent sight — dozens of freshly opened oysters dipped in beaten egg and rolled in crushed cracker crumbs. On the stove would be two huge iron skillets with a half inch of bubbling butter in each one, waiting to brown the delicate morsels as soon as we were seated at the table.

It was the man of the house who always cooked these oysters. He would never trust the women or the cook to do the job properly. Such perfection of cookery I have seldom encountered since, and the smell of those early morning oyster fries has stayed in my memory and enchanted me for years.

Here, so far as I can remember, is Mr. Hamblet's oyster recipe:

Butter
3 eggs
3 tablespoons heavy cream
1 quart oysters (not too big)

Freshly rolled cracker crumbs,
    preferably saltines
Salt
Freshly ground black pepper

Melt plenty of butter in your skillet — it should be about ½ inch deep. (I usually use part oil so the butter will not burn.) Beat the eggs lightly and combine with the cream. Dip the oysters in the egg mixture, then in the crumbs, and arrange on wax paper (far enough apart so they do not touch) and let them stand for a few minutes before cooking. They should be cooked just long enough to brown delicately and get a little crisp. Salt and pepper to taste and serve with lemon wedges or with tartar sauce (pages 35–36).

OYSTER SAUTÉ

Oysters may be dipped in flour and sautéed in butter very quickly. You may season them with chopped herbs or a little white wine, or simply with salt and freshly ground black pepper. They are particularly good with tarragon and a little white wine, or with equal amounts of chives and parsley and a little white wine. They will cook in 3 or 4 minutes — be careful not to overcook them.

VARIATIONS

1. Sauté oysters in butter and serve on fried toast with a sauce made as follows: To the juices in the pan add 4 tablespoons butter, 1 clove garlic finely minced, and 3 tablespoons finely chopped parsley. Pour this over the oysters on the toast. Six or 7 oysters fixed in this manner will make a good serving for a first course at dinner or a main course at luncheon.

2. Sauté 24 oysters and arrange them on thin slices of frizzled ham. Garnish with sautéed mushroom caps and chopped parsley.

3. Sauté a chicken in butter with a little parsley and some white wine. Sauté 24 oysters in butter and combine with the chicken. This is an excellent combination of flavors.

4. Combine sautéed oysters with broiled fillets of any white-meated fish, such as sole. Grill the fillets or sauté them in butter and smother them with the oysters. Sprinkle with freshly ground black pepper and chopped parsley.

FRENCH-FRIED OYSTERS

Fat for frying (*or* oil)
2 eggs
3 tablespoons of cream
1 teaspoon salt
½ teaspoon freshly ground black
   pepper

Bread *or* cracker crumbs *or* corn
   meal
1 quart oysters
Flour

Heat fat to 380°. Beat the eggs with the cream; add the seasonings. Roll the crumbs very fine. Dip the oysters in flour, then in the egg mixture, and then in the crumbs. Fry for about 2 minutes or until delicately browned. Drain on absorbent paper. Salt and pepper.

VARIATION

Add 1 tablespoon curry powder to the egg mixture or to the crumbs.

HANGTOWN FRY

This mixture of eggs and oysters is made in several ways. Here are three popular methods.

1. Beat eggs with cream and seasonings, using 2 eggs for 4 large oysters. Sauté oysters in a skillet and pour the egg mixture over them. Continue cooking until the eggs are set. Turn out on a platter.

2. This is an Italian version, similar to a frittata. Fry the oysters until just delicately browned. Mix 2 eggs and 1 tablespoon cream for each 4 oysters and combine with 3 tablespoons

grated Parmesan cheese. Pour over the oysters and place under the broiler until the eggs are set.

3. Fold fried oysters into scrambled eggs just before they are ready to serve.

Scallops

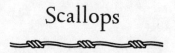

The scallop is a mollusk that is so named because of its beautifully fluted and scalloped shell. There are two types found along most American shores. The tiny bay scallop is tenderer and more delicately flavored, and is so popular that the supply has been greatly depleted. Then there is the larger deep sea scallop, which is more generally available.

In Europe, where they are called by the French term Coquilles St. Jacques, scallops are eaten whole. In this country, only the muscle that controls the shell movement is used — no one seems to know why — and the rest of the meat is used for bait or fertilizer. One pound will supply 3 average or 2 large servings.

SCALLOPS AS AN APPETIZER

Raw scallops are delicious, although few people eat them this way — possibly the idea has never been suggested to them. Serve with a sauce rémoulade (page 35), a sauce gribiche (pages 36–37), or perhaps a sauce Béarnaise (page 26). The bay scallops, tiny and tender, served like oysters with lemon, salt, and pepper, have delightful and unusual flavor.

BROILED SCALLOPS

Place the scallops on a flat tin — a baking sheet or pie tin. Dot them with butter and sprinkle lightly with salt and freshly ground black pepper. Place under the broiler, about 3 inches from the flame. They will take from 5 to 6 minutes to broil and become delicately browned. Serve with lemon juice.

SAUTÉED SCALLOPS

1½ pounds scallops	Salt
Flour	Freshly ground black pepper
6 tablespoons butter	¼ cup chopped parsley

Wash the scallops and pick out any bits of shell. Dry and dust lightly with flour. Melt the butter in a skillet, and add the scallops. Let them cook quickly and not too long or they will get tough and lose their delicious flavor. They should just heat through and brown lightly. Salt and pepper to taste, sprinkle with chopped parsley, and serve with lemon wedges. Serves 4.

SCALLOPS SAUTÉ PROVENÇALE

1½ pounds bay scallops	Salt
Flour	Freshly ground black pepper
6 tablespoons olive oil	½ cup chopped parsley
2 or 3 cloves garlic, finely chopped	

Wash and dry the scallops and roll them in flour. Heat the olive oil, add the scallops and cook them very quickly, tossing them lightly in the hot oil. While they are cooking add the chopped garlic and mix it in well. Then salt and pepper to taste, and just before taking the pan from the stove, add the parsley and toss it around so that the scallops are nicely coated with it.

Serve with lemon wedges. Scallops Provençale are often served in shells — a very attractive dish.

VARIATION

Peel, seed, and chop 3 medium tomatoes. Sauté them in butter until soft and thick. Serve with the scallops.

SCALLOPS SAUTÉ FINES HERBES

Follow the same procedure as for scallops Provençale, omitting the garlic and adding 1 teaspoon chopped tarragon and 1 teaspoon chopped chives with the parsley.

SCALLOP QUICHE

White wine *or* dry vermouth
½ pound scallops
9 to 12 small mushroom caps
1 cup light cream
½ cup heavy cream

Cayenne pepper
Salt
Freshly ground black pepper
3 eggs
1 9-inch pastry shell

Partially pre-bake the pastry shell for 10 to 12 minutes in a 400° oven, and brush the inside lightly with an egg yolk. Return the shell to the oven for an additional 2 minutes. Poach scallops and mushroom caps in enough white wine to barely cover, until scallops and mushrooms are just cooked through. Drain scallops and mushrooms and pat dry. Arrange in a starburst pattern, starting from the center and moving to the outer edge of the pastry shell alternating scallops with mushroom caps, or lining rows of scallops next to rows of mushroom caps. Combine the light cream, heavy cream, salt, pepper, a dash of cayenne, and the eggs. Beat together until thoroughly blended. Carefully pour custard into the pie shell. Bake in a 375° oven for 25 to 30 minutes, or until the quiche is well puffed and brown and tests done.

SCALLOP STEW

See oyster stew, page 433.

FRIED SCALLOPS

2 pounds scallops	Salt
Beer batter (page 99)	Freshly ground black pepper
Fat *or* oil	

Wash, drain, and dry scallops on a dry cloth. Prepare the beer batter. Heat fat or oil for deep frying to 370°. Dip the scallops into the beer batter and drop by spoonfuls into the hot fat. Cook for 3 to 5 minutes, or just long enough for them to brown nicely. Drain on absorbent paper. Season to taste and serve with tartar sauce (pages 35–36).

SCALLOPS MORNAY

2 pounds scallops	Sauce Mornay (page 22)
White wine to cover	Buttered crumbs
Bouquet garni (onion, parsley, thyme)	Grated Parmesan cheese

Poach the scallops in white wine with the bouquet garni for 3 to 5 minutes — until they are just cooked through. Drain them and use some of the white wine to prepare the sauce Mornay. Arrange the scallops in shells or small ramekins and cover with the sauce. Sprinkle with buttered crumbs and a little grated Parmesan cheese. Heat under the broiler for a few minutes to glaze the tops.

There is usually enough seasoning in the sauce; however, it is wise to taste for seasoning before you fill the ramekins.

VARIATIONS

1. Line individual casseroles with thin slices of frizzled smoked ham. Place scallops on top. With the aid of a pastry tube squeeze a ruffle of Duchess potatoes around the edge. Cover the scallops with sauce Mornay and sprinkle liberally with buttered crumbs. Bake in a 450° oven for 10 or 15 minutes to give a pleasant glaze to the sauce and brown the potatoes.

2. Poach the scallops in white wine. Prepare the sauce Mornay. Line a shallow oval baking dish with a border of Duchess potatoes piped through a pastry tube. Alternate scallops and mushroom caps that have been sautéed in butter for 6 minutes. Correct the seasoning and cover the scallops and mushrooms with the sauce Mornay. Sprinkle with crumbs and grated Parmesan and Gruyère. Bake at 450° for 10 minutes or until nicely browned.

SCALLOPS DUXELLES

2 pounds scallops	9 tablespoons butter
2 cups white wine	4 tablespoons flour
Salt	½ cup tomato sauce
Freshly ground black pepper	1 cup bouillon from the scallops
1 onion, finely chopped	Buttered crumbs
1 pound mushrooms, finely chopped	

Poach the scallops for 6 minutes in white wine to cover. Salt and pepper to taste. Drain and save the bouillon. Sauté the onion and half the mushrooms in 6 tablespoons of the butter until they cook down thoroughly and are almost a paste. Add a little of the wine bouillon if necessary. Spread the bottom of shells or ramekins with this mixture.

Melt the remaining 3 tablespoons of butter in a small skillet and add the rest of the mushrooms. Cook for 3 minutes, add the flour, and mix well. Add the tomato sauce and bouillon and stir until the sauce is well blended and thickened. If it does not thicken enough add a little beurre manié (page 475). Correct the seasoning. Cover the mushroom paste in the ramekins with scallops and top with the sauce. Sprinkle with crumbs and brown quickly in a very hot oven — 500° — or under the broiler.

VARIATION

Use part scallops and part shrimp, mussels, or clams. I like this dish made with a third scallops, a third shrimp, and a third oysters for a change. Poach the shrimp and scallops in white wine and add the oysters to the sauce at the last minute.

COQUILLES ST. JACQUES MONTEIL

1½ pounds bay scallops	Juice of 1 lemon
7 tablespoons butter	½ teaspon salt
6 shallots *or* green onions, chopped	¼ teaspoon freshly ground black pepper
Bouquet garni (parsley, onion, celery leaves, thyme, bay leaf)	2 or 3 tablespoons flour
	4 egg yolks
1½ cups white wine	1 cup heavy cream
12 mushrooms, finely chopped	Grated Parmesan cheese
⅓ cup water	Bread crumbs

Wash the scallops and place in a saucepan with 2 tablespoons of the butter, the shallots, and the bouquet garni. Barely cover with white wine and simmer for about 4 to 6 minutes until the scallops are done. Drain and save the cooking liquid. When the scallops are cool enough to handle, cut them into small pieces.

Melt 2 more tablespoons of butter and add the mushrooms. Add the water, lemon juice, salt, and pepper. Let this cook for about 5 or 6 minutes over low heat. Drain the mushrooms and save the liquid.

Prepare a beurre manié with the remaining 3 tablespoons butter and the flour. Add the combined cooking liquids from the scallops and mushrooms and stir over a medium flame until thickened. Correct the seasoning. Add the scallops and let them heat in the sauce. Cool slightly. Combine the egg yolks and cream and stir into the mixture. Continue stirring over a low flame until it is well thickened, but take care that the mixture does not boil. Add the mushrooms. The sauce will be quite thick — stiff enough to be heaped into shells or individual casseroles. Sprinkle with bread crumbs and grated Parmesan cheese and glaze under the broiler.

VARIATION

You may use half scallops and half some other seafood.

SCALLOPS AND BACON EN BROCHETTE

Intertwine scallops and rashers of bacon on skewers. Put the bacon on first, then a scallop, then bacon, then a scallop, and so on. Brush the scallops well with butter, salt and pepper them, and broil until they are delicately browned and the bacon is cooked. Serve with lemon wedges.

Cold Cooked Scallops

SCALLOPS IN MAYONNAISE

2 pounds scallops	Lettuce
White wine	Potato salad
Bouquet garni (onion, parsley, thyme)	Mayonnaise
	Capers

Poach the scallops in white wine with the bouquet garni. Drain and let them cool. Arrange a bed of finely shredded lettuce. Cover it with a layer of sliced potato salad. Top with the scallops and mask with mayonnaise. Decorate with capers.

SCALLOP SALAD

Poach the scallops in white wine with the bouquet garni (see recipe above). Drain and let them cool. Pour over them a sauce vinaigrette and let them stand for 2 hours. Arrange Boston lettuce and romaine in a bowl, add thinly sliced onion rings and quartered tomatoes and hard-cooked eggs. Put the scallops in the center. Decorate with capers and sliced cucumbers and serve with additional vinaigrette sauce (page 36).

Shrimp

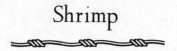

More shrimp, either fresh or canned, are sold in this country than any other type of shellfish. The fresh shrimp in our markets range in size from 6 to 8 to the pound, 12 to 16 to the pound, or 18 to 25 to the pound, down to the tiny Maine and Pacific shrimp which are extremely small. As for the tiny shrimp, I think they are much underrated in this country. They are remarkably good in salads and are excellent in many cooked dishes. A huge bowl of tiny shrimp, shelled, makes a perfect snack with cocktails.

You can now buy quick-frozen shrimp in nearly all parts of the country. They are obtainable both cooked and raw. In the raw state, they may be a greenish-gray color, pale pink, or brown.

Cooked shrimp are sold in shells, shelled, and sometimes both shelled and deveined. In my opinion, shrimp that have been shelled and deveined before cooking are more delicate in flavor and less apt to be gritty. Shelling is a simple job — just push the shell with your thumb and forefinger and it comes off easily. You should leave the tails on for certain types of cookery, especially in preparing barbecued or grilled shrimp. While it is not necessary to devein shrimp, most people prefer to serve them that way. Use a sharp-pointed knife to cut along the curve in the body, removing the black vein. If you are making "butterfly" shrimp, by all means devein before cooking to enhance the appearance of the dish. Cut well through each shrimp so that the two halves nearly divide.

The unpardonable fault in preparing shrimp is overcooking. They should be cooked just long enough to give them color and firmness — about 3 to 5 minutes, certainly no longer. If you are adding shrimp to a sauce, don't cook them before adding them or they will be overcooked. If a recipe calls for bouillon from the shrimp, cook the shells and a couple of fish heads to get the required amount of broth. For shrimp to be served as hors d'oeuvre or in salads, poach them in a strong court bouillon.

Practically all shrimp sold in the markets have been decapitated, but in certain localities in the South and the West, you may find small sweet shrimp that are sold with their heads on. These are what the French call *bouquet* and are excellent served in shell as hors d'oeuvres — without sauce. The flavor is very delicate, and overwhelming them with sauces is unthinkable.

It is very difficult to tell you how many shrimp to buy per person. Sometimes I can eat a half pound as a first course at dinner, and for a main course I would want the same amount. So, if the appetites are very good, you might gauge about 1 pound of shrimp for two persons. If you are mixing the shrimp with a great deal of sauce, you may be able to make a pound stretch for 4 servings.

Shrimp as a First Course – Cold

In addition to the small shrimp, poached and served without sauce, there are almost endless ways in which shrimp may be used as appetizers. Large shrimp, cooked in court bouillon (page 18) and cooled, may be served either shelled or unshelled. Arrange them on plates of greens and pass:

1. Sauce rémoulade (page 35)
2. Sauce vinaigrette (page 36)
3. Sauce mayonnaise (page 34)
4. Sauce verte (page 34)
5. Mustard sauce (page 23)

You may use a cocktail sauce if you wish; personally I like to get as far away as possible from the bottled tomato sauce that is served so much as cocktail sauce. It smothers the flavor of the shrimp. So I give it a little dressing up (see page 38).

TOMATO SHRIMP APPETIZER I

For each person, peel, seed, and hollow out a large ripe tomato. Into the bottom place a cold egg which has been poached in boiling salted water until the yolk has not quite set. Cover the egg with shrimp. Top with mayonnaise (page 34) and garnish with finely chopped parsley, chives, and tarragon.

TOMATO SHRIMP APPETIZER II

Hollow the tomato out as above, put in the egg, and add the shrimp. Cover with a tomato aspic and chill until very firm. Prepare mayonnaise jelly (page 34) with equal quantities of mayonnaise and aspic and cover each tomato with this sauce. Garnish with finely chopped egg, red pepper, and parsley.

CUCUMBER SHRIMP APPETIZER

For each person make a cucumber boat. Cut a strip from one side of the cucumber and remove all the seeds, hollowing it out. Then cut a thin slice from the bottom so that the cucumber boat will stand steady on the plate. Salt and pepper the inside, and rub with olive oil and vinegar. Chill for 2 hours.

Fill the boats with well-seasoned shrimp that have been cooked in a court bouillon and chilled. Cover with a mayonnaise sauce, and garnish with slices of tomato, hard-cooked egg, and finely chopped fresh dill.

Season the cucumber boats well with chopped fresh dill and chives. Fill with the cooked shrimp, cover with dill-flavored sour cream, and garnish with chopped hard-cooked egg and capers.

SHRIMP ASPIC RING

2 quarts court bouillon (page 18)
3 pounds large shrimp
3 envelopes gelatin
12 eggs, hard-cooked
1 small onion, chopped
6 mushrooms, chopped
12 ripe olives, chopped
Mayonnaise

2 cucumbers
Romaine lettuce
2 or 3 knob celery (celery root), grated
Sauce rémoulade (page 35)
Pimientos, olives, and other garnish

Prepare the court bouillon. Poach the shrimp for 4 minutes and remove them from the bouillon to cool. Reduce the bouillon to 1 quart and strain. Dissolve the gelatin in ½ cup of cold water and combine with the bouillon. Cool, but do not let it set.

Cut 6 eggs in half the long way and 6 the round way; remove the yolks. Crush the yolks with the onion, mushrooms, and ripe olives. Moisten with mayonnaise. Fill the egg halves with this paste piped through the large rosette end of a pastry tube. Chill.

Arrange the shelled shrimp in the bottom of a ring mold — making a solid ring of shrimp. Cover with a layer of the jelly and chill until firm. Score the skin of the cucumbers by running the tines of a fork the long way, from tip to tip, in order to form scalloped edges on the cucumber slices. Then slice them evenly. Arrange a layer of the cucumber slices in an overlapping ring on top of the shrimp and jelly. Add another layer of shrimp and cover with more aspic. Chill. Cover each stuffed egg with aspic and chill.

Arrange romaine on a large platter and unmold the ring on top. Fill the center with the celery root mixed with sauce rémoulade. Decorate the stuffed eggs with pimientos and olives cut in slices or designs and arrange them around the edge of the platter. Serve with more rémoulade.

CUCUMBER ASPIC WITH SHRIMP

White wine court bouillon (pages 18–19)
2 pounds shrimp
1½ envelopes gelatin
2 or 3 cucumbers, peeled and sliced

Romaine
Green peppers
Russian salad (pages 409–410)

Prepare the court bouillon. Add shrimp shells and cook for ½ hour over a brisk flame to blend the flavors. Poach the shrimp for the last 4 minutes and remove from the bouillon to chill. Reduce the bouillon to 3 cups and strain through a linen napkin.

Dissolve the gelatin in ¼ cup of cold water. Combine it with the bouillon and season to taste with fresh tarragon or dill.

Arrange the cucumber in overlapping slices in the bottom of a ring mold. Add a little of the gelatin mixture and let it set. Pour the remaining gelatin over it and chill until firm. Arrange romaine on a round platter and unmold the ring on top. Fill the center with the cold poached shrimp. Decorate with strips of green pepper and surround with pepper cups filled with Russian salad. Serve with sauce verte (page 34).

INDIVIDUAL SHRIMP ASPICS

Court bouillon (page 18)
2 pounds shrimp
2 envelopes gelatin
Fresh *or* dried tarragon
4 truffles

6 hard-cooked eggs
4 pounds asparagus
4 pimientos
Mayonnaise (page 34)

Prepare the court bouillon. Peel and devein the shrimp and poach them for 4 minutes. Remove to cool. Reduce the bouillon by half and strain through a linen cloth. Dissolve the gelatin in ½ cup of cold water. Combine with the bouillon and add a few leaves of fresh or dried tarragon. Taste for seasoning. Chill, but do not let it set.

Line individual molds with a large slice of truffle surrounded with slices of hard-cooked egg. Add a spoonful of the jelly mixture and let it set. Arrange the cooked shrimp in the molds in an even design. Place another slice of truffle in the center and cover with more jelly. Chill.

Clean the asparagus and cook in boiling salted water until just barely tender. Drain and cool. Arrange in a half sunburst on a large platter and garnish with strips of pimiento. Unmold the aspics and arrange them on the platter. Serve with mayonnaise.

SHRIMP BOATS

1½ pounds shrimp	¼ cup olive oil
Court bouillon (page 18)	3 avocados
2 cloves garlic	Russian dressing (page 35)

Shell and devein the shrimp. Prepare the court bouillon and poach the shrimp for 4 minutes. Cool.

Crush the garlic in a mortar or chop exceedingly fine and combine with the olive oil. Cut the avocados in half and remove the pits. Dress each one with a little of the oil and garlic mixture. Fill the centers with cold shrimp and serve with a Russian dressing.

PICKLED SHRIMP

These may be prepared with either shelled or unshelled shrimp and may be kept for quite a while in the refrigerator if you store them in covered fruit jars. They are exceedingly good with beer and cocktails and make a wonderful late evening snack with a bottle of chilled white wine. I like heavy rye or pumpernickel bread with them.

For 3 pounds of shrimp you will need 1 cup wine vinegar (the white is better, but the red does add color), a cup of either olive oil or peanut oil, 2 cups wine (white or red, depending upon the vinegar you use), a like amount of water, and a bouquet garni of 2 leeks or large green onions cut in pieces, 2 or 3 hot red peppers, a handful of parsley, some celery leaves, 6 to 8 whole peppercorns, 2 or 3 cloves, a sprig of fresh tarragon or a teaspoon of the dried, a sprig of thyme, 1 tablespoon brown sugar, and a piece of stick cinnamon.

Cook this bouillon all together for about 15 minutes after it has started to simmer. Add the shrimp and cook 5 more minutes. Let the shrimp cool in the broth and store in jars until you wish to use them.

Hot Shrimp Hors d'Oeuvre

FRENCH-FRIED SHRIMP

Fat for frying	Salt
2 pounds shrimp	Freshly ground black pepper
1 teaspoon curry powder	Corn meal
1 teaspoon chili powder	3 eggs, beaten

Heat fat in your automatic fryer or deep fryer to 365°. Shell and devein the shrimp, leaving the tails on. Mix the seasonings with the corn meal. Dip the shrimp in the eggs and then roll in the corn meal. Fry a few at a time in the hot fat. Drain on absorbent paper. Serve with mayonnaise (page 34).

SHRIMP STRAWS PEKINESE

1 pound shrimp	Freshly ground black pepper
¼ pound fresh ginger, finely chopped	2 egg whites
1 large onion, finely chopped	Slices of stale bread
Salt	Crumbs
	Deep fat for frying

Shell and clean the shrimp and chop very fine. Mix with the vegetables, season to taste, and moisten with egg whites. Spread the mixture on stale bread cut into fingers. Dip in fine crumbs and fry in fat heated to 375° for 3 minutes. Drain on absorbent paper.

BUTTERFLY SHRIMP

2 pounds shrimp	Soy sauce
2 eggs, beaten	Mustard
¾ cup milk	Kumquat chutney
Soft bread crumbs	

Heat the fat in your French fryer to 360°. Shell and devein the shrimp, leaving the tails on. Split them almost in two and flatten them out. Beat the eggs with the milk. Dip the shrimp in the eggs and milk, then in the crumbs, and fry 2½ to 3 minutes, or until brown. Drain on absorbent paper. Serve with bowls of soy sauce, hot mustard, and kumquat chutney.

TEMPURA

2 pounds shrimp	1 cup sifted flour
2 eggs, separated	1 tablespoon soy sauce
¾ cup beer	1 teaspoon mustard
1 tablespoon olive oil	Flour

Heat the fat in your French fryer to 365° or slightly over. Shell and devein the shrimp, leaving the tails intact. Beat the egg yolks with the beer, oil, flour, and seasonings and blend well. Beat the whites until stiff and fold them in. Dip the shrimp in flour and then into the egg batter. Lower them into the frying basket by spoonfuls. Cook 4 minutes. Drain on absorbent paper and serve with soy sauce and hot mustard. Thin slices of large white radish go well with this.

Wrap the shrimp in half slices of bacon.

SHRIMP FRITTERS

1 pound shrimp	3 teaspoons baking powder
3 cups chopped parsley	2 eggs, well beaten
1 tablespoon fresh dill	½ cup milk
1 cup flour	Dash of Tabasco
½ teaspoon salt	

Cook and clean the shrimp. Chop them and mix with the parsley
and dill. Sift the dry ingredients; add the eggs and the milk and
mix until smooth. Combine with the shrimp and herbs and add
a dash of Tabasco. Drop by spoonfuls into shortening heated to
380°. Fry until brown and crisp. Drain on absorbent paper. Serve
as a first course. If you serve these as a cocktail snack, drop them
from a small teaspoon into the fat.

BROILED BARBECUED SHRIMP

2 pounds shrimp	1 tablespoon tomato sauce *or*
1 cup olive oil	chili sauce
1 teaspoon salt	1 teaspoon freshly ground black
3 tablespoons chopped parsley	pepper
1 tablespoon basil	1 tablespoon wine vinegar
2 cloves garlic, minced	

Shell and devein the shrimp, but leave the tails on. Make a
sauce by mixing all the other ingredients together. Arrange the
shrimp in a shallow pan — 9 by 14 inches — and pour the sauce
over them. Marinate for several hours. Broil for 5 to 8 minutes.
Arrange the shrimp on a serving dish or serve them in the broiling pan. Eat them by picking them up by the tail and dipping
them into the hot sauce, so plates and plenty of paper napkins
are needed with this dish.

BROILED SHRIMP ITALIAN

½ cup olive oil
2 pounds large shrimp
2 cloves garlic, chopped
¼ pound prosciutto, shredded
1 cup tomato sauce
1 teaspoon salt

1 teaspoon dry mustard
1 teaspoon oregano
1 teaspoon freshly ground black pepper
½ cup red wine

Shell and clean the shrimp, leaving the tails intact. Heat the olive oil in a skillet and add the garlic. Sauté it gently without browning. Add the ham and cook 2 minutes. Add the tomato sauce, seasonings, and red wine and blend well. Cool. Arrange the shrimp in a 9-by-14-inch pan and pour the sauce over them. Marinate for 2 hours. Broil in the sauce for about 7 to 9 minutes.

BROILED SHRIMP

2 pounds shrimp
2 cloves garlic, finely chopped
½ cup peanut oil
¼ cup soy sauce

1 tablespoon lemon juice
3 tablespoons chopped parsley
¼ cup chili sauce

Shell and devein the shrimp, leaving the tails on. Combine the other ingredients. Marinate the shrimp in this mixture for 2 hours. Broil in the sauce for 7 to 8 minutes.

VARIATION

Leave the shells on the shrimp and let them soak in the marinade for 2 hours. Arrange them in a grill or on skewers and grill over or under coals or under the broiler. They should broil in about 5 minutes. Serve with plenty of napkins and plates, of course. Heat the marinade separately to be used as a dip, and let each person shell his own shrimp and dip them in the sauce.

SHRIMP EN BROCHETTE

Any of the preceding recipes for broiling may be used for broiling *en brochette*. Remove the shrimp from the marinade and arrange them on the skewers. Brush them with oil or butter and broil for about 5 minutes. Heat the sauce separately and serve as a dip.

SHRIMP AND MUSHROOM EN BROCHETTE

Alternate large shrimp and mushrooms on a brochette. Salt and pepper and brush well with olive oil or butter. Broil about 5 minutes.

HELEN EVANS BROWN'S STUFFED
BROILED SHRIMP

Shell and clean the shrimp and cut them almost in half — as for butterfly shrimp. Poach them in court bouillon (page 18). Place an anchovy fillet between the halves of each shrimp and press them together tightly. Wrap each shrimp in half a slice of bacon. Arrange 3 to 5 of these shrimp on a skewer and bake in a moderate oven or broil until the bacon is crisp. Serve as a first course with broiled tomato or with a cucumber salad.

Shrimp as a Main Course

SHRIMP IN CREAM

Shell and devein 2 pounds of shrimp and cook for 3 minutes in salted water. Prepare a shellfish velouté (page 21) or béchamel (page 23) and combine with the cooked shrimp. Heat until the fish is hot through and the flavors are blended. Serve with croustades, toast, patty shells, or vol au vent. Garnish with finely chopped hard-cooked egg.

SHRIMP WIGGLE

This dish, which used to be the delight of the chafing dish and the standby of the girls' dormitory, can be delightful if correctly prepared.

Combine 1 large can of French peas (*petits pois*), which have been heated with 4 tablespoons of butter and 1 teaspoon of onion juice, with the recipe above for shrimps in cream. Use the liquid from the peas in preparing the velouté or béchamel.

SHRIMP SAUTÉ IN CREAM

2 pounds shrimp
Flour
3 tablespoons butter
3 tablespoons olive oil
Salt

Freshly ground black pepper
1 tablespoon minced onion
1 tablespoon minced parsley
1 tablespoon minced tarragon
1½ cups heavy cream

Shell and devein the shrimp. Dredge them with flour. Melt the butter, add the oil, and sauté the shrimp until lightly browned and cooked through — about 3 or 4 minutes. Salt and pepper to taste. Add the seasonings and toss with the shrimp. Gradually pour in the cream, stirring carefully, and continue stirring until the sauce is thickened and thoroughly blended.

VARIATION

When the sauce is slightly thickened, pour the mixture into an ovenproof serving dish and sprinkle with 4 ounces of grated Gruyère or good Cheddar cheese. Run under the broiler to melt the cheese and glaze the top.

SHRIMP NEWBURG

Follow directions for lobster Newburg (pages 396–397).

SHRIMP À L'AMÉRICAINE

Follow directions for lobster à l'Américaine (page 391).

SHRIMP CREOLE

2 pounds shrimp
⅓ cup olive oil
3 cloves garlic, cut in fine strips
2 onions, cut in fine strips
2 pounds tomatoes, peeled, seeded, and chopped
2 green peppers, seeded and chopped

3 stalks celery, cut in fine strips
1 carrot, cut in fine strips
Bouquet garni (thyme, parsley, fennel)
1 cup white wine
½ cup tomato paste
Salt
Freshly ground black pepper

Shell and clean the shrimp and keep the shells. Heat the olive oil in a large kettle and add the garlic and onion and brown lightly. Add the tomatoes, shrimp shells, peppers, celery, carrot, bouquet garni, and wine. Cover and simmer for 1 hour. Strain through a fine sieve with the aid of a wooden spoon, or put through a puree machine. Add the tomato paste and season to taste.

Return to the stove and bring to a boil. Add the shrimp and let them cook for 5 minutes in the sauce. Serve with rice prepared in your favorite fashion. This will serve 6 people.

NEW ORLEANS SHRIMP CREOLE

4 tablespoons butter
2 onions, finely chopped

3 green peppers, finely chopped
1 clove garlic, finely chopped

2 cups stewed *or* canned tomatoes	Salt
1 teaspoon paprika	Freshly ground black pepper
	1½ pounds shrimp

Melt the butter in a large skillet or Dutch oven. Add the onions, peppers, and garlic and cook slowly until tender. Add the tomatoes and simmer for 30 minutes. Add the paprika, season to taste, add the shrimp, shelled and cleaned, and cook for 5 minutes. Serve with rice.

JAMBALAYA WITH SHRIMP

I have found that a great many of the recipes for jambalaya do not specify ham. Evidently almost any type of smoked meat was considered *jambon* in the old days.

4 tablespoons butter, lard, *or* bacon fat	Salt
2 tablespoons flour	Freshly ground black paper
3 onions, chopped	2 pounds shrimp
1 clove garlic, chopped	2 cups rice
¼ pound ham, cut in strips	3 cups liquid (water, broth, *or* fish stock)
2 cups cooked *or* canned tomatoes	

Melt the fat in a large Dutch oven and blend in the flour. Add the onions, garlic, and ham and cook just until the onion grows translucent. Add the tomatoes and cook them down for a few minutes. Salt and pepper to taste.

Shell and clean the shrimp. Wash the rice well and add with the shrimp to the sauce. Pour over it enough boiling water or stock to cover 1 inch above. Cover and simmer until the rice is cooked. It may be necessary to add more liquid as the rice cooks.

VARIATIONS

1. Some recipes omit the tomatoes and use more stock or liquid.

2. Some recipes include chili powder or gumbo file.

3. I prefer to add the shrimp during the last 5 minutes of cooking time when I make this dish. It is my opinion that the seafood is overcooked in the original recipe.

POTTED SHRIMP

Melt and clarify some butter. Mix with tiny Pacific or Maine shrimp. The imported canned shrimp can be used here, if fresh shrimp are not available. Season with grated mace, a little nutmeg, a few drops of Tabasco, and a drop of lemon juice. Put the shrimp into pots, pour the clarified butter over them, and chill. When the butter has congealed, pour a little additional butter over the top to smooth it off. Serve as an appetizer or first course.

LIZ LUCAS'S SHRIMPS

3 pounds or more cooked and shelled shrimp	Salt
3 medium onions, thinly sliced	Freshly ground black pepper
3 or 4 lemons, thinly sliced	¼ teaspoon Tabasco
Chopped parsley	Olive oil
	3 bay leaves

Combine layers of shrimp, onion, lemon slices, and parsley in a casserole or serving dish. Add seasonings and olive oil to cover. Top with bay leaves. Marinate 6 to 8 hours or overnight. Serve in a casserole or serving dish with cocktails — or as an appetizer for a first course arranged on a bed of greens.

SHRIMP KIEV

Shell jumbo shrimp, leaving the tails on. Allow 4 to 6 shrimp per person. Split shrimp on the *inside,* flatten and pound slightly between waxed paper. Place tiny pieces of frozen butter on the inside of the shrimp and roll them around the butter. First dip the shrimp in flour, then in beaten egg — allow about one egg per person — and finally, in very fine bread crumbs. Chill well, or freeze. Deep fry at 370° until nicely browned. These may be served with mustard mayonnaise (page 34) or with lemon wedges.

SHRIMP DE JONGHE

No one seems to know where this dish originated, but it is very popular in the South and parts of the Middle West.

2 cloves garlic, minced	Pinch each of nutmeg, mace,
1 teaspoon each of chopped	freshly ground black pepper
parsley, chopped chervil,	¼ pound butter
chopped shallots, chopped	⅔ cup bread crumbs
tarragon	½ cup dry sherry
Salt	2 pounds shrimp

Gradually work the garlic and other seasonings into the butter. Work in the crumbs and sherry.

Shell and clean the shrimp and cook in boiling salted water for 3 minutes. Butter 6 to 8 ramekins or individual baking dishes. Arrange layers of the shrimp and the herbed crumb mixture alternately in the ramekins. Top with buttered crumbs and bake in a 400° oven for 10 to 15 minutes.

PAIN DE CREVETTES — SHRIMP LOAF

For this recipe you will need 1 pound of shelled raw shrimp, which should be about 1½ pounds of shrimp before shelling.

1 pound shelled shrimp	½ cup heavy cream
1 teaspoon salt	1 whole egg
½ teaspoon freshly ground black	2 egg yolks
pepper	Pinch of nutmeg
2 cups cold, thick sauce	
béchamel (page 23)	

Clean the shrimp, grind them twice, and pound them in a mortar or work them with a heavy wooden spoon. They must be thoroughly mashed and as smooth as possible. Add the salt, pepper, béchamel sauce, cream, egg, egg yolks, and nutmeg. Blend thoroughly and force through a fine sieve.

Pour the mixture into a buttered mold, place it in a pan of hot water, and bake at 350° for 25 to 30 minutes, or until the mixture is set. Unmold on a hot platter, decorate with whole cooked shrimp, and serve with a Hollandaise sauce (pages 25–26) or a shrimp sauce (page 21).

This recipe will serve 6 people amply.

SHRIMP POLENTA

Polenta is an Italian version of our old-fashioned corn-meal mush. It is actually a European adaptation of an original American dish with a Creole and perhaps a Mexican background.

2 pounds shrimp	1½ teaspoons salt
2 slices salt pork	1 onion, chopped
6 tomatoes, peeled and chopped	1 green pepper, chopped
2 tablespoons butter	2 tablespoons chili powder
4 cups boiling water	⅔ cup grated Cheddar or Jack
1 cup yellow corn meal	cheese

Shell and devein the shrimp. Try out the salt pork until crisp. Cook the tomatoes with the butter for 25 to 30 minutes.

Stir 1 cup of the boiling water into the corn meal; when it boils add the remaining 3 cups and salt to taste. Let it simmer for 10 minutes, stirring constantly to keep it smooth. Add the salt pork, onion, green pepper, tomatoes, and chili powder and cook over hot water for 20 minutes.

Butter an earthenware casserole well. Place a thin layer of the polenta in the bottom, then a layer of shrimp and a slight sprinkling of cheese. Repeat this pattern until all the ingredients are used, but be sure that the top layer in the casserole is polenta. Sprinkle with cheese and dot well with butter. Bake in a 350°

oven for 20 to 25 minutes. Serve with a well-seasoned tomato sauce, spiked with additional chili.

SHRIMP CURRY

2 pounds shrimp
Court bouillon (page 18)
1 onion, finely chopped
1 green pepper, finely chopped
2 cloves garlic, finely chopped

3 tablespoons butter
1 tablespoon curry powder
1 teaspoon cumin
Beurre manié (page 475)

Shell and devein the shrimp and keep the shells to use in the bouillon. Prepare a court bouillon, add the shells and shrimp, and cook for 5 minutes. Remove the shrimp and reduce the broth by half.

Sauté the onion, pepper, and garlic in the butter until just soft, but not browned. Add the curry powder and cumin and blend well. If the curry powder is too bland, spike it with a little cayenne or Jamaica ginger.

Strain the bouillon and add it to the curry mixture. Taste for seasoning. If you wish a thickened sauce, add beurre manié. Add the shrimp and cook just long enough to heat through. Serve with rice pilaf, crisp fried onions, and chutney.

SHRIMP AND MUSHROOM SAUTÉ POLONAISE

1 pound shrimp
1 pound mushrooms
4 tablespoons butter
2 tablespoons olive oil
6 to 8 shallots, chopped
¼ cup chopped parsley

¼ cup sherry *or* Madeira
Salt
Freshly ground black pepper
Paprika
1 cup sour cream

Shell and devein the shrimp. Remove the stems from the mushrooms.

Melt the butter, add the oil, and sauté the shallots for 2 minutes. Add the mushrooms and sauté gently for 10 minutes, tossing them frequently. Add the parsley and wine. Let it come to the boiling point and add the shrimp. Cook for 4 to 5 minutes, or until the shrimp turn pink. Season to taste with the salt, pepper, and paprika. Stir in the sour cream and heat thoroughly but do not boil. Serve with a rice pilaf or with kasha.

VARIATION

Omit the mushrooms and add more shrimp.

SHRIMP AND ASPARAGUS MORNAY

2 pounds shrimp
Court bouillon (page 18)
1½ cups sauce béchamel (page 23)
Salt
Few grains cayenne pepper

24 large asparagus tips, *or* 36 medium ones
2 egg yolks
½ cup grated Gruyère cheese
3 tablespoons heavy cream

Shell and clean the shrimp. Cook in a court bouillon for 3 to 5 minutes. Remove to a hot dish. Reduce the bouillon to 1 cup and strain. Prepare a sauce béchamel using the fish broth and a little milk. You will need about 1½ cups of sauce. Season to taste with salt and cayenne.

Cook the asparagus tips and arrange them on the bottom of a large oval baking dish. Top with the shrimp. Combine the sauce with the egg yolks and cheese and heat until the cheese is melted. *Do not let it boil.* Add the cream and pour over the shrimp, but leave the tips of the asparagus uncovered. Top with additional cheese, run under the broiler to brown, and serve at once.

VARIATION

This may be prepared with broccoli instead of asparagus.

SHRIMP FLORENTINE

1 pound shrimp	Salt
1 package frozen chopped	Freshly ground black pepper
spinach	Pinch of nutmeg
2 tablespoons butter	2 teaspoons chopped parsley
2 tablespoons flour	2 teaspoons minced onion
2 cups milk	¼ cup grated Parmesan cheese
4 egg yolks, slightly beaten	

Shell and clean the shrimp and cook in boiling salted water for 3 to 5 minutes. Cook spinach according to the directions on the package. Melt the butter in a saucepan. Stir in the flour and make a smooth paste. Gradually add the milk and continue stirring until the sauce thickens. Add the egg yolks and heat the mixture through, but do not let it boil. Season to taste and add the nutmeg, parsley, and onion. Butter 4 individual casseroles and place a layer of spinach in the bottom of each one. Add a layer of shrimp and pour the sauce over the top. Sprinkle with the grated cheese. Bake in a 400° oven for about 10 minutes, or brown under the broiler.

SHRIMP AND CORN SAUTÉ

This is a delicious dish to make in the summer when fresh corn is in season.

1 green pepper, finely chopped	½ cup heavy cream
4 to 6 tablespoons butter	Salt
1½ cups corn kernels	Freshly ground black pepper
1½ cups cooked shelled shrimp	Paprika

Sauté the green pepper in the butter. Add the corn and let it heat through. Add the shrimp and the cream and mix thoroughly. Cover the pan and let it simmer for 3 or 4 minutes. Season to taste with salt, pepper, and paprika.

FRENCH-FRIED SHRIMP LOAF

1-pound loaf of unsliced bread (Italian, French, *or* regular)
¼ pound butter
1 clove garlic, minced
French-fried shrimp (page 450)

Curry (pages 22, 29) *or* Hollandaise sauce (pages 25–26)
or
Russian (page 35) *or* Louis dressing (page 36) with greens, olives, pickles

Cut the top off the loaf of bread and scoop out the center, leaving a wall about ½ inch thick. Brush well with the butter mixed with the garlic. Toast in a slow oven until nicely browned and crisp, but not hard.

Fry the shrimp and stuff the loaf with them, using a little additional melted butter if needed.

This dish may be served hot with a curry or Hollandaise sauce or cold on a bed of greens with an olive and pickle garnish, and Russian or Louis dressing.

Shrimp Salads

SHRIMP SALAD I

Shell and clean 2 pounds of shrimp. Cook in a court bouillon (page 18) for 5 minutes. Remove and chill. Combine with a well-seasoned mayonnaise and arrange in a bowl lined with greens. Garnish with sliced hard-cooked eggs and onion rings.

VARIATION

Add walnut halves.

SHRIMP SALAD II

Combine cooked, chilled shrimp with greens in a salad bowl and toss with a sauce vinaigrette (page 36), well flavored with dry mustard.

1. Shrimp may be added to any tossed salad.
2. Combine shrimps with anchovy fillets and toss with greens. Dress with an olive oil dressing heavily laced with garlic.

SHRIMP AND ORANGE SALAD

Combine cooked, chilled shrimp with orange sections and onion rings and toss with a sauce vinaigrette (page 36). Serve on romaine or endive.

OLD-FASHIONED SHRIMP SALAD

I remember from childhood the shrimp salad that was always served at our family's favorite resort hotel. Its sauce was, I realize now, a true old-fashioned boiled dressing.

Combine 2 cups of broken pieces of cooked, chilled shrimp with 2 cups of finely chopped cabbage. Dress with a boiled dressing (page 37) and add a little sour cream. Let it stand for 1 hour.

SHRIMP LOUIS

Make beds of shredded lettuce or other greens on salad plates. Top with cooked, chilled shrimp. Dress with a Louis dressing (page 36) and decorate with tomato wedges and quartered hard-cooked eggs.

I think that the smaller shrimp are much better for this dish than the larger varieties.

SHRIMP SALAD EDWARDIAN

Marinate 2 cups cooked shrimp in a vinaigrette sauce (page 36) heavily flavored with dill. Let it stand for 2 hours. Drain, and combine with 1 cup finely cut celery, 2 tablespoons grated onion, and enough mayonnaise to bind the salad. Serve with asparagus tips and quartered hard-cooked eggs.

Terrestrial Animals
Prepared like Fish

Frogs' Legs

There are plenty of wild frogs in this country for people who enjoy the sport of catching and skinning them. Fortunately for most of us, frogs are also grown commercially in the Middle West and in Florida, Louisiana, and California. Besides our native product, we receive some frogs' legs shipped frozen from Japan.

Frogs' legs come in many sizes — for my taste the small ones are by far the best. They are delicately flavored, tender, and cook very quickly. About 6 pairs of the small sort are a good portion.

Frogs' legs are better if soaked in milk for an hour or more before cooking.

FROGS' LEGS SAUTÉ

Sautéing is by far the most common way of preparing frogs' legs. There are a number of variations, but the general procedure is the same. It's a good idea to use half butter and half olive oil. The oil prevents burning and adds a great deal of flavor to the frogs' legs.

Use one or two good-sized spatulas to turn the legs. They are very tender and are apt to stick to the pan. Cook them quickly — they need only about 5 minutes. Flavor them at the last, just before serving.

For a plain sauté, soak frogs' legs in milk for an hour or more. Dry them on a towel, then roll in flour and sauté very quickly in butter and olive oil mixed, turning them so that they become delicately browned on all sides. Salt and pepper to taste and serve with lemon wedges.

FROGS' LEGS SAUTÉ FINES HERBES

Soak the frogs' legs in milk. Dry on a clean towel and roll in flour. Chop parsley, chives, and tarragon very fine and add to toasted buttered bread crumbs. (For four people use 1 cup of crumbs and 2 tablespoons each of the herbs.)

Melt butter and olive oil in a skillet. Sauté the legs very quickly and, when they are nicely browned, add the herbed crumbs. Mix these well with the frogs' legs, salt and pepper to taste, and serve with lemon wedges.

FROGS' LEGS SAUTÉ PROVENÇALE

Soak the frogs' legs in milk, dry and roll them in flour. Sauté them very quickly in olive oil (omitting the butter). When nicely browned, add chopped garlic and parsley and blend well. (Use about 1 clove of garlic for each portion. Plenty of parsley, of course.) Salt and pepper to taste.

FROGS' LEGS SAUTÉ NIÇOISE

Follow the recipe for sauté Provençale above. For each person, peel, seed, and chop one tomato. Cook the tomatoes down in butter until they are a paste. Add a spoonful or so of this paste to each serving of frogs' legs.

FROGS' LEGS SAUTÉ ITALIENNE

Soak the frogs' legs in milk, dry them, and roll them in flour. Sauté in olive oil. Just before they are done, add mushrooms and onion, very finely chopped, to the pan. Salt and pepper to taste and serve sprinkled with chopped parsley.

DEVILED FROGS' LEGS

Soak the frogs' legs in milk and dry them. Roll them in flour, dip them in beaten egg, and roll in crumbs. Sauté in butter and olive oil. When nicely browned remove from the pan. Add salt, pepper, lemon juice, dry mustard, Worcestershire sauce, and a dash of brandy or whiskey to the pan. Swirl it around and mix well. Pour this sauce over the frogs' legs.

FROGS' LEGS POULETTE

Poach frogs' legs for about 5 minutes in just enough white wine to cover them. Serve with a sauce poulette (page 25), using some of the white wine broth as a base.

FROGS' LEGS VINAIGRETTE

For this dish you really must have the small frogs' legs. Use about 3 pairs per serving as a first course at dinner or as a main luncheon course.

Poach the legs in a light court bouillon (page 18) for about 5 minutes. Or poach them in a mixture of half white wine and half water. Season to taste with salt and freshly ground black pepper. Chill.

Serve on romaine or Boston lettuce leaves and top with the following very highly seasoned sauce vinaigrette:

For 4 servings:

1 cup olive oil
¼ cup wine vinegar, *or* half vinegar and half lemon juice
½ teaspoon salt
½ teaspoon freshly ground black pepper
½ teaspoon dry mustard

¼ teaspoon oregano
1 tablespoon chopped shallot *or* green onion
1 tomato, peeled, seeded and finely chopped
1 tablespoon capers
3 tablespoons chopped parsley

Mix all together thoroughly. You may add anything you choose to this sauce — chopped pickle, hard-cooked egg, chopped olives. Spoon the sauce over the frogs' legs.

SOUTHERN-FRIED FROGS' LEGS

Soak the frogs' legs in milk. Roll them in flour, dip in the milk again, and roll in dry bread crumbs or cracker crumbs. Melt 6 tablespoons butter and 5 tablespoons oil in a large skillet. Sauté the frogs' legs quickly in the hot fat and, when nicely browned, remove them to a hot platter. Pour off all but 4 tablespoons of the fat. Combine this with 4 tablespoons flour and mix well, being sure to scrape up all the bits of brown from the pan. Add 1½ cups light cream and stir until thickened. Season to taste with salt and freshly ground black pepper and pour over the frogs' legs or serve separately.

VARIATION

Add 3 tablespoons of sherry or Madeira to the sauce just before pouring over the frogs' legs.

FRIED FROGS' LEGS I

Soak frogs' legs in milk for 30 minutes. Roll in flour, dip in beaten egg and milk, and roll in crumbs. Heat fat for deep frying to 370°. Fry the legs for 2 minutes or until brown. Remove to absorbent paper and sprinkle with salt and freshly ground black pepper. Serve with lemon or with tartar sauce (pages 35–36).

FRIED FROGS' LEGS II

Soak frogs' legs in milk for 30 minutes. Dip them in beer batter (page 99). Fry in deep fat heated to 375° for 3 or 4 minutes or until brown and crisp. Drain on absorbent paper and serve with a sauce rémoulade (page 35) or a tartar sauce (pages 35–36).

NOTE: It is my opinion that frying frogs' legs robs them of their delicate flavor and their delightful juiciness. I much prefer one of the methods for sautéing, frogs' legs poulette, or vinaigrette.

Snails

Snails can be terrestrial, freshwater, or marine. The terrestrial variety, which is the most commonly eaten, is admittedly not a shellfish, but a land-loving vegetarian. It is included in this book because it is similar in many ways to the sea snail, or periwinkle, and because all snails, whether native to land or water, may be cooked by the same recipes.

Most snails eaten in this country come canned, accompanied by a bag of polished shells so that they may be served in the approved way. Moroccan and Tunisian snails are available fresh in the markets, along with a smaller quantity of periwinkles.

French cookbooks give startling directions for cooking snails, and some of the French dishes take days or even weeks to achieve. Complicated procedure is not necessary for preparing and cooking the fresh snails found in American markets. Soak them in warm water just long enough to break the membrane that covers the shell. Any snails that do not emerge should be discarded. The remaining snails should be brought to a boil in salted water or court bouillon. They can then be used in several fashions.

SNAILS BOURGUIGNONNE
(WITH CANNED SNAILS)

1 cup creamed butter	3 or 4 garlic cloves, minced
½ cup minced parsley	Salt to taste

Cream the above ingredients together to make a *beurre d'escargots* (snail butter). Rinse the snails with ½ cup of white wine. Butter the inside of each shell lightly. Insert a snail and cover the entrance of the shell with the snail butter. Arrange on snail platters or on a large baking sheet, and let them stand for several hours before you cook them, if you have the time. About 10 minutes before serving, place the snails in a 450° oven and let them heat through thoroughly. Serve with plenty of good crisp French bread and white wine.

VARIATION
Prepare the snails as above and add ½ cup of white wine to the pan in which you heat them.

SNAILS BOURGUIGNONNE
(WITH FRESH SNAILS)

Soak the snails until they come out of their shells and put them in salted water or court bouillon (see above). After you have brought this to a boil, remove them from their shells and rinse them with a little cold water or white wine. Wash the shells, and then follow the preceding recipe for canned snails.

SNAILS LASSERE

48 mushroom caps (medium size, about 1 inch across)	48 snails
	⅔ cup walnuts, coarsely
6 tablespoons butter	chopped
Snail butter (above)	Fried toast

Sauté the mushroom caps in butter until just slightly tender. Prepare the snail butter. Arrange the mushrooms, cup side up, on a baking sheet. Place a snail in each mushroom cup, cover with a little snail butter, and sprinkle with chopped nuts. Cook in a 400° oven for about 10 minutes, or until thoroughly heated through. Serve on fried toast.

FRESH SNAILS POULETTE

Fresh snails
White wine and water mixed
1 large onion stuck with 2 cloves
1 bay leaf
Pinch of thyme
3 medium onions, finely chopped
2 cloves garlic, finely chopped

8 tablespoons butter
3 tablespoons flour
½ cup heavy cream
3 egg yolks
1 tablespoon lemon juice
¼ cup chopped parsley

Prepare the fresh snails as for snails Bourguignonne with fresh snails (page 474). After you have removed them from the boiling salted water, transfer them to a mixture of half white wine and half water. Add the onion stuck with cloves, the bay leaf, and the thyme. Bring to a boil and simmer for 35 to 40 minutes. Sauté the onions and garlic in 6 tablespoons of the butter until they are soft but not browned. When the snails are tender, remove them from the bouillon, and keep them hot in their shells in a hot serving dish.

Remove the onion and bay leaf from the bouillon and taste for seasoning. Add the sautéed onions, bring to a boil, and simmer for 15 minutes. Make beurre manié by kneading the remaining 2 tablespoons of butter with 3 tablespoons of flour. Mix the heavy cream with the egg yolks; add the beurre manié and the cream-egg mixture to the broth. Stir until well blended and thickened, but do not let it boil. Add the lemon juice and chopped parsley and pour over the snails. Serve with plenty of hot French bread.

Turtle, Tortoise, and Terrapin

Turtles come in many different sorts, sizes, and colors, and once the word *turtle* covered all of them. Now some people restrict the term just to the sea turtles. A *tortoise* is a turtle that prefers the land, and a *terrapin* is a variety of turtle that inhabits rivers and coastal swamps along the Eastern seaboard and the Gulf.

Green turtle is the most famous of sea turtles, and the turtle soup that comes from it is extraordinary. If you have never tasted thick, gelatinous turtle soup, freshly made, then you have a great treat awaiting you. The canned green turtle soup is also excellent. Look for brands with turtle fat or meat in the jar or tin; add a little Madeira or sherry to the soup, heat, and serve with a thin slice of lemon and finely chopped parsley.

Commercial fishing for green turtle is centered around Key West, and turtle steak is much fancied in the South. I have eaten it when it resembled the finest veal. Also delicious is turtle liver, which, ideally, should be sautéed in butter with shallots and parsley. Neither steak nor liver reaches the markets very often, so there is not much use longing for them.

Diamondback terrapin has always had enthusiasts in the Eastern part of the country. It was expensive even around the turn of the century — about \$120 a dozen. Now it is very scarce, and red-bellied turtle is marketed in Eastern cities as a substitute. Snapper turtle, which is found all through the East in lakes, rivers, and canals, is very popular in some areas, especially eastern Pennsylvania.

TURTLE STEAK FLORIDIAN

Have 1½ pounds of turtle cut paper-thin. Pound the steaks with the edge of a plate. Dip them in flour. Melt 6 tablespoons butter in a skillet that has a cover, and brown the pieces of turtle very quickly. Salt and pepper them to taste and add 1 tablespoon paprika. Pour over them ½ cup white wine, cover, and simmer for 1 hour. Remove the pieces of turtle to a hot platter. Add 1 cup sour cream to the pan and stir well until it is heated through and blended. Pour the sauce over the turtle steaks and sprinkle with paprika and chopped parsley.

TERRAPIN MARYLAND

Terrapin is a food that people either like tremendously or dislike violently. If you can stand the rather unique odor, you may enjoy it. To me, terrapin is offensive.

For this recipe, 1 terrapin will serve 3 people.

Bring a kettle of water to a rolling boil and toss the terrapin in alive. Let it boil for 5 minutes. Remove it from the water and rub it with a coarse towel — preferably a Turkish towel — to take the skin off the feet and head. Cook it in boiling salted water until the feet fall off and the shell is cracked. Remove it from the water and place it on its back.

When it is cool enough to handle, draw the nails from the feet. Cut under the shell and remove the meat. Be careful in removing the gall bladder, the sandbags, and the large intestines. These are to be discarded. Cut the meat into 1-to-2-inch strips. Cut up the liver and the small intestines and add them to the meat. Add the eggs, if there are any. Add ¾ cup of the broth and simmer for 25 minutes. Add 4 tablespoons butter, salt and freshly ground black pepper to taste, and a dash of cayenne pepper.

Combine a little of the broth with 2 slightly beaten egg yolks and stir it in carefully. Add ¼ cup of Madeira or sherry to the mixture just before serving.

VARIATION

Terrapin, Philadelphia Style. Cut the meat very fine, add the broth, and simmer for 25 minutes. Make 1 cup of velouté (page 21) with some of the broth and cream. Add this to the terrapin. Beat 2 egg yolks with ½ cup cream, and stir this into the mixture slowly. Do not let it boil. Add sherry or Madeira just before serving. You may add 1 cup sautéed mushrooms if you wish.

SOUTHERN TERRAPIN STEW

Boil and pick 3 terrapin according to the directions given above. Strain and clarify the stock and add a little concentrated turtle broth to it.

Rub the yolks of 6 hard-cooked eggs through a sieve and combine them with 3 tablespoons flour and ½ pound butter to form a paste. Season with ¼ teaspoon freshly grated nutmeg, 2 tablespoons grated onion, 1 tablespoon Worcestershire sauce, the grated rind of 1 orange, and the juice of 1 lemon. Heat 3 cups of turtle broth until boiling, stir in the seasoned paste, reduce the heat and continue stirring until well blended. Add 1 cup Madeira and 1 pint heavy cream and continue stirring until the mixture is thickened and smooth. Be careful not to burn or curdle it. Add the heated terrapin eggs, the meat, and the chopped whites of the 6 hard-cooked eggs. Heat thoroughly and taste for seasoning. Serve with hot buttered toast.

TURTLE FINS

The flippers or fins of the sea turtle are excellent eating. They must be simmered in boiling water until tender and then skinned. After this initial preparation they can be prepared in various ways:

1. Dip the fins in seasoned flour and brown them in butter or oil. When they are nicely browned, add a little white wine and a pinch each of tarragon and fennel. Simmer until tender.

2. Dip in seasoned flour and brown in butter or oil. When brown add white wine and sauce à l'Américaine (page 28). Simmer until tender.

3. Brown the turtle fins as above, add white wine and simmer until nearly done. At the last add a little sauce Mornay (page 22), sprinkle with grated cheese, and run under the broiler to brown.

SNAPPER TURTLE SOUP

Cut off the head of a 10-pound snapper turtle and let it bleed. Wash it thoroughly, scrubbing it with a stiff brush. Run a sharp knife around each shell, pull out the legs, pull the shells open, and extract the meat.

To the shell, skin, and bones of the turtle, add several veal knuckles cracked into pieces. Place this mixture in a large oven-proof pan with 1 cup butter, 2 or 3 chopped onions, several stalks of celery chopped, several chopped carrots, a pinch of thyme, 1 bay leaf, 4 cloves, and salt and freshly ground black pepper to taste. Roast in a hot oven until brown. Stir in 1 cup flour and cook for 30 minutes longer.

Place this mixture in a large kettle, add 3 quarts beef broth and 2 cups canned tomatoes, strained. Simmer for 2 hours. Strain the broth. Cut the turtle meat into small pieces and add these to the strained broth. Add 1 cup sherry and simmer for 10 minutes or until the turtle meat is tender. Taste for seasoning. Serve garnished with chopped hard-cooked egg and lemon slices.

MINORCA GOPHER STEW

Marjorie Kinnan Rawlings in her book *Cross Creek Cookery* has a mouthwatering recipe for what she calls gopher (turtle) stew:

"Wash the decapitated gopher. Cut the shell away from the meat. Scald the feet until the skin and claws can be removed. Discard entrails. Cut meat in two-inch pieces. Simmer until thoroughly tender in two cups water to every cup of meat, adding one half teaspoon salt and a dash of pepper to every cup of meat.

"In a deep kettle or Dutch oven, heat fat, preferably olive oil, allow one quarter cup of fat to every cup of meat. Brown in fat one large chopped onion to every cup of meat, one small can of tomatoes and one green pepper, finely cut. Simmer gently while gopher is cooking. More tomatoes may be added if mixture cooks down too much. When gopher is tender, turn the sauce into the gopher pot. There should be enough liquid to make plenty of gravy. Thicken by mashing the yolks of hard-boiled eggs, two eggs to every cup of meat, and stirring into the stew. Add more salt and pepper to taste. Stir in three tablespoons dry sherry to every cup of meat. Serve at once, preferably directly from pot.

"Thin corn sticks make a good bread to serve with the stew, and spring onions, ripe olives and a green salad usually accompany it."

TURTLE EGGS

Turtle eggs are a rare delicacy and hard to get, but if you ever happen to come on some, here is what Marjorie Kinnan Rawlings has to say about them:

"They are boiled in heavily salted water for twenty minutes. The white never solidifies, but the hard-boiled yolk is rich, rather grainy, with a fine and distinct flavor. They are eaten 'out of hand,' from the shell, breaking off the top of the shell, dotting the egg with salt and pepper and butter, and popping the contents of the shell directly into the mouth. A dozen turtle eggs, with plain bread and butter and a glass of ale, make all I ask of a light luncheon or supper."

Index

Abalone, 353–355
  Canned, Chinese style, 355
  Chowder, 354
  Fried, 354
  Sauté, 353
    Breaded, 354
  Stuffed, 354–355
Alaska crab. *See* King crab
Albacore, 286–290. *See also* Tuna
  Baked, 289
    Marinated, 289–290
  Canned, 290
  Poached, 290
  Sautéed, with tarragon and wine, 287–288
Aspics (Jellied dishes)
  Court bouillon for, 18–20
  Decoration, 34, 131, 199, 342–343

Baking. *See* Cooking methods
Barracuda, 69–72
  Baked, 70
    California, 70
    Niçoise, 71
  Braised, Santa Barbara, 71
  Broiled, 69
  Charcoal-broiled, 69–70
  Roe, 72
  Sautéed, 70
Bass, freshwater, 305–306. *See also* California black sea bass; Sea bass; Striped bass
  Baked, 306
  Broiled, 306
  Pan-fried, 306
Beurre manié, 25
Bloaters, 140–141
Blowfish (Sea squab), 73–74
  Broiled, 74
  Cleaning and preparing, 73–74
  Fried, 74
  Sautéed, 74

Bluefish, 74–76
  Baby, 76
  Baked, 75–76
  Broiled, 75
  Sautéed, 75
  Stuffed, baked, 75–76
Bluegill sunfish, 306–307
Bouillabaisse. *See* Soups and stews
Bowfin, 307
Braising. *See* Cooking methods
Breakfast, smoked fish, 349
Bream, 306
Broiling. *See* Cooking methods
Buffalo fish, 307–308
Burbot, 308
Butter sauces and spreads
  Anchovy, 32
  Beurre noir (black butter), 32
  Beurre noisette (brown butter), 31
  Black, 32
  Browned, 31
  Caviar, 33
  Crawfish, 387
  Herb, 33
  Lemon, 32
  Lime, 32
  Lobster, 32
  Maitre d'hotel, 31
  Parsley, 33
  Tarragon-chive, 33
Butterfish, 77–79
  Baked, en papillote, 79
  Broiled, 77
  in Cases, 78
  with curry and tomatoes, 78
  Niçoise, 78
  Pan-fried, 79
  Sautéed, 77–79
  Smoked, 79
Buying and preparing. *See also* individual fish entries
  Cleaning and dressing, 5–6

Buying and preparing (*Cont.*)
  Filleting, 6
  Fresh, 3
  Frozen, 3–4, 54
  How much to buy, 4
  Scaling, 5

California black sea bass, 80–81
    See also Sea bass
  Baked, 80
  Barbecued steaks, 81
  Broiled, 80
  Fillets Pacific, 215
  Jewfish steaks tropical, 81
California kingfish, 82–83. *See also*
    Kingfish
  Baked
    with anchovies, 83
    Italian, 83
  Broiled, 82
  French-fried, 82
California whitefish, 84–85. *See also*
    Whitefish, freshwater
  Baked, au gratin, 84
  Broiled, 84
  Poached, Hollandaise, 85
Canadian cooking theory, 6–8, 353*n*
Canapés. *See* Hors d'oeuvre and
    appetizers
Carp, 308–317
  Alsatian, with sauerkraut, 310
  Aspic, 315
  Baked, Hungarian style, 311
  au Bleu, 310
  Braised
    Jewish fashion, 315
    Mexican, 311
    Provençale, 309–310
  Broiling, 10
  de Cahors, 312
  à la Chambord, 313–314
  Cold, 315–316, 317
  Fillet, Spencer method, 309
  Gefilte fish, 317
  Marinated, 314
  Pâté chaud, 312–313
  Poached, with sauces, 315–316
  Potted, 316
  Smoked, 317
  Stuffed (de cahors), 312
    à la Chambord, 313–314
  Sweet and sour, 315–316

Catfish, 318–320
  Fried, 319
  Pan-fried, 319
  Poached, 319
  Sautéed, 318
  Skinning, 318
  Soup, 320
Caviar, 275–279
  Blinis with, 277
  Butter, 33
  Cheese, 278
  Dip, 278
  Eggs, 279
  Hors d'oeuvre, 276–278
  Omelet, 278
  Red, 206, 275, 278–279
  Whitefish, 345
Chowders. *See also* Soups and stews
  Abalone, 353
  Caribbean, 58–59
  Clam, 55–56, 356
    Manhattan, 56–57
    Win's, 57
  Fish, 57–58
  Oyster, 431–432
Chub, 321
Cioppino, 13, 48–49
Clams, 355–368
  Appetizers. *See* Hors d'oeuvre and
    appetizers
  Baking and broiling method, 359
  Bisque, 61–62
  Batter-fried, 366–367
  Cakes, 362
  Canned, 356
  Chowders and soup, 55–56, 356, 358
  Fried, 366–367
  Fritters, 361–362
  on Half Shell, 356–357
  Hash, 361
  with Noodles, 367
  Pan roasts, 365–366
  Pie, 363–364
  Quiche, 364
  with Rice, Spanish style, 365
  Sauce, 21, 129, 243, 368
  Sauté, 366
  Scalloped, 363
  Soufflé, 362–363
  Spaghetti sauce, 368
  Steamed, 358
    à la Marinière, 358–359

Clams (*Cont.*)
  on Toast, 359
  Stuffed, 360–361
  Stuffing, 117, 126
Cleaning and dressing, 5–6
Cocktail sauce I, 38; II, 38
Cod, fresh, 85–91. *See also* Cod,
  salt; Ling cod
  Baked, 88
    Baker fashion, 89
    with Cream, 89
    Steaks, in wine, 87
    Stuffed, 88
  Brochettes, Italian, 86
  Broiled, 86
  Cold, poached, 91
  Curried (Indian style), 86–87
  Custard, 90
  Florentine, 91
  Kedgeree, 194–195
  Loaf, 89–90
  New England turkey, 88–89
  Pickled, 64
  Poached, 90, 91
  Sautéed, 86
    Indian style, 86–87
  Steaks, in wine, 87
  Stuffed, 88–89
Cod, salt, 91–101. *See also* Cod,
  fresh; Ling cod
  Armenian, 93–94
  Béchamel, 92–93
  Benedictine, 101
  Brandade de morue, 100–101
  Cakes I, 98–99; II, 99; III, 100
  Carcassone, 96
  Croquettes, 98
  Fried strips, 95
  Hors d'oeuvre, 100
  Lyonnaise, 95
  Marseillaise, 96–97
  Poached, 92
  Portugaise, 97
  Salad, 97–98
  Salt removal, 91–92
  Soufflé, 94–95
  Spanish style, 94
Conch, 368–369
  Fried, 369
  Fritters, 368–369
  Stewed, 369
  Tenderizing, 368

Cooking methods. *See also* Buying
  and preparing
  Baking, 7, 8
    in Foil or paper, 8
    Spencer method, 309
    Stuffed fish, 8
  Braising, 7, 11
  Broiling, 7
    Charcoal grilling, 8–9
    Oven, 9–10
  Canadian cooking theory, 6–8, 353n
  in Court Bouillon, 12
  Flavoring, 8
  Frozen fish, 8–9, 12
  Frying
    Breading for, 252
    Canadian cooking theory, 7
    Deep, 10–11
  Pan frying, 7, 10
  Poaching, 7, 12, 20
  Sautéing, 7, 10
  Shellfish, 353n, 359
  Spencer method, 309
  Steaming, Chinese style, 152, 347
Coquilles St. Jacques Monteil, 442–
  443
Coulibiac, of salmon, 189–191
  of sturgeon, 274
Court bouillon, 17–20
  for Cold dishes, 18–19
  Cooking in, 12
  Creole, 165
  New Orleans, 53–54
  Red wine, 19
  for Shellfish, 20
  Simple I, 18; II, 18
  White wine, for aspics, 19–20
Crab, 369–386. *See also* Crab legs;
  Crab, soft-shelled; King crab;
  Stone crab
  à l'Américaine, 378–379
  Appetizers. *See* Hors d'oeuvre and
    appetizers
  Avocado stuffed with, 372–373
    and Lobster, à la Ritz, 412
  Cakes, 377–378
  Cocktail, 371
  Cooking, 370
  in Cream, 375–376
  Creole, 380
  Curried, 373, 376
  Deviled, 374–375

Crab (*Cont.*)
  Florentine, 376
  Gumbo, 52–53
  Hongroise, 376
  Indienne, 376
  Louis, 372
  Marseillaise, 373
  Mornay, 376
  Mushrooms stuffed with, 376
  with Mussels, 373
  Pilaf, 378
  Quiche, 380–381
  and Rice, 380
  Salads. *See* Salads
  Sauce, 21
  Sautéed, with almonds, 373
  Soufflé, 377
  Soup, Margaret Jennings's, 59
  Stuffing, 41, 158, 268, 324
  Vinaigrette, 371
Crab legs, 370
  Broiled, 384
  Mayonnaise, 384
  Palace Court, 372
  Rémoulade, 384
Crab, soft-shelled, 370, 381–383
  à l'Américaine, 383
  Broiled, 382–383
  Fried, 383
  Sautéed
    Amandine, 382
    in Cream, 382
    Grenobloise, 382
    Meunière, 381–382
Crappies, 321–322
  Broiled, 322
  Pan-fried, 322
  Sauté meunière, 322
Crawfish, 386–388
  Bordelaise, 386–387
  Butter, 387
  Cold, spiced, 388
    Rémoulade, 388
  Gratin d'écrevisses, 387–388
  Serving, 386
Crayfish
  Bisque, 61–62
Croaker, 102
  Broiled, 102
  Pan-fried, 102
  Sauté meunière, 102
Cusk, 103

Decorating fish, 11, 182, 281
  Cold dishes, 34, 131, 199, 342–343
Drum, 72–73
  Baked, 73
  Broiled, 73
Duxelles, 27

Écrevisses. *See* Crawfish
Eels, 103–110
  Baked, New England, 107
  Bordelaise, 106–107
  Canned, 110
  Cold, 109–110
  Commachio, 105
  Flemish green, 109–110
  Marinated, 108
  Matelote of, Normandie, 51–52
    Provençale, 106
  Napolitana, 104–105
  Pan-fried, 104
  Poached, 107–108
  Skinning, 104
  Smoked, 110
  Stew, Normandie, 51–52
  Stifle, New England, 106
Eggs
  Benedictine, 101
  Caviar, 279
  Stuffed, 261
  and oysters, 436–437
Escabeche, 65, 149–150, 210, 241–242
Escargots. *See* Snails
Essence, of fish, 19, 20

Finnan haddie, 113, 120–122
  Broiled, 120
    in milk, 120
  Cakes, 122
  Kedgeree (Cadgery), 194–195
  Poached, 121
  Soufflé, 121
  Vinaigrette, 122
Fish cakes, 64
Flounder. *See* Sole
Fluke, 110–111
Forcemeat, 41–42
Fritters
  Clam, 361–362
  Conch, 368–369
  Mussel, 418
  Oyster, 427
  Shrimp, 452

Frogs' legs, 469–473
 Cold, vinaigrette, 471–472
 Deviled, 471
 Fried I, 472; II, 473
  Southern, 472
 Poached, 471
 Poulette, 471
 Sauté, 469
  Fines herbes, 470
  Italienne, 470
  Niçoise, 470
  Provençale, 470
 Vinaigrette, 471–472
Frying. *See* Cooking methods

Garnishes. *See* Decorating fish
Gefilte fish, 317
Groupers, 80, 111–112
Grunion, 112–113
 Broiled, 112
 Fried, 113

Haddock, 113–120. *See also* Finnan
  haddie
 Baked
  in Cream sauce, 115
  in Paper cases, 116
  in White wine and tarragon, 115
  Provençale, 117–118
  Stuffed, 117, 118
 Boiled, New England, 118
 Broiled, 113
 Cold, 120
 Custard, 119
 Fried, 114
 Kedgeree, 194–195
 Loaf, 119–120
 Pie, 119
 Sautéed, 114
 Smoked. *See* Finnan haddie
 Stuffed, 116, 117, 118
 Turbans, with lemon sauce, 114
 Véronique, fillets, 114–115
Hake, 122–123
 Cold, 123
 Salt, 123
Halibut, 123–132
 Baked, 125
 Broiled, 124
 Cheeks, 124
 Cold, 131–132
 Fried, 128

Halibut (*Cont.*)
 au Gratin, 130
 with Lobster, 130
 Mousse, 129
 Pickled, 64
 Poached, 128–129
 Pudding, 63
 Sauté, 124–125
 Soufflé, 130
 Stuffed steaks, 125–128
 Timbale, 63
Hangtown Fry, 436–437
Hash
 Clam, 361
 Fish, Marc Parson's, 62–63
Herring, 132–141, 208
 Baked
  Boulangère, 134
  Spiced, 135–136
 Bloaters, 140–141
 in Brine, 137–139
 Cold, 135–138
  Spiced, 135–136
 English fashion, 133–134
 Fried, 134
 Grilled, 133
 Hors d'oeuvre, 136–138
 Kippered, 140–141
 Marinated, 138
 in Oil, 140
 Pickled, 138–139
 River, 171–172
 Roe, 136
 Rollmops, 137
 Salad, 139
  Russian style, 140
 Sautéed, 133–134
 Smoked, 139–141
 Smothered, 135
Homard, 388–389
Hors d'oeuvre and appetizers
 Blinis with caviar, 277
 Butterfish, smoked, 79
 Carp, pâté, 312–313
  Smoked, 317
 Caviar, 276–279
 Clams
  Dips and spreads, 357
  on Half Shell, 356–357
  Steamed, 358–359
  Stuffed, 360–361
 Codfish balls and cakes, 100

Hors d'oeuvre and appetizers (*Cont.*)
Crab
Avocado stuffed with, 372–373
Cocktail, 371
Legs, Palace Court, 372
Mushrooms stuffed with, 376
Quiche, 380–381
Crawfish, 388
Eels, Flemish green, 109–110
Smoked, 110
Herring, 136–139
Escabeche, of flounder, 241–242
of Mackerel, 149–150
Fish forcemeat balls, 41–42
Lobster
Avocado stuffed with, 412
Cold, 407–408
Mousse, 404–405
Mackerel, escabeche of, 149–150
Mussels, Ravigote Pascal, 415
Oysters, 421
Angels on Horseback, 429
Devils on Horseback, 428–429
on Half Shell, 420
Stuffed, 421–426
Pâté chaud de carpe, 312–313
Pickled fish, 64, 138–139, 343–344,
449–450
Salmon
Cheeks, 205–206
Kippered, 206
Marinated (Gravad lax), 196–197
Roe, 206
Smoked, 196, 203–205
Tartare, 183
Sardines
in Escabeche, 210
First course, in a hurry, 212
Norwegian spread, 213
Puffs, 211
Turnovers, 212
Scallops, 437
Shrimp
Aspics, 447–449
Avocado stuffed with, 449
Barbecued, 452
Boats, 446–447, 449
Bouquet, 445
Broiled, 452–453
Cucumber, 446–447
Fritters, 452
Marinated, Liz Lucas's, 458

Pickled, 449–450
Potted, 458
Straws Pekinese, 450–451
Tomato I, 446; II, 446
Smelt Oriental, 232
Sole, julienne of, 253
Striped bass, cold, 271
Trout, smoked, 344
Tuna
Canned, 290
Fried fingers, 288
Spread, 291
Whitefish, cold, 348
Smoked, 349
How much to buy, 4. *See also in-
dividual fish entries*

Jambalaya, 457–458
Jewfish, 80
Steaks tropical, 81

Kedgeree (Cadgery), 194–195
King crab, 370, 383–385
à l'Américaine, 384
Broiled, 384
Mayonnaise, 384
Newburg, 385
Rémoulade, 384
Salad, 384
Soufflé, 385
Thermidor, 385
Kingfish, 141–143. *See also* California
kingfish
Baked
Steaks, au gratin, 142
Whole, 143
Broiled steaks, 141
Cold, 143
Sautéed, 142
à l'Anglaise, 142
Stew, 143
Kippers, 140–141

Lake herring, 322–323
Langouste, 389
Cold, 407–408
North African, 401–402
Leftovers, 62–65
Escabeche, 65
Fish cakes, 64
Hash, Marc Parson's, 62–63
Pickled fish, 64

Leftovers (*Cont.*)
  Pie, 63
  Pudding, steamed fish, 63
  Quiche, 62
  Salad
    Bean, Florentine, 65
    Fish and coleslaw, 64
Ling cod, 144–146
  Baked
    Deviled, 145
    Fines herbes, 144
    Mornay, 145
  Broiled, 144
  Poached, 145
  Timbales, 145–146
Lobster, 388–412
  à l'Américaine, 391–393
  Aspic, 409–410, 411
  aux Aromates, 399
  Baked, Italian, 400
  en Bellevue, Parisienne, 408–409
  Bisque, 61
  Broiled live, 390
  Butter, 32
  Cardinal, 402–403
  Chausson of, 392
  Civet of, 393
  Cleaning, 389, 390
  Cold, 407–409
  in Cream, 395
  Curry, 395, 401
  Deviled, 400
  Fra Diavolo, 392–393
  Franco-American, 394
  au Gratin, 394
  Hungarian, 395
  Italian, 400
  Mornay, 395
  Mousse, 404–405
  Newburg, 396–397
  North African, 401–402
  Omelet, 392
  Phoceenne, 397
  Salad. *See* Salads
  Sauce, 21
  Sautéed
    with curry, 401
    Fines herbes, 403
    Louisiana, 404
    Mexican, 403–404
    with tomatoes, 402
    with Sole, 247

Lobster (*Cont.*)
  Soufflé, 405–406
    Plaza-Athenée, 406–407
  Stew, 407
  Stuffed, Drouant, 397
  Thermidor, 398
    American, 399
    Quick, 399
  Tomalley, 389
  Turnover (Chausson), 392

Mackerel, 146–152. *See also* Spanish
    mackerel
  Baked, 150
  Broiled, 146
  Chinese style, 152
  Escabeche (cold), 149–150
  Fried, 146
  Hors d'oeuvre, 149–150
  Poached I, 147; II, 147–148
  Sautéed fillets
    Florentine, 148–149
    Italian, 148
    Meunière, 147
  Stuffed I, 150; II, 151
    with white wine, 151
Mirepoix, 20, 387
Mousses
  Halibut, 129
  Lobster, 404–405
  Pike, 327
  Salmon, 195
Mullet, 152–154
  Baked, a l'Anglaise, 153
    Split, 153–154
  Broiled, 153
  Sautéed, 153
Mussels, 413–418
  Barbecued, 417
  in Crabmeat Marseillaise, 373
  in Cream, 418
  Creole, 416–417
  Curried, 416
  Fritters, 418
  Marinère, 413–414
  Poulette, 414
  Ravigote Pascal, 415
  Salad, 415
  Spaghetti sauce, 418
  Steamed, 416
  Stuffed, 415
    Provençale, 417–418

New England turkey (cod), 88–89
Newburg, Lobster, 396–397

Ocean perch, 154–159
  Amandine, 155
  Baked, Espagnole, 155–156
  Broiled, 154
  Cold jellied, 158–159
  Curried, 156–157
  Deviled, 157
  Fried, 155
  Loaf, Polonaise, 156
  Mornay, 157
  Polonaise, 156
  Sauté meunière, 155
  Stuffed, Foyot, 158
Ocean sunfish, 159–160
  Italian, 160
Omelets
  Caviar, 278
  Lobster, 392
  Oyster, 431
  Sole, 248–250
  Tunafish, 292–293
Oysters, 419–437
  Angels on Horseback, 429
  Bisque, 62
  Breton, 424
  en Brochette, 429–430
  Casino, 426
  Chowder, 431–432
  Cocktail, 421
  with Crabmeat Mornay, 376
  Creamed, 430
  Croustades, 427–428
  Crumbed, 425
  Curried, 425
  Devils on Horseback, 428–429
  Florentine, 424
  Fried, 434–435
    French-, 436
  Fritters, 427
  au Gratin, 424
  on Half Shell, 420
  Hangtown Fry, 436–437
  Hors d'oeuvre. *See* Hors d'oeuvre
    and appetizers
  Kirkpatrick, 422–423
  Loaf, 426–427
  Omelet, 431
  Pan roast, 428
  Paprika, 425

Oysters *(Cont.)*
  Puree, 430–431
  Remick, 423
  Rockefeller, 422
  Sandwiches, club, 432
    Open-faced, 421
  Sauce, 21, 128
  Sautéed, 435–436
  Scalloped, 432
  Stew I, 433; II, 433
    Zelma Seton's, 433
  Stuffed, Casenave, 421–422
  Stuffing, 40, 88, 127, 168–169

Parsley, fried, 253
Pâté chaud de carpe, 313
Perch. *See* Ocean perch; Pike perch;
    Surf perch; Yellow perch
Pickled fish, 64, 138–139, 343–344,
    449–450
Pickerel. *See* Pike
Pies
  Clam, 363–364
  Fish, 63
  Haddock custard, 119
  Salmon, 191–192
Pike, 323–330
  Aspic, 329
  Baked stuffed, 324
  Braised stuffed, 324–325
  Broiled, 323–324
  Cold, 329
  Mousse, 327
  Poached, 328
  Pudding (Mold), 327
  Quenelles, 325–327
    with Red snapper, 171
  Roasted, Izaak Walton, 329–330
Pike perch, 331–332
  Baked, 332
  Oven-fried, 332
  Pan-fried, 332
  Sauté meunière, 331–332
Poaching. *See* Cooking methods
Pollock, 160
Pompano, 161–163
  Baked, 162
  Broiled, 161
  California, 83
  en Papillote, 162–163
  Sauté meunière, 161

Porgy, 163
  Pan-fried, 163
  Sautéed, 163

Quenelles
  Pike, 325–327
  Red snapper, 171
Quiches
  Clam, 364
  Crab, 380–381
  Leftovers used in, 62
  Salmon, smoked, 204
  Scallop, 439
  Shad roe, canned, 224

Redfish, 154, 164–167
  Baked, Creole, 165
  Broiled, 164
  Cold, 166
    Bayou, 166–167
  Court bouillon, Creole, 165
  Pan-fried, 164
  Poached, 166
Red snapper, 167–171
  Baked
    Florida, 169–170
    Stuffed, 168–169
  Broiled, 167
  Cold poached, 170
  Court bouillon, New Orleans,
    53–54
  Fillet, amandine, 168
  Poached, 170
  Quenelles, 171
  Sautéed, 167–168
  Stuffed, 169
    with seafood, 168–169
Rockfish. *See* Striped bass

Sablefish, 172–175
  à l'Anglaise, 173
  Baked, 173
    Creole, 174
  Broiled, 172
    Smoked, 175
  Curried, 174
  Deviled, 173
  Kippered, 173
  Poached, 174
  Sautéed, 173
  Smoked, 175
    Broiled, 175
    in Cream, 175

Salad dressings
  Boiled, 37
  Gribiche, 36–37
  Mayonnaise, 34, 348
    Green (Sauce Verte), 34–35
    with Jelly (aspic), 34
    Tomato (Sauce Andalouse), 34
  Russian, 35
  Thousand Island, 35
  Vinaigrette, 36, 471–472
Salads
  Bean, Florentine, 65
  Caviar eggs, 279
  Codfish, 97–98
  Coleslaw and fish, 64
  Crab
    Avocado stuffed with, 372–373
    King, 384
    Legs, mayonnaise, 384
      Palace Court, 372
      Rémoulade, 384
    Louis, 372
    Vinaigrette, 371
  Eel, canned, 110
  Finnan haddie vinaigrette, 122
  Herring, 139–140
  Lobster, 409–412
    Aspic, 409–410, 411
    Avocado stuffed with, 412
    English Garden Party, 412
    Parisienne, 411
    Rémoulade, 412
    Traditional, 410–411
  Mussel, 415
  Orientale, 261
  Pickled fish, 64
  Potato, 140, 294, 348
  Rice, 259, 261
  Russe, 372
  Russian, 140, 294, 409–410
  Salmon, 201–202
    Boats, 202
    Celery, 202
    Mayonnaise, 202
  Sardine, 212–213
  Scallop, 443–444
  Shrimp I, 464; II, 464–465
    Aspics
      Cucumber, 448
      Individual, 448–449
      Ring, 447–448
      Tomato II, 446

Salads (Cont.)
  Boats
    Avocado, 449
    Cucumber, 446–447
    Edwardian, 466
    Louis, 465
    Old-fashioned, 465
    and Orange, 465
    Tomato appetizers, 446
  Skate, 227–228
  Striped bass, 271–272
  Tuna
    Bean, Florentine, 65
    Buffet plate, 294
    Niçoise, 293
    Old-Fashioned, 294
    Plate, 291
    Supreme, 293
  Vegetable, 131
  Whitefish, 348
Salmon, 176–206
  in Aspic, 198–201
  Baked
    with Mushrooms and seafood,
      185
    Oregon, 183
    Planked, 182
    Scandinavian, 184
    in Sour cream, 184
  Belly, 205
  à la Bernard, 195
  Boiled, in egg sauce, 187–188
  Breaded, Niçoise, 181–182
  Braised
    à l'Américaine, 187
    Burgundian, 185–186
    in White Wine, 186
  Broiled, 178
  Canapé Danois, 203
  Canned, 192–195, 201– 202
  Caviar, red (Roe), 206
  au Chambertin, 198–199
  Cheeks, 205–206
  Cold, 183, 196–201
  Cornucopias, 203
  Coulibiac of, 189–191
  Curry, quick, 192–193
  Cutlets, 194, 199–200
  Gravad lax, 196–197
  Hors d'oeuvre. See Hors d'oeuvre
    and appetizers
  Kedgeree, 194–195

Salmon (Cont.)
  Kippered, 206
  Loaf, molded, 200–201
  Marinated, Swedish, 196–197
  Mousse, 195
  Paprika, 187
  Parisienne, jellied, 201
  Pie, 191–192
  Planked, 182
  Poached, 179
    Cold, 179, 197–198
    with Sauces, 189
  Quiche, 204–205
  Roe, 206
  Roll (Coulibiac), 189–191
  Rolls, 196
  Salad. See Salads
  Salt, 205
  Sandwiches, 204
  Sautéed, 178–179
    with Cream, 180
    with Curry sauce, 180–181
    Florentine, 180
    with Mushroom puree, 181
  Scalloped, 193–194
  Smoked, 194–196, 203–205
  Soufflé, 192–193
  Spiced, cold, 198
  Stew (Solianka), 49–50
  Stuffed, 179, 184
  Tartare, 183
Sand dabs, 206–207
  Baked, 207
  Broiled, 207
  Sautéed, 207
Sardines, 208–213
  Appetizer, Norwegian, 213
  Baked, 209
  Canned, 208, 210–213
  Escabeche, 210
  Fried, 209
  Grilled, 211
  Hors d'oeuvre, 211–213
  Puffs, 211
  Salad, 212–213
  Sautéed, 209
  Supper, quick, 212
  Turnovers, 212
Sauces, 21–38
  Aïoli, 33–34
  à l'Américaine, 28, 379
  Anchovy, 24

Sauces (*Cont.*)
Onion, 30–31
Andalouse, 34
Aurore, 22
Barbecue, 30, 282, 452
Béarnaise, 27
Tomate, 27
Béchamel, 23–24
Bordelaise, 23
Bourguignonne, 25–26
Brown, basic, 23
Butter. *See* Butter sauces and spreads
Cardinal, 24
Cheese, 24
Clam, 21, 129, 243
Cocktail I, 38; II, 38
Crabmeat, 21
Cream, 24
Cucumber, 37–38
Curry, 29, 180–181, 235, 243–244, 253
French, 22
Tomato-, 24
Diable, 30
Dill, 24, 343
Duxelles, 27–28
Egg, 24, 188
Espagnole, 23
Fine herbes, 23
Hollandaise, 26
Horseradish, 25
and Walnut, 198
Italienne, 29
Lobster, 21
Louis, 36
Mignonette, 420
Mornay, 22
Mousseline, 26
Mustard, 24, 197
Newburg, 396–397
Oyster, 21, 128
Parsley, 24
Piquant, 24
Poulette, 25
Provençale, 31
Rémoulade, 35
for Salads. *See* Salad dressings
Shrimp, 21, 128, 242
Soubise, 22
Sour cream, 38

Sauces (*Cont.*)
Sweet and sour, 274
Tartar, 36
Tomate, Béarnaise, 27
Tomato, 24
-curry, 24
Velouté, 21
Verte, 34–35
Villeroi, 25
Wine, white, 24
Sautéing. *See* Cooking methods
Scallops, 437–444
Appetizers, 437
and Bacon, en brochette, 443
Broiled, 438
Coquilles St. Jacques Monteil, 442–443
Duxelles, 441–442
Fried, 440
in Mayonnaise, 443
Mornay, 440–441
Quiche, 439
Salad, 443–444
Sautéed, 438
Fine herbes, 439
Provençale, 438–439
with Sole, 240–241, 252
Stew, 440
Sculpin, 213
Sea bass, 214–216. *See also* Bass, freshwater; California black sea bass; Striped bass
Baked, amandine, 216
Braised, Italian, 214–215
Broiled, sesame, 216
Quenelles, with red snapper, 171
Sautéed, 215
Fillets Pacific, 215
Sea perch, 154, 279
Sea squab, 73–74
Sea trout, 217–219
Baked, 219
Scandinavian, 219
Broiled, 217
Charcoal (Outdoors), 218
Flambé, 217
Pan-fried, 218
Sautéed, with almonds, 218
Meunière, 217
with tarragon, 218
Shad, 219–222. *See also* Shad roe

Shad (*Cont.*)
  Baked, 220
    in Cream, 222
  Broiled, 220
  Marinated, 221–222
  Sautéed, 220
  Stuffed, 221–222
Shad roe, 222–224
  Baked, en papillote, 224
  Broiled, 223
  Canned, 224
  Smothered, 223
  Soufflé, 223–224
Sheepshead, 225–226. *See also* Sheeps-
    head, freshwater
  Baked, 226
  Broiled, 225
  Sautéed, 225
  Stuffed, 226
Sheepshead, freshwater, 333
Shrimp, 444–466
  à l'Américaine, 456
  Appetizers. *See* Hors d'oeuvre and
    appetizers
  and asparagus Mornay, 462
  Aspics, 446–449
  Avocado boats, 449
  Barbecued, 452
  Bisque, 61–62
  and Broccoli Mornay, 462
  en Brochette, 454
    with Mushrooms, 454
  Broiled, 453
    Barbecued, 452
    Italian, 453
    Stuffed, 454
  Creole, 456
    New Orleans, 456–457
  and Cucumber appetizer, 446–447
    Aspic, 448
  Curry, 461
  Florentine, 463
  Fried
    Butterfly, 451
    French-, 450
      Loaf, 464
    Kiev, 458–459
  Fritters, 452
  Jambalaya, 457–458
  de Jonghe, 459
  Loaf, 459–460, 464
  Marinated, Liz Lucas's, 458

Shrimp (*Cont.*)
  Newburg, 456
  Pain de crevettes, 459–460
  Pickled, 449–450
  Polenta, 460–461
  Potted, 458
  Salads. *See* Salads
  Sauce, 21, 128, 242
  Sauté, with corn, 463
    in cream, 455
    and mushroom Polonaise, 461–
      462
  Straws Pekinese, 450–451
  Stuffed broiled, 454
  Stuffing, 168–169
  Tempura, 451–452
  Wiggle, 455
Skate, 226–228
  Beurre noir, 227
  Cold, rémoulade, 227–228
  with tomato sauce, 227
Smelt, 228–232
  Baked, au gratin, 231
  en Brochette, 230
  Broiled, 229
  Cold, Oriental, 232
    Spiced, 231–232
  Fried, 230–231
    Piquant, 230–231
    Rolled, 230
  Sautéed, 229–230
Snails, 473–475
  Bourguignonne, 474
  Canned, 473, 474
  Lassere, 474–475
  Poulette, 475
  Preparation, 473
Sole, 233–261
  Fillet of
    Benedictine, 242–243
    in Blankets, 248–249
    Bonne femme, 250
    Broiled (grilled), 234
    Buying, 233
    Casanova, 243–244
    Cassis, 239
    à la Cecily, 236
    Cold dishes, 258–261
    Clovisse, 243
    Creole, 244
    with Curry, 235, 237, 243, 253
    Dugléré, 251

Sole (*Cont.*)
  Escabeche, 241–242
  Fried, 253
    Deep-, 252
    Ginger, 239
  Gavarni, 236–237
  Goujons, 253
  à l'Indienne, 237
  Jellied, with fine herbes, 258
    Niçoise, 259
    with Tarragon, 260
    Wheel, 260–261
  Julienne, 253
  Lobster, 247
  Marguery, 246
  Meunière, 234–235
  Mirabeau, 249–250
  Mornay, 247
  Niçoise, 245
  Omelets, 248–250
  Paysanne, 240
  à la Piemontese, 237–238
  Pilaf, Italian, 238
  Poached, 241–252, 256
  with Rice, Italian, 238
  Rolled, 254–255
    Herbed, 255
    Niçoise, 257
    with Salmon stuffing, 256
    with Shrimp sauce, 256
    Toad in the Hole, 257–258
  St. Jacques, 240–241
  with Scallops Mornay, 252
  Sautéed, 234–240
  in Shells, 248
  with Shrimp sauce, 242, 256
  Stuffed, 254–255
    Cassis, 239
  à la Tsarovitz, 235–236
  au Vermouth, 245
  Wheel of, 260–261
Omelets
  in blankets, 248–249
  Mirabeau, 249–250
  Sole stuffed, 250
Whole
  Broiled, 10, 234
  Poached, 241
  Sautéed, 234
    Meunière, 234–235
  with Shrimp sauce, 242

Solianka, 49–50
Soufflés
  Clam, 362–363
  Codfish, 94–95
  Crab, 377
  Finnan haddie, 121
  Halibut, 130
  Lobster, 405–406
    Plaza-Athenée, 406–407
  Salmon, 192–193
  Shad roe, 223–224
Soups and stews. *See also* Chowders
  Aigo-sau, 43–44
  Bisques, 61–62
  Bouillabaisse, 42–43
    Borgne, 44
    Breton, 44–45
    Cotriade, 44–45
  Bouillinade des pêcheurs, 47
  Bourride I, 45–46; II, 46
  Catfish head, 320
  Chiberta, 45–46
  Cioppino, 48–49
  Clam, 358
  Crab, Margaret Jennings's, 59
    Gumbo, 52–53
  Creole court bouillon, 165
  Eel, matelote of, 51–52, 106
  Gopher stew, Minorca, 479–480
  Gumbo, crab, New Orleans, 52
    Western, 53
  Kingfish stew, 143
  Lobster stew, 407
  Marseillaise, 54
  à la Marsellaise, 55
  New Orleans court bouillon, 53–54
  Oyster stew, 433–434
  Russian fish stew, 50
  Salmon stew (Solianka), 49–50
  Seafood, cream of, 59–60
  Scallop stew, 440
  Snapper turtle, 479
  Solianka, 49–50
  Terrapin stew, southern, 478
  Turtle, 476, 479
  Ukha, 51
  Zuppa di pesce, 47–48
Spaghetti, sauce, 292, 368, 418
  Sautéed, 239
Spanish mackerel, 261–264. *See also*
  Mackerel

Spanish mackerel (*Cont.*)
  Baked, 262–264
  Broiled, 262
  Sautéed, 262
Spencer cooking method, 309
Spot, 264
Spot bass, 164
Squid, 265–266
  Baked, 266
  Fried I, 265; II, 265–266
Stews. *See* Soups and stews
Stone crab, 385–386
  Legs beurre noir, 385
  Sauté Florida, 385–386
Striped bass, 266–272. *See also* Sea
    bass
  Baked, 269
  Broiled, 266–267
  Cold, 271
  Flambé, 267
  en Papillote, 270
  Pickled, 64
  Poached, 270
    Curry, 270
  Salad, 271–272
  Sauté, 269
  Stuffed, 267–269
Stuffings, 39–42
  Anchovy (Scandinavian), 41
  Bread, simple, 39
  Clam, 117, 126
  Crabmeat, 41, 158, 268, 324
  Forcemeat, 41–42
  Ham, 324–325, 347
  Oyster, 40, 88, 127, 168–169
  Pungent, 40
  Salmon, 256
  Scandinavian, 41, 184
  Shrimp and oyster, 168–169
  Vegetable, 40
Sturgeon, 272–275
  Baked, Scandinavian, 273
    Steaks, with cream, 275
  Braised, 272–273
    Sweet and sour, 274
  Caviar (Roe), 275–278
  Coulibiac, 274
  Sauté meunière, 273–274
Sucker, 333–335
  Braised, 334
  Broiled, 334
  Cold poached, 335

Sucker (*Cont.*)
  Pan-fried, 334
  Poached, 334–335
Surf perch, 279–280
  Broiled, 280
  Sautéed, 280
Swordfish, 280–285
  Baked, 283
    Castilian, 284–285
    with Mushrooms, 284
  Barbecued, 282
  Broiled, 280–281
  Cold, 281
  Marinated, 281
  with Pepper or rosemary, 282–283
  Pickled, 64
  Planked, 281–282

Tautog, 285–286
  Baked, 286
  Broiled, 286
  Sautéed, 285
Tempura, 451–452
Terrapin, 476–478. *See also* Turtle
  Maryland, 477
  Philadelphia style, 477
  Stew, 478
Tortoise, 476
Trout, 335–344. *See also* Sea trout
  Amandine, Casenave, 336–337
  à l'Anglaise, 338
  au Bleu, 341–342
  Charcoal-broiled, 338–339
  en Chemise, 337–338
  Cold, with dill sauce, 343
    in jelly, 342–343
  French-fried, 338
  with Mushrooms, 341
  Outdoors method, 337
  en Papillotes, 339–340
  Pickled, 343–344
  Poached, 342
  Sauté meunière, 336
  Smoked, 344
  Stuffed, 339–340, 340–341
Tuna
  Canned, 286, 290–294
    Curry, 291
    Hors d'oeuvre, 290
    Omelet, 292–293
    Plate, 291
    Salad. *See* Salads

Tuna (*Cont.*)
    Sauce, for spaghetti, 292
    Scalloped, 292
    Spread, 291
    Fresh, 286–290
        Baked, 289
        Barbecued, 287
        Cold poached, 290
        Fried fingers, 288
        Grilled with sauces, 286–287
        Marinated, 289–290
        Pickled, 64
        Poached, 290
        Sautéed, amandine, 287
            with Tarragon and wine, 287–288
Turtle, 476–480. *See also* Terrapin
    Eggs, 480
    Fins, 478
    Soup
        Canned, 476
        Snapper, 479
    Steak, Floridian, 476–477
    Stew, Monorca gopher, 479–480

Weakfish. *See* Sea trout
Whitebait, 294–296
    Fried, 295
    Italian, 296

Whitebait (*Cont.*)
    Pancakes, 296
    Sautéed, 295
Whitefish, freshwater, 344–349. *See also* California whitefish
    Baked, 346
    Broiled, 345
    Chinese steamed, 347
    Cold, 348
    Oven-fried fillets, 345–346
    Poached, 348
    Roe, 345, 349
    Sauté meunière, 345
    Smoked, 349
        for Sunday breakfast, 349
    Stuffed, 346–347
Whiting, 296–299
    Creole, 299
    Fried, 298
    Grilled, 297
    Poached, 298
    Sauté meunière, 297
    Stuffed rolled, 299
Wines, 13–17

Yellow perch, 350
Yellowtail, 300–301
    Baked, 300–301
    Broiled, 300

From Very Famous Chefs